The
Greenwood Library
of
American Folktales

The Greenwood Library of American Folktales

VOLUME III

The Southwest, The Plains and Plateau, The West

Edited by Thomas A. Green

GREENWOOD PRESS
Westport, Connecticut • London

Library of Congress Cataloging-in-Publication Data

The Greenwood Library of American folktales / edited by Thomas A. Green.
    p. cm.
  Includes bibliographical references and index.
  ISBN 0-313-33772-1 (set : alk. paper)—ISBN 0-313-33773-X (vol. 1 : alk. paper)—ISBN 0-313-
33774-8 (vol. 2 : alk. paper)—ISBN 0-313-33775-6 (vol. 3 : alk. paper)—ISBN 0-313-33776-4 (vol.
4 : alk. paper) 1. Tales—United States—History and criticism. 2. Legends—United States—
History and criticism. 3. United States—Folklore. I. Green, Thomas A., 1944–
  GR105.G75 2006
  398.20973—dc22   2006022952

British Library Cataloguing in Publication Data is available.

Library of Congress Catalog Card Number: 2006022952
ISBN: 0-313-33772-1 (set)
       0-313-33773-X (vol. I)
       0-313-33774-8 (vol. II)
       0-313-33775-6 (vol. III)
       0-313-33776-4 (vol. IV)

First published in 2006

Greenwood Press, 88 Post Road West, Westport, CT 06881
An imprint of Greenwood Publishing Group, Inc.
www.greenwood.com

Printed in the United States of America

The paper used in this book complies with the
Permanent Paper Standard issued by the National
Information Standards Organization (Z39.48–1984).

10 9 8 7 6 5 4 3 2 1

Contents

VOLUME III

Contents

Contents

THE SOUTHWEST

Introduction

For purposes of *The Greenwood Library of American Folktales*, the Southwest is limited to Texas, New Mexico, and Arizona. The landscape of these states varies from thickly forested areas of the piney woods in East Texas to cedar and oak as one moves further into the state or into the mountains of New Mexico. The Gulf Coast of Texas is contrasted with the deserts of New Mexico and Arizona. The plains give way to rolling hill country and mountains crop up at various locations in this region.

With its dramatic extremes of blasting heat, temperatures reaching as high as 125 degrees in the Sonoran desert, and bitter cold in the higher elevations of the Rocky Mountains in Arizona and New Mexico, the climate itself has inspired the folk imagination—particularly tall tales. "Them Petrified Buzzards" (p. 98) tells the story of a desert heat so dry that buzzards ossified while wheeling through the sky in search of a meal; the buzzards continued their petrified hovering, though, unable to change altitude because of their stone wings. Other features of the landscape received similar treatment. According to "Meteor Hell! Cicero Done It!" Meteor Crater—near Arizona cities Winslow and Flagstaff—was the work not of a meteorite's impact with Earth, but resulted from the efforts of a Paiute goat named Cicero.

The Southwestern region's ecology has in turn given rise to a variety of occupations and the lifestyles attendant upon them. Fertile flatlands and river bottoms, the coasts, the open plains, and mountain ranges supported farming, commercial and subsistence fishing, gathering, ranching, mining, subsistence hunting and—before the virtual extermination of the great bison herds—hide hunting. Each of these vocations has left its mark on oral tradition. "Range Life in Texas" (p. 86) provides the details of a working Texas cowboy, while "Booger Red" (p. 68) takes Samuel Thomas ("Booger Red") Privett from his boyhood on a spread in Dublin, Texas, to starring in the most well-known circuses and wild west shows of the turn of the century. Gunfighters and lawmen of New Mexico are celebrated equally in the oral autobiography of Mexican American folk hero Elfego Baca (p. 63), as are Buffalo Hunters who, in the words of Manuel Jesus Vasques, "never held one single penny in his hand" while his patron lived (see "History of a Buffalo Hunter," p. 79). Elsewhere in the state, miners toiled and prospectors searched for the "mother load" as described in "The Adams Diggings" (p. 92). The business of raising crops under difficult situations is explored from the European American perspective in "Victorio's Raid" (p. 83), and the sacred nature of the same enterprise emerges from the Native American "Origin of Acoma" (p. 7).

While it is an extreme oversimplification, particularly in the twenty-first century, to claim that the Southwest Region has been marked by the coming together of three cultures—the Native American, the Hispanic, and the Anglo American—these cultures traditionally have been recognized as having exerted early and profound influence on the region. Before turning to these, however, it should be noted that Americans of African, Asian, continental European, and Middle Eastern descent have made their unique impressions of the Southwest. Moreover, to presume that there is a uniform "Native American" culture among the various indigenous cultures—Pueblo, Athabascan, Plains, and others that inhabited the area—does an equal disservice. With this disclaimer, it is now possible to consider a sample of the folktales that arose from the mix of cultures in Texas, New Mexico, and Arizona.

Turning first to the Native American, a concern with the origin of the environment and those elements of it that provide subsistence becomes immediately apparent. In "Origin of Acoma" (p. 7)—the origin myth of village dwelling Native American horticulturists—the maturation of the world mimics the growth of the corn plant and outlines the social principles necessary to farm in the middle of the desert. Occupying the same region with overlapping territory but different lifestyles, the Athabascan Jicarilla Apaches in "Origin of the Apaches" (p. 17) and the Navajo in "Noqoìlpi, the Gambler: A Navajo Myth" (p. 35) offer different views of the history and construction of the universe. "The Turkey Herd" (p. 77), a Pueblo "Cinderella," and "How Sheep and Horses and Burros Came to the Zuni" (p. 24) result from creative culture contact between Native American and Hispanic Cultures. Unfortunately, many of these native cultures were displaced and some were eradicated by the arrival of the next groups to arrive in the Southwest.

The Spanish culture, in the person of Álvar Núñez Cabeza de Vaca, was the first European element to enter the Southwest Region (1528). After Cabeza de Vaca's travels through Texas and New Mexico, he returned to Spain with the stories of vast riches that led to the introduction of not only the Spanish language and culture, but also the livestock that generated the Zuni narrative mentioned in the preceding paragraph. The horse, in particular, when taken up by the Southern Plains Shoshoneanses and Athabascan people (the Comanche and Apache, respectively), caused a cultural revolution that inevitably appeared in the folktales of the Southwest and at a somewhat later date in the culture of the Plains and Plateau Region. With the Spanish came both European folklore and Roman Catholicism. Individually and in combination with Native American perceptions of the supernatural, **belief tales**, personal experience narratives, and **legends** such as "Witch Flights" (p. 121), "Witches Discovered" (p. 122), "Curanderas and Brujas" (pp. 124 and 125), and "The Ghost Penitente" (p. 127) produced a potent mix of both religion and magic and also mysticism and medicine that was preserved in narratives.

The Anglo American presence was introduced to the Southwest in Texas in 1823 with the founding of a colony on the Brazos River by Stephen F. Austin. In 1846, during the Mexican War, United States troops were led by General Stephen W. Kearny into Santa Fe and occupied the city in. The United States took possession of New Mexico and most of Arizona at the end of the war in 1848. Settlement of the area accelerated after the end of the Civil War in 1865, thus, increasing the "Anglo" population (a population that consisted not simply of Anglo Americans, but also African Americans and other ethnic groups). In the context of the present collection of American folktales, the cowboy, the farmer, the prospector and the lawman—who was compelled to keep order among them (all of whom have been mentioned in earlier paragraphs)—stand out protagonists.

Each of these groups has memorialized in folk narrative its heroes, its antagonists and its human symbols. Each of these figures represents the response to the Southwestern environment, dictated by their worldview, their ambitions, and their historical niche.

SUGGESTED READINGS

Boatright, Mody Coggin. *Mody Boatright, Folklorist: A Collection of Essays.* Austin: University of Texas Press, 1973.

5

Espinosa, Aurelio. *The Folklore of Spain in the American Southwest: Traditional Spanish Folk Literature in Northern New Mexico and Southern Colorado.* Edited by J. Manuel Espinosa. Norman: University of Oklahoma Press, 1985.

Farrer, Claire. *Thunder Rides a Black Horse: Mescalero Apaches and the Mythic Present.* 2nd edition. Prospect Heights, IL: Waveland Press, 1996.

Matthews, Washington. *Navajo Legends.* Memoirs of the American Folklore Society 5. New York: American Folklore Society, 1897.

Parsons, Elsie Clews. *Kiowa Tales.* Memoirs of the American Folklore Society 22. New York: American Folklore Society, 1929.

———. *Tewa Tales.* Memoirs of the American Folklore Society 19. New York: American Folklore Society, 1926.

Weigle, Martha and Peter White. *The Lore of New Mexico.* Albuquerque: University of New Mexico Press, 1988.

West, John O. *Mexican-American Folklore.* Little Rock, AR: August House, 1988.

ORIGINS

ORIGIN OF ACOMA

Tradition Bearer: Unavailable

Source: Stirling, Matthew W. Pages 1–10 in *Origin Myth of Acoma and Other Records.* Bureau of American Ethnology Bulletin 135. Washington, DC: U.S. Government Printing Office, 1942.

Date: 1928

Original Source: Acoma Pueblo (New Mexico)

National Origin: Native American

As with all myths of origin, this one from Acoma Pueblo details the ways in which the orderly universe develops from primal chaos. The physical environment and its life forms are created, as are technology, religious practice, and elements of the social structure. The residents of Acoma are traditionally farmers who rely on the meager New Mexico rainfall rather than on the irrigation used by the Pueblos farther to the east. The image used to depict the development of the current order suggests maturation and emergence from an underground world; it is derived from the model of the growing corn plant—the primary Acoma crop and, therefore, the basis of traditional subsistence. The central place of the plant in practical and ceremonial life and the role of the sun in the nurturing of the plant are depicted in the **myth**. The kiva, the underground site of Pueblo religious life, re-creates Shipapu, which is identified in this narrative as the original source of life. The primacy of the sacred number "four" is reflected in, for example, the presence of four directions, four kinds of pine trees, four seeds, and four mountains. The Acoma, like the rest of the Western Pueblos, emphasize clans related through the female line and women own both houses and gardens. The female gender of the primal pair establishes these kinship and ownership patterns. The two sisters embody messages concerning traditional ethics and morality, as well. Iatiku's altruistic behavior is regarded as more appropriately Pueblo than is Nautsiti's self-absorption and hoarding. Thus, in a later **myth**, Nautsiti eventually "disappears into the East"—her behavior becoming increasingly less appropriate by Western Pueblo standards—while Iatiku remains to establish clans, ceremonies, and other features of Acoma culture.

In the beginning two female human beings were born. These two children were born underground at a place called Shipapu. As they grew up, they began to be aware of each other. There was no light and they could only feel each other. Being in the dark they grew slowly.

After they had grown considerably, a Spirit whom they afterward called Tsichtinako spoke to them, and they found that it would give them nourishment. After they had grown large enough to think for themselves, they spoke to the Spirit when it had come to them one day and asked it to make itself known to them and to say whether it was male or female, but it replied only that it was not allowed to meet with them. They then asked why they were living in the dark without knowing each other by name, but the Spirit answered that they were nuk'timi (under the earth); but they were to be patient in waiting until everything was ready for them to go up into the light. So they waited a long time, and as they grew they learned their language from Tsichtinako.

When all was ready, they found a present from Tsichtinako, two baskets of seeds and little images of all the different animals (there were to be) in the world. The Spirit said they were sent by their father. They asked who was meant by their father, and Tsichtinako replied that his name was Ûch'tsiti and that he wished them to take their baskets out into the light, when the time came. Tsichtinako instructed them, "You will find the seeds of four kinds of pine trees, lā'khok, gēi'etsu (dyai'its), wanūka, and lă'nye, in your baskets. You are to plant these seeds and will use the trees to get up into the light." They could not see the things in their baskets but feeling each object in turn they asked, "Is this it?" until the seeds were found. They then planted the seeds as Tsichtinako instructed. All of the four seeds sprouted, but in the darkness the trees grew very slowly and the two sisters became very anxious to reach the light as they waited this long time. They slept for many years as they had no use for eyes. Each time they awoke they would feel the trees to see how they were growing. The tree lǎ'nye grew faster than the others and after a very long time pushed a hole through the earth for them and let in a very little light. The others stopped growing, at various heights, when this happened.

The hole that the tree lǎ'nye made was not large enough for them to pass through, so Tsichtinako advised them to look again in their baskets where they would find the image of an animal called dyu·pi (badger) and tell it to become alive. They told it to live, and it did so as they spoke, exclaiming, "A'uha! Why have you given me life?" They told it not to be afraid nor to worry about coming to life. "We have brought you to life because you are to be useful." Tsichtinako spoke to them again, instructing them to tell Badger to climb the pine tree, to bore a hole large enough for them to crawl up, cautioning him not to go out into the light, but to return, when the hole was finished. Badger climbed the tree and after he had dug a hole large enough, returned saying that he had done his work. They thanked him and said, "As a reward you will come up with us to the light and thereafter you will live happily. You will always know how to dig and your home will be in the ground where you will be neither too hot nor too cold."

Tsichtinako now spoke again, telling them to look in the basket for Tāwāi'nū (locust), giving it life and asking it to smooth the hole by plastering. It too was to be cautioned to return. This they did and Locust smoothed the hole but, having finished, went out into the light. When it returned reporting that it had done its work, they asked it if it had gone out. Locust said no, and every time he was asked he replied no, until the fourth time when he admitted that he had gone out. They asked Locust what it was like outside. Locust replied that it was just tsī'ītī (laid out flat). They said, "From now on you will be known as Tsi·k'ǎ. You will also come up with us, but you will be punished for disobedience by being allowed out only a short time. Your home will be in the ground and you will have to return when the weather is bad. You will soon die but you will be reborn each season."

The hole now let light into the place where the two sisters were, and Tsichtinako spoke to them, "Now is the time you are to go out. You are able to take your baskets with you. In them you will find pollen and sacred corn meal. When you reach the top, you will wait for the Sun to come up and that direction will be called ha'nami (east). With the pollen and the sacred corn meal you will pray to the Sun. You will thank the Sun for bringing you to light, ask for a long life and happiness, and for success in the purpose for which you were created." Tsichtinako then taught them the prayers and the creation song, which they were to sing. This took a long while, but finally the sisters followed by

9

Badger and Locust, went out into the light, climbing the pine tree. Badger was very strong and skillful and helped them. On reaching the earth, they set down their baskets and saw for the first time what they had. The earth was soft and spongy under their feet as they walked, and they said, "This is not ripe." They stood waiting for the Sun, not knowing where it would appear. Gradually it grew lighter and finally the Sun came up. Before they began to pray, Tsichtinako told them they were facing east and that their right side, the side their best aim was on, would be known as kū'āimē (south) and the left ti dyami (north) while behind at their backs was the direction pūna'me (west) where the Sun would go down. They had already learned while underground the direction nŭk'ŭmi (down) and later, when they asked where their father was, they were told tyu-nami (four skies above.)

And as they waited to pray to the Sun, the girl on the right moved her best hand and was named Iatiku, which meant "bringing to life." Tsichtinako then told her to name her sister, but it took a long time. Finally Tsichtinako noticed that the other had more in her basket, so Tsichtinako told Iatiku to name her thus, and Iatiku called her Nautsiti, which meant "more of everything in the basket."

They now prayed to the Sun as they had been taught by Tsichtinako, and sang the creation song. Their eyes hurt for they were not accustomed to the strong light. For the first time they asked Tsichtinako why they were on earth and why they were created. Tsichtinako replied, "I did not make you. Your father, Uchtsiti made you, and it is he who has made the world, the Sun which you have seen, the sky, and many other things which you will see. But Uchtsiti says the world is not yet completed, not yet satisfactory, as he wants it. This is the reason he has made you. You will rule and bring to life the rest of the things he has given you in the baskets." The sisters then asked how they themselves had come into being. Tsichtinako answered saying, "Uchtsiti first made the world. He threw a clot of his own blood into space and by his power it grew and grew until it became the earth. Then Uchtsiti planted you in this and by it you were nourished as you developed. Now that you have emerged from within the earth, you will have to provide nourishment for yourselves. I will instruct you in this." They then asked where their father lived and Tsichtinako replied, "You will never see your father, he lives four skies above, and has made you to live in this world. He has made you in the image of himself." So they asked why Tsichtinako did not become visible to them, but Tsichtinako replied, "I don't know how to live like a human being. I have been asked by Uchtsiti to look after you and to teach you. I will always guide you." And they asked again how they were to live, whether they could go down once more under the ground, for they were afraid of the winds and rains and their eyes were hurt by the light. Tsichtinako replied that Uchtsiti would take care of that and would furnish them means to keep warm and change the atmosphere so that they would get used to it.

At the end of the first day, when it became dark they were much frightened, for they had not understood that the Sun would set and thought that Tsichtinako had betrayed them. "Tsichtinako! Tsichtinako! You told us we were to come into the light," they cried, "why, then, is it dark?" So Tsichtinako explained, "This is the way it will always be. The Sun will go down and the next day come up anew in the east. When it is dark you are to rest and sleep as you slept when all was dark." So they were satisfied and slept. They rose to meet the Sun, praying to it as they had been told, and were happy when it came up again, for they were warm and their faith in Tsichtinako was restored.

Tsichtinako next said to them, "Now that you have your names, you will pray with your names and your clan names so that the Sun will know you and recognize you." Tsichtinako asked Nautsiti which clan she wished to belong to. Nautsiti answered, "I wish to see the Sun, that is the clan I will be." The spirit told Nautsiti to ask Iatiku what clan she wanted. Iatiku thought for a long time but finally she noticed that she had the seed from which sacred meal was made in her basket and no other kind of seeds. She thought, "With this name I shall be very proud, for it has been chosen for nourishment and it is sacred." So she said, "I will be Corn clan." They then waited for the Sunto come up. When it appeared, Tsichtinako once more advised them to sing the first song and to pray, not forgetting their name and their clan name in starting their prayer. After the prayer they were to sing the second song.

When the Sun appeared it was too bright for Iatiku and it hurt her eyes. She wondered if Nautsiti's eyes hurt her, too, so she put her head down and sideways, letting her hair fall, and looked at Nautsiti. By doing this the light did not strike her squarely in the face and her hair cast a shade. Tsichtinako said, "Iatiku, the Sun has not appeared for you. Look at Nautsiti, see how strongly the light is striking her. Notice how white she looks." And although Iatiku turned to the Sun, it did not make her as white as Nautsiti, and Iatiku's mind was slowed up while Nautsiti's mind was made fast. But both of them remembered everything and did everything as they were taught.

When they had completed their prayers to the Sun, Tsichtinako said, "You have done everything well and now you are both to take up your baskets and you must look to the north, west, south, and east, for you are now to pray to the Earth to accept the things in the basket and to give them life. First you must pray to the north, at the same time lift up your baskets in that direction. You will then do the same to the west, then to the south and east." They did as they were told and did it well. And Tsichtinako, said to them, "From now on you will rule in every direction, north, west, south, and east."

They now questioned Tsichtinako again so that they would understand more clearly why they were given the baskets and their contents, and Tsichtinako replied, "Everything in the baskets is to be created by your word, for you are made in the image of Uchtsiti and your word will be as powerful as his word. He has created you to help him complete the world. You are to plant the seeds of the different plants to be used when anything is needed. I shall always be ready to point out to you the various plants and animals."

The sisters did not realize that they were not taking food and did not understand when Tsichtinako told them they were to plant seeds to give them nourishment. But they were always ready to do as Tsichtinako, asked, and she told them to plant first that which would maintain life, grains of corp. "When this plant grows," said Tsichtinako, "it will produce a part which I will point out to you. This will be taken as food." Everything in the basket was in pairs and the sisters planted two of each kind of corn.

The corn grew very slowly so Tsichtinako told them to plant ĭsthĕ (the earliest plant to come up in the spring; gray with a small white flower; dies quickly) and to transmit its power of early ripening to the corn.

They were very interested in the corn and watched it every day as it grew. Tsichtinako showed them where the pollen came out. "That you will call kū'ăch'tīmu," she said, "there the pollen win [will?] appear. When the pollen is plentiful, you will gather it, and with it and corn meal you will pray to the rising Sun each morning." This they did always, but Nautsiti was sometimes a little lazy.

After some time the corn ripened. Tsichtinako told them to look at it and to gather some. They saw that the corn was hard and they picked four ears. Iatiku took two ears carefully without hurting the plant, but Nautsiti jerked hers off roughly. Iatiku noticed this and cautioned her sister not to ruin the plants. They took the ears of corn to Tsichtinako saying, "We have brought the corn, it is ripe." Tsichtinako agreed and explained that the corn ears when cooked would be their food. They did not understand this and asked what they would cook with. Tsichtinako then told them that Uchtsiti would give them fire. That night as they sat around they saw a red light drop from the sky. After they had seen it, Tsichtinako told them it was fire, and that they were to go over and get some of it. They asked with what, and she told them to get it with a flat rock because it was very hot and they could not take it in their hands. After getting it with a rock, they asked what they were to do with it, and were told they were to make a fire, to go to the pine tree they had planted, to break off some of the branches and put them in the fire. They went to the tree and broke some of the twigs from it. When they got back to the fire, they were told to throw the twigs down. They did so and a large pile of wood appeared there. Tsichtinako told them this wood would last many years till there was time for trees to grow, and showed them how to build a fire. She told them that with the flames from the fire they would keep warm and would cook their food.

Tsichtinako next taught them how to roast the corn. "When it is cooked," she explained, "you are to eat it. This will be the first time you have eaten, for you have been fasting for a long time and Uchtsiti has been nourishing you. You will find salt in your baskets; with this you will season the corn." They began to look for this and Tsichtinako pointed it out to them. As soon as they were told this, Nautsiti grabbed some corn and salt. She was the first to taste them and exclaimed that they were very good, but Iatiku was slower. After Nautsiti had eaten part, she gave it to Iatiku to taste. When both had eaten, Tsichtinako told them that this was the way they were going to live, and be nourished. They were very thankful, saying, "You have treated us well," They asked if this would be their only food. Tsichtinako said, "No, you have many other things in your baskets; many seeds and images of animals, all in pairs. Some will be eaten and taken for nourishment by you." After they had used the salt, they were asked by Tsichtinako to give life to this salt by praying to the Earth, first in the north direction, then in the west, then in the south, and then in the east. And when they did so, salt appeared in each of these directions. Tsichtinako then instructed them to take always the husks from the corn carefully and to dry them. They were then instructed to plant hǎ'mi (tobacco). When the plant matured, they were taught how to roll the leaves in corn husks and to smoke it. (Even now in ceremonies the corn husks must be torn with the fingers and tied in the center with a little strip of corn husk. It may not be cut by artificial means. You smoke in order to make your prayers merge into the minds of the gods to whom prayer is addressed. This will also compel obedience. If a man smokes when a request is made of him, he must obey that request.) They were then told to place the tobacco with the pollen and the corn meal and to remember that these three were always to be together, and to be used in making prayers.

Now they were told that they were to give life to an animal whose flesh they were going to use for food. Tsichtinako named this animal as Ba'shya (kangaroo mouse) and also taught them the first song to be sung to animals. She told them to sing this song in order to make the images alive, and pointed out the images to them in the basket.

They did everything as they were taught. They sang the song to the image and with the word, "Come to life, Bashya," it came to life. As it did so it asked, "Why have I come to life?" Tsichtinako told it not to ask any questions because,

13

"It is you that is going to give life to other life." After this was done, Nautsiti and Iatiku, told this animal that it was going to live on the ground and said to it, "Go now and increase." After the animal increased, Tsichtinako told the sisters to kill one of the animals. "Now eat the two together, the corn and the field mouse, and also the salt to see how it tastes." She had already told them never to let out the fire that had been given to them. They acted according to Tsichtinako's instructions. They roasted their corn and roasted the flesh of the field mouse with some salt on it. After it was cooked, Tsichtinako told them to pray with the food, not with all of it, but with little pieces from each—corn, flesh, and salt. Each sister did this and prayed to Uchtsiti, the creator of the world, who lives up in the fourth sky. Tsichtinako told them they were to do this always before eating. After this they ate the food. There was not very much of the meat, but it was good. They did not know that there were to be bones but these were not hard and they broke them with their teeth. They liked the flesh so well that they asked Tsichtinako if they might have something larger that would yield more flesh. Tsichtinako answered that they would find other things in their baskets. They went back to them, and Tsichtinako said they would find Tsū'na (rat) and another animal Katsa (mole) and also Nī te (prairie dog). "Go, make these images alive," said Tsichtinako, pointing them out according to their names. They were to do this in the same way as with Bashya. Tsichtinako also told them that these animals were to be used as food and that they must tell each of these animals to live in the ground because as yet there was no shade on earth to live in. "But before you give life to them," said Tsichtinako, "it is necessary that you plant seeds of grass which will be the food for them." Tsichtinako pointed out the seeds they were to plant, and they took the seeds of the grasses and scattered them first to the North, next to the West, then some to the South, and then to the East. And immediately grass covered the ground. They then took the images and prayed to the cardinal points, and, according to the instructions of Tsichtinako, gave life to all of these animals, giving them names as they came to life. Each one as it came to life asked why it had come to life but Tsichtinako told them not to ask questions, that they would give life to other life. As before, the sisters told the animals to increase. After all of this was done, they proceeded to eat the new animals after praying with them, doing just as they did before. The two sisters were now very happy, they had plenty and some to spare. "It is not yet time for the larger animals to be given life," said Tsichtinako, "first the world must have sufficient plants and small animals to feed them."

After a long time, Tsichtinako spoke to them, "What we are going to do now concerns the earth. We are going to make the mountains." She told them to remember the words she was going to say. They were to say, "Kaweshtima kōti

(North Mountain), appear in the north, and we will always know you to be in that direction." Tsichtinako also pointed out an article in the basket that she named ya'ōni (stone) and instructed them to throw the stone to the north direction as they spoke the words. When they did so, a big mountain appeared in the north. After they had done this, Tsichtinako instructed them to do the same thing in the west, but to name this mountain Tsipīna koti, and in the south, naming it Da'ōtyuma koti, and in the east, naming it G'ūchana koti.

After all this was done, Tsichtinako spoke again and told them, "Now that you have all the mountains around you with plains, mesas, and canyons, you must make the growing things of these places." Tsichtinako told them to go back to the trees which they had planted underground, lakhok, geietsu, wanuka, and lă'nye. She told them to take the seeds from these trees, and they did so. Following her instructions they spread some to each of the four directions, naming the mountains in each direction, and saying, "Grow in North Mountain, grow in West Mountain, etc." Tsichtinako said to them, "These are going to be tall trees; from them you will get logs. Later you will build houses and will use these." They asked if that was all that was going to grow on the mountains, and Tsichtinako said, "No, there are many other seeds left in your baskets. You have seeds of trees which are going to yield food. You will find *dyai'its* (pinon tree), *sē'isha* (kind of cedar), *hapani* (oak, acorn) and *maka'yawi* (walnut)." She again instructed them what to do and taught them the prayer to use, which was: "From now on, grow in this mountain and yield fruit which will be used as food. Your places are to be in the mountains. You will grow and be useful." When everything had been done well, Tsichtinako told (them) that there were many smaller seeds left in the baskets and she gave a name to each, telling them to fill the rest of the land. These seeds were planted on every one of the four mountains and in the rest of the world. Tsichtinako spoke to the sisters again and told them, "You still have seeds in your baskets which you will know as scuts'ōibewi (wild fruits). These trees you will grow around you and care for." But they mistook the instructions and instead of instructing them to grow nearby, they named the mountains, and that is where they grew. But there were also some that grew close around. It is not known how long they had to wait for these things to happen, but it was a very long time. They noticed that the wild plants grew very fast and produced much fruit, but Tsichtinako had not told them whether or not to eat these, so they left them alone.

They saw that there were still seeds and images in their baskets, and asked Tsichtinako how many more kinds there were. Tsichtinako, said there were yet many other seeds, which would also be important food. They would grow quickly and easily and she named them squash and beans. They were instructed to act with them as with the other seeds, and these also grew into plants. After

15

a time, when they were ripe, Tsichtinako pointed out the parts of the plants which they were to use as food.

Iatiku later asked Tsichtinako, "What remains in my basket?" and she was answered, "You have still many animals; these will be multiplied to populate the mountains." And as the two grew larger, they required more food. Tsichtinako saw this and told them that they were now to bring to life larger animals. She said they would find in their baskets cottontails, jackrabbits, antelope, and water deer. They were told to give life to these animals and to send them into the open plains. Everything was done as before, and when they killed the animals for food they were always careful to pray to their father as before. As they again asked Tsichtinako what remained in their baskets, Tsichtinako said, "You have images of the still bigger game. You will find deer, elk, mountain sheep, and bison." Iatiku asked where these animals were to be told to live and Tsichtinako told them that the elk and deer were to live in the lower mountains and the mountain sheep higher and in the rougher places. The bison, however, were to live on the plains. They followed the instructions and gave life to these animals and told them to go to these places to live and multiply. They again tried all these different animals for food. Their flesh was very good and always they prayed to Uchtsiti before tasting them.

In Nautsiti's basket there were many more things left than in Iatiku's. Nautsiti was selfish and hoarded her images, but Iatiku was ready to let her seeds and images be used. She was more interested in seeing things grow. They again asked what remained, and Tsichtinako replied, "You will find lion, wolf, wildcat and bear. These are strong beasts; they are going to use as food the same game that you also use. There is now game enough for them." When all these had been selected they were brought to life in the same manner as before.

The sisters again asked what was in their baskets, and they were told, "You will find birds which will fly in the air. These birds win also use small game for their food. You will find in the basket the eagles and the hawks." Tsichtinako pointed these out to them and they brought them to life. The birds flew up into the high mountains and over the plains. The sisters told the birds to use small game for food, and again Iatiku asked what was in the basket. Tsichtinako pointed out smaller birds, which would populate the country, each living in a different kind of region. They were then given life, as the animals before them. The birds were of many and bright colors, some were blue. The wild turkey was among them and they were instructed to tell it not to fly easily like the others. They were told to tell these birds that their food was to be the different seeds on the mountains and the plains. And all these, animals were sampled for food after they had been given life. Again Iatiku asked what remained in the baskets, because she found things there that were thorny. Tsichtinako told them their names. They were the various cacti and were said to be very good for food. But Tsichtinako explained that most were intended for animals to eat. All these were planted as before and tried for food, and they found that some tasted good. After they asked again what was left, Tsichtinako pointed out to them that there were still fish, water snakes, and turtles, of which there were many kinds of each. They gave life to them as before and told them all to live in the water as instructed. Tsichtinako pointed out several that were to be used for food. They tried them all for food, and they found that some were good, and others poor, but offered prayers to all and gave thanks to Uchtsiti. So it happened that many animals came alive in the world and they all increased.

ORIGIN OF THE APACHES

Tradition Bearer: Laforia

Source: Russell, Frank. "Myths of the Jicarilla Apaches." *Journal of American Folklore* 11 (1898): 253–54.

Date: ca. 1898

Original Source: Jicarilla Apache (New Mexico)

National Origin: Native American

The following **myth** varies from "When the World Was Formed" (Bourke 1890, 209–12), also a Jicarilla narrative. Differences in the "same" sacred narrative when related by different tradition bearers is not unusual in those cultures in which there are "competing" myths owned by different lineages, clans, or holy persons. Although there are references to physical features of the Jicarilla world and the deification of wind, the primary concern of this narrative is on human relations ranging from the evil caused by witchcraft to the scattering of the original people into the various Apache bands and distinct languages associated with each. The emergence of the people from an underground world may result from the influence of the neighboring Pueblo cultures (compare this **myth** to "Origin of Acoma," p. 7).

In the under-world, *Un-go-ya-yen-ni*, there was no sun, moon, or light of any kind, except that emanating from large eagle feathers which the people carried about with them. This method of lighting proved unsatisfactory, and the head men of the tribe gathered in council to devise some plan for lighting the world more brightly.

One of the chiefs suggested that they make a sun and a moon. A great disk of yellow paint was made upon the ground, and then placed in the sky. Although this miniature creation was too small to give much light, it was allowed to make one circuit of the heavens ere it was taken down and made larger. Four times the sun set and rose, and four times it was enlarged, before it was "as large as the earth and gave plenty of light."

In the underworld dwelt a wizard and a witch, who were much incensed at man's presumption, and made such attempts to destroy the new luminaries that both the sun and the moon fled from the lower world, leaving it again in darkness, and made their escape to this earth, where they have never been molested, so that, until the present time, they continue to shine by night and by day.

The loss of the sun and moon brought the people together, that they might take council concerning the means of restoring the lost light. Long they danced and sang, and made medicine. At length it was decided that they should go in search of the sun.

The Indian medicine men caused four mountains to spring up, which grew by night with great noise, and rested by day. The mountains increased in size until the fourth night, when they nearly reached the sky.

Four boys were sent to seek the cause of the failure of the mountains to reach the opening in the sky, through which the sun and moon had disappeared. The boys followed the tracks of two girls who had caused the mountains to stop growing, until they reached some burrows in the side of the mountain, where all trace of the two females disappeared.

When their story was told to the people, the medicine-men said, "You who have injured us shall be transformed into rabbits, that you may be of some use to mankind; your bodies shall be eaten," and the rabbit has been used for food by the human race down to the present day.

All then journeyed to the tops of the mountains, where a ladder was built that reached the aperture in the sky or roof of the underworld. The badger was then sent out to explore the earth above; the messenger soon returned, and reported water everywhere except around the margin of the opening. The legs of the badger were covered with mud, which accounts for their dark color at the present day. Four days later, the turkey was sent to see if the waters had subsided. The turkey reported no land yet to be seen above. As the turkey came in contact with the foam of the flood surrounding the opening, his tail became wet and heavy; in shaking this he scattered filmy drops upon his wings, and that is why the feathers of the turkey to the present day present an iridescent play of colors.

Then the Wind came to the anxious people and said, "If you will ask me to help you, I will drive back the water for you." Thus the first prayers came to be addressed to the Wind, which yet remains a powerful deity.

When the Wind had rolled back the waters to the limits of the present ocean, the Indians began to ascend the ladder; four times the ladder broke with them, and four times it was replaced by a new one.

All the people reached the new world except one old woman, too old and infirm to climb the ladder, who said to them: "I do not wish to leave the land of my youth. Go your way and leave me here; you will come back to join me when you die. You have forgotten one thing; you will soon discover what it is."

For four days after their emergence no one could sleep; then the people remembered the warning of the old woman, and two boys were sent down to the under-world to learn what it was that had been forgotten.

The old woman said in reply to their question, "You forgot to take lice with you; without them you cannot sleep." She took two black ones from her hair and two white ones from her body, saying, "These will be all you will need, for they will increase night and day." So it has happened that the Apaches sleep well to this day because they harbor these parasites upon their bodies.

So well had the Wind performed his task of drying up the waters, that none remained for the people to drink; but prayers addressed to that deity were answered by the appearance of the present springs and rivers. The few lakes that occur in the Apache country are remnants of the primeval ocean. All the inhabitants of the earth were then Apaches, but the Cheyennes and Utes were soon created from willows.

The supreme god, *Yi-na-yes-gon-i*, directed the people westward; as they journeyed, small parties became separated, and settled by the wayside. These were given different names and languages.

ORIGIN OF THE ANIMALS

Tradition Bearer: La Foria

Source: Russell, Frank. "Myths of the Jicarilla Apaches." *Journal of American Folklore* 11 (1898): 259–61.

Date: ca. 1898

Original Source: Jicarilla Apache (New Mexico)

National Origin: Native American

The **myth** "Origin of the Animals" resumes the narrative of the creation of the Jicarilla world where "Origin of the Apaches" (p. 17)—also performed by La Foria—left off, because while the latter is concerned with the creation of the first physical state of the cosmos by deities and **culture heroes**, this tale turns to human efforts to secure the game animals needed to survive through magic and guile. Just as human cleverness obtained access to game, however, human peevishness destroyed the short-lived harmony between man and animals.

When the Apaches emerged from the under-world, they traveled southward on foot for four days. They had no other food than the seeds of two plants from which they made a sort of flour by grinding between stones. When they camped for the fourth time, one of the tipis stood somewhat apart from the others. While the owner and his wife were absent from this lodge, a Raven brought a bow and a quiver of arrows, and hung them upon the lodge poles. The children within took down the quiver, and found some meat in it; they ate this, and at once became very fat.

When the mother returned, she saw the grease on the hands and cheeks of the children, and was told how the food had been obtained. The woman hastened to her husband with the tale. Marveling at the appearance of the children, the people gathered to await the reappearance of the Raven, which subsisted upon such remarkable food.

When the Raven found the food had been stolen from the quiver, he flew away toward the eastward; his destination was a mountain just beyond the range of vision of the Indians. A bat, however, followed the flight of the Raven, and informed them where the Raven had alighted.

That night, a council of the whole tribe was held, and it was decided that they should go to the home of the Raven, and try to obtain from him the food which had wrought such a miraculous change in those who had partaken of it.

At the end of four days they came to a place where a large number of logs were lying in irregular heaps. Many ravens were seen, but they avoided the Indians, and no information could be obtained from them. At one point they discovered a great circle of ashes where the ravens were accustomed to cook their meals.

Again a council was held, and they talked over the problem of how to spy upon the ravens, and learn whence they obtained the precious animal food. That night the medicine men transformed a boy into a puppy, and concealed him in the bushes near the camp.

After the Indians had departed, next morning the ravens came, as is their habit, to examine the abandoned camp. One of the young ravens found the puppy, and was so pleased with it that he exclaimed, "This shall be my puppy!" When he carried home his prize his parents told him to throw it away. He begged permission to keep it, but agreed to give it up if the puppy winked when a splinter of burning wood was waved before its eyes. As the puppy possessed much more than canine intelligence, it stared during the test without the quiver of an eye-lid. So the young raven won consent to keep the puppy, which he placed under his own blanket, where it remained until evening.

At sunset the puppy peeped from his cover, and saw an old raven brush aside the ashes of the fireplace, and take up a large flat stone which disclosed an opening beneath; through this he disappeared, but arose again with a buffalo, which was killed and eaten by the ravens.

For four days the puppy remained at the camp of the ravens, and each evening he saw a buffalo brought up from the depths and devoured. Satisfied that he had discovered the source from which the ravens derived their food, the puppy resumed the form of a boy on the morning of the fifth day, and, with a white eagle feather in one hand and a black one in the other, descended through the opening beneath the fireplace, as he had seen the ravens do.

In the under-world in which he found himself he saw four buffaloes. He placed the white eagle-feather in the mouth of the nearest Buffalo, and commanded it to follow him, but the Buffalo told him to go on to the last of the four and take it. This the boy tried to do, but the fourth Buffalo sent him back to the first, in whose mouth the boy again thrust the feather, declaring it to be the king of animals. He then returned to the world above, followed by all the animals at present upon the surface of the earth, except those specially created later, such, for example, as the horse and aquatic animals.

As the large herd of animals passed through the hole, one of the ravens awoke, and hastened to clap down the stone covering the opening, but he was too late to prevent their escape. Seeing that they had passed from his control into that of man, he exclaimed, "When you kill any of these animals you must at least leave their eyes for me."

Attended by the troop of beasts of many species, the boy followed the track made by the departing Apaches. On the site of their first camp he found a fire stick or poker of which he inquired, "When did my people leave here?"

"Three days ago," was the reply. At the next camping-place was an abandoned ladder of which he asked, "When did my people leave here?"

"Two days ago," replied the ladder. Continuing his journey the boy soon reached the third camping-place, where he questioned a second fire stick, and learned that the people had been gone but one day.

At the fourth camp another ladder answered his question, with the news that the Indians had left there that morning. That evening he overtook them and entered the camp, the herd of animals following him like a flock of sheep. One old woman who lived in a brush lodge became vexed at the deer, which ate the covering of her rude shelter. Snatching up a stick from the fire, she struck the deer over the nose, to which the white ashes adhered, causing the white mark, which we see on the nose of that animal at the present time. "Hereafter you shall avoid mankind; your nose will tell you when you are near them," said she.

Thus terminated the brief period of harmony between man and the beast; they left the camp at once, going farther each day, until on the fourth they disappeared from sight. That night the Apaches prayed for the return of the animals, that they might use them for food, and that is why animals approach nearer the camps now at night than at any other time. They never come very close, because the old woman told them to be guided by their noses and avoid the Indians.

ORIGIN OF FIRE

Tradition Bearer: Laforia

Source: Russell, Frank. "Myths of the Jicarilla Apaches." *Journal of American Folklore* 11 (1898): 261–62.

Date: ca. 1898

Original Source: Jicarilla Apache (New Mexico)

National Origin: Native American

Fox is given the role of **culture hero** in the following **myth**. In contrast to Coyote, who plays a similar role in "When the World Was Formed"

(Bourke 1890, 209–12), Fox maintains more of the qualities of **trickster**. He tries to acquire the cry and flying ability of the geese, but is unable to exercise sufficient restraint to do so. The inventiveness, coupled with deceit fueled by curiosity—is a cross-cultural combination in **trickster** figures—allows him to successfully steal fire. His theft, however, seems little more than a prank in contrast to other mythological fire-stealers, such as the Greek Prometheus.

At that early day the trees could talk, but the people could not burn them, as they were without fire. Fire was at length obtained through the instrumentality of the Fox.

One day Fox went to visit the geese whose cry he wished to learn. They promised to teach him, but it would be necessary for him to accompany them in their flights, in order to receive instruction. They gave him wings with which to fly, but cautioned him not to open his eyes while using them.

When the geese rose in flight Fox flew with them. As darkness came on, they passed over the enclosure where the fireflies lived. Some gleams from their flickering fires penetrated the eyelids of Fox, causing him to open his eyes.

His wings at once failed to support him, and he fell within the walls of the corral in which were pitched the tents of the fireflies. Two flies went to see the fallen Fox, who gave each a necklace of juniper berries to induce them to tell him where he could pass the wall that surrounded them.

The fireflies showed Fox a cedar tree that would bend down at command and assist anyone to pass over the wall. In the evening Fox went to the spring where the fireflies obtained water, and found colored earths suitable for paint, with which he gave himself a coat of white.

Returning to the camp, he told the fireflies that they ought to have a feast; they should dance and make merry, and he would give them a new musical instrument. They agreed to his proposal, and gathered wood for a great camp-fire, which they ignited by their own glow.

Before the ceremonies began, Fox tied shreds of cedar bark to his tail, and then made a drum, the first ever constructed, which he beat for some time. Tired of beating the drum, he gave it to one of the fireflies and moved nearer the fire, into which he thrust his tail, in opposition to the advice of those about him, who said it would surely burn.

"I am a medicine-man," said Fox, "and my tail will not burn." However, he kept a close watch upon it, and when the bark was burning well he said, "It is too warm for me here; stand aside and let me go where it is cooler."

Fox ran away with tail blazing, followed by the fireflies, who cried, "Stop, you do not know the road; come back."

Straight to the cedar-tree Fox ran, and called, "Bend down to me, my tree, bend down." The tree lifted him out of the enclosure, and on he ran, still pursued by the fireflies. As he passed along, the brush and wood on either side was ignited by the sparks, which fell from the burning cedar, and fire was widely spread over the earth.

Fox became fatigued from running, and gave the firebrand to the hawk, which carried it on, and finally delivered it to the brown crane. This bird flew far southward, but not so far but that one tree was not reached, and it will not burn to this day.

The fireflies pursued Fox to his burrow and informed him that, as punishment for having stolen fire from them and spread it abroad over the land, he should never be permitted to use it himself.

HOW SHEEP AND HORSES AND BURROS CAME TO THE ZUNI

Tradition Bearer: Tsatiselu

Source: Parsons, Elsie Clews. "Pueblo Indian Folk-tales, Probably of Spanish Provenience." *Journal of American Folklore* 31 (1918): 245–55.

Date: ca. 1918

Original Source: Zuni Pueblo (New Mexico)

National Origin: Native American

This is an extraordinary narrative that mixes plot elements of the European **ordinary folktale**, such as a cruel father-in-law and the reversal of fortune on the part of the protagonist, with Native American traditional beliefs like Kolowisi the water serpent who lives in and protects underground springs, the cornmeal road from Zuni ritual, and the magical use of the deer heart. An appropriately Pueblo moral about the virtue of dedication and hard work is substituted for the European "happily ever after" conclusion. The opening of the tale with "Sonachi" is a **formulaic** introduction for Zuni tales.

S*onachi* long ago, in the village of Heshshotoula, the son of a priest married a girl of another village. After they were married, he saw that her moccasins were all worn out, so he told her he would make her a new pair. After he had finished one for her left foot, she put it on to see if it fitted. She kept it on. With it on, she went down the hill to sit down.

Over at Alahohankwi Kyatolunnapkwi lived a Water Serpent who stole all the girls he could. Says he to himself, "Hey! There lives a girl married to the son of a priest, and I see her alone. I am going to get her." So he stretches himself, and lands by the side of the girl, who was sitting down; and he says, "I have come after you."

She asks, "Where do you live?"

He says, "Just over the way. I will bring you back in a little while." She did not want to go with him, but the Water Serpent said, "You must go, I won't go without you."

The girl said, "How am I to go?" He told her to get on his back and shut her eyes. She got on his back and shut her eyes, and the Water Serpent stretched himself, and they reached his home. He told her to open her eyes. "We are here. You wanted to come, so you will have to stay, although you have on just one moccasin." The Water Serpent puts a chair in the middle of the room, and the girl sits down. The Water Serpent wraps him-self around her so his face is near hers, and they sit there and talk.

The husband finished the other shoe, and waited for his wife to come in. She did not come. He asks, "Where is the elder sister?"

The younger sister says, "I don't know."

They all went out to look for her. They found where she had sat down, but she was nowhere to be seen. The young man says, "To-morrow I will go and search for her. Maybe I shall find her or die."

The next morning his mother gave him a bundle of meal, and he started out towards the east; and he prayed, "I am going out to find my wife, and I want you to show me the way." He sprinkled the meal, and it made a road before him, and he followed it. He went on until noon, when he sat down to eat his lunch.

While he was eating, a big eagle from his home by the ocean, saw him sitting there; and he said to himself, "I wonder who that can be! It must be the husband of the girl who was stolen by the Water Serpent. He must be looking for her. I will fly down and see him."

So the eagle flew to where the young man sat, and said, "*Konotewananate.*"

The man said, "*Ketsanishi.*"

The eagle asked, "Why are you sitting here alone and so sad?"

The young man replied, "I am hunting for my wife; someone stole her yesterday."

The eagle said, "Don't be sad! You are on the right road, and you will find her. This road leads to the ocean, and she is in the home of the Water Serpent. He is the one that stole her from you. You keep on this road; and when you get there, don't do anything until I come; then I will tell you what to do. You will be on the road four days."

"But my lunch is about all gone," replied the young man. The eagle said, "Never mind! You will be taken care of." Then the eagle flew back to his home. The young man went on until night. He rested, and he went on the next day and the next, and he went on until the morning of the fourth day. He went on until he came to a place of sand, and he sat down and ate the last of his lunch. Then he went on until night.

He reached the side of the ocean, and he said, "This must be the place." He sat down by a large tree. When he hears the flapping of wings, he says to himself, "You are coming. Who else can it be?"

The eagle alighted at his feet. He says, "My child, have you come?"

"Yes. Is this the place?"

"Yes. Is your lunch all gone?"

"Yes." The eagle says, "I have brought you something to eat;" and he gave the young man something like a deer-heart, saying, "After you eat this, you will never want for anything to eat." While the young man was eating, the eagle by his magic took the young man's heart out and put in its place the heart of a Negro.

The eagle says, "My child, your wife is here, but you are not to have her yet. You are to go towards the east; and whatever you find to do, you are to do without asking any questions. When it becomes dark, wherever you are, you are to spend the night, whether you are in a house or out of doors in the woods. Then, when you are tired of wandering around, you are to come back to this place, and I will see you again." So the eagle flew back to his home.

The young man went on for a while; and he looked down at his clothes, and they had become rags, and he had been turned into a ragged Mexican. He went on until the sun went down. He sat down in a grassy place, and said, "I will stay here for the night."

He looked around, and up out of the ground plates of food appeared; and he said, "This must be for me." So he ate; and when he had enough, the things went back into the ground.

When he got sleepy, he turned around, and he saw a bed before him; and he said, "This must be for me. This is what the eagle meant when he said that I would be taken care of." He lay down and went to sleep. Next morning he woke up and built a fire; and his bed had gone away, and his breakfast was before him. He ate, and then went on until he got to where Ley had his sheep.

He got to a little knoll, and looked down and saw the sheep and the herder. Says he to him-self, "I wonder whose sheep these are! There are only a few. They must belong to Ley. But last year the country was full of Ley's sheep, of his cattle, horses, and burros, and now there is only a small herd left. I wonder what became of them! I will talk to the herder."

He goes up to the herder, and says, "How are you?"

And the herder looks up, and sees a very ragged man standing there, and he says, "Who are you, and where are you from?"

The young man says, "I am just going about the country." The herder asks, "What are you doing? Do you work?"

The young man says, "Yes, I do any-thing I find to do. Whose sheep are these?"

The herder says, "They belong to Ley."

The young man asks, "Are you working for Ley?"

The herder says, "Yes, but my time is up, and I am just waiting for the over-seer to find someone to take my place. Won't you help me to-morrow? The over-seer will be here, and maybe he will let you take my place." They spent the night with each other. The next day the overseer says to Ley, "The herder's time is up. Who is to take his place?"

Ley says, "I do not know. You had better go and see him, and maybe he will stay a while longer."

The overseer hitches up the team and goes to the camp. When he gets there, he sees two men sitting there. "I wonder who the other man is! I never saw him before," says he to himself. He drives up, and says, "Halloo! How are you?"

"We are well," they answer. The overseer says, "Who is this man, and where is he from?"

"He came yesterday," says the herder.

The overseer asks the Zuni, "Where are you from?"

The Zuni says, "I am from the west. I am just working at anything I find to do."

"Will you work for us?" asks the overseer.

"Yes, I will."

"All right!" says the overseer. "But you must not go on the side of the hill where the ocean is. You can graze everywhere but on that side."

"All right! I will do what you say." The overseer and the herder got into the buggy and went back to Ley's house. The Zuni took the sheep out to graze; and after a while he saw another man like himself, a man all in rags, coming towards him.

When the man got near, the Zuni said, "Who are you, and where did you come from?"

The man said, "This way am I come. I do anything I find to do."

"All right!" says the Zunii. "You are to call me 'elder brother,' and you are to be my younger brother. To-morrow Ley's overseer will be here, and maybe he will let you help me."

The next day the overseer comes, and sees the other man, and asks who he is; and the Zuni says, "My younger brother, and he wants to help me."

"All right!" says the overseer. "He may help; but you must not go near the ocean, for that is where Ley lost all his sheep."—"We won't go near there," they replied. The overseer went home, and the two herded until night. The next morning the elder brother says, "Younger brother, you are to herd the horses and cattle, and I will herd the sheep." And the Zuni, by his magic heart, caused a big horse, saddle, and cowboy clothes, to appear a little ways from them.

And as the other man turned around, he saw them, and he said, "Elder brother, whose horse is that standing there?"

And the elder brother said, "It is yours. That is the horse and clothes that you are to use in herding Ley's cattle and horses. You can't herd in those rags. So go get the horse and bring him here, and take off those rags and put on the other clothes."

The younger brother did as he was told, and he got on the horse and rode away after the cattle. After he had gone, the elder brother turned the sheep out; and says he to himself, "I am going over the way they told me not to go, to see why it is that they do not want me to go over there."

He goes over the hill, and he sees nothing but water. He says to himself, "I can't do anything alone. I shall have to have someone to help me. [He, having the magic heart, saw where all Ley's herds had gone to.] So I shall have to call on my father Cougar to help me."

He calls to the cougar; and he comes and he says, "My child, why have you called me?"

The elder brother says, "Water Serpent has been killing all of Ley's sheep, cattle, and horses, and I want you to help. When I go into the water and he starts after me, I want you to grab him."—"All right!" says the cougar. The young man takes off his clothes, sprinkles the meal, and goes into the water. Water Serpent sees him, and makes a leap at him. Before he gets to the man, the cougar grabs him by the jaws and begins to drag him out. When he drags him out, Ley's sheep begin to come out of Water Serpent's stomach, all that had been eaten months before. He kept pulling at him, and all the sheep came; then the burros with herder's packs on their backs came out; then the cattle began to come. He was just about half way out, when the cougar said, "I am getting tired. I can't hold any longer."

So the man said, "Turn him loose." So he let go, and Water Serpent went back into the water. They looked around, and the whole place was full of sheep and cattle. The elder brother calls to his younger brother to come and get the cattle and put them with the others.

The younger brother says, "Whose are these?"

The elder brother says, "They are ours. They belong to Ley." The younger brother took the cattle and put them with the others. The elder brother says, "See, my father. Look around for the biggest sheep you can find, kill it, and take it home, so you can eat it and be strong, for to-morrow we are to fight again. They are not all out yet."

The cougar catches a big sheep and goes home. Next day the younger brother takes the cattle out to graze, and the elder brother takes his sheep and goes where they told him not to. He calls to his father Cougar to come.

He comes, and says, "My child, *konotewananate.*"

"*Ketsanishi,* father," says he. "We are to fight again." And he pulls his clothes off and goes into the water. Water Serpent sees him; and just about the time he is going to eat the young man, the cougar grabs him by the jaws and begins to pull him out. When he is half way out, the sheep, cattle, burros, and horses come out.

"I am getting tired," says the cougar. "I can't hold him any longer."

"Turn him aloose," the man says. So the cougar turns him loose, and he goes back into the water. The man tells the cougar to catch another sheep, so that he can have a good meal and be ready for a fight again the next day. He catches one and goes home. The elder brother takes his sheep and goes back to the corral; but there are so many, they can't all get into it. The whole country was full of sheep, cattle, burros, and horses. The men ate their supper and went to bed.

The next day the overseer came; and he saw a fine horse saddled, and a man with nice clothes on, and the place full of herds. He asks, "Whose horse is this, and whose sheep, cattle, and horses are these?"

And the elder brother says, "They are Ley's. Go and see if they are his. You know those that were lost."

The overseer went and looked at them; and he comes back, and says, "Where did all these come from? Most of them were killed long ago."

The elder brother says, "They did not come from anywhere. We just found them. We know how to herd."

"Thanks," says the over-seer. "Even if Ley has four rooms filled with gold and silver, maybe he will have enough to pay you; for you have found all of his stock, and made him a rich man again. I will go and tell him; and if he does not believe me, I will bring him, so that he may see for himself. I am going."

After he had gone, the herders sat down and ate. When they got through, the younger brother got on his horse and went after his cattle. The elder brother took his sheep and went to the ocean, and called for his father to come.

When he reached there, the elder brother said, "This is our last fight." He pulled his clothes off and went into the water. Water Serpent leaped at him, but the cougar has him by the jaws, and begins to pull him until he is almost out. The horses all begin to come out; and when all that were in had come out, the young man cried to the cougar to let him go. "His face is so sore, he won't be able to kill anything else." The cougar let go, and he went back into the water.

While they had been fighting, Ley had come to the camp, and, not finding anyone, started out to hunt them, and met them as they were coming over the hill. They all went back to camp. Ley says, "Thanks, my child! A long time ago Ley had lots of stock, but they most all were killed. Where did you get all these sheep?"

The young man says, "I did not get them anywhere. I just found them. Look around for yourself and see if they are all here."

Ley looks, and finds that they are all back again, and says, "You must know how to herd. Thanks! Maybe I shall have enough to pay you. No matter how much you want, I won't say no. When is your time up?"

"Two days from now," the young man replies.

"All right!" says Ley. "Maybe I can find someone to take your place. We must go now; and when I find someone, I will bring him, and take you back with me."

The next day they found a man to take their place. The next day they took the new herder to the camp; and the two men went back with the overseer, who said, "Maybe Ley can pay you what he owes. We will see when we get there."

Before they reached Ley's house, the elder brother says, "Younger brother, how is it to be? What are we to ask for?"

The younger brother says, "I don't know. Whatever you say."

The elder brother says, "What do we want with money? I want no money, but I want the handkerchief of his eldest daughter."

The younger brother says, "I want the gold cup the youngest daughter drinks out of."

"All right! That is what we shall ask for." When they got there, Ley's overseer set out gold chairs for them to sit on. In the other room they could hear them rattling the dishes, getting ready their dinner. When it was ready, they were asked to eat. After they had gotten through eating, they came into the room where Ley, his wife, and the overseer were sitting. They were asked to sit down. After they sat down, Ley says, "Because of you we have all of our stock back, and we are as well off as we were before. I have four rooms filled with gold and silver. Maybe I shall have enough to pay you. Tell me how much you want. Name your price."

The elder brother says, "We do not want any money. All I want is the handkerchief of your eldest daughter."

Ley says, "Are you crazy? If that is all you want, you may have it." He says to the overseer, "Go into the other room and ask the elder sister to give it to you."

He goes into the other room and asks the elder sister for it; and she laughs, and says, "He wants it. Give it to him." And she hands him her handkerchief. He takes it and gives it to the elder brother, who takes it and puts it in his pocket, with an end sticking out.

Ley turns to the other and asks what he wants; and he says, "I want the gold cup that the younger sister drinks out of."

The overseer goes into the ether room and tells the younger sister that he wants her gold cup. She gives it to him, and says, "If that is all he wants, let him have it." He takes the cup and gives it to the younger brother.

They both rose, and said, "We have got all the pay we want. We are going." They went out. Ley and his family did not know what to think.

Four days the two men wandered around in the streets, and at night they would sleep in Ley's chicken-coop with the chickens. Ley sent word out that in four days he wanted all the young men from everywhere to come to his place, and his daughters would choose from the crowd two men whom they would marry. On the fourth day the Americans, Mexicans, and all were there from everywhere.

Ley asked if all were there, and they said, "Yes." The two girls were sitting on two gold chairs on a porch that had been built for them, and the men were all to pass before them. When all was ready, the men passed by, and no one was selected. The girls would not have any of them. None were left but the two herders.

"Come," says the elder brother, "let's try! Maybe we shall be chosen."

They went; and as they passed by the nice-looking men, the men said, "Look at those two ragged men! Do they think they will be chosen after all we fine ones have been refused?"

But they did not heed anyone; and when they got to where the sisters were, both the sisters rose, and said to the two men, "You are our choice. You have our handkerchief and cup in your pockets. Come, let's go into the house!" They went into the house and told their father they had chosen these two.

Ley was angry, and said, "No, I don't want them for sons-in-law. They are too dirty and ragged. They are nothing but herders."

His daughters said, "But for them, you would not have all your stock again. You must think what they have done for you."

Ley told them, "If you want them, you will have to leave my house. You are no longer my daughters. If you want to be poor, go with them." He turned them all out.

They wandered around during the day, and at night they would sleep in Ley's chicken-house. After a few days Ley wrote them a note, saying, "I have sent for all my soldiers, and you are to be killed."

The elder brother sent a note, saying, "All right! We are not afraid." The night before they were to be killed, the elder brother selected a big open space where there were no houses, and told the others that they would spend the night there instead of in the chicken-coop. They all lay down; and the men wrapped up in the skirts of their wives and went to sleep.

After the others were asleep, the elder brother got up and went to the middle of the place, and called to his father, who lived four worlds below, whose heart he had, and said, "I want soldiers, a big fine house with everything in it, servants and all, plenty of big black horses; for tomorrow we are going to fight, and see who is the stronger." Then he went back to sleep, for he knew by his magic heart that everything would be as he asked.

Next morning, when they woke up, they were in a fine house, with everything they could wish for. They looked out, and the whole place was covered with black soldiers. The wife of the elder brother said, "Whose house and horses and soldiers are these?"

And he said, "They are ours. Today your father is to have us killed. I borrowed these soldiers from the underworld. They are not real people. They are raw people (non-Zunis)."

At noon Ley's over-seer brought over a note, saying they were to be killed. They wrote a note back, saying, "All right! We are not afraid, for you can't kill our soldiers."

After dinner Ley brought out his soldiers and lined them up. There were eight lines. Then the elder brother lined up his, and there were nine lines. The Whites shot at the Blacks, but not one fell. They shot at them until all their shells were shot. Now the Blacks began to shoot at the others; and all Ley's soldiers were killed, and the people all fled to the hills. No one was left but Ley and his wife.

Ley's sons-in-law went to him, and said, "We have come to kill you ourselves."

"You started the fight, we did not." Ley said, "My children, if you will spare me, I will become your herdsman. All of my money, houses, stock, and everything are yours if you will not kill me. You will become Ley, and I shall be you."

They granted him his wish; and Ley went to herding sheep, and his wife went with him as cook. The two herders became Ley. At night the elder brother told his soldiers to go back to their home. They had done as he wanted them, so they went back. After a few days the elder brother said, "Younger brother, you are to be Ley. I am going back to my home. It is not to be that I live here. I am of another people." His wife wanted to go with him; but he told her she could not go, that he was to go alone.

He started out; and when he had gone a ways, he saw a crowd around a pole. On top of the pole was a shoe with five dollars in gold in it, and whoever climbed up there and got the money won. They all had tried, but no one had climbed up.

Someone said, "Here comes a man. Maybe he can climb and get it." He began to climb; and as he was climbing, he prayed to his fathers of the underworld to help him. He went up and got the shoe, and brought it down.

He goes again on his way. As he goes along, he says to himself, "I wonder how far I am from my wife! I should like to see her." At night he comes to a grassy place, and he builds a fire; and a table with everything to eat appears, and he eats, and the table disappears; and when he gets sleepy, the bed comps up, and he goes to sleep. He gets up and he goes on.

After four days, he gets to where his wife is. He sits there and waits for the eagle to come. And while he is sitting there, the eagle flies down to where he is. He says, "My child, have you come? And what is in your mind?"

The young man says, "I want my wife. I love her; and if you can help me, I shall be glad."

"All right!" says the eagle. "But you will have to be brave and not give up. I shall go first and see how things are. Maybe she is dead. When you were at Ley's, the one that stole her you almost killed. He is sick now. When the cougar caught him, she was looking from the window at you."

The eagle went, and found Water Serpent dead. The girl was sitting beside him, for there was no way for her to get out. The eagle went in, and said, "How are you, my child, and how is your husband?"

"He is dead," she said.

The eagle said, "Your husband wants you, but how can he come in when you have people here watching you?"

She said, "You must find a way to get him here, and then we will try and get away."

So the eagle flew back to where the young man was sitting, and said, "I have come after you to take you to your wife. Get on my back, and we will go." The young man got on his back and flew to his wife.

He got off, and he said, "I have come for you. I started a long time ago; but our father, the eagle, changed my road. We will go home."

She says, "All right! I love you, and will do as you say." He calls all the Zuni from the different directions, and tells them he has come for his wife, and asks if he may take her.

They say, "Yes;" and they bring them beads, white and coral and turquoise; and one brought *a shule* (a blanket made of reeds), and they wrapped the beads in it and gave it to them. They told him he was not to sleep with his wife, and not for anything was he to leave her or the beads alone at any time on his way. "If you do, we shall get her again."

The young man said, "I want the heart of Water Serpent to take with me." So they gave him the heart with the beads. They got on the back of the eagle, and they flew out of the house of the Water Serpent. The eagle put them down, and told them not to forget what they had been told.

They went on their way. At night they did not sleep together, and he slept with the beads under his head. Next day they went on; and the next day, as they were just a little way from home, they stopped; and the man told his wife, "You sit on these beads while I look around some." She sat down on the beads, and he passed out of sight.

Water Serpent, by his magic (*aiuchiana*), sees her sitting there alone, and he stretches himself and lands where she is, and says, "I have come after you. Your husband does not love you. He did not do as he was told." And he takes her and the beads back to his home.

The young man saw a deer; he killed it, and took out the heart. He made a bundle of the meat. When he went back to where he left his wife, she was not there. Then he remembered what he had been told, and he knew where she had gone. He knew he had done wrong in leaving her alone.

The eagle saw him, and he flew to where he was sitting, and said, "How are you?"

And the young man said, "I am happy and not happy, for I have lost my wife. I did wrong in leaving her; but I saw a deer and ran after it, and when I came back, she was gone."

"Too bad," says the eagle, "and you so near home too. What have you on the fire?"

And the young man says, "The heart of the deer."

"Give it to me," says the eagle. And he gave it to him. The eagle kept it a little while, then gave it to him, and said, "Eat it; and when you have eaten it, the heart I gave you will come back to me, and you will have your own heart again. As you go home, whatever you find, know that I have sent it to you. As you go home, you will find something. Tomorrow go to the west, the next day go to the south, the next, to the east; and whatever you see, know that I have taken pity on you and sent it."

The eagle flew away, and the young man started on. Pretty soon he saw a flock of sheep; and he said, "This must be what you were going to give me." He goes behind them and drives them home. Before he gets home, his little sister sees him, and she tells the others that the elder brother is coming and bringing something with him. But they did not believe her.

Her father comes out, and sees him, and goes to meet him, and says, "My child, have you come home, and what are these?"

His son says, "They are sheep."

"But what are sheep?" he asks. "They are good to eat; and if we are careful, we shall have many. Put them into a corral, and to-morrow you can take them out to graze."

After supper they ask him if he found his wife. He tells all about Ley and where he had been, and how he had almost brought his wife home. But he had not done as he was told, and she was taken back again.

"Too bad," they said. "You did not love her enough to do as you were told. She did right in going back."

The next morning he went out, and he saw a big deer. He killed it. He turned around, and he saw a horse with a saddle on. He went up to it and caught it. He thinks, "This must be what I was to get." He puts his deer-meat on its back and goes home.

His little sister was looking for him, and she says, "Elder brother is coming and leading something." They go to meet him, and ask what he has. He tells them it is a horse. They ask him what a horse is. He tells them that it is to ride.

The next day he went out, and he killed a deer and found a mule. The next day he went out, and he found a burro and brought it home. They had never seen any-thing like them, and they did not know their names. So by the good-ness of his father the eagle he became rich. Thus it happens, that if anyone tries hard enough, he will be able to find something. Thus ends the story.

NOQOÌLPI, THE GAMBLER: A NAVAJO MYTH

Tradition Bearer: Unavailable

Source: Matthews, Washington. "Noqoìlpi, the Gambler: A Navajo Myth." *Journal of American Folklore* 2 (1889): 89–94.

Date: ca. 1889

Original Source: Navajo (New Mexico)
National Origin: Native American

According to folklorist Washington Matthews, "In the cañon of the Chaco, in northern New Mexico, there are many ruins of ancient pueblos which are still in a fair state of preservation, in some of them entire apartments being yet, it is said, intact. One of the largest of these is called by the Navajos Kintyèl or Kintyèli, which signifies 'Broad-house.' It figures frequently in their legends." These are ruins of dwellings built by the Anasazi who occupied the area from about 1 CE to 1300 CE, farming corn, beans, and squash. There are varied opinions concerning the reasons for the abandonment of the cliff dwellings and the fragmenting of the Anasazi culture; their descendants are probably the modern Zuni Pueblo. Some scholars contend that the Navajo migrated to the area as early as 1000 CE, which would place them in the area before the Anasazi abandonment. At the time of their arrival, the Navajo, like the Apache, were hunters and gatherers. They were strongly influenced by the sedentary Pueblo farmers, which wrought changes in areas such as their means of obtaining subsistence and their religious life. The **formulaic** use of the number four is common not only in Navajo tradition, but also among the majority of Native American groups. The story of "Noqoìlpi, the Gambler" is a single episode in the Navajo **myth** of the creation and their migration to the Southwest.

Some time before, there had descended among the Pueblos, from the heavens, a divine gambler or gambling-god, named Noqoìlpi, or He-who-wins-men (at play); his talisman was a great piece of turquoise. When he came, he challenged the people to all sorts of games and contests, and in all of these he was successful. He won from them, first their property, then their women and children, and finally some of the men themselves.

Then he told them he would give them part of their property back in payment if they would build a great house; so when the Navajos came, the Pueblos were busy building in order that they might release their enthralled relatives and their property. They were also busy making a racetrack, and preparing for all kinds of games of chance and skill.

When all was ready, and four days notice had been given, twelve men came from the neighboring pueblo of *Kinçolij* (Blue-house) to compete with the great gambler. They bet their own persons, and after a brief contest they lost themselves to Noqoìlpi. Again a notice of four days was given, and again twelve men of *Kinçolij*—relatives of the former twelve—came to play, and these also lost themselves. For the third time an announcement, four days in advance of a game, was given; this time some women were among the twelve contestants, and they too lost themselves. All were put to work on the building of *Kintyèl* as soon as they forfeited their liberty. At the end of another four days the children of these men and women came to try to win back their parents, but they succeeded only in adding themselves to the number of the gambler's slaves. On a fifth trial, after four days' warning, twelve leading men of Blue-house were lost, among them the chief of the pueblo. On a sixth duly announced gambling-day twelve more men, all important persons, staked their liberty and lost it. Up to this time the Navajos had kept count of the winnings of Noqoìlpi, but afterwards people from other pueblos came in such numbers to play and lose that they could keep count no longer. In addition to their own persons the later victims brought in beads, shells, turquoise, and all sorts of valuables, and gambled them away. With the labor of all these slaves it was not long until the great *Kintyèl* was finished.

But all this time the Navajos had been merely spectators, and had taken no part in the games. One day the voice of the beneficent god *Qastcèyalçi* was heard faintly in the distance crying his usual call "hu`hu`hu`hu`." His voice was heard, as it is always heard, four times, each time nearer and nearer, and immediately after the last call, which was loud and clear, *Qastcèyalçi* appeared at the door of a hut where dwelt a young couple who had no children, and with them he communicated by means of signs.

He told them that the people of *Kinçolij* had lost at game with Noqoìlpi two great shells, the greatest treasures of the pueblo; that the Sun had coveted these shells, and had begged them from the gambler; that the latter had refused the request of the Sun and the Sun was angry. In consequence of all this, as *Qastcèyalçi* related, in twelve days from his visit certain divine personages would meet in the mountains, in a place that he designated, to hold a great ceremony. He invited the young man to be present at the ceremony, and disappeared.

The Navajo kept count of the passing days; on the twelfth day he repaired to the appointed place, and there he found a great assemblage of the gods. There were *Qastcèyalçi*, *Qastcèqogan* and his son, *Níltci*, the Wind, *Tcalyèl*, the Darkness, *Tcàapani*, the Bat, *Klictsò*, the Great Snake, *Tsilkàli* (a little bird),

Nasísi, the Gopher, and many others. Beside these, there were present a number of pets or domesticated animals belonging to the gambler, who were dissatisfied with their lot, were anxious to be free, and would gladly obtain their share of the spoils in case their master was ruined. *Níltci*, the Wind, had spoken to them, and they had come to enter into the plot against *Noqoìlpi*. All night the gods danced and sang, and performed their mystic rites, for the purpose of giving to the son of *Qastcèqogan* powers as a gambler equal to those of *Noqoìlpi*. When the morning came they washed the young neophyte all over, dried him with corn meal, dressed him in clothes exactly like those the gambler wore, and in every way made him look as much like the gambler as possible, and then they counseled as to what other means they should take to out-wit *Noqoìlpi*.

In the first place, they desired to find out how he felt about having refused to his father, the Sun, the two great shells.

"I will do this," said *Níltci*, the Wind, "for I can penetrate everywhere, and no one can see me;" but the others said, "No, you can go everywhere, but you cannot travel without making a noise and disturbing people. Let *Tcalyèl*, the Darkness, go on this errand, for he also goes wherever he wills, yet he makes no noise."

So *Tcalyèl* went to the gambler's house, entered his room, went all through his body while he slept, and searched well his mind, and he came back saying, "*Noqoìlpi* is sorry for what he has done."

Níltci, however, did not believe this; so, although his services had been before refused, he repaired to the chamber where the gambler slept, and went all through his body and searched well his mind; but he too came back saying *Noqoìlpi* was sorry that he had refused to give the great shells to his father.

One of the games they proposed to play is called *çàka-çqadsàç*, or the thirteen chips; it is played with thirteen thin flat pieces of wood, which are colored red on one side and left white or uncolored on the other side. Success depends on the number of chips, which, being thrown upward, fall with their white sides up.

"Leave the game to me," said the Bat; "I have made thirteen chips that are white on both sides. I will hide myself in the ceiling, and when our champion throws up his chips I will grasp them and throw down my chips instead."

Another game they were to play is called *nanjoj*; it is played with two long sticks or poles, of peculiar shape and construction (one marked with red and the other with black), and a single hoop. A long many-tailed string, called the "turkey-claw," is secured to the centre of each pole.

"Leave *nanjoj* to me," said the Great Snake; "I will hide myself in the hoop and make it fall where I please."

Another game was one called *tsínbetsil*, or push-on-the-wood; in this the contestants push against a tree until it is torn from its roots and falls.

"I will see that this game is won," said *Nasísi*, the Gopher; "I will gnaw the roots of the tree, so that he who shoves it may easily make it fall."

In the game of *tcol*, or ball, the object was to hit the ball so that it would fall beyond a certain line.

"I will win this game for you," said the little bird, *Tsilkáli*, "for I will hide within the ball, and fly with it wherever I want to go. Do not hit the ball hard; give it only a light tap, and depend on me to carry it."

The pets of the gambler begged the Wind to blow hard, so that they might have an excuse to give their master for not keeping due watch when he was in danger, and in the morning the Wind blew for them a strong gale. At dawn the whole party of conspirators left the mountain, and came down to the brow of the *canyon* to watch until sunrise.

Noqoìlpi had two wives, who were the prettiest women in the whole land. Wherever she went, each carried in her hand a stick with something tied on the end of it, as a sign that she was the wife of the great gambler.

It was their custom for one of them to go every morning at sunrise to a neighboring spring to get water. So at sunrise the watchers on the brow of the cliff saw one of the wives coming out of the gambler's house with a water jar on her head, whereupon the son of *Qastcèqogan* descended into the *canyon*, and followed her to the spring. She was not aware of his presence until she had filled her water-jar; then she supposed it to be her own husband, whom the youth was dressed and adorned to represent, and she allowed him to approach her. She soon discovered her error, however, but deeming it prudent to say nothing, she suffered him to follow her into the house. As he entered, he observed that many of the slaves had already assembled; perhaps they were aware that some trouble was in store for their master. The latter looked up with an angry face; he felt jealous when he saw the stranger entering immediately after his wife. He said nothing of this, however, but asked at once the important question, "Have you come to gamble with me?" This he repeated four times, and each time the young *Qastcèqogan* said "No." Thinking the stranger feared to play with him, Noqoìlpi went on challenging him recklessly.

"I'll bet myself against yourself;"

"I'll bet my feet against your feet;"

"I'll bet my legs against your legs;" and so on he offered to bet every and any part of his body against the same part of his adversary, ending by mentioning his hair.

In the mean time the party of divine ones, who had been watching from above, came down, and people from the neighboring pueblos came in, and among these were two boys, who were dressed in costumes similar to those worn by the wives of the gambler. The young *Qastcèqogan* pointed to these and said, "I will bet my wives my against your wives."

The great gambler accepted the wager, and the four persons, two women and two mock women, were placed sitting in a row near the wall. First they played the game of thirteen chips. The Bat assisted, as he had promised the son of *Qastcèqogan*, and the latter soon won the game, and with it the wives of Noqoìlpi.

This was the only game played inside the house; then all went out of doors, and games of various kinds were played. First they tried *nanjoj*. The track already prepared lay east and west, but, prompted by the wind god, the stranger insisted on having a track made from north to south, and again, at the bidding of the Wind, he chose the red stick. The son of *Qastcèqogan* threw the wheel: at first it seemed about to fall on the gambler's pole, in the "turkey-claw" of which it was entangled; but to the great surprise of the gambler it extricated itself, rolled farther on, and fell on the pole of his opponent. The latter ran to pick up the ring, lest Noqoìlpi in doing so might hurt the Snake inside; but the gambler was so angry that he threw his stick away and gave up the game, hoping to do better in the next contest, which was that of pushing down trees.

For this the great gambler pointed out two small trees, but his opponent insisted that larger trees must be found. After some search they agreed upon two of good size, which grew close together, and of these the wind-god told the youth which one he must select. The gambler strained with all his might at his tree, but could not move it, while his opponent, when his turn came, shoved the other tree prostrate with little effort, for its roots had all been severed by the Gopher.

Then followed a variety of games, on which *Noqoìlpi* staked his wealth in shells and precious stones, his houses, and many of his slaves, and lost all.

The last game was that of the ball. On the line over which the ball was to be knocked all the people were assembled: on one side were those who still remained slaves; on the other side were the freedmen and those who had come to wager themselves, hoping to rescue their kinsmen. Noqoìlpi bet on this game the last of his slaves and his own person. The gambler struck his ball a heavy blow, but it did not reach the line; the stranger gave his but a light tap, and the bird within it flew with it far beyond the line, where at the released captives jumped over the line and joined their people.

The victor ordered all the shell beads and precious stones and the great shells to be brought forth. He gave the beads and shells to *Qastèyalçi*, that they might be distributed among the gods; the two great shells were given to the Sun.

In the mean time *Noqoìlpi* sat to one side saying bitter things, bemoaning his fate, and cursing and threatening his enemies: "I will kill you all with the lightning. I will send war and disease among you. May the cold freeze you! May the fire burn you! May the waters drown you!" he cried.

"He has cursed enough," whispered *Níltci* to the son of *Qastcèqogan*. "Put an end to his angry words."

So the young victor called Noqoìlpi to him, and said, "You have bet yourself and have lost; you are now my slave and must do my bidding. You are not a god, for my power has prevailed against yours."

The victor had a bow of magic power named the Bow of Darkness; he bent this upwards, and placing the string on the ground, he bade his illustrious slave stand on the string; then he shot Noqoìlpi up into the sky as if he had been an arrow. Up and up he went, growing smaller and smaller to the sight till he faded to a mere speck, and finally disappeared altogether. As he flew upwards he was heard to mutter in the angry tones of abuse and imprecation, until he was too far away to be heard; but no one could distinguish anything he said as he ascended.

He flew up in the sky until he came to the home of *Bekotcic-e*, the god who carries the moon, and who is supposed by the Navajos to be identical with the god of the Americans. He is very old, and dwells in a long row of stone houses. When Noqoìlpi arrived at the house of *Bekotcic-e*, he related to the latter all his misadventures in the lower world and said, "Now I am poor, and this is why I have come to see you."

"You need be poor no longer," said *Bekotcic-e* "I will provide for you."

So he made for the gambler pets or domestic animals of new kinds, different than those he had in the Chaco valley; he made for him sheep, asses, horses, swine, goats, and fowls. He also gave him *bayeta*, and other cloths of bright colors, more beautiful than those woven by his slaves at *Kintyèli*. He made, too, a new people, the Mexicans, for the gambler to rule over, and then he sent him back to this world again, but he descended far to the south of his former abode, and reached the earth in old Mexico.

Noqoìlpi's people increased greatly in Mexico, and after a while they began to move toward the north, and build towns along the Rio Grande. Noqoìlpi came with them until they arrived at a place north of Santa Fe. There they ceased building, and he returned to old Mexico, where he still lives, and where he is now the *Nakài C-igíni*, or God of the Mexicans.

THE ANTELOPE BOY

Tradition Bearer: Unavailable

Source: Lummis, Charles. "The Antelope Boy." Pages 12–21 in *Pueblo Indian Folk-Stories*. New York: Century, 1910.

Date: 1910.

Original Source: Isleta Pueblo (New Mexico)

National Origin: Native American

The Tiwa of Isleta, like the Acoma (see "Origin of Acoma," p. 7), developed an agricultural way of life based on raising corn, beans, and squash. The diet provided by these crops was supplemented by hunting, as was the case with Acoma. Eastern, or Rio Grande, Pueblos such as Isleta—unlike the Western Pueblo of Acoma—relied on irrigation for their crops and thus developed a strong village identity and loyalty. The village was divided into halves, called moieties: the Summer People and the Winter People. Each of the moieties had a cacique (principal religious authority) who governed the village's religious life for half the year. The caciques were elders who were chosen for wisdom, even temperament, and their ability to maintain village harmony. They stood in polar opposition to the witches who play so prominent a role in the following **myth.** The cigarettes smoked by Antelope Boy to create rain clouds are the equivalent to the pipe that is familiar to other Native American traditions. The power of Antelope Boy comes from both his animal spirit helpers and from his marginal status as a human who was raised by antelopes. This marginality is also an attribute of **trickster.**

Once upon a time there were two towns of the Tiwa, called White Village and Yellow Village. A man of White village and his wife were attacked by Apaches while out on the plains one day, and took refuge in a cave, where they were besieged. And there a boy was born to them. The father was killed in an attempt to return to his village for help; and starvation finally forced the mother to crawl forth by night seeking roots to eat. Chased by the Apaches, she escaped to her own village, and it was several days before she could return to the cave—only to find it empty.

The baby had begun to cry soon after her departure. Just then a Coyote was passing, and heard. Taking pity on the child, he picked it up and carried it across the plain until he came to a herd of antelopes. Among them was a Mother-Antelope that had lost her fawn; and going to her the Coyote said: "Here is a poor thing that is left by its people. Will you take care of it?"

The Mother Antelope, remembering her own baby, with tears said "Yes," and at once adopted the tiny stranger, while the Coyote thanked her and went home.

So the boy became as one of the antelopes, and grew up among them until he was about twelve years old. Then it happened that a hunter came out from White village for antelopes, and found this herd. Stalking them carefully, he shot one with an arrow. The rest started off, running like the wind; but ahead of them all, as long as they were in sight, he saw a boy!

The hunter was much surprised, and, shouldering his game, walked back to the village, deep in thought. Here he told the Cacique what he had seen. Next day the crier was sent out to call upon all the people to prepare for a great hunt, in four days, to capture the Indian boy who lived with the antelopes.

While preparations were going on in the village, the antelopes in some way heard of the intended hunt and its purpose. The Mother-Antelope was very sad when she heard it, and at first would say nothing, but at last she called her adopted son to her and said: "Son, you have heard that the people of White village are coming to hunt. But they will not kill us; all they wish is to take you. They will surround us, intending to let all the antelopes escape from the circle. You must follow me where I break through the line, and your real mother will be coming on the northeast side in a white *manta* (robe). I will pass close to her, and you must stagger and fall where she can catch you."

On the fourth day all the people went out upon the plains. They found and surrounded the herd of antelopes, which ran about in a circle when the hunters closed upon them. The circle grew smaller, and the antelopes began to break through; but the hunters paid no attention to them, keeping their eyes upon the boy. At last he and his antelope mother were the only ones left, and when she broke through the line on the northeast he followed her and fell at the feet of his own human mother, who sprang forward and clasped him in her arms.

Amid great rejoicing he was taken to White village, and there he told the *principales* (Council of advisors) how he had been left in the cave, how the Coyote had pitied him, and how the Mother-Antelope had reared him as her own son.

It was not long before all the country round about heard of the Antelope Boy and of his marvelous fleetness of foot. You must know that the antelopes never comb their hair, and while among them the boy's head had grown very bushy. So the people called him *Pée-hleh-o-wah-wée-deh* (big-headed little boy).

Among the other villages that heard of his prowess was Yellow Village, all of whose people "had the bad road." They had a wonderful runner named *Pée-k'hoo* (Deer-foot), and very soon they sent a challenge to White village for a championship race. Four days were to be given for preparation, to make bets, and the like. The race was to be around the world. Each village was to stake all its property and the lives of all its people on the result of the race. So powerful were the witches of Yellow Village that they felt safe in proposing so serious a stake; and the people of White village were ashamed to decline the challenge.

The day came, and the starting-point was surrounded by all the people of the two villages, dressed in their best. On each side were huge piles of ornaments and dresses, stores of grain, and all the other property of the people. The runner for the Yellow Village was a tall, sinewy athlete, strong in his early manhood; and when the Antelope Boy appeared for the other side, the witches set up a howl of derision, and began to strike their rivals and jeer at them, saying, "We might as well begin to kill you now! What can that little thing do?"

At the word "*Hái-ko!*" ("Go!") the two runners started toward the east like the wind. The Antelope Boy soon forged ahead; but Deer-foot, by his witchcraft, changed himself into a hawk and flew lightly over the lad, saying, "We do this way to each other!" The Antelope Boy kept running, but his heart was very heavy, for he knew that no feet could equal the swift flight of the hawk.

But just as he came halfway to the east, a Mole came up from its burrow and said: "My son, where are you going so fast with a sad face?"

The lad explained that the race was for the property and lives of all his people; and that the witch-runner had turned to a hawk and left him far behind.

"Then, my son," said the Mole, "I will be he that shall help you. Only sit down here a little while, and I will give you something to carry."

The boy sat down, and the Mole dived into the hole, but soon came back with four cigarettes. Holding them out, the Mole said, "Now, my son, when you have reached the east and turned north, smoke one; when you have reached the north and turn west, smoke another; when you turn south, another, and when you turn east again, another. Go!"

The boy ran on, and soon reached the east. Turning his face to the north he smoked the first cigarette. No sooner was it finished than he became a young antelope; and at the same instant a furious rain began. Refreshed by the cool drops, he started like an arrow from the bow. Halfway to the north he came to a large tree; and there sat the hawk, drenched and chilled, unable to fly, and crying piteously.

"Now, friend, we too do this to each other," called the boy-antelope as he dashed past. But just as he reached the north, the hawk—which had become dry after the short rain—caught up and passed him, saying, "We too do this to each other!"

The boy-antelope turned westward, and smoked the second cigarette; and at once another terrific rain began. Halfway to the west he again passed the hawk shivering and crying in a tree, and unable to fly; but as he was about to turn to the south, the hawk passed him with the customary taunt. The smoking of the third cigarette brought another storm, and again the antelope passed the wet hawk halfway, and again the hawk dried its feathers in time to catch up and pass him as he was turning to the east for the homestretch. Here again the boy-antelope stopped and smoked a cigarette—the fourth and last. Again a short, hard rain came, and again he passed the water-bound hawk halfway.

Knowing the witchcraft of their neighbors, the people of White village had made the condition that, in whatever shape the racers might run the rest of the course, they must resume human form upon arrival at a certain hill upon the fourth turn, which was in sight of the goal. The last wetting of the hawk's feathers delayed it so that the antelope reached the hill just ahead; and there, resuming their natural shapes, the two runners came sweeping down the home stretch, straining every nerve. But the Antelope Boy gained at each stride. When they saw him, the witch-people felt confident that he was their champion, and again began to push, and taunt, and jeer at the others. But when the little Antelope Boy sprang lightly across the line, far ahead of Deer-foot, their joy turned to mourning.

The people of White village burned all the witches upon the spot, in a great pile of corn; but somehow one escaped, and from him come all the witches that trouble us to this day.

The property of the witches was taken to White village; and as it was more than that village could hold, the surplus was sent to Isleta, where we enjoy it to this day; and later the people themselves moved here. And even now, when we dig in that little hill on the other side of the pool, we find charred corncobs, where our forefathers burned the witch-people of the Yellow Village.

HEROES, HEROINES, TRICKSTERS, AND FOOLS

THE HERO TWINS

Tradition Bearer: Unavailable

Source: Lummis, Charles. "The Hero Twins." Pages 206–14 in *Pueblo Indian Folk-Stories*. New York: Century, 1910.

Date: 1910.

Original Source: Isleta Pueblo (New Mexico)

National Origin: Native American

According to Charles Lummis, who collected the following **myth** at Isleta Pueblo, the narrative was imported into the Tiwa village by Keres (Quères) speakers from the villages of Laguna and Acoma that were given refuge from crop failure brought on by a drought and stayed to become residents of Isleta. The Hero Twins are prominent figures in Pueblo **myth** as **tricksters** and **culture heroes**. Similar twin figures, in fact, are found throughout Native North America (see, for example, the Wichita "The Two Boys Who Slew the Monsters and Became Stars," p. 212). For further discussion of Isleta religious life, see "The Antelope Boy" (p. 41).

Máw-Sahv and Oó-yah-wee, as the Hero Twins are named in Quères, had the Sun for a father. Their mother died when they were born, and lay lifeless upon the hot plain. But the two wonderful boys, as soon as they were a minute old, were big and strong, and began playing.

There chanced to be in a cliff to the southward a nest of white crows; and presently the young crows said: "Nana, what is that over there? Isn't it two babies?"

"Yes," replied the Mother-Crow, when she had taken a look. "Wait and I will bring them." So she brought the boys safely, and then their dead mother; and, rubbing a magic herb on the body of the latter, soon brought her to life.

By this time Máw-Sahv and Oó-yah-wee were sizable boys, and the mother started homeward with them. "Now," said she when they reached the edge of the valley and could look across to that wondrous rock whereon stands Acoma, "go to yonder town, my sons, for that is where live your grandfather and grandmother, my parents; and I will wait here. Go ye in at the west end of the town and stand at the south end of the council-grounds until someone speaks to you; and ask them to take you to the Cacique, for he is your grandfather. You will know his house, for the ladder to it has three uprights instead of two. When you go in and tell your story, he will ask you a question to see if you are really his grandchildren, and will give you four chances to answer what he has in a bag in the corner. No one has ever been able to guess what is in it, but there are birds."

The Twins did as they were bidden, and presently came to Acoma and found the house of the old Cacique. When they entered and told their story, he said: "Now I will try you. What is in yonder bag?"

"A rattlesnake," said the boys.

"No," said the Cacique, "it is not a rattlesnake. Try again."

"Birds," said the boys.

"Yes, they are birds. Now I know that you are truly my grandchildren, for no one else could ever guess." And he welcomed them gladly, and sent them back with new dresses and jewelry to bring their mother.

When she was about to arrive, the Twins ran ahead to the house and told her father, mother, and sister to leave the house until she should enter; but not knowing what was to come, they would not go out. When she had climbed the big ladder to the roof and started down through the trap-door by the room-ladder, her sister cried out with joy at seeing her, and she was so startled that she fell from the ladder and broke her neck, and never could be brought to life again.

Máw-Sahv and Oó-yah-wee grew up to astounding adventures and achievements. While still very young in years, they did very remarkable things; for they had a miraculously rapid growth, and at an age when other boys were toddling about home, these Hero Twins had already become very famous hunters and warriors. They were very fond of stories of adventure, like less precocious lads; and after the death of their mother they kept their grandmother busy telling them strange tales. She had a great many anecdotes of a certain ogre-giantess who lived in the dark gorges of the mountains to the South, and so much did Máw-Sahv and Oó-yah-wee hear of this wonderful personage—who was the terror of all that country—that their boyish ambition was fired.

One day when their grandmother was busy they stole away from home with their bows and arrows, and walked miles and miles, till they came to a great forest at the foot of the mountain. In the edge of it sat the old Giant-woman, dozing in the sun, with a huge basket beside her. She was so enormous and looked so fierce that the boys' hearts stood still, and they would have hidden, but just then she caught sight of them, and called: "Come, little boys, and get into this basket of mine, and I will take you to my house."

"Very well," said Máw-Sahv, bravely hiding his alarm. "If you will take us through this big forest, which we would like to see, we will go with you."

The Giant-woman promised, and the lads clambered into her basket, which she took upon her back and started off. As she passed through the woods, the boys grabbed lumps of pitch from the tall pines and smeared it all over her head and back so softly that she did not notice it. Once she sat down to rest, and the boys slyly put a lot of big stones in the basket, set fire to her pitched hair, and hurriedly climbed a tall pine.

Presently the Giant-woman got up and started on toward home; but in a minute or two her head and manta were all of a blaze. With a howl that shook the earth, she dropped the basket and rolled on the ground, grinding her great head into the sand until she at last got the fire extinguished. But she was badly scorched and very angry, and still angrier when she looked in the basket and found only a lot of stones. She retraced her steps until she found the boys hidden in the pine-tree, and said to them: "Come down, children, and get into my basket, that I may take you to my house, for now we are almost there."

The boys, knowing that she could easily break down the tree if they refused, came down. They got into the basket, and soon she brought them to her home in the mountain. She set them down upon the ground and said: "Now, boys, go and bring me a lot of wood, that I may make a fire in the oven and bake you some sweet cakes."

The boys gathered a big pile of wood, with which she built a roaring fire in the adobe oven outside the house. Then she took them and washed them very carefully, and taking them by the necks, thrust them into the glowing oven and sealed the door with a great, flat rock, and left them there to be roasted.

But the Trues were friends of the Hero Twins, and did not let the heat harm them at all. When the old Giant-woman had gone into the house, Máw-Sahv and Oó-yah-wee broke the smaller stone that closed the smoke-hole of the oven, and crawled out from their fiery prison unsinged. They ran around and caught snakes and toads and gathered up dirt and dropped them down into the oven through the smoke-hole; and then, watching when the Giant-woman's back was turned, they sneaked into the house and hid in a huge clay jar on the shelf.

Very early in the morning the Giant-woman's baby began to cry for some boy-meat. "Wait till it is well cooked," said the mother; and hushed the child till the sun was well up. Then she went out and unsealed the oven, and brought in the sad mess the boys had put there. "They have cooked away to almost nothing," she said; and she and the Giant-baby sat down to eat. "Isn't this nice?" said the baby; and Máw-Sahv could not help saying, "You nasty things, to like that!"

"Eh? Who is that?" cried the Giant-woman, looking around till she found the boys hidden in the jar. So she told them to come down, and gave them some sweet cakes, and then sent them out to bring her some more wood.

It was evening when they returned with a big load of wood, which Máw-Sahv had taken pains to get green. He had also picked up in the mountains a long, sharp splinter of quartz. The evening was cool, and they built a big fire in the fireplace. But immediately, as the boys had planned, the green wood began to smoke at a dreadful rate, and soon the room was so dense with it that they all began to cough and strangle. The Giant-woman got up and opened the window and put her head out for a breath of fresh air; and Máw-Sahv, pulling out the white-hot splinter of quartz from the fire, stabbed her in the back so that she died. Then they killed the Giant-baby, and at last felt that they were safe.

Now the Giant-woman's house was a very large one, and ran far back into the very heart of the mountain. Having got rid of their enemies, the Hero Twins decided to explore the house; and, taking their bows and arrows, started boldly down into the deep, dark rooms. After traveling a long way in the dark, they came to a huge room in which corn and melons and pumpkins were growing abundantly. On and on they went, till at last they heard the growl of distant thunder. Following the sound, they came presently to a room in the solid rock, wherein the lightning was stored. Going in, they took the lightning and played with it awhile, throwing it from one to the other, and at last started home, carrying their strange toy with them.

When they reached Acoma and told their grandmother of their wonderful adventures, she held up her withered old hands in amazement. And she was nearly scared to death when they began to play with the lightning, throwing it around the house as though it had been a harmless ball, while the thunder rumbled till it shook the great rock of Acoma. They had the blue lightning, which belongs in the West; and the yellow lightning of the North; and the red lightning of the East; and the white lightning of the South; and with all these they played merrily.

But it was not very long till Shée-wo-nah, the Storm-King, had occasion to use the lightning; and when he looked in the room where he was wont to keep it, and found it gone, his wrath knew no bounds. He started out to find who had stolen it; and passing by Acoma he heard the thunder as the Hero Twins were playing ball with the lightning. He pounded on the door and ordered them to give him his lightning, but the boys refused. Then he summoned the storm, and it began to rain and blow fearfully outside; while within the boys rattled their thunder in loud defiance, regardless of their grandmother's entreaties to give the Storm-King his lightning.

It kept raining violently, however, and the water came pouring down the chimney until the room was nearly full, and they were in great danger of drowning. But luckily for them, the Trues were still mindful of them; and just in the nick of time sent their servant, Tee-oh-pee, the Badger, who is the best of diggers, to dig a hole up through the floor; all the water ran out, and they were saved. And so the Hero Twins outwitted the Storm-King.

South of Acoma, in the pine-clad gorges and mesas, the world was full of Bears. There was one old She-Bear in particular, so huge and fierce that all men feared her; and not even the boldest hunter dared go to the south—for there she had her home with her two sons.

Máw-sahv and Oó-yah-wee were famous hunters, and always wished to go south; but their grandmother always forbade them. One day, however, they stole away from the house, and got into the canyon. At last they came to the She-Bear's house; and there was old Quée-ah asleep in front of the door. Máw-sahv crept up very carefully and threw in her face a lot of ground chile, and ran. At that the She-Bear began to sneeze, ah-hútch! Ah-hútch! She could not stop, and kept making ah-hútch until she sneezed herself to death.

Then the Twins took their thunder-knives and skinned her. They stuffed the great hide with grass, so that it looked like a Bear again, and tied a buckskin rope around its neck.

"Now," said Máw-sahv, "We will give our grandma a trick!"

So, taking hold of the rope, they ran toward Acoma, and the Bear came behind them as if leaping. Their grandmother was going for water; and from the top of the cliff she saw them running so in the valley, and the Bear jumping behind them. She ran to her house and painted one side of her face black with charcoal, and the other side red with the blood of an animal; and, taking a bag

51

of ashes, ran down the cliff and out at the Bear, to make it leave the boys and come after her.

But when she saw the trick, she reproved the boys for their rashness—but in her heart she was very proud of them.

HOW THE TWINS OF WAR AND CHANCE FARED WITH THE UNBORN-MADE MEN OF THE UNDERWORLD

Tradition Bearer: Waí-hu-si-wa

Source: Cushing, Frank Hamilton. "A Zuni Folk-tale of the Underworld." *Journal of American Folklore* 5 (1892): 49–56.

Date: 1892

Original Source: Zuni (New Mexico)

National Origin: Native American

The Zuni like the people of Acoma are dryland farmers with an extremely sophisticated system of metaphysics. According to their view, the universe was generated from the darkness by the action of light, which generated haze. In their philosophy, beings pass through stages of "becoming," analogous to the growth of plants from green to mature to the finished state of death. As the following **myth** notes, the phases are cyclical and circular, like the seasons on which the Zuni depend: the first stage of infancy and the last stages of the elderly are identical in many features. Similarly, as folklorist Frank Hamilton Cushing writes, the "unmade were misty inversions of humans" and other "Made" beings such as the Twins of War and Chance.

It seems—so the words of the grandfathers say—that in the Underworld were many strange things and beings, even villages of men, long ago. But the people of those villages were unborn—made—more like the ghosts of the dead than ourselves, yet more like our-selves than are the ghosts of the dead, for as the dead are more finished of being than we are, they were less so, as smoke, being hazy, is less fine than mist, which is filmy; or as green corn, though raw is soft, like cooked corn which is done (like the dead), both softer than ripe corn which, though raw, is hardened by age (as we are of meat).

And also, these people were, you see, dead in a way, in that they had not yet begun to live; that is, as we live, in the daylight fashion.

And so, it would seem, partly like ourselves, they had bodies, and partly like the dead they had no bodies, for being unfinished they were unfixed. And whereas the dead are like the wind, and take form from within of their own wills, these people were really like the smoke, taking form from without of the outward touching of things, even as growing and unripe grains and fruits do.

Well, in consequence, it was passing strange what a state they were in! Bethink ye! Their persons were much the reverse of our own, for wherein we are hard, they were soft, pliable. Wherein we are most completed, they were most unfinished; for not having even the organs of digestion, whereby we fare lustily, food in its solidity was to them destructive, whereas to us it is sustaining. When, therefore, they would eat, they dreaded most the food itself, taking thought not to touch it, and merely absorbing the mist thereof. As fishes fare chiefly on water and birds on air, so these people ate by gulping down the steam and savor of their cooked things whilst cooking or still hot; then they threw the real food away, forsooth!

Now, the Twain Little-ones, Á-hai-yú-ta and Má-tsai-lé-ma, were ever seeking scenes of contention; for what was deathly and dreadful to others was lively and delightful to them; so that cries of distress were ever their calls of invitation, as to a feast or dance is the call of a priest to us.

On a day when the world was quiet, they were sitting by the side of a deep pool. They heard curious sounds coming up through the waters, as though the bubbles were made by moans of the waters affrighted.

"Uh!" said the elder. "What is that?"

The younger brother turned his ear to the ground and listened. "There is trouble down there, dire trouble, for the people of the Underworld are shrieking war-cries like daft warriors and wailing like murder-mourners. What can be the matter? Let us descend and see!"

"Just so!" said Á-hai-yú-ta.

Then they covered their heads with their cord-shields—turned upside down—and shut their eyes and stepped into the deep pool.

"Now we are in the dark," said they, "like the dark down there. Well then, by means of the dark let us go down," for they had wondrous power, had those twain; the magic of in-knowing-how-thought had they.

Down like light through dark places they went; dry through the waters; straight toward that village in the Underworld.

"Whew! The poor wretches are already dead," said they, and rotting,—for their noses were sooner accustomed to the dark than their eyes which they now opened.

"We might as well have spared ourselves the coming, and stayed above," said Á-hai-yú-ta.

"Nay, not so," said Ma-tsai-1e-ma. "Let us go on and see how they lived, even if they are dead."

"Very well," said the elder; and as they fared toward the village they could see quite plainly now; for they had made it dark—to themselves—by shutting their eyes in the daylight above, so now they made it light—to themselves—by opening their eyes in the darkness below, and simply looking. It was their way, you know!

"Well, well!" said Má-tsai-lé-ma as they came nearer and the stench doubled. "Look at the village; it is full of people; the more they smell of carrion the more they seem alive!"

"Yes!" exclaimed Á-hai-yú-ta. "But look here! It is food we smell; cooked food, all thrown away, as we throw away bones and corncobs because they are too hard to eat and profitless withal! What, now, can be the meaning of this?"

"What, indeed! Who can know save by knowing," replied the younger brother. "Come, let us lie low and watch."

So they went very quietly close to the village, crouched down and peered in. Some people inside were about to eat. They took fine food steaming hot from the cooking pots and placed it low down in wide trenchers; then they gathered around and sipped in the steam and savor with every appearance of satisfaction; but they were as chary of touching the food or of letting the food touch them as though it were the vilest of refuse.

"Did you see that?" queried the younger brother. "By the delight of Death, but..."

"Hist!" said the elder. "If they are people of that sort, feeding upon the savor of food, then they will hear the suggestions of sounds better than the sounds themselves, and the very Demon Fathers would not know how to fare with such people or to fight them, either!"

Hah! But already the people had heard! They set up a clamor of war, swarming out to seek the enemy; as well they might, for who would think favorably of a sneaking stranger under the shade of a house wall watching the food of another! Why, dogs growl even at their own offspring for the like of that!

"Where? Who? What is it?" cried the people, rushing hither and thither like ants in a shower. "Hah! There they are! There! Quick!" said they, pointing to the Twain who were cutting away to the nearest hillock. And immediately they fell to singing their war-cry as they ran headlong toward the two, and then they began shouting:

"Tread them both into the ground! Smite them both! Fan them out!"

But the Twain laughed and quickly drew their arrows and loosed them amongst the crowd. Pit! Tsok! Sang the arrows through and through the people, but never a one fell!

"Why, how now is this?" cried the elder brother.

"We'll club them, then!" said Má-tsai-lé-ma, and he whipped out his war-club and sprang to meet the foremost, whom he pummelled well and sorely over the head and shoulders. Yet the man was only confused (he was too soft and unstable to be hurt); but another, rushing in at one side, was hit by one of the shield-feathers and fell to the ground like smoke driven down under a hawk's wing!

"Hold, brother, I have it! Hold!" cried Á-hai-yú-ta. Then he snatched up a bunch of dry plume-grass, and leaped forward. Swish! Two ways he swept the faces and breasts of the pursuers. Lo! Right and left they fell like bees in a rainstorm, and quickly sued for mercy, screeching and running at the mere sight of the grass straws.

"You fools," cried the brothers. "Why, then, did ye set upon us? We came for to help you and were merely looking ahead as becomes strangers in strange places, when you come running out like a mess of mad flies. Call us coyote-sneaks, do you? But there! Rest fearless! We hunger; give us to eat."

So they led the Twain into the court within the town, and quickly brought steaming hot food for them.

They sat down and began to blow the food to cool it; whereupon the people cried out in dismay: "Hold! Hold, ye heedless strangers; do not waste precious food like that! For shame!"

"Waste food? Ha! This is the way we eat!" said they; and clutching up huge morsels they crammed their mouths full and bolted them almost whole. The people were so horrified and sickened at sight of this, that some of them sweated furiously, which was their way of vomiting, whilst others, stouter of thought, cried, "Hold! Hold! Ye will die; ye will surely sicken and die if the stuff do but touch ye!"

"Ho! Ho!" cried the two, eating more lustily than ever. "Eat thus and harden yourselves, you poor, soft things you!"

Just then there was a great commotion. Everyone rushed to the shelter of the walls and houses, shouting to them to leave off and follow quickly.

"What is it?" asked they, looking up and all around.

"Woe, woe! The gods are angry with us this day and blowing arrows at us. They will kill you both! Hurry!" A big puff of wind was blowing over, scattering slivers and straws before it; that was all!

"Brother," said the elder, "this will not do. These people must be taught to eat and be hardened. But let us take a little sleep first, then we will look to this."

They propped themselves up against a wall, set their shields in front of them, and fell asleep. Not long after they awakened suddenly. Those strange people were trying to drag them out to bury them, but were afraid to touch them now, for they thought them dead stuff—more dead than alive.

The younger brother punched the elder with his elbow, and both pretended to gasp, then kept very still. The people succeeded at last in rolling them out of the court, like spoiling bodies, and were about to mingle them with the refuse when they suddenly let go and set up a great wail, shouting, "War! Murder!"

"How now?" cried the two, jumping up. Whereupon the people stared and chattered in greater fright than ever at seeing the dead seemingly come to life!

"What's the matter, you fool people?"

"Akaa! Kaa!" cried a flock of jays.

"Hear that!" said the villagers. "Hear that, and ask 'What's the matter?' The jays are coming; whoever they light on dies!—run you two! Aii! Murder!" And they left off their standing as though chased by demons. On one or two of the hindmost some jays alighted. They fell dead as though struck by lightning!

"Why, see that said the elder brother, "these people die if only birds light on them!"

"Hold on there!" said the younger brother. "Look here! You fearsome things." So they pulled hairs from some scalplocks they had, and made snares of them, and whenever the jays flew at them, caught them with the nooses until they had caught everyone. Then they pinched them dead and took them into the town and roasted them.

"This is the way," said they, as they ate the jays by morsels.

And the people crowded around and shouted "Look! Look! Why they eat the very enemy—say nothing of refuse!" And although they dreaded the couple they became very conciliatory and gave them a fit place to bide in.

The very next day there was another alarm. The two ran out to learn what was the matter. For a long time they could see nothing, but at last they met some people fleeing into the town. Chasing after them was a cooking pot with earrings of onions. It was boiling furiously and belching forth hot wind and steam and spluttering mush in every direction. If ever so little of the mush hit the people they fell over and died.

"He!" cried the Twain. "As if food-stuff were made to make people afraid!" Whereupon they twitched the earrings off the pot and ate them with all the mush that was in the pot, which they forthwith kicked to pieces vigorously.

Then the people crowded still closer around them, wondering to one another that they could vanquish all enemies by eating them with such impunity, and they begged the Twain to teach them how to do it. So they gathered a great council of the villagers, and when they found that these poor people were only half finished, they cut vents in them (such as were not afraid to let them), and made them eat solid food, by means of which they were hardened and became men of meat then and there, instead of having to get killed after the manner of the fearful, and others of their kind beforetime, in order to ascend to the daylight and take their places in men born of men!

And for this reason, behold! A newborn child may eat only of wind-stuff until his cord of viewless sustenance has been severed, and then only by sucking milk, or soft food first and with much distress.

Behold! And we may now see why like new-born children are the very aged; childish withal—not only toothless too, but also sure to die of diarrhea if they eat ever so little save the soft parts and broths of cooked food. For are not the babes new-come from the Shi-u-na (hazy, steam-growing) world; and are not the aged about to enter the Shi po-lo-a (mist-enshrouded) world, where cooked food unconsumed is never needed by the fully dead?

HOW THE TWINS VISITED THE SUN

Tradition Bearer: Unavailable

Source: Fewkes, J. Walter. "The Destruction of the Tusayan Monsters." *Journal of American Folklore* 8 (1895): 136–37.

Date: ca. 1895

Original Source: Hopi (Arizona)

National Origin: Native American

The Hopi was a farming culture that relied on rainfall to grow crops of corn, beans, and squash. Given the fact that they were at the mercy of forces of nature, great energy was devoted to religious ceremonies that literally caused natural acts such as rainfall to occur. Religious life was developed through the religious societies and clans headed by strong females. Spider-Woman, the mother of the Twins, was an especially powerful female figure. Hopi witches who were believed to be possessed of "two hearts" were traced back to mythic times and Spider-Woman (or Grandmother Spider as she is sometimes called) who brought both death and witchcraft into the lives of the people.

T he Twins lived with Spider-Woman, their mother, on the west side of Mt. Taylor, and desired to see the home of their father. Spider-Woman gave them as a charm a kind of meal, and directed that when they met the guardians of the home of the Sun, to chew a little and spurt it upon them.

The Twins journeyed far to the sunrise where the Sun's home is entered through a canon in the sky. There Bear, Mountain Lion, Snake, and "Canyon Closing" keep watch. The sky is solid in this place, and the walls of the entrance are constantly opening and closing, and would crush any unauthorized person who attempted passing through.

As the Twins approached the ever fierce watchers, the trail lay along a narrow way; they found it led them to a place on one side of which was the face of a vertical cliff, and on the other a precipice which sunk sheer to the Below (Underworld). An old man sat there, with his back against the wall and his knees drawn up close to his chin. When they attempted to pass, the old man suddenly thrust out his legs, trying to knock the passers over the cliff. But they leaped back and saved themselves, and in reply to a protest the old man said his legs were cramped and he simply extended them for relief. Whereupon the hero remembered the charm which he had for the southwest direction, and spurted it upon the old man and forced the malignant old fellow to remain quite still with legs drawn up, until the Twins had passed.

They then went on to the watchers, guardians of the entrance to the Sun's house, whom they subdued in the same manner. They also spurted the charm on the sides of the cliff, so that it ceased its oscillation and remained open until they had passed.

These dangers being past, they entered the Sun's house and were greeted by the Sun's wife, who laid them on a bed of mats. Soon Sun came home from his trip through the underworld, saying, "I smell strange children here; when men go away their wives receive the embraces of strangers. Where are the children whom you have?" So she brought the Twins to him, and he put them in a flint oven and made a hot fire. After a while, when he opened the door of the oven, the Twins capered out laughing and dancing about his knees, and he knew that they were his sons.

HOW THE TWINS KILLED THE GIANT ELK

Tradition Bearer: Unavailable

Source: Fewkes, J. Walter. "The Destruction of the Tusayan Monsters." *Journal of American Folklore* 8 (1895): 135–36.

Date: ca. 1895

Original Source: Hopi (Arizona)

National Origin: Native American

Moving beyond the role of mischievous young **tricksters** that they embodied in "How the Twins Visited the Sun" (p. 57), the Hopi Twins mature into **culture heroes** in this **myth**. They do so by ridding the land of a monster and giving Chipmunk its distinctive markings.

Great Elk was one day lying down in a valley near Mount Taylor (one of the San Francisco mountains), and the Twins went out against him. Mole met them and said, "Do not encounter him, for he is mighty, and may kill you; wait here, and I will help you." Mole then excavated four chambers in the earth, one below the other, and made the Twins remain in the upper one.

He dug a long tunnel, and coming up under Elk, plucked a little soft hair from over his heart, at which Elk turned his head and looked down, but Mole said, "Be not angry, I only want a little soft down to make a bed for my children." So Elk allowed him to continue the plucking. But Mole took away enough fur to leave the skin quite bare over the heart. He returned to the Twins and told them what he had done.

Then each Twin threw his lightning, and wounded Elk, who sprang to his feet, and charged them, but the Twins concealed themselves in the upper chamber, and when Elk tried to gore them. His horns were not long enough; again he charged, and thrust his horns downward, but the Twins had safely retreated to the second chamber; again he tried to reach them, but they were safe in the third room. They retreated to the fourth chamber, and when Elk made another attempt he fell dead.

Chipmunk hurried to them, and after thanking the Twins said he had come to show them how to cut up the monster's body, which with his sharp teeth he soon accomplished. One of the Twins thanked Chipmunk, and stooping he dipped the tips of the first two fingers of his right hand in Elk's blood, and, drawing them along the body of Chipmunk, made on it the marks that he still bears.

HOW TIYO PUNISHED MAN-EAGLE

Tradition Bearer: Unavailable

Source: Fewkes, J. Walter. "The Destruction of the Tusayan Monsters." *Journal of American Folklore* 8 (1895): 132–37.

Date: ca. 1895

Original Source: Hopi (Arizona)

National Origin: Native American

Tiyo, in the following Hopi **myth**, is not a **culture hero** like the Twins. Although he serves one of the functions associated with the **culture hero** when he destroys the monster Man-Eagle, he does so only because he has enlisted powerful allies. The familiar figure Spider-Woman shows her abilities as a shape-shifter (a trait associated with witches), as well as her knowledge of medicines such as "charm flour" (bewitched corn meal). In contrast to his role in European culture, Mole has been shown to be an important character in Pueblo mythology. He is an underground hunter who demonstrates talents as a **trickster** as he works behind the scenes in Tiyo's physical contests against Man-Eagle. The ravages of Man-Eagle extended over the whole earth and afflicted all people. He carried off their women and maids, and took them to his home in the sky, where he slept with them as he wished during four nights and then devoured them.

The Youth, while on his way to the San Francisco mountains, met at the foothills the Pinon Maids, dressed in mantles of pinon bark and grass. There likewise he found Spider-Woman and Mole. After they had greeted him and bade him be seated, they inquired where he was going. He replied that Man-Eagle had carried off his bride, and that he sought to bring her back.

"I will aid you," said Spider-Woman, and told the Pinon Maids to gather pinon gum, wash it, and make a garment in exact imitation of the flint arrowhead armor, which Man-Eagle is said to wear. The Pinon Maids bathed themselves, gathered and washed the gum, and made the desired garment for Spider-Woman, who gave it with charm flour to the Youth. Then she changed herself into a spider, so small as to be invisible, and perched on the Youth's right ear, that she might whisper her advice.

Mole led the way to the top of the mountains, but the Pinon Maids remained behind. When they reached the summit, Eagle swooped down; they got on his back, and he soared aloft with them until he was tired; Hawk came close by, they were transferred to his back, and he carried them still higher in the sky. When he was weary, Gray Hawk took them and mounted the heavens with them, until he could go no farther, and Red Hawk received the burden; thus for an immense distance upward they flew, until the adventurers reached a passageway through which the Youth, Spider-Woman, and Mole passed, and saw the white house in which Man-Eagle lived.

Spider-Woman advised the Youth, before mounting the ladder that led into this house, to pluck a handful of sumac berries and give them to Lizard, who received them with thanks, chewed them, and gave him back the cud. The ladder of the house had for each rung a sharp stone like a knife, which would lacerate the hands and feet of anyone who attempted to climb it. The Youth rubbed these sharp edges with the chewed berries and instantly they became dull, and he was able to climb the ladder without cutting himself.

Upon entering the house of Man-Eagle, one of the first objects which met his eye was the fabulous flint arrow-head garment hanging on a peg in a recess, and he at once exchanged it for his own, the imitation which the Pinon Maids had manufactured. Glancing into another recess, he saw Man-Eagle and his lost wife. He called out to her that he had come to rescue her from the monster, and she replied that she was glad, but that he could not do so as no one ever left the place alive. Youth replied, "Have no fear; you will soon be mine again."

So powerful was Spider-Woman's charm that it prevented Man-Eagle from hearing the conversation, but he soon awoke and put on the imitation flint garment without detecting the fraud. He then for the first time became aware of the Youth's presence, and demanded what he wished.

61

"I have come to take my wife home" responded the hero. Man-Eagle said, "We must gamble to decide that, and you must abide the consequences, for if you lose I shall slay you," to which the Youth agreed. Man-Eagle brought out a huge pipe, larger than a man's head, and having filled it with tobacco gave it to the hero, saying: "you must smoke this entirely out, and if you become dizzy or nauseated, you lose." So the Youth lit the pipe and smoked but exhaled nothing. He kept the pipe aglow and swallowed all the smoke, and felt no ill effect, for he passed it through his body into an underground passageway that Mole had dug. Man-Eagle was amazed, and asked what had become of the smoke. The Youth going to the door showed him great clouds of dense smoke issuing from the four cardinal points, and the monster saw that he had lost.

But Man-Eagle tried a second time with the hero. He brought out two deer antlers, saying: "We will each choose one and he who fails to break the one he has chosen loses." The antler that he laid down on the northwest side was a real antler, but that on the southeast was an imitation made of brittle wood. Spider-Woman prompted the Youth to demand the first choice, but Man-Eagle refused him that right. After the Youth had insisted four times, Man-Eagle yielded, and the hero chose the brittle antler and tore its prongs asunder, but Man-Eagle could not break the real antler, and thus lost a second time.

Man-Eagle had two fine large pine-trees growing near his house, and said to the hero, "You choose one of these trees and I will take the other, and whoever plucks one up by the roots shall win." Now Mole had burrowed under one of them, and had gnawed through all its roots, cutting them off, and had run through his tunnel and was sitting at its mouth, peering through the grass anxious to see Youth win. The hero, with the help of his grandmother, chose the tree that Mole had prepared, and plucked it up, and threw it over the cliff, but Man-Eagle struggled with the other tree and could not move it, so he was unhappy in his third defeat.

Then Man-Eagle spread a great supply of food on the floor and said to Youth that he must eat all at one sitting. Tiyo (the Youth) sat and ate all the meat, bread, and porridge, emptying one food basin after another, and showed no sign of being satisfied before all was consumed; for Mole had again assisted him, and dug a large hole below to receive it, and the Youth was a winner the fourth time.

Man-Eagle then made a great wood-pile and directed Tiyo to sit upon it, saying he would ignite it, and that if the Youth were unharmed he would submit himself to the same test. The Youth took his allotted place, and Man-Eagle set fire to the pile of wood at the four cardinal points, and it speedily was ablaze. The arrowheads of which the flint armor was made were coated with ice, which melted so that water trickled down and prevented Youth from being burnt, and all the woodpile was consumed, leaving Tiyo unharmed.

The monster was filled with wonder, and grieved very much when he saw Youth making another great pile of wood. Still, thinking that he wore his fireproof suit, he mounted the woodpile, which Youth lit at the four cardinal points. The fuel blazed up, and as soon as the fire caught the imitation garment of gum, it ignited with a flash and the monster was consumed. At the prompting of Spider-Woman Tiyo approached the ashes, took the charm in his mouth and spurted it over them, when suddenly a handsome man arose. Then Spider-Woman said to him, "Will you refrain from killing people, will you forsake your evil habits?"

Man-Eagle assented with a fervent promise, and the Youth rejoicing ran to his wife, embraced her and set free all the captive women wives of the Hopi and other peoples, of whom there were many. Eagle and Hawk carried them to the earth.

ELFEGO BACA

Tradition Bearer: Elfego Baca

Source: Smith, Janet. "Interview of Elfego Baca." *American Life Histories: Manuscripts from the Federal Writers' Project, 1936–1940.* Manuscript Division, Library of Congress. 12 October 2005. http://memory.loc.gov/ammem/wpaintro/wpahome.html.

Date: 1936

Original Source: New Mexico

National Origin: Mexican American

Elfego Baca (1865–1945) was a lawman, gunfighter, lawyer, and politician at various points in his life. The Frisco Affair mentioned in passing refers to an incident that took place in Frisco, New Mexico, when Baca was nineteen. Baca was deputized by the local deputy sheriff to arrest a gang of cowboys that had turned murderous. The ensuing events included a gunfight, an arrest, and the death of one of the men whose horse fell on top of him during the excitement. The arrested cowboy was fined for disorderly conduct, and later Baca was compelled to hold off a reputed eighty cowboys from a refuge in a shack for thirty-six hours. He survived by lying flat on the dirt floor, dug below ground level. From this legendary event his reputation grew for the next sixty years. In 1958, Disney Studios made a film of his life.

I never wanted to kill anybody," Elfego Baca told me, "but if a man had it in his mind to kill me, I made it my business to get him first."

Elfego Baca belongs to the six-shooter epoch of American history. Those were the days when hard-shooting Texas cowboys invaded the territory of New Mexico, driving their herds of longhorns over the sheep ranges of the New Mexicans, for whom they had little liking or respect. Differences were settled quickly, with few words and a gun. Those were the days of Billy the Kid, with whom Elfego, at the age of seventeen, made a tour of the gambling joints in Old Albuquerque. In the words of Kyle Crichton, who wrote Elfego Baca's biography, "the life of Elfego Baca makes Billy the Kid look like a piker." Harvey Ferguson calls him "a knight-errant from the romantic point of view if ever the six-shooter West produced one.

And yet Mr. Baca is not a man who lives in his past. "I wonder what I can tell you," he said when I asked him for pioneer stories. "I don't remember so much about those things now. Why don't you read the book Mr. Crichton wrote about me?"

He searched about his desk and brought out two newspaper clippings of letters he had written recently to the *Albuquerque Journal* on local politics. The newspaper had deleted two of the more outspoken paragraphs. Mr. Baca was annoyed.

I tried to draw Mr. Baca away from present day politics to stories of his unusual past, but he does not talk readily about himself, although he seemed anxious to help me. Elfego Baca is a kindly courteous gentleman who is concerned to see that his visitor has the coolest spot in the room.

He brought out books and articles that had been written about him, but he did not seem inclined to reminiscing and answered my questions briefly. "Crichton tells about that in his book" or "Yes, I knew Billy the Kid."

Finally I asked him at random if he knew anything about the famous old Manzano Gang which I had frequently seen mentioned in connection with Torrance County.

He replied that he broke up that gang when he was Sheriff of Socorro County.

"There were ten of them," he said, "and I got nine. The only reason I didn't get the other one was that he got over the border and was shot before I got to him. They used to go to a place near Belen and empty the freight cars of grain and one thing and another. Finally they killed a man at La Jolla. Contreros was his name. A very rich man with lots of money in his house, all gold. I got them for that. They were all convicted and sent to the Pen."

Mr. Baca settled back in his chair and made some remark about the late Senator Cutting whose photograph stood on his desk.

I persisted about the Manzano Gang. "I wish you'd tell me more about that gang. How you got them, and the whole story."

"Well," he said, "after that man Contreros was shot, they called me up at my office in Socorro and told me that he was dying. I promised to get the murderers in forty-eight hours. That was my rule. Never any longer than forty-eight hours."

Mr. Baca suspected certain men, but when a telephone call to Albuquerque established the fact that they had been in that city at the time of the killing, his next thought was of the Manzano Gang.

Accompanied by two men, he started out on horseback in the direction of La Jolla. Just as the sun was rising; they came to the ranch of Lazaro Cordova. They rode into the stable and found Cordova's son-in-law, Prancasio Saiz already busy with his horse.

"Good morning," said Elfego, "what are you doing with your horse so early in the morning?"

Saiz replied that he was merely brushing him down a little. Mr. Baca walked over and placed his hand on the saddle. It was wet inside. The saddle blanket was steaming. He looked more closely at the horse. At first sight it had appeared to be a pinto, white with brown spots. Mr. Baca thought he remembered that Saiz rode a white horse.

"What happened to that horse?" he asked.

The man replied that the boys had had the horse out the day before and had painted the spots on him with a kind of berry that makes reddish-brown spots. "Just for a joke," he added.

"Where's your father-in-law?" asked Mr. Baca.

Saiz said that his father-in-law had gone the day before to a fiesta at La Jolla and had not returned.

"I understand you're a pretty good shot," said Sheriff Baca. "You'd better come along, and help me round up some men I'm after for the killing of Contreros in La Jolla."

Saiz said that he had work to do on the ranch, but at the insistence of Mr. Baca, he saddled his horse and rode out with the three men.

65

"About as far as from here to the station," went on Mr. Baca, "was a grave-yard where the gang was supposed to camp out. I rode over to it and found where they had lunched the day before. There were sardine cans and cracker boxes and one thing and another. Then I found where one of them had had a call to nature. I told one of my men to put it in a can. Saiz didn't know about this, and in a little while he went over behind some mesquite bushes and had a call to nature. After he came back I sent my man over, and by God it was the same stuff—the same beans and red chili seeds! So I put Saiz under arrest and sent him back to the jail at Socorro with one of my deputies, although he kept saying he couldn't see what I was arresting him for."

Mr. Baca and his other deputy proceeded in the direction of La Jolla. Before long they saw a man on horseback coming toward them.

"He was running that horse like everything. When we met I saw that he was a Texan. Doc Something or other was his name. I can't remember now. But he was a pretty tough man."

"You a Sheriff?" he said to Mr. Baca.

"No," replied Mr. Baca, "no, I'm not a Sheriff. Don't have nothing to do with the law, in fact.

"You're pretty heavily armed," remarked the man suspiciously.

"I generally arm myself this way when I go for a trip in the country," answered Baca, displaying his field glasses. "I think it's safer."

"Well, if you want fresh horses, you can get them at my ranch, a piece down the road," said the Texan.

Mr. Baca figured that this was an attempt to throw him off the trail, so as soon as the Texan was out of sight, he struck out east over the mountains for Manzano. Just as he was entering the village he saw two of the gang coming down the hill afoot leading their horses. He placed them under arrest and sent them back to Socorro with his other deputy.

It was about two o'clock in the morning when Mr. Baca passed the Cordova ranch again on his way back. He roused Lazaro Cordova, who had returned from La Jolla by that time, and told him to dress and come with him to Socorro.

"The old man didn't want to come," said Mr. Baca, "and kept asking what you want with me anyhow?' I told him that he was under arrest, and on the way to Socorro I told him that unless he and his son-in-law came across with a com-plete statement about the whole gang, I would hang both of them, for I had the goods on them and knew all right that they were both in on the killing of Contreros. I put him in the same cell with his son-in-law, and told him it was up to him to bring Saiz around. They came through with the statement. I kept on catching the rest of the gang, until I had them all. All but the one who got himself shot before I caught up with him."

"If you ever go to Socorro you ask Billy Newcomb, the Sheriff down there now to show you the records. You might see the place on the way down where they buried a cowboy I shot. It's a little way off the main road though.

"That was a long time before I was a real Sheriff. In those days I was a self-made deputy. I had a badge I made for myself, and if they didn't believe I was a deputy, they'd better believe it, because I made 'em believe it."

"I had gone to Escondida a little way from Socorro to visit my uncle. A couple of Texas cowboys had been shooting up the town of Socorro. They hadn't hurt anybody that time. Only frightened some girls. That's the way they did in those days—ride through a town shooting at dogs and cats and if somebody happened to get in the way—powie!—too bad for him. The Sheriff came to Escondida after them. By that time they were making a couple of Mexicans dance, shooting up the ground around their feet. The Sheriff said to me 'Baca, if you want to help, come along, but there's going to be shooting.'"

"We rode after them and I shot one of them about three hundred yards away. The other got away—too many cottonwood trees in the way.

"Somebody asked me what that cowboy's name was. I said I didn't know. He wasn't able to tell me by the time I caught up with him."

I asked what the Sheriff's name was, and when Mr. Baca said it was Pete Simpson, I said, "The one you were electioneering for the time of the Frisco affair when you held off about 80 cowboys for over 36 hours." This is the one of Mr. Baca's exploits that has been most frequently written about.

"Hell, I wasn't electioneering for him," he said. "I don't know where they got that idea. I couldn't have made a speech to save my life. And I didn't wear a Prince Albert coat either. They didn't have such things in this country in those days."

"Is it true that you ate dinner afterward with French and some other men who had been shooting at you, and talked the affair over," I asked.

"I ate dinner with some men afterward but I don't remember who they were now. I don't think that man French was there at all, although he must have been in the neighborhood, as he seemed to know all about it. But I don't remember him. Jim Cook was one that was shooting at me though. He was a pretty tough man, but he came near getting it."

He showed me a photograph that Jim Cook had sent him recently. The picture showed an old man who still looks as though he could not be easily trifled with. It was inscribed "To Elfego Baca in memory of that day at Frisco."

"Did you see the letter that Englishman wrote to Crichton? He wanted to hang me. 'Why don't you hang that little Mexican so-and-so?' he asked. I said,

'Why don't you be the one to do it?' and pulled my guns, and wooo, he wasn't so eager. You know I surrendered only on condition that I keep my guns. They placed six guards over me, but they rode 25 steps ahead of me all the way to Socorro.

"Those were great old days. Everything is very quiet now, isn't it?" said Mr. Baca looking up. "I think I'll run for something this fall, but I don't know what yet."

BOOGER RED

Tradition Bearer: Mollie Privett

Source: Doyle, Elizabeth. "Interview of Mollie Privett." *American Life Histories: Manuscripts from the Federal Writers' Project, 1936–1940.* Manuscript Division, Library of Congress. 12 October 2005. http://memory.loc.gov/ammem/wpaintro/wpahome.html.

Date: 1938

Original Source: Texas

National Origin: European American

The following oral biography of Samuel Thomas ("Booger Red") Privett narrated by his widow, Mollie Privett, is composed of **legends** from Booger Red's early life and Mrs. Privett's **personal experience narratives** after their marriage 1895. The collected tales present a remarkable history of life in the Southwest and on the circus and wild-west show circuit during the late nineteenth and early twentieth centuries. The **family saga** takes Booger Red from his early days on a Texas ranch to his career as an independent performer and as a star in such famous shows as Al G. Barnes Circus, the Hagenbeck-Wallace Circus (in its heyday the second largest circus in the world next to the Ringling Brothers and Barnum & Bailey Circus), and even Buffalo Bill Cody's Wild West Show.

It is admitted by all that the movies have produced some wonderful horsemen but the master of them all was never filmed," so says the old timer in any crowd of rodeo fans. They hold one name over all others as the greatest bronc rider that America has ever produced. Few people ever knew his real name which was Samuel Thomas Privett, but his nickname, "Booger Red" was famous and for a quarter of a century he was known to thousands as the greatest master of outlaw horses in America.

He was born on a ranch near Dublin, Erath County, Texas, December 29, 1864 and as a youth seemed to possess all the vim, vigor, and vitality that makes the red-head outstanding. At the age of 10 he began riding wild calves on his father's ranch and by the time he was 12-years of age he was widely known as the Red-Headed Kid Bronc Rider and was already on the road to fame. He was the youngest of a large family and was always trying to imitate some stunt of his older brother's.

In attempting to make his own fireworks on his 13th Christmas as he had seen others do, he and a pal crammed a lot of gun powder into a hole bored into an old tree stump and when it exploded it killed his friend and blew him about twenty feet. His face was hopelessly burned and for six months he did not see daylight. His eyes were cut open three times and his mouth and nose twice. As he was being carried to the hospital in a farm wagon, a small boy friend hopped on the side of the wagon, looked over at Red and thoughtlessly remarked, 'Gee, but Red is sure a booger now, ain't he?' Thus, the famous "Booger Red" nickname, which went with him to his grave.

His parents died when he was 15 years old and he started out in the world to make his own way at the job which he loved most, that of breaking wild horses. None were too bad for him to tackle and he made a name for himself in a country where there were plenty of bronc scratchers. By the time he was grown he had saved enough to buy and stock a small ranch near Sabinal, Texas, but he soon sold that and purchased the wagon yard in San Angelo, Texas. He married Mollie Webb at the little west Texas town of Bronte, in 1895. She and their six children who became famous in show life were great assets to the show business, which he established later. He died of Bright's disease at Miami, Oklahoma, in 1924. His widow Mrs. Mollie Webb Privett who lives with her aged mother in San Angelo, Texas, relates the following:

"While we were running the wagon yard in San Angelo, people from all over the southwest would bring wild horses to Mr. Privett to ride. He had never been thrown and of course there were those who were envious and wanted to see his laurels hauled down. One man even brought along a camera with his outlaw horse, so sure was he that no one could ride him; he was going to take a picture of Booger Red as he was thrown. The picture was not taken and during the ride the man himself became so excited that he threw away his camera and joined in the applause.

"Booger Red had the utmost confidence in his ability to ride and he wasn't afraid to back it up with cash. One year during a San Angelo Fair a man imported a famous young horse from Montana and bet his whole bankroll that Booger Red could not ride him. Other bets were piled up and excitement ran high. The horse was a dun color with a black stripe right down his back and the same black stripes encircled his legs. He was sixteen hands high and altogether a magnificent looking creature. As Booger Red mounted him he was very cautious not to excite him and the horse actually stood dead still for a moment, then Booger Red yelled to the crowd, 'Folks, he's come all the way down here from Montana to get a booger on his back and here we go.' With that he thumbed him in the neck and the battle was on. So was Booger at the end of the ride but I'll have to admit that there were times I believe that I had as much confidence in his ability to ride as he did himself but this was the toughest number I had ever seen him tackle.

"The money won was used to buy the horse and we called him Montana Gyp. This was only one of the many battles between Booger Red and Montana Gyp, as each ride was only a temporary conquering and the spirit of Montana Gyp was never conquered. For twenty-three years almost daily, some times ten or fifteen times daily this battle was renewed. Old Montana never threw Booger Red but he tried, just as hard the last time as he did the first.

"I often think of when he rode him here once at a San Angelo Fair. He bucked all over the grounds then broke through the fence and out through a bunch of horses that were tied on the outside. One horse became so frightened that he reared up and fell on his head and broke his neck. Booger was with him when he stopped, though, and rode him back on the tracks. As he rode by the grandstand he said, 'Ladies and Gentlemen, I knew I was ugly but I never knew before that I was ugly enough to scare a horse to death.' They tried to pay the man for his horse but he wanted an exorbitant price and refused any reasonable offer, saying that he had rather have nothing at all than less than he asked.

"Another time at the Fair here he rode a big old white steer that was said to be ride proof. Many bronc busters had tried him but had been thrown. He was so wild that the rider had to climb up on the gate and drop on his as he came through. Booger Red hit on him backwards, so he grabbed him by the tail and pulled it up over his shoulder with one hand and used the other to fan himself with his big white hat, as he came by the grandstand. He really got a hand on that ride.

"I used to have to exercise the show horses around the tracks when we were not showing. Ella and Roy were little shavers then but I usually left Roy at the grandstand with Ella but not without a squall. He would cry to ride in the little two-wheeled carriage I drove. 'Stick him down in the foot of that thing and let the horses out,' his daddy said to me one morning, 'one time will do him.' I stuck his feet through the slats in the bottom of the thing and put the horses out at their best. When we got back to the grandstand you couldn't tell what that kid was. His eyes, nose, and mouth were filled with dirt and as his daddy predicted he was cured of wanting to ride.

"The children were already as fond of horses as their father was. We got them a little paint horse when he was 2 years old and kept him until he was 25. All six of the children learned to ride on little Prince. He was the smartest horse I ever saw. One of his many intelligent acts was to stop at a railroad crossing if he heard a train blow, and no amount of whipping could force him to cross until he saw the train go by. The children could ride just as long as one could stick on anywhere. We kept him twenty-three years and when he died at Miami, Oklahoma, we buried him with much grief and ceremony.

"After we bought old Gyp and he and Mr. Privett became the attraction at every show, the idea of a Wild West Show of our own was born in our minds, so we got our small possessions together and started out with two bucking horses, a covered wagon, and two buggies. The teams and little Prince were just family equipment.

"Mr. Privett originated the act of riding with his thumbs in his suspenders and looking back at the crowd. It had always been the custom up to then for the bronc rider to keep his eye directly on the mount in an effort to anticipate his next movement but Booger Red would tuck his thumbs in his suspenders and look all about, talking to his audience as he rode.

"We started off showing in ball parks with a 25¢ admission charge and did well from the beginning. Our success always out-balanced the usual knocks and bumps encountered.

"Booger was a proud, clean fellow, always so jovial and witty that he made everyone, including himself, either forget his misfortune or regard it only as an asset to his business. His announcements were always wound up with, 'Come and see him ride, the ugliest man dead or alive, Booger Red.'

"We had lots of fun and many good times. We put on a show once at a church in Midlothian, Texas. The 'old man' (Booger Red) was always donating our exhibitions to some charitable cause and on this particular occasion a woman rider was needed and I could not fill the place, so Booger put on my skirt and hat and a good wig and would have fooled everyone, I believe, if he had not failed to fasten them on rights; but when the horse made two or three rounds, off came his entire disguise. The crowd went wild when they saw that it was Booger Red himself.

71

"Our camp life was our most fun while we traveled in wagons, camping on streams and in the most beautiful places we could find. We always had a general clean up, even to washing the harness at such times.

"Each Saturday night we would have Kangaroo Court. There were regular rules to be obeyed and when they were broken the victim was put on trial in regular cowboy style. On one occasion the 'old man' (Booger Red) was the offender. He had gotten about half sore one morning when the boys were late to breakfast and had rung a third bell after the first for rising, and the second for breakfast had been rung. He was tried, found guilty and sentenced to ten licks with the chaps as he was bent over a wagon tongue. He was a good sport and started off taking his medicine like a man, when Jack Lewis who loved him like a daddy ran into the guy, caught his arm and stopped the punishment. This created the great excitement and Jack was then tried for contempt of court and sentenced to double punishment. The usual punishment was to have to buy candy for the ladies or cigars for the men.

"Many people try to say that show people are no good, etc., but I've seen more honesty and true principle shown by show people than many so-called higher-ups. I was just talking the other day about a boy we had with us down in East Texas. We called him Texas Kid and loved him like one of the family. He took sick down there and Mr. Privett sent him to the hospital in Little Rock, Arkansas. We continued with our shows but one night when we had a nice crowd, we all kept feeling so depressed that we couldn't seem to get going. Even the band couldn't play right and just before we were to start everything the 'old man' received a telegram stating that Texas Kid was dead. We all just went to pieces and Mr. Privett went out and read the message to the crowd, offering them a free pass the next night if they would excuse us and come back. They removed their hats and filed out of the tent in respectful order. The next night the crowd was almost double and not one would accept the free pass. 'Use the extra money to defray funeral expenses,' they would say, and that was what was done.

"Many were the kind deeds I have seen the 'old man' perform. He was a fun-loving, witty man and carried on a lot in a joking way but when it came right down to principle and honesty he couldn't be beat. I have seen him go out to a little bunch of ragged children and say, 'Boys, aren't you coming in the show?' 'We'd sure love to, Mr. Red,' they would reply, 'but we ain't got no money.' 'Come on in,' he would say, 'and bring me some money next year when I come back here.' It was surprising how many little shavers would walk up to him at different towns and offer him money, long after he had forgotten all about them. He always gave the money back to them but that was his lesson in honesty for them. The same was true of old or trampy people who could not pay their way into the show and many times I have seen him call back the customers for change, which in their excitement they would leave at the ticket window.

"Booger Red was not a drinking man but he was broadminded and lenient with his boys. On Christmas Eve, one year, he told all the boys that if they would perform good that night they could have four days for celebration, with the lid off. That was the funniest four days I ever spent. The "old man" (Booger Red) set a keg of beer on the Christmas table and every fellow had his own cup. It seemed each one had an extra stunt all his own to pull off.

"The boys all called me Mother and they took a notion for hot biscuits one day. I cooked their biscuits in a dutch oven aver an open campfire. 'Why, I can't cook biscuits today, boys.' I said, 'it is raining and will put out the fire.' 'Make 'em, Mother, make 'em,' they all shouted, 'we will get out there and hold our slickers over you and the fire while you cook them.' That was too much and I made up the dough while they built the fire under the canopy of slickers and we cooked and ate biscuits like that until every one was filled.

"At one time we were at Mill Creek, Oklahoma, during a big picnic and the crowd insisted that we put on a morning as well as an afternoon show. We tried it but somehow the usual time of day for the performances threw us off balance and every thing went wrong. Several riders were thrown and the whole thing was a flop. We felt sure that we would have no audience that afternoon but I guess our reputation was bigger than our blunders for the crowd very soon outgrew the tent and Mr. Privett raised the side walls and told them to stack up, all outsiders free. Pretty soon all the trees around the tent were filled and I believe we put on one of the best shows we ever produced.

"Booger Red always advertised ahead of his appearances for people to bring in anything they could lead, drive, drag, or ship, and he would ride it or pay the standing forfeit of $100.00. He never had to pay off and there were plenty of bad horses brought in. He won twenty-three first prizes in all and rode at the World's Fair at T. Louis forty years ago when Will Rogers and Tom Mix made their first public appearance.

"His bronc riding saddle was merely a frame or tree, certainly no fancy affair but almost as famous as the 'old man' himself.

"In a rodeo contest in Fort Worth once he won $500.00 and a fine saddle. When he went to the hotel with the rest of the crowd he took both his old and new saddle with him and hastily checked the new saddle as his buddies were rushing him to come on and eat. He pitched the old one in as he rushed after the boys. 'Come back,' yelled the clerk, 'you haven't checked your other saddle.' 'That's all right,' Booger shouted back, 'if anyone uglier than I comes along just give it to him.'

"Our show was growing all the time. He now had twenty-two broncos, twelve saddle horses and thirty-two wagons and had become known as the best Wild West Show on the road. It was then that the circus sought us out. He sold everything except our best bucking horses and went with the circus. We traveled by rail then and our good old wagon days were over. At different times we were with Al G. Barnes, Hagenbeck-Wallace, Buffalo Bill, and others.

"I have to laugh every time I think of an incident which took place while we were with the Barnes Circus. Booger had twenty-five or thirty bucking horses, all good performers and with them and our crew we put on the Wild West part of the show. He wanted a strong line in the parade so we dressed up every thing available and put them on horses. Old Frog Horn Clancy was our announcer and when he came out to tell them of the fame of Booger Red's wife it was pitiful how he spread it on. In truth I was not much of a rider but the way Frog Horn Clancy told them of the loving cups and handsome prizes I had won would have convinced the most skeptical. His blarney extended into "time" and my horse became very restless, so when he finally did close his spiel with, 'Behold the famous Mrs. Privett in action,' my horse lurched forward with an impatient gesture that sent me right off on my head. Wonder of wonders that I was not killed but I was hardly hurt. Tickled at my plight, but shamed to tears, I gathered myself up with all possible haste and ran from the tent as the applause died upon the lips of my spectators.

"In show life there is sadness as well as gladness; lots of fun and some sorrow, like when we were to show in Wichita Falls (Texas) once. We were approaching the town and were met out on the highway by Pat Flynn's brother who knew we were coming in and who had come on out to meet his brother in an effort to persuade him to quit the bronco riding business. Booger Red had taught little Pat to ride and he was good, also crazy about riding, much to the objection of his family. We were all crazy about Pat and hated to see him leave us but he had already promised his brother that he would go home with him the next day. A few hours before the show we all began to feel some of our old signs of depressed feelings returning. We couldn't account for this but it was so noticeable that we all commented on it. Pat's brother begged him not to ride that night. 'Ah, just this last time,' begged Pat, 'you know we are going home tomorrow and I want to ride for the last time.' 'O.K.,' said his brother, 'if you will let me hold the horse.' Mr. Privett knew he did not know how to stub a horse and he insisted that he keep out of it. Nothing else would do him however, and in getting off to an awkward start the horse became excited and broke away in a wild run, tangling himself in the rope and falling. He slung little Pat's head against a tent pole and crushed his skull. Feeling the sense of depression that I had before the show began, I had remained at the wagon. When I noticed the awful stillness, the hushed exclamations, and then the agonized groans of the audience, I knew the thing had happened but who the victim was I was not to know until Thomas, my son, came running out to the wagon and said, 'Oh! Mama, little Pat is killed.' He was not really dead right then but he never regained consciousness and died about two hours later. Mr. Privett rushed to him and held his bleeding head on his lap until the inquest was held. No means of cleaning ever removed that dying blood from the 'old man's' chaps and jacket. The body was sent to the boy's hometown in Oklahoma and we all felt that we had lost one of our best boys.

"While we were with the Barnes Circus, Mr. Privett had Alexander here in San Angelo (Texas) make him a fine silver mounted saddle and ship it to him. Of course it had 'Booger Red' and our address, all over the big wooden box. When it arrived at the station and was being unloaded the children all gathered around and began saying to each other, 'Booger Red has arrived, he's in that box.' Excitement grew until I really believe some of the grown-ups believed it too. Booger Red enjoyed the joke so much that he would walk around the box and tell the children that they should have Booger Red some thing there to eat when he came out, that he would be hungry. By the time the box was opened the kids had enough peanuts, candy, milk, and sandwiches there to feed several people. When the box was opened and the saddle taken out, the look of disappointment on the poor little kiddies' faces was pitiful. The 'old man' enjoyed the joke so much that her repeated it in several towns where he showed.

"Booger had many wonderful horses and riders in his different shows but always it took Montana Gyp and Booger Red to produce the star act in any show. We kept the old horse over twenty years and when he died we had another funeral and the family grief was not far different from our experience when little Prince died.

"Some of our famous horses were: Flaxy, Moon, Texas Boy, Rocky Mountain Steve, Black Diamond, Grey Wolf, Hell Set, and old Pay Day. Texas Boy was the one that never pitched twice the same way and Booger Red maintained a standing offer of $50.00 per minute to anyone who stayed on him but he was the only one ever to win the money. They were all bad horses but none ever equalled old Montana Gyp with the 'old man.' He held one grudge against the horse though, until his dying day. In 1915 he won the world's championship at the San Francisco World's air and received a $750.00 silver mounted saddle and one day after he had ridden his old horse down and thought he was conquered for that once, he made an extra lunge just as the 'old man' was dismounting, causing the rowel of his spur to make an ugly scratch across the seat of his beautiful saddle. He often remarked that he would never forgive the horse for this one deed.

"Booger Red's last performance was at the Fat Stock Show at Fort Worth (Texas) in 1924 just a short time before he died. He had retired and went to Fort Worth just to see the show. To keep from being recognized he wore a cap instead of his big white hat, and low quarters instead of boots and slipped in on the top seat of the grandstand. He was enjoying the performances when trouble arose in the arena with an outlaw horse. The rider was thrown and the crowd yelled, 'Give us Booger Red.' He sat as still as a mouse until an old lady at his elbow recognized him and shrieked, 'Here he is!' The crowd went wild and would not be put off. He made his way calmly down through the audience until he reached the bottom step where he was hoisted on the shoulders of the cheering throng and carried to the arena. He rode the old horse to a finish and many said it was the prettiest riding they ever saw. He was at that time probably the oldest man on record to make such a ride.

"He had lots of trouble during the last years of his performances with Movie Companies trying to steal pictures of him. Many were the times he would start into the arena and see a machine set up in some obscure place, but they never tricked him. If he had lived until the picture business became more prominent he would have been as famous in the Movie world as he was in the show life of his day.

"He always thought of his family first and was a kind husband and father, doing all the good he could wherever he was.

"He died in March 1924, at Miami, Oklahoma, with these words on his lips, 'Boys, I'm leaving it with you. Take good care of mama and little Bill. Always be honest, for it pays in the long run. Have all the fun you can while you live, for when you are dead you are a long time dead.'

"After his death the children and I went back to the Buchanan Shows and tried to carry on but it was never the same any more. Ella, the eldest girl who had done a beautiful riding and roping act with her father for sometime, rushed from the arena in tears the first time she attempted to put on the act without her father.

"All the children were taught the riding and roping acts and were called famous by many.

"We are all pretty well scattered now though, Ella married one of her father's performers by the name of Linton and they are with the Tom Mix Circus in California. Roy never went back to the show after the World War. He has a nice family and is in the oil business in Electra, Texas. Thomas is with the Ringland Circus in New York. Luther is in California. Alta, who suffered a broken leg in the Hagenbeck-Wallace Circus, married a Mr. Fuch and lives in San Angelo; and Little Bill as we all call the baby who weighs only 115 pounds, trains race stock on the Santa Anita track at Arcada, California.

"Thomas and a bunch of boys went to Belgium in 1937 and put on a Wild West Show in answer to a request from there and when they were through showing they wouldn't pay them. They had to sell all of their saddles and equipment to live until relatives could send for them. It cost over $100.00 to get Thomas back across the 'pond.'

"They then attempted to pull the same stunt with Tom Mix but before he started he asked them to put up a forfeit. When they refused he broke up the plans and never went.

"I've never learned to drive an automobile. I didn't take any hat off to any man when it came to handling a team but I tell them when they start making cars without fenders so I can see where my wheels are going I will learn to drive then."

THE TURKEY HERD

Tradition Bearer: Tsatiselu

Source: Parsons, Elsie Clews. "Pueblo Indian Folk-tales, Probably of Spanish Provenience." *Journal of American Folklore* 31 (1918): 234–35.

Date: ca. 1918

Original Source: Zuni Pueblo (New Mexico)

National Origin: Native American

The following Zuni folktale is likely to be a **variant** of the European tale best known to contemporary readers as "Cinderella" (AT510A). This adaptation stresses the heroine's subjugation to her sisters far less than it stresses her alliance with the animal world in the form of a flock of turkeys. The latter **motif** is stressed in many European versions; in the German version of the tale "Ash Girl," for example, Ash Girl is aided in her endeavors by pigeons. As folklorist Elsie Clews Parsons suggests, this tale is more likely to have been borrowed from Spanish sources than to have been Native American in origin.

Long ago at Kyakima lived a girl who spent all her time herding turkeys. She never did anything for her sisters. Nobody would comb her hair. It was all in a snarl. Her sisters would tell her to cook. They would say, "Why do you so love the turkeys?" She did not answer. After her sisters had cooked, she would take the bread and go out and tend the turkeys.

At Matsaki they were dancing lapalehakya. They were dancing for the third time, when the turkey-girl said, "Younger sisters!"

The turkeys said, "What?"

The girl said, "I want to go and see the dance."

The turkeys said, "You are too dirty to go."

She repeated, "I want to go."

The turkeys said, "Let us eat the lice out of her hair!" Then each ate lice from her hair. Then an elder-sister turkey clapped her wings, and down from the air fell women's moccasins (mokwawe). Then her younger sister (ikina) clapped her wings, and down from the air fell a blanket dress (yatone). Then another elder sister clapped her wings, and down from the air fell a belt (ehnina). A younger sister clapped her wings, and a pitone fell down. An elder sister clapped, and a blanket (eha) fell down. The little younger sister (an hani tsanna) clapped, and a hair belt (tsutokehnina) fell down.

An elder sister turkey said, "Is this all you want?"

The girl said, "Yes." She put on the moccasins and the clothing. The turkeys put up her hair in a queue.

She said to the turkeys, "I will comeback before sundown." She went to her house, and made a little cloth bag, and filled it with meal. Then she went on to Mat-saki. Her sisters said, "Has she gone to the dance?"

One said, "Yes."

"She is too dirty to go." After she reached Matsaki, as she stood there, the dance-director asked if she would dance.

She said, "Yes." She danced all day.

When the sun set, she finished dancing, and ran back to the turkeys. The turkeys had said, when she did not come, "We must not go on living here. Our sister does not love us."

When she arrived, they were not there. They were on top of a little hill, singing,—

"Kyana to to
kyana to to
kyana to to ye
uli uli uli to to to to."

They flew down to Kyakima. They went on as fast as they could until they came to turkey-tracks. There they drank at the spring. Their tracks were from north, south, east, west. After they drank, they flew to Shoakoskwikwi. They reached a high rock. They sat on it, and sang,—

"Kyana to to
kyana to to
kyana to to ye
uli uli uli to to to to."

When Turkey Girl arrived, the turkeys were not there. She saw their tracks. She followed the tracks on a run. At Tonateanawa she saw where they had drunk. She ran on. Then she lost their tracks.

She went back to her house. The turkeys had flown to Shoakoskwikwi, to the spring there. That is why at Shoakoskwikwi you see wild turkeys. The girl came back to her house crying.

Her sisters said, "Don't cry! You did not return on time. You did not love them." The girl stayed and cooked for her sisters. Thus it was long ago.

HISTORY OF A BUFFALO HUNTER

Tradition Bearer: Manuel Jesus Vasques

Source: Tejada, Simeon. "Interview of Manuel Jesus Vasques." American Life Histories: Manuscripts from the Federal Writers' Project, 1936–1940. Manuscript Division, Library of Congress. 12 October 2005. http://memory.loc.gov/ammem/wpaintro/wpahome.html.

Date: 1939

Original Source: New Mexico

National Origin: Mexican American

The passing of the great bison, or buffalo, herds on the Plains has been incorporated into every American school child's history text. The image of the white hide hunters and their Sharps rifles is a staple of pop culture in media from the "dime novel" to the Hollywood feature film. The reality of this life has not survived with these media depictions. Manuel

Jesus Vasques—hunting with a lance from horseback, making his patron a wealthy man while "never holding a single penny in his hand"—knew the reality of the buffalo hunter and horse trader intimately. His account is contained in the following **personal experience narrative**.

Don Manuel Jesus Vasques was born in the settlement of Chamisal, Taos County, New Mexico on the 31st day of January of the year 1856. He himself does not know how he came to live at the home of Don Juan Policarpio Romero of the village of Penasco but at the age of eight he was herd-boy for a flock of goats belonging to Don Juan Policarpio Romero and continued as such until he married Rosario Fresquez of Penasco.

After he was married he practiced carpentry, making coffins for the dead, during the great smallpox plague of the year 1875. There were days in which four or five deaths occurred and Don Manuel could not make coffins enough to supply the demand and there was no other carpenter in Penasco. Some of the dead were placed on poles and dragged to the cemetery by burros.

While the epidemic raged Don Manuel continued making coffins and when it had subsided in Penasco, Don Juan Policarpio sent him to Ocate, Chacon, and Santa Clara, now known as Wagon Mound, to make coffins at those places.

In the year 1877 Don Policarpio sent Don Manuel Jesus Vasques in company with other men to the plains on a buffalo hunt. He left Penasco with a Navajo Indian called Juan Jesus Romero, whom Don Policarpio Romero had raised. Alvino Ortega and Jesus Maria Ortega of the settlement of El Llano de San Juan (Plains of Saint John) as well as some thirty other men went with them on the buffalo hunt. They took with them fifteen ox drawn carts, the oxen's horns were tied securely to the yokes with straps of ox-hide. This group of men met in Penasco on the 15th of November, 1877 before setting out on the hunt.

They set the same day for Mora, there they were joined by more men and more carts, from there they went to Ocate and there also, they were joined by more men and more carts. From this place they traveled as far as the Colorado River, which they crossed below what is now the town of Springer in Colfax County. At that time there was not a single house there, or at least they saw none, nor did they see any footprints and there was no trail of any kind.

They were traveling towards the state of Oklahoma and reached Chico, also in Colfax County, New Mexico. At this place they camped for a few days in order to rest their oxen. A meeting was called with the object of placing some-one of them at the head of the expedition; votes were cast and Don Alvino

Ortega of the Llano de San Juan received a majority of votes and was given the title of "Comandante," Commander.

From this time on nothing was done except at the express command of Don Alvino Ortega, he ordered the oxen to be yoked, he gave the order to make camp, to water the animals, he also ordered mounted men to ride ahead to scout for signs of Indians who might cause them trouble, and to reconnoiter ahead for water for since there was no road over the prairies it was quite possible and dangerous that at any moment they might suddenly come upon a deep canon or swollen stream which they would not be able to cross. These scouts would ride ahead of the caravan, returning to the camp each night.

They passed close to the site of the city of Clayton by way of a spring called El Ojo del Cibolo (Buffalo Spring) and continued across Texas to enter Oklahoma at a point called Punta de Agua (Waterhole). It took them a month to reach buffalo country. At a point called Pilares a buffalo bull was killed which furnished them meat for a few days.

From Pilares the expedition traveled for three or four days more until it reached a river called Rio de las Nutrias (Beaver River). They camped a short ways down the stream and began hunting buffaloes.

The hunt continued until they had killed enough buffaloes to fill fifty carts with the meat. Only the meat that could be cut into large strips was used, that is, the hindquarters, the hump. The buffalo fat was saved also.

The hunt was conducted on horseback and lances were the weapons used. The commander would order the men to form a line placing the hunters mounted on the swifter horses at each end so that when they advanced on a herd of buffalo the ends of the line would lead the rest in an encircling movement of the beasts.

When the men were formed in line and before they launched themselves on the buffalo the Commander would ask that they all pray together and ask the Almighty God for strength in the impending hunt. When the Commander was heard to say, "Ave Maria Purissima" (Hail Holy Mary) the line would move forward as one man the end men on their swifter horses outdistancing the rest so as to encircle the herd, which was to be attacked.

Some of the men designated as skinners followed the hunt driving burros before them. These men skinned the fat cows only for the dead animals were so plentiful that they would ignore the bulls and lean cows.

They would pack the buffalo meat into camp where they would cut it into convenient sized strips after which they would slice it very t thin and hang it up to dry on poles. The "cecina" or jerked meat was prepared in the following manner; long strips were cut from the carcasses, for this, men expert at the job were selected. After the meat had cooled it was spread on hides and tramped on until it was drained of blood and then as we have already stated the cecinas were hung on poles to dry in the sun. After it had dried they would stack it up like cordwood, each pile containing enough meat to load three or four carts.

As soon as the Commander thought that sufficient meat had been prepared to fill all of the ox-carts he would give orders to cease killing buffaloes. He then would assign three or four carts to each pile of meat and he himself would divide the meat according to the different kinds, larger pieces, meat from the hump and the tallow; the smaller pieces were anybody's property in any quantity desired.

In loading the meat the same method was used as in loading fodder, some would load the meat on the cart while the owner of the cart would trample it down so as to get as much of a load on the cart as he possibly could and all that the oxen would be able to haul home.

After the carts were loaded a party of ten Plains Indians of the Kiowa tribe suddenly rode into camp. The Indians asked for something to eat and their request was complied with. After they had eaten some of the party thought it would be a good idea to kill the Indians, arguing that they were only ten in number and could be safely dispatched whereas if they were allowed to leave they might apprise others of their tribe and return in larger numbers to kill the members of the hunting party and steal the meat. Don Manuel Jesus Vasques opposed this plan. The Indians were ordered out of camp. They retired a short distance but followed the homeward bound caravan for a long distance. The following morning on orders of the Commander the long trek home was begun in earnest.

At the crossing of the Nutrias River the ox-cart belonging to the only American in the party became stuck in midstream. This American lived in Ocate. After all the rest of the ox-carts had safely crossed the river, all of the party helped in extricating the American's cart from the river and onto dry land. The actual hunting of the buffaloes lasted one month, the trip to and from the hunting grounds required a month's travel each so that the whole trip lasted three months. It took three months of that winter for the entire trip.

This expedition was free of any dispute or fight of any kind, whatever Don Manuel ordered was executed and the whole expedition got along very agreeably.

When Don Manual Jesus Vasquez returned to Penasco preparations were being made for another expedition to the country of the Comanches and Cayguas (Kiowas) towards Kansas. Don Manual Jesus Vasques went on this trip also. The object of this trip was the buying of horses from the Comanches and Kiowas.

On this trip burros loaded with bread were taken along. The bread was a certain kind of bread called Comanche bread. This bread was made of wheat flour but without yeast so that the bread was as hard or harder than a rock; and was traded to the Indians for horses. The Indians were Kiowas and Comanches. A "trinca" of bread was given for each horse. A "trinca" was half a sack of bread or in other words a sack of bread for a pair of horses. At this time the Indians already were receiving some aid from the government and they would feed those who went to trade with them, they had plenty of coffee and sugar. Twenty men went on this trading expedition and they brought fifteen horses back to Penasco with them.

The most of the men who went on this expedition worked for wages, small wages however, no one of them ever made more than 50¢ a day. Yet Don Juan Policarpio Romero never paid Don Manuel Jesus Vasques a single cent for his labors, as shepherd for his flock of goats nor for the making of coffins, nor for his services as a buffalo hunter or horse trader with the Indians, but he did keep Don Manuel and his family. While his patron lived Don Manuel never held one single penny in his hand.

Don Manuel Jesus Vasques who is alive today at the age of 83 says that he never recollects having seen the inside of a school house, but that his patron taught him how to sign his name. Don Juan Policarpio left or designated Don Manuel as one of his heirs and the sons of Don Juan Policarpio Romero gave him four goats and asked him to sign a paper which attested that he had received his share of the inheritance, and he not knowing how to read signed. The Probate Judge at Taos called him before him and asked Don Manuel if he was content and satisfied and upon his answering that he was, he signed the paper or document.

VICTORIO'S RAID

Tradition Bearer: Maurice Coates

Source: Totty, Francis. "Interview of Maurice Coates." American Life Histories: Manuscripts from the Federal Writers' Project, 1936–1940. Manuscript Division, Library of Congress. 12 October 2005. http://memory.loc.gov/ammem/wpaintro/wpahome.html.

Date: 1938

Original Source: New Mexico

National Origin: European American

Victorio's War against the European Americans who moved into the Southwest after the Civil War lasted from 1879 to 1880. The cause of the war was the repeated breaking of a promise to provide Victorio's Warm Springs Apache in New Mexico Territory with its own reservation. Ultimately, Victorio led his band throughout the New Mexico and Arizona Territories waging guerilla warfare, terrorizing residents, and fleeing across the border into Mexico to evade the U.S. Army forces sent to subdue him. It was in Mexico that Victorio and the remainder of his band—by then numbering fewer than eighty—were penned in and killed in 1880. At its greatest strength, his band numbered fewer than two hundred. The following **legend** is important both for its account of one of the events in this campaign and also for the clash of cultures the narrator's words reveal.

In 1878 Jim Keller, Maurice Coates, John Roberts, W. H. Beavers, Robert Stubblefield and Morris Smith and family left Prescott Arizona for the Frisco Valley, where they settled.

Late in May of 1879 we were out in the field plowing when a roving band of Apaches, five in number, fired upon us. We made a rush for the house and after getting our guns we crossed the Frisco river up into the Cedars, we were at the present site of Glenwood when we saw the Indians coming. Deming was going on down the valley to warn the settlers and Houston, Beaver, Keller and I hid, after staking out a horse as a decoy.

We fired on the Indians when they came in sight for they had made for the horse as they were all afoot. Deming came back as he was afraid that the Indians were heavily armed and he was taking too much of a risk to continue on down the valley. We fired too low and broke three of the warriors' legs, one of the warriors had been left on the hill to watch, and the others when we fired ran up the hill to escape.

We camped for the night and the next morning took the trail of the Indian that we had injured that went over the hill; we saw an Indian up in the hill covered with a blanket. Mr. Foster thinking that the warrior was dead lifted up the blanket and was surprised to find that the man had been asleep. Mr. Foster raised his gun to shoot. The Indian began to beg for his life, but Foster was so disgusted with the raids of the Indians that he pulled the trigger and blowed the Indian's head off.

Terrible was a son-in-law of Victorio and was killed by us during the fight, we soon heard that Victorio was on the warpath as he was going to revenge the death of his son-in-law.

During the month of April, 1880, there were many rumors that Victorio was out. Steve, a sub-chief of the Apaches, was up in the hills, was up in the [White?] Rocks country camping for Indians on the warpath. Steve was on a hunting trip when Victorio arrived on the scene and tried to get him to throw in with him to attack the settlers in the territory. Victorio became angry with Steve because he wouldn't attack the whites, and attacked the sub-chief. Three of Victorio's warriors were killed and Steve left the region.

On April the 28th Victorio made his presence known by appearing at the location of the Conney Mine killing two men. The rest of the party hid out and brought the news into the camp that the Indians had attacked and killed two of their group. Jim Cooney and Jack [Chick?] went to give the alarm while another group went Clairmont to give the alarm. George Doyle and John Lambert remained on the grounds. The tribe soon took over the mining camp and burned the cabins. Around noon one of the braves took a mirror and tied it around his neck. The squaws were soon fighting for a chance to get a glimpse of their dirty features in the mirror.

When Chick and Conney arrived with the news that Brightman and one other had been killed, we began at once to get out and round up the live stock. We spent the entire night on the range hunting the stock.

Conney and Chick went to the Meader ranch to carry the news, and Mr. Meader made the remark that, "Well we have the garden planted and I don't think the Indians are going to bother us." Mrs. Meader remarked that she believed the report and started at once to mold bullets. Conney desired to return to camp, and Mrs. Meader begged him to not leave, but he insisted that he was going and it was not long until the horses of Chick and Conney returned without riders.

When the horses were seen without their riders the alarm was sent out at once. Mr. Elliot rushed over to the Meader ranch and gave the alarm. The Meader family started at once for the Roberts ranch. On the way over the Indians fired upon the family and as the wagon was between the house and the Indians there wasn't much that the people in the cabin could do to help the family. Agnes Meader Snyder had an arrow shot through her bonnet, was as near as the Indians came to hitting any of the members of the family. Mrs. Meader had the people to fill of the barrels and tubs with water before the water was cut off, and it was only a short time after the vessels were filled that the ditch was cut.

Five of we men decided to go behind the house and shoot at the Indians. They were out there only a short time when they were fired upon. We made a run for the house. I lost my belt of cartridges and pistol.

There was a horse picketed some forty feet from the house. An Indian tried to get the horse. When he raised up to cut the rope, he was surprised with a shot from Jim Keller's gun. Some time later when it was decided safe to go out to where the Indian was it was found that he had on the gun that had been lost earlier in the day. The body of the Indian was removed during the night from where it was laying.

Wilcox raised up to look over the barricade and was shot through the heart. The only member of the party to be killed after the fight started.

A rescue party was sent from Silver City to the aid of the besieged, but as the Indians left the morning after the fight they were not to be found.

RANGE LIFE IN TEXAS

Tradition Bearer: Jack Robert Grigsby

Source: Angermiller, Florence. "Interview of Jack Robert Grigsby." American Life Histories: Manuscripts from the Federal Writers' Project, 1936–1940. Manuscript Division, Library of Congress. 12 October 2005. http://memory.loc.gov/ammem/wpaintro/wpahome.html.

Date: 1938

Original Source: Texas

National Origin: Anglo American

Most of the historical accounts that find their way into print chronicle significant turning points in political careers, national crises, and major encounters between political systems. The autobiography that follows includes a **personal experience narrative** that includes the notorious figures Billy the Kid and William H. Bonney (1859?–1881). It also makes passing references to lesser known, but no less deadly, gunmen, Bill (William Preston) Longley (1851–1878), notorious for his hate crimes against Blacks after the Civil War, and George Gladden, a central figure in what came to be known as the Mason County War. The Mason County War, also known as the Hoodoo War, took place in Texas in the decade after the Civil War. More importantly, however, the following are the vivid memories of a fairly average man caught up in the turmoil of Reconstruction and the changes brought by the turn of the twentieth century. This is a life that many lived in the Southwest, but few have passed along to the twenty-first century.

I was born in Tyler, Texas, August 26, 1854, coming to this country in November, 1870. I was about sixteen years old when I came here. I was raised an orphan. I don't ever remember seeing my mother, and my father died when I was six or seven years old. After that I lived first one place and another till I came out here.

I started work on a ranch when I first got to this country, working for Will Pruitt. I just lived in the woods, for there were very few people here at that time. I worked for Mr. Pruitt about six years, just working for my board and clothes, and it wasn't many clothes either.

I went part of the way up the trail to Oklahoma, twice with stuff for Will Pruitt. But he would always turn me back at Red River. He knew that I had a half brother living on up in Oklahoma and I always thought he did this so I wouldn't find my brother and stay with him, for he wanted me to work for him. I would come all the way back from Red River alone. Sometimes I would meet up with herds on the way and sometimes I would ride all the way back without seeing anyone.

I have had all kinds of ups and downs in the cattle business. Once we took a bunch of cattle to the old Woodhull ranch out south of Spofford. Part of the herd belonged to Mr. Furness. He had come up here and bought them up, and we got twenty-five cents a head for all we delivered, and furnished ourselves. But we had to pay for all we lost. One night we had camped about where Cline is now and had put the herd in a corner of a pasture for the night. We were herding them too, but along in the night something scared them and they run through all three of those wire fences. As we would turn them from one string they would go into another. But we only lost two. One broke its shoulder and one got away. It was a steer that belonged to old Man Vogel and three years later Millard Parkerson caught him and sold him for old Man Vogel. But the one that got its shoulder broke didn't cost us anything for it belonged to one of the boys in the bunch.

Our boss wanted to get there with the cattle looking good. So after we crossed Turkey Creek, we heard the train coming and he asked us to take the cattle a mile or so away from the track so the train wouldn't stampede 'em. Well, we all had cattle in the outfit and we made it up to hold them right to the track. So we took our slickers from behind our saddles and whipped the herd right up to the track. We had to do some riding for about two miles, for those cattle really did run. But we stayed with 'em. The boss sure got red but it didn't do him any good.

The next day we got to the ranch and was going down on a creek to camp, and one of the boys roped the pack horseman and he went to pitching and scattered skillets, frying pans, coffee pots and all our grub everywhere. But we got everything back but our grub. So we went up to the house and told Mr. Furness what had happened. He told us to come on up to the house and stay. So we helped him brand out his cattle, and he give us enough grub to get back home.

Yes, we always used a packhorse to carry our grub for we worked in this rough country and there were no roads, so we had no use for a chuck wagon. Except one time when we made a trip up on the divide above Leakey. Well, there was no road and the wagon broke down. We had gotten ahead with the herd, so some of the boys went back to see what was wrong and to get some corn from the wagon to feed the horses. The man saw a light out across the country and came back and told us it was Indians. So we had to get out and round up the horses. We built a brush pen to put them in and guarded them all night. The next morning we had gotten breakfast and started to eat. But it was always the custom then, when the cowboys were eating, for someone to keep watch for Indians. Well, one of the boys got up to look and saw a big bunch of men coming. He says, 'Boys, here they come!' But it turned out to be soldiers and they had seen us and thought we were Indians. So the boss got up and hollered at them to wait and the officer in charge come on up to the camp. We had killed a beef the evening before, so we gave them part of that and they gave us about twenty-five pounds of coffee.

One time Joe Pan Pelt came to work with our outfit down here about Rio Frio. Well, we always turned all the horses loose at night except one or two we kept to ride after the others next morning. We never cared what we kept up to ride—just anything, no matter how they were. The boys always took it turn about going after the horses in the morning, so it came Joe's time to get the horses. It was a cold, frosty morning and he said he didn't want to get on the horse. But I told him yes, he must go. So he got on the horse and he began pitching and finally turned a somersault with him. He got up and said he couldn't ride the horse again. But I told him we had those horses there to ride and if he didn't ride him I couldn't keep him for I couldn't afford to keep a hand that could not ride the horses. So he got on him again and that time he rode him.

Joe Collins used to come out in this country and buy fat cattle and take them to New Orleans and ship them from there. I have seen him ride into cow camp with a *morral* (nose bag) full of gold and go off and leave it there maybe all night and no one ever bothered it. I guess if someone had taken it he would have just been killed and that would have been all there would have been to it. There wasn't any court. Uvalde was the nearest post-office.

Old Man Schwartz used to come to the cow camps with his hack peddling dry goods and lots of times he would stay all night. He always went prepared to camp, for them days you couldn't always make it to a house for the night. But he would always sell something to the cowboys, such as gloves and if they didn't have the money they got them just the same. And I don't believe those cowboys ever beat him out of a quarter. He was sure a fine old man. I thought a lot of him.

When I first commenced work for myself I had some awful mean horses. I traded for the meanest ones I could get, so the boys wouldn't ride 'em when I was gone. I had one I only rode every three days. Well, he was so mean I would have to tie him to a tree and beat him up before I could get a bridle on him, for he sure would fight.

I broke a horse down here once for Mart Pruitt. He finally traded him to Calvin Bowles. The horse was getting tender-footed so I met Calvin one day and told him his horse needed shoeing. He said yes, but he was too mean to shoe. But the old blacksmith in Leakey come out and said he could handle him. Well, they brought the horse down and the old blacksmith fooled around him a little while and finally dropped the rope. I said, 'Don't do that; he'll run off.' He told me to just let him alone he would handle him. So he went in and got his nails and hammer and horseshoes and put the shoes on him and the horse never moved. I don't know what he did to the horse for after that he was just as mean to kick anyone else as he ever was.

Yes, times are quite different now to what they used to be. I remember when Old Man Hanson come in here and taken up a preemption of a hundred and sixty acres. Hatten Elms come along and wanted to trade him out of it. Elms asked him what he would take for it and he said, 'Two cows and calves,' which meant about eight dollars for a cow and calf. Well, they traded for about a week, and then Elms backed out. So you can imagine about what land was worth then.

Once the Indians come into the country and was stealing horses. Well, we heard of them and the settlers got together and took their trail down here about Rio Frio. We followed them on across the Seco to the Sabinal Canyon and on to Frio Town, down by Old Man Westfall's ranch, which was a big cow ranch. And when we crossed the Frio near where Loma Vista is now, we had run out of food and were sure hungry. We hadn't had anything to eat for several days but a little coffee. There didn't seem to be any stock in that country then. But we finally met a Mexican sheepherder with a herd of sheep and asked him for one. He said we would have to go see the boss. We didn't have time to fool around hunting the boss. So Joe Van-Pelt jumped off his horse and shot at a big old mutton and killed two. We took them on down to a little creek and cooked them and the eighteen of us ate every bit of those two sheep.

The Indians killed nineteen people before they reached the Rio Grande. Well, we went on for a day or two without overtaking them and some of the men got discouraged and kept dropping out till there was only five of us left. We had appointed Henry Patterson as captain. So he decided it was best to go back to Uvalde and wire Lieutenant Bullis for help so he met us here with his Seminole Indian soldiers and we took up the trail again and followed it on to the Rio Grande. But they had already gone across. We could see men riding back and forth and we were satisfied it was these Indians, but we were not allowed to go after them.

They killed one man by the name of Byrd and about five of his men who was herding sheep for him. Mr. Byrd was in his buggy when the Indians overtaken him and after they killed him, they taken everything he had in the buggy and his buggy harness. They cut the leather harness up in little pieces and scattered it along the way. Of course it was of no value to them. But we found it as we followed the trail. They had also gone by the Mount Woodward ranch and killed two or three men there. We didn't see anyone as we passed the ranch. We wasn't bothered about seeing people—we was just following that Indian trail.

Another time we followed a bunch of Indians over on Dry Frio. They had killed a man by the name of Terry and captured his two children a little boy and a little girl. The girl's name was Mattie and the boy's name was Joe. But Joe had fought them so hard they knocked him in the head and left him for dead, right before his little sister's eyes. But he didn't die. Well, we rode all night that night till daylight. At daylight we took up the trail again and overtaken them just before noon. They didn't offer to fight for it was raining and their bowstrings were wet. They couldn't shoot and that gave us the best of them. One old Indian was off ahead of the others and they were crossing a creek when we begin to shoot at them. We followed them on into a shin-oak thicket. After awhile we come into a little opening and just as we got to this opening we saw the little girl. It looked like she had just been kicked off of the horse by the old Indian she was riding behind. She had an Indian blanket wrapped around her and when she saw us she started to run. But we told her to wait, we wouldn't hurt her, so she sat down on the blanket and waited.

We went on after the Indians, still shooting at them every chance we got. Finally we got so close to the old Indian that had dropped the little girl that we could see him kick his horse every jump trying to make him go faster. Anyway, he had a bed tick around him and we found that full of bullet holes and bloody. I don't know if we killed any or not but there was plenty of blood along the trail.

He ran on till he got to a ridge and when he went over this ridge and into another thicket, we was close enough to see he carried a long lance in his hand. None of us wanted him bad enough to go in there after him, for you know they can throw those old lances through you.

We got the little girl and started back home. On the way back we found a lot of stuff the Indians had lost, such as goat hides and one buffalo robe. It was cold and everything was wet. So we picked them up and took them to camp and used them for bedding. Just before night someone said, 'Do you suppose these things have lice?' But we slept on them just the same. Yes, we got plenty lice.

When we got back to Old Man Shores' where we were in cow camp, we took a big wash pot, got off down on the river and cleaned up. We boiled all our clothes and tied the buffalo robe in the river for about three days. Jim Avant took the little girl on to his home, but he had to stay in camp with the rest till he got rid of those lice. Mrs. Avant took the little girl and combed and washed the lice out of her hair, and washed the paint off of her face that the Indians had put on it. And she put clean clothes on her.

Every family in the whole country wanted the little girl, but she didn't want to stay with any of them. She wanted to stay with us men who had rescued her from the Indians. When they did take her back to her mother, she went with a herd of fat cattle that Pruitt was taking to San Antonio. When they got to San Antonio, she wouldn't get on the stage coach to go home unless one of the cowboys went along, so one of them got on the coach up with the driver and put the little girl back inside with the mail. There was a little window in the top where she could see the cowboy sitting up on top. Well, when they got down the road a piece, they picked up another passenger so the cowboy slipped off and this man took his place. The little girl didn't know the difference. But I never saw her after that.

I knew Billy the Kid. He stayed in camp with us down here about Hackberry once for about a week. He rode into camp one day and his horse was rode down. He told us his name was Word and he wanted to stay a few days. I told him all right. So he stayed on and helped us round up cattle till one day he got into a fight with a Negro we had working with the outfit. Billy cut the Negro across the side of the face and down the back with a long butcher knife. The Negro finally run. And when he stopped, I walked over to where he was and he said, 'Mr. Jack, please don't let him hurt me any more!' About that time Billy came up and said, 'Oh, shut your damn mouth. I have already done all to you that I want to.' Billy stood there and wiped the blood off of the knife with his hands and looked at the cut on the man as unconcerned as if he hadn't done a thing. But he left after that. He was afraid the officers would hear of this and would get him for other things he was wanted for.

When he left camp he went on up to Bill Patterson's ranch and got a job going up the trail to Kansas that spring. They said he stayed with them part of the way back home, but stopped one day away out on the prairie and took his bed but turned his horse a-loose. So they left him right there without a horse. They said they guessed he didn't want to get any closer to Texas.

I knew several other desperados. Among them was Bill Longley, George Gladden, John Beard and Lew Sawyers. They all come through this one winter at different times. They didn't do any kind of work while they was here but they took in all the dances.

There was one man, a desperado, come in to this country one time. I can't remember his name right now. Anyway he stayed over on the West Prong a lot. I don't know what he had done, no telling what. Anyway, while he was staying up on the West Prong, he shot a Mexican one day just to try out his gun. The Mexican was about two hundred and fifty yards away and as he stooped over to dig a hole this man shot him in the hip. I met the man about a mile down the road just after it had happened but he didn't say a word about what he had done. Well, the (Texas) Rangers come in and got after him and caught him away from home without a horse. But he got away from them and Old Man Lyman Smith helped him get out of the country by exchanging clothes with him so he would be disguised and wouldn't get caught. Those fellows were very peaceful and nice unless trouble come up.

I was married to Miss Jennie Horton in January 1888. We were married right up the river here about a half-mile in my wife's parent's home. We walked on down here after the wedding and have been here ever since. But I had to give a dance at Leakey in the courthouse that night to keep the boys from shivareeing us. We had a big supper and danced till about four o'clock, then it came up a big, snow storm and we had to go home to keep from freezing. It was one of the biggest snowstorms I ever saw in this country. I guess me getting married caused it.

THE ADAMS DIGGINGS

Tradition Bearer: E. V. Batchler

Source: Batchler, E. V. "Autobiographcial Account by E. V. Batchler." American Life Histories: Manuscripts from the Federal Writers' Project, 1936–1940. Manuscript Division, Library of Congress. 12 October 2005. http://memory.loc.gov/ammem/wpaintro/wpahome.html.

Date: 1938

Original Source: New Mexico
National Origin: European American

The following is one of the many **legends** of lost treasures and gold mines that circulated throughout the Southwest. Many were lured by the tales, but virtually all came away disappointed.

Since I came to New Mexico, eighteen years ago, I have heard stories of the wealth of the famous, old, lost Adams Diggings Mine. I have heard at least a dozen different stories and each succeeding story made the mine richer both in actual gold value and romantic interest. As is often the way with lost mines of this type, it all depends on who you listen to, whether the mine gets richer or not. It always seemed strange to me that nearly every old-timer will swear that he knows more about a fabulously rich, lost mine than any other old prospector. He will try to discredit other prospectors who have searched for the mine and in an effort to tell something "bigger," magnify its riches by many times what others have estimated it at. In reality, none of them know or have the slightest idea as to the value of the lost mine, because it has never been found.

The current story based on a story from the *El Paso Herald* is that a bunch of men, among them Edward Adams, who purportedly found the mine that was later named for him, organized an expedition to go to California. Their probable starting place was Magdalena. They traveled in a northwesterly direction, until somewhere between Magdalena and old Fort San Rafael, they camped on a little stream.

One of the men noticed gold in the stream and excitedly revealed his discovery to the rest. Adams, who knew a little more about mining than his companions, decided that the gold washed into the stream from a rich outcropping above the camp. Taking his partner, a man by the name of Davidson with him, he left camp and traveled up the canyon about a mile to try to discover the "mother lode." A little while after they had disappeared around a bend in the creek, the expedition was attacked by Apaches, and as they caught the encampment totally unprepared, the Indians massacred every man in camp.

Adams and Davidson heard the firing, and guessed its cause, took to the cover of the bushes on the nearby hillside. After hiding for several hours, the two men cautiously made their way over the hill and saw that the Apaches had left, secure in the belief that they had killed all the men of the expedition, and had taken all the mules and horses with them.

After burying all the dead, Adams and Davidson knocked a few pieces of gold-bearing ore off an outcropping of quarts that they believed to be the "mother lode." They then purported made their way to Fort San Rafael, where they said they asked for aid to go back and find the gold and were refused by the officer in charge.

They then made their way afoot and after perilous hardships and a great deal of suffering, came into the little town of Reserve, in what is now Catron County. It is said that they showed the ore to several of the natives, and then after borrowing some money on the strength of the richness of the ore, bought horses and went to Pima, Arizona, where Adams had friends whom he thought had enough money to properly outfit an expedition to return to the place where he had found the gold.

The expedition was organized, and traveled from Pima to Alma and thence to the immediate locality where Adams was supposed to have found the gold. But through some freak of nature or loss of direction, they could not find the gold, or even the place where the men had been massacred. Perhaps it was because Adams and Davidson both were notoriously poor in remembering directions. Many expeditions have been organized since then, but to this day, the Adams Diggings remains as much a mystery as when Adams first told of it.

Now I am going to tell a story that is almost completely at variance with the story printed by the *El Paso Herald*. It is a first-hand story from the lips of Bob Lewis, pioneer, old-time prospector, cowboy and for the better part of his manhood, a frontier peace officer and a personal friend of Edward Adams. Bob is a big man, well over six-feet and weighing in the vicinity of two hundred pounds. He always have a jovial greeting and manner, and has the map of Ireland printed all over his face. Big, rough and burly, he has been the bane of many crooks and lawbreaker in his County. He lives in Magdalena. He has been over nearly every section of the southwestern corner of the State of New Mexico, and knows its rugged terrain as well or better than nearly any other man. He is renowned for his lack of fear, and truthfulness. That is why I believe his account of the Adams Diggings far more than any of the others I have heard. Here is the story in his own words:

"Sure I knowed old Adams. I knowed him before he left Magdalena, and after he came back. Never was a bigger old liar. He'd tell a lie when the truth would fit better. He was used to braggin' and stretchin' the truth. He was drinkin' man too. I knowed him to stay drunk six months out of the year, and then go on and throw a big drunk the rest of the year."

It was in the early part of August, 1864, when Adams and about seven other men organized a trappin' expedition and started up in the northwestern part of the state to trap beaver. They started early and intended to get their camp set up before cold weather came. They camped on a little stream not far from old Fort San Fafael, which is now Fort Wingate and has been moved a few miles from the old site of Fort San Rafael.

Now I don't know this for certain, but I believe from events, which I will try to explain later, that just about dark, a caravan from California stopped and threw camp with Adams party. They had stopped at Fort Wingate two days before and had told the commanding officer that they were transporting between sixty and eighty thousand dollars in placer gold from California to some of the Eastern states. I know that they were never seen after the time Adams party was wiped out by the Indians, so I believe that they camped with Adams party and met the same fate.

I know from Adams personal character, that he was not above ambushing such a caravan. I did not know Davidson, but as he was Adams sidekick, I believe he throwed in with Adams and the two of 'em made plans to hijack the California outfit and steal their gold.

An encampment like that, in those days, usually got us an hour or two before daylight, in order to make an early start. It is said that Adams and Davidson made an excuse to go and gather some wood, as wood had been scarce the evening before and they had not been able to obtain a sufficient supply. I believe that Adams and Davidson absented themselves from camp, so they could go down country a few miles and find a suitable place for waylaying the California outfit.

While they were gone, and it must have been just as good daylight came, because that is the time when Indians usually attack, a big bunch of Apaches attacked the camp. So complete must have been the surprise, that the white men could not have had a very good chance to grab their guns and defend themselves. Every man in that camp was killed, scalped and their bodies mutilated, and all their provisions, horses and mules stolen by the Apaches.

When Adams and Davidson returned to camp, they must have congratulated themselves on the luck that had caused them to absent themselves from camp. Rummaging around among the supplies, Adams must have found the gold the California outfit had been carrying. As proof of this, I later saw a handful of this gold that Adams had save when he buried the rest and it was a quality entirely foreign to that part of New Mexico and identical with some I had seen from California Diggin's. The pellets were about the size of a pinhead, up to as big as a pinto bean, and I knew that nobody ever found that kind of gold in the parts of New Mexico I have prospected over.

After burying the gold in what they considered a safe place, the two made their way afoot, supposedly, to Fort San Rafael, where they said they reported the massacre to the authorities in charge and petitioned aid from the command-ing officer to go back and help them relocate a mine they had found and to view the remains of the Indian attack.

I do not believe this last part, because many years later, I happened to be in Evans [?], in March 1890, where Adams, who had been drinkin' pretty heavy, related a story of how he had gone to Fort San Rafael, on a certain day (he men-tioned the exact date, which I can not now remember) in August, 1864, and petitioned the commanding officer for aid to return to give decent burial to the massacred party and offer him and Davidson protection while they tried to relo-cate a rich gold claim.

There happened to be an old, retired Army officer in the saloon who had listened intently to Adams story. This man was Captain Sanborn, who was con-sidered a heavy drinker. However, he did not appear to be drunk at this partic-ular time, and he answered Adams:

"Sir, since the latter part of your speech concerns me, and it is most damag-ing to my character, I now take it upon myself to refute your statements and call you a contemptible, damned liar. I happened to be the commanding officer of Fort San Rafael at the time of which you are talking. I recall the day of which you speak very clearly and to my knowledge you never set foot in that Fort in your life. It could never be said truthfully that Cap Sanborn ever refused aid to anybody within a weeks march of my post who needed it."

"Who's a damn liar?" bellowed Adams. "Yuh better eat them words cap, or me an' you are agoin' to tangle right here an' now. Bigod! I don't like army offi-cers anyway, so I might as well wipe up th' floor with one of 'em right now." Saying which, he started for Sanborn.

Cap Sanborn ran behind the lunch counter and grabbed a big butcher knife and jumped over the counter. Adams ran out the front door and Sanborn chased him for a couple of blocks shouting that Adams was the dirtiest liar that ever lived. He could not catch Adams, and returned to the saloon, where he again told everybody in hearing distance that Adams had not ever been to Fort San Rafael.

From the above incident I drew the conclusion that Adams and Davidson never went to Fort San Rafael at all, but passed a considerable distance to the south in an effort to avoid it. They limped into the little town of Reserve, sore-footed and half-starved.

It was in Reserve that Adams showed a couple of pieces of ore in quartz form that was exceedingly rich, and stated that it was from the mine he had found before the Indians had massacred his party. He made no mention of the California expedition.

I later saw the same samples Adams had shown in Reserve and recalled that Adams had showed me one of the samples before he left Magdalena in 1864. He had told me then that he had given an Indian some whiskey for the samples and had promised him more if he would show him where he got the samples. If Adams story he told in Reserve about these samples had been true, there would indeed have been a substantial claim to his having found a rich mine. But to my knowledge, no ore of similar quality has ever been found, and the Indian who gave the samples to Adams must be long since dead and the place he found the samples will probably never be found.

Adams didn't dare show any of the gold at that time he had stolen and buried. Therefore he and Davidson separated, Adams going to Pima, Arizona to obtain money and supplies from friends to outfit an expedition to later come back and salvage the gold. Davidson went on a supposed visit to see some relatives in Louisiana.

Adams was successful in his attempt to raise an expedition, and he sent for Davidson who returned from Louisiana and the expedition met him in Alma, a little town just south of Reserve. They could not find any gold, and Adams later made several solitary trips in search of it, but never had any luck.

Several expeditions have been organized and sent forth in an effort to find the Adams Diggings, but all have met with defeat. It was in 1818 that I decided to see if I couldn't find the bodies of the men who were massacred in Adams' party. Adams had told me that they had camped about fifteen miles north of three peaks that rose up from the plain and were a considerable distance from any other mountains. I got to thinkin' and the only three peaks I knew of between Gallup and Magdalena, were the Tres Montosas, which are only about fifteen miles west of Magdalena. Figuring about fifteen or twenty miles north of there, I went to North Lake. A few miles north of North Lake, I found the bodies of five men, all buried in one hole. I could find no clue to any gold from anything in the vicinity, so I came back to town and reported the finding of the bodies. It is my belief that the bodies I found were the remains of part of Adams expedition, but of course I can't prove this. But there is one thing I do know. That is that an old fellow I know, found about twenty thousand dollars buried about five miles north of North Lake, and only a few miles from the place I discovered their bodies. This mans name is Jose Maria Jaramillo, and this what he told me. But when I asked him if the twenty thousand was in gold dust, he would not tell me.

"That's the way a lot of their old, 'rich-nice' stories get started," finished old Bob. "I've heard that the definition of a miner is a damn liar with a hole in the ground. And a prospector is a damn liar without anything but a dang good imagination. You can talk to most of 'em, and dang near ever' one of 'em tells you about some rich prospect they struck. But they're always broke and beggin' a grubstake. If their mines was half as rich as their imaginations, they could take a handpick, and a gold pan and make more money in a month than most bank presidents could by wearin' out a half a dozen fountains pens. It's true that sometimes a prospector does hit it rich, but when he does, he generally don't talk and brag on it, but gets busy and gets some capital interested and starts workin' it. That's my story of the Adams Diggings. It is one of the richest mines in the world in the mind of a danged old liar like I knowed Ed Adams to be, and in the minds of a bunch of old, dream-crazy prospectors who ain't got no more sense than to believe in it."

THEM PETRIFIED BUZZARDS

Tradition Bearer: Harry Reece

Source: Bowman, Earl. "Interview of Harry Reece." American Life Histories: Manuscripts from the Federal Writers' Project, 1936–1940. Manuscript Division, Library of Congress. 12 October 2005. http://memory.loc.gov/ammem/wpaintro/wpahome.html.

Date: 1938

Original Source: Arizona

National Origin: European American

This tale, attributed to Steve Robertson and recounted by his nephew Harry Reece, develops a typical **tall tale** theme in its exaggerated focus on the rigors of the Arizona climate. More than a playful attempt to enhance a regional reputation, a narrative of this sort, by implication, increases the stature of those who are able to survive the rigorous natural elements they describe. In the present case, the survivors overcome a blistering summer whose heat petrifies buzzards in mid-air. Therefore, it functions as tongue-in-cheek bragging. The repudiation of lies and liars that precedes and follows this tale is a typical way of **framing** such narratives. Moreover, Uncle Steve's tale, in relying on the audience's ignorance of the West, is typical of the tall tales included in explorers' accounts of their exploits. See, for example, the literary contributions of Karl Friedrich Hieronymus Baron von Münchhausen, an eighteenth-century German aristocrat so noted for telling tall tales that his name became synonymous with the **genre**.

My Uncle Steve Robertson was a native of the State of Missouri or Arkansas; he was not certain which, because he said he was born so close to the line that sometimes he thought it was on one side and sometimes on the other.

He also said that one reason he didn't remember which State it was, was because he started Out West when he was so young that it really didn't matter whether he was born in Missouri or Arkansas; he was satisfied just to be born, and was willing to let it go at that.

Anyway, my Uncle Steve Robertson was a great pioneer in his day, before any government irrigation projects were built in the West, and he knew all about shooting bear and deer and fighting Indians, and settling in out-of-the-way places where people had to depend mostly on themselves and each other and there were not any electric lights or telephones or radios or WPA's or PWA's or AAA's or things like that to distract their attentions, and post offices were quite far apart indeed. So, people depended to a large extent upon themselves and not to any great extent to or on anything else.

My Uncle Steve's idea of "Out West" was anywhere west of the east line of the Indian Territory (Uncle Steve never did get around to calling it "Oklahoma" because he said that that did not seem natural!)—he also thought that "Out West" was bounded on the south by the Big Bend country of the Rio Grande and on the north by the last peak of the Bitterroot Mountains in Idaho and which leaned over into Canada. So, Uncle Steve had quite a large idea of what "Out West" really was, and he also had quite a lot of experience with it.

Naturally, also, my Uncle Steve Robertson accumulated a vast knowledge of and quite a few strange experiences during the many years he was a great "pioneer of the far 'Out West'" and which, I am sorry to say, quite a lot of people in New York, and especially around the Washington Square district, do not yet realize ever existed—or for that matter may still exist to some extent.

Also, my Uncle Steve used to say that the one damned thing he could not endure was … "a danged double talkin' liar … one of them 'rubber-tongued' persons who could stretch the truth till she would crack, and keep on stretchin' it, and still expect people to believe it."

My Uncle Steve always began his "tall tales," (for I am afraid that they were "tall" tales, and some of them very tall indeed!) with the preliminary statement that he 'just couldn't stand any damn person that "'zagerates!"

When we were on a fishing trip one time he told me about how the petrified forests of Arizona happened to be petrified—and also about 'the petrified buzzards' … It was a hot and dry season and I had mentioned it because the water in the creek where we were fishing was almost all dried up, and that was Uncle Steve's excuse to tell me about a really hot and dry season he once experienced in Arizona.

"It was back in … now danged if I remember jest which year it was back in," Uncle Steve said, "but anyhow it was the year that old Geronimo was loaded on the train at Bowie, Arizona, when the government sent him to Florida to keep him from butchering people in Arizona. Well, that was the year that it was in, and it shore-as-hell was a hot and dry year in Arizona.

"Bob White an' me had a little cow outfit in partnership down close to the Mexican line, and we was gettin' along pretty well. We'd took up some land … about two sections … and dug some wells and built some ditches so we could irrigate a little ground around the place. We had windmills to pump water out of the wells into a pond and the ditches, and our nine or ten hundred head of cattle had pretty good feed on the range. And outside of havin' to shoot a few Apaches now and then, before the government got rid of them, we was doin' fairly well and was contented enough, I reckon.

"At first, 'Mam' White, that was Bob's wife, was a little lonesome because there wasn't no frogs to croak down by th' pond or along th' ditches at night. She said she plumb missed frogs a-croakin' an' if there was jest some frogs she could hear croak of a' evenin' she'd be about as happy as she used to be back in Slippery Elm County, Arkansas, where she was born, and her pa and ma still lived. Well, Bob was always sentimental and he fixed it for Mam. He sent back to Arkansas and had a few settin's of frog eggs sent out to her. So, Mam set 'em an' they hatched out jest fine, and before long, when the sun went down behind old Apache Peak of an' evenin', frogs was croakin' all over th' place and Mam was plumb happy.

"Like I said, everything was goin' smooth an' pleasant and we was prosperous till it began to get hot and dry one summer … hotter an' dryer, I-Gawd, than anybody'd ever knowed it to be in that part of Arizona before, an' the first thing me realized them damn pumps wasn't suckin' nothing out of them wells but hot air, and th' alfalfa was withered and Mam's marigolds she'd planted by the side of the house was all dead and dried up, too.

"And in addition to that, them nine or ten hundred head of cattle Bob an' me had out there on th' range was staggerin' around, so cussed thirsty an' dried out, that when they'd walk their livers and hearts and lungs or whatever was loose inside of them would rattle against their hides like seeds shakin' around in a ripe gourd. Yeah, that's jest th' way they'd sound! And when one of them got tired walkin' around, hearin' hisself or herself as the case might be, rattlin' like a gourd that ain't got nothin' in it but some seeds, and finally laid down, well, danged if he or she or it didn't jest naturally petrify, plumb solid. That's when them poor buzzards got a awful shock.

"They'd be wheelin' around, jest wheelin' around watchin' for a cow or a steer brute to topple over, and as soon as they'd see one topple, down they'd swoop thinkin' they'd make a meal on it, and when they'd try to take a bite out of that petrified carcass they'd bust their poor bills off, and there they was ... plumb helpless, so they'd topple over, too—and in a minute they'd be petrified themselves!

"Well, the rest of them damn buzzards that hadn't come down and was still wheelin' 'round up there in the hell-blisterin' heat and dryness, would wonder what th' hell had happened to their brother buzzards, layin' down there all petrified beside them petrified cattle; they'd be scairt to come down, and jest keep on wheelin' and wheelin' and gettin' more and more bewildered till damned if they wouldn't petrify themselves up there in the sky without ever knowin' it— and that's the way it was.... Thousands and thousands, hell, millions of buzzards jest wheelin' and wheelin' around 'way up in that hot, sizzlin' Arizona atmosphere—and all so damned petrified they couldn't do nothin' but keep on wheelin' and wheelin' without ever makin' a sound or flappin' a doggone wing— Gawd, it was a gruesome sight!

"Yeah, them damned buzzards—all petrified and everything jest wheelin' and wheelin' around up there in th' sky, was a terrible thing to look at, but, I-Gawd, bad off as they was they didn't suffer as much as them poor wild hydrophobia cats that got so dry that they couldn't even foam at th' mouth when they'd have hydrophobia fits.... That was one of the pitifullest sights I ever seen. A poor hydrophobia cat tryin' to foam at th' mouth when he's havin' a fit, and not be able to do nothin' only spit out a little stream of dry, kind of chalky dust, instead of good rich foam like he'd naturally do! It sure as hell was pitiful to look at...

"But them hydrophobia cats wasn't no worse off than all them poor ants jest crawlin' around on the sand under th' blazin' sun, without a drop to drink, jest swelterin' and dryin' up till eventually they'd be in such agony they'd double over an' bite themselves on their own belly-band, an' commit suicide an' perish in misery ... Gawd, I'll bet ten billion ants ... damn nice big red Arizona ants committed suicide on our ranch alone! It's a awful thing to see a poor damn ant so thirsty an' hot an' dried out that it doubles over an' gnaws its own belly-band in two ... It sure is.

"Still, I reckon th' worst sufferin' was done by them miserable danged frogs; all them frogs Mam had hatched out from them settin's of frog eggs Bob had had sent out from Arkansas ... They got so dry, they jest kind of shriveled up and all wrinkled sort-of-like, well, like a prune that has been layin' out in th' sun too long. That's jest th' way their hides looked—jest shriveled up an' wrinkled like a prune, or worse. But th' worst of it was when they didn't have no water to waller in any more, and sort of soak 'em up; I-Gawd, when the sun would go down behind old Apache Peak an' them poor frogs would open their mouths and try to croak, like Mam loved to hear 'em do of an evenin', all th' poor damn things could do was jest sort of whistle.... It was terrible, th' most agonizin' and heart-wrenchin' thing anybody can imagine. Yes, sir, I-Gawd, if you ever saw a poor shriveled frog tryin' to croak, and not be able to get anything out but jest a measly little damn whistle, it's th, saddest thing you ever saw!

"It sure was distressin'.... Them poor frogs gaspin' out little dinky whistles instead of good solid croaks, was what settled it. When it got that dry, Mam, Bob's wife, couldn't stand it no longer. She'd listen to them frogs tryin' to croak—and jest break down with grief. She jest couldn't stand it. So, finally, after all then buzzards was petrified and most of them ants had committed suicide and them hydrophobia cats 'most plumb forgot how to foam at the mouth, and at last them helpless cussed frogs was whistlin' 'stead of croakin', Mam said to me an' Bob one day: "We're goin' to move out of this cussed place, Bob White and Steve Robertson. When it gets so danged dry that even a buzzard petrifies and even a frog can't croak, I-Gawd, it's time to go somewhere else." That's what Mam said. And Bob an' me always did believe in lettin' the women folks have their way, so, I-Gawd, we moved. An' damned if I know whether it ever did rain an' bust th' dry spell, or not. Maybe it did an' maybe it didn't. But while we was present it was *one hell of a dry spell*—and I imagine if anybody went down there to that part of Arizona they could still see some of them petrified trees layin' around on the ground ('cause—while I didn't mention it before—even most of th' damn trees got to be petrified, too, before things was done with)— an' I also imagine that anybody would probably see some of them poor petrified buzzards still wheelin' an' wheelin' and wheelin' around and around, 'way up there in the air ... never makin' a sound an' never flappin' a wing ... Jest petrified as hell, an' unable to do anything about it!"

My Uncle Steve Robertson was a very great pioneer in his day, and no doubt had many wonderful and thrilling experiences in the very far Out West, and—as I said before—he was one of those sturdy old ex-Rebel soldiers who could not *"endure a danged liar an' depised any ornery man that 'xaggerates."* Perhaps that is why I loved him; he was my favorite Uncle ... the one with whom I liked best to go fishing, or on camping-out trips.

METEOR HELL! CICERO DONE IT

Tradition Bearer: Harry Reece

Source: Bowman, Earl. "Interview of Harry Reece." American Life Histories: Manuscripts from the Federal Writers' Project, 1936–1940. Manuscript Division, Library of Congress. 12 October 2005. http://memory.loc.gov/ammem/wpaintro/wpahome.html.

Date: 1939

Original Source: Arizona

National Origin: European American

As was the case with the previous narrative, "Them Petrified Buzzards" (p. 98) this **tall tale** is attributed to "Uncle" Steve Robertson and recounted by his nephew Harry Reece. Like "Buzzards," "Meteor Hell" is a typical in its exaggerated focus on the rigors of the Arizona climate. The narrator further adopts a persona who lies with the greatest sincerity while cursing "some danged liars." As is commonly the case with tall tales, this story abounds with pseudo-verifications as in the tale's quote, "if they don't believe you, take 'em out there an' show them th' Hole, its still there ain't it? They can see for themselves th' damned thing's there—An' that ought to be proof enough for anybody."

My Uncle Steve Robertson told me how the "Great Hole" (which some people think was made by a meteor) happens to be out in the very middle of the vast, almost level Arizona desert. He told me about it one night when we were camped over in the Lost River country where we had gone with a pack outfit, aiming ultimately to get up into the Stanley Basin part of the Sawtooth Mountains and perhaps get ourselves a mountain sheep or, if our luck was good, maybe a mountain goat.

My Uncle Steve was such a great pioneer in the very Far West that there were few things indeed whether of natural, human or animal phenomenon of those early-settler days which he could not tell about and that too with the greatest of sincerity.

So, Uncle Steve told me about the "Big Hole."

We had been out through the "lavas" where there are many strange sink-holes, lava-pots, and other weird and ghostly formations in the volcanic desolation of that mighty interesting corner of Idaho. (I think that it has been made into a National Park by the Government and is now called "The Craters of The Moon"). Anyhow, it's fascinating and one kind of feels like he is ... on the desolate Moon when he is wandering around in the silence that is always there.

After supper, both of us entirely full of Little Lost River trout, we were lying by the camp fire listening to the coyotes and just sort of thinking ... maybe about what we'd seen that day, so I mentioned to Uncle Steve that once down in Arizona I had come onto a Great Hole, several hundred feet deep and nearly a mile across from lip to lip, right out there in the flat desert and as far as I could see there wasn't the slightest excuse for it being there.

But some people, I told my Uncle Steve, had the idea that a big meteor had fallen there one time and caved in the earth and that probably that was why the hole was there.

My Uncle Steve then told me just how it happened.

"Yeah, I-Gawd, since you mention it, I remember that damned hole out there in Arizony," my Uncle Steve exclaimed. "In fact, by gosh, Bob White and me was right there and practically saw it made.... But, Meteor, hell, Cicero done it. 'Twant no dammed meteor a-tall!

"But maybe, to be plumb reliable an' truthful an' not 'xaggerate an' stretch things like some danged liars does, Bob an' me wasn't on the 'xact spot where th' hole is when she was made, an' maybe we didn't 'xactly *see* th' cussed thing made, but I-Gawd we was as clost as anybody ought to be an' we sure as hell *heard* her when she was made. They ain't no doubtin' that!

"An' like I said, twasn't no cussed 'meteor' that made it. 'Cicero' which was Bob's and my goat done it an' he done a hell of a good job when he done it.

"That was one thing I admired about 'Cicero.' He was one of th' thoroughest damned goats I ever seen an' when he done anything whether it was eatin', or buttin' or, I-Gawd, even smellin' he done it right or he didn't do it a-tall.... Fer instance, if Cicero started to eatin' anything he et it all 'fore he'd quit, if he started to buttin' anything he'd keep buttin' the danged thing till he busted it or butted it out of his way, that's all there was to it; an' when it come to smellin', well, hell there jest ain't no describin' how p'rsistent he was about that!

"But Cicero was a Papago Injun goat (to be plumb honest an' truthful, Bob an' me stole him from some Papago Injuns an' thats how we come to have him in the' first place) an' that's that way the Papago Injun goats is. They ain't nothin' they won't undertake an' when they undertake it, I-Gawd they finish it up.

"Bob an' me'd never possessed a goat back in Arkansas an' natcherally when him an' me an' Mam (she was Bob's wife) went out to Arizony an' we heard about th' buttin' power of them Papago Injun goats, Bob an' me thought that by rights we ought to git ourselves one jest to see if all we'd heard about 'em was th' truth, besides we figgered that probably we'd need one some time.... 'Cause we'd heard how powerful they was in an emergency when it come to buttin'. Why, I-Gawd all th' freighters haulin' ore from Bisbee an' so forth always had a Papago Injun goat in their outfit so's when they'd git stuck in th' sand with a load of ore an' their six or eight mule-team couldn't budge it they'd jest take their Papago Goat back a ways an' turn him loose an' tell him to butt th' hind end of their wagon an' I' Gawd he'd butt her a couple of butts an' away they'd go! What them six or eight mules couldn't do, that danged Papago Injun goat could accomplish with jest a few brief butts.

"So, when Bob an' me got a chance we stole Cicero an' took him home.

"Mam (Bob's wife) wasn't so hellish enthusiastic about Cicero when she first saw him.

"'My Gawd,' Mam says when she saw Bob an' me leadin' Cicero up to the ranch, 'what have you danged fools gone an' brang home now? Ain't there enough disagreeable features on this cussed desert out here in Arizony without you goin' an' gittin' a doggone Papago Injun goat for a body to be dodgin' an' also smellin' all th' time? Jest when I'm gittin' used to smellin' Arizony skunks an' Arizony vinagaroons an' Arizony carrion when a steer or cow dies an' the buzzards let it ripen too long before cleanin' it up, I-Gawd you go an' bring home a danged Papago Injun goat for me to also smell. When I married you, Bob White, I promised to "love, honor an' obey" but darned if I promised to smell Papago Injun goats for you! So, you can take him right back where you got him or take him out behind th' corral an' shoot him, I don't give a dang which, before he butts th' britches off of you an' Steve Robertson an' smells me out of house an' home!'

"But Bob he always had a soothin' way with wimmen so he jest said, 'Why, Mam, Steve an' me thought Cicero would be a kind of surprise to you an' we stole him jest so you could have somethin' else to smell a while besides them other things an' he'd be a sort of change for you—But now you go an' scold us for bringin' him home! You've plumb hurt our feelin's Mam 'cause we brung him home jest for you an' now you go an' ... an' ... resent him! I-Gawd, you see, Steve,' Bob says, 'that's the way it is—A Man goes an' does his damndest to do somethin' for a woman like stealin' a goat for her to smell or something an' then she gives him hell for it! That's th' way wimmen is, they never appreciate nothin' an' I-Gawd I don't blame you for shyin' off from 'em like you do Steve an' never gittin' married or nothin'....'

"Bob winked at me when he said it an' 'course I knowed he was jest 'soft-talkin' Mam but I-Gawd it worked an' Mam repented and said, 'Alright, dadgum you, Bob White—you know cussed well no woman can resist that, danged honey-tongue-of yourn—If it hadn't been for it I'd still be down in Arkansas enjoyin' paw-paws an' persimmons in Mam an' Pap's peaceful home down on th' old Sac River! So, you an' Steve Robertson can keep your cussed Papago Injun goat but I'm promising you one thing and that is that if he ever butts me once I'll bust him twice! I'll smell Him ... but I'll be danged if I'll be butted by him, that's all there is to it, Bob White!'

"So, Bob an' me kept Cicero an' if we hadn't there probably wouldn't be that damned Big Hole out in th' middle of that Arizony desert you mentioned a while ago.

"To start with, that danged hole wasn't a hole but was Injun Head Butts ... one of them cussed mountains that sticks itself right up all alone as if it doesn't want any other mountain neighbors close to it.... Sort of like Big Butte, over there th' other side of Lost River Sinks, where we was today.

"An' Injun Butte was practically solid rock to begin with ... jest a great big bump of rock stickin' up out of the' desert.... Then, I Gawd, Cicero turned that damned Butte into a hole in th' ground!

"Yeah, it wasn't no danged 'Meteor,' Cicero done it.

"I-Gawd, I ought to know. Bob White an' Mam an' me an' Cicero was there when it happened ... After it happened, well, Bob an' Mam an' me was still there but where th' hell Cicero was ... that's a mystery nobody ain't ever solved yet an' I don't reckon they ever will!

"It happened th' year before th' big dry spell, th' one I told you about, maybe you remember it, when it got so dry an' hot that even th' damned buzzards wheelin' around up in th' sky an' practically everything else includin' th' cattle an' the trees out in th' forest jest up an' petrified from th' heat and th' dryness.

"Well, Bob an' Mam an' me decided to take a trip up to North Arizony an' see if maybe there wasn't better grazin' for our cattle up there than there was down along th' Santa Cruz river in south Arizony where we'd started our cow-outfit when we come out from Arkansaw, so we travelled up there.

"Natcherally, Cicero went along. Bob an' me had trained him to go along with us wherever we went with a wagon-outfit so if we got stuck in the sand he could butt us out like th' ore freighters had their Papago Injun goats do when they got stuck.

"So, we got up there to where there was a little spring ... Arsenic Springs they called it 'cause th' water would physic anybody worse than hell but it was all there was an' they had to drink it anyhow ... about two miles from old Injun Head Butte an' we camped there.

"Everything would a' been all right only there was a couple of prospectors already camped there who was figgerin' on doin' some prospectin' on Injun Head Butte 'cause a old Hopi Injun Chief had told 'em there was a lost gold mine somewhere on th' Butte.

"Them damned prospectors had a whole burro load of dynamite with them an' had spread it out in th' shade of a Joshua tree to sort of cool off and ... well, to make a long story short, while Bob an' Mam an' me was gittin' our camp set an' not payin' much attention to Cicero th' damn fool found that dynamite an' 'fore he quit he'd et every last cussed stick of it! Th' first thing Bob an' me knowed about what had happened was when one of th' prospectors ... Dirty Shirt Smith was his name ... caught Cicero jest swallerin' th' last damned stick of dynamite they had, an' he come runnin' over to our camp yellin'—'Hey, your cussed doggone goat has et up all our dynamite every damned drop of it! Now, how th' hell is Solemn Johnson (that was th' other prospector's name) an' me goin' to do any balstin' to find that damned lost gold mine that old Injun Chief told us was on Injun Head Butte? How th' hell are we goin' to—You gotta pay us for that dynamite your goat et!'

"I ain't worryin' about payin' for your damned dynamite,' Bob up an' told him. 'What I'm worryin' about is that cussed goat runnin' loose around here with all that high explosive in him. If he ever gits th' idea that 'cause our wagon's standin' still we're stuck an' need buttin' out, or if he starts in to practicin' buttin' like Pago Injun goats does, well, Gawd help us all, that's all I can say!'

"Mam she got excited too an' says, 'Bob White, for Gawd's sakes, you an' Steve Robertson figger out some scheme to keep that goat from stirrin' around much till he either sweats all that dynamite out of his system or digests it or something. If he goes off anywheres clost to us there wont be nothin' but fragments of us left! For Gawd's sake tie him up or something but do it an far away from camp as possible—Maybe you'd ought to give him a dose of castor oil, that might help!' Mam says.

"'Yeah,' Bob says, 'an' who th' hell would straddle him an' hold him while I'm givin' it to him ... an' take a chance of him goin' off while they're straddle of him?'

"Mam realized th' danger of it an' didn't insist on us givin' Cicero castor oil.

"So Bob an' took Cicero an' tied him to a Joshua tree about a hundred yards from camp an' everything seemed safe an' sound for th' time being.

"Mam, she quieted down an' after supper we all went to bed ... lettin' the' white Arizony moonlight stream over th' desert calm an' serene like.

"Fore I went to bed I looked out where Cicero was tied an' he was layin' there peaceful an' quiet as if eatin' sixty or seventy sticks of dynamite was jest a incident an' didn't have no significance a-tall.

"Bout three o'clock in th' mornin' I reckon it was I waked up all of a sudden with a sort of p'resentiment—I think that's what you call it when you think somethin' terrible's about to happen—pressin' down on me. Anyhow, I felt it i' my marrow that Gawd only knowed what might take place any minute.

"Natcherally, when I was a little awaker I remember about Cicero eatin' that dynamite an' the first thing I done was to peer out through th' moonlight an' see if he was still tied to th' Joshua tree an' still keepin' still till th' dynamite was absorbed out of his system—

"I-Gawd, that's when I got a shock. Cicero was gone.

"He'd gnawed his rope in two an' escaped.

"Then I snuck over to where Bob was sleepin' an' shook him an' says, 'Bob, fer Gawd's sake wake up! Cicero's loose an' prowlin' around somewhere with all that dynamite in him an' Gawd only knows what's liable to happen!'

"Bob waked up and says, 'My Gawd, Steve, don't wake Mam ... she's tired an' needs her rest (Bob was always like that, awful considerate of Mam) an' besides if she wakes up an' realizes Cicero's loose she'll raise hell an' I'm too dammed worried to have any woman raisin' hell with me at this time of night! But where th' hell do you reckon Cicero's gone to, Steve?'

"'Danged if I know,' I told Bob, 'but th' chances is he's wanderin' around in th' moonlight huntin' something to practice buttin' on—Only, I-Gawd,' I says, 'if he find it I hope to Gawd it's a good ways from camp!'

"'I-Gawd, so do I,' Bob said. An' then it happened—

"Sounded jest exactly like th' world had come to a end.

"Th' long an' th' short of it was, th' next mornin' there wasn't no danged Injun Head Butte out there on th' Arizony desert. There was jest a hell of a big hole in th' ground where she had been. Bob an' me knowed what had happened.

"Cicero had wandered around huntin' somethin' to practice butting on an' in that moonlight he'd saw Injun Head Butte. She looked danged good an' solid so he thought he'd practice on her. An', natcherally, when he hit here with all that dynamite in him he jest went off. That's all there was to it.

"An' when he went off he jest ripped old Injun Head Butte out by th' roots ... an' there couldn't be nothin' left but jest a hole where she had been!

"So, that's the way it was—An' I don't give a dang what anybody says— even them cussed 'scientists' that thinks they know such a hell of a lot ... an' [calim] that that Big Hole out in Arizony was made by a meteor... [They] gits crazy ideas sometimes. They jost don't know th' inside story of them things like us Pioneers of th' Far West does, that's all.

"But th' next time anybody tells you that that hole was made by a 'meteor' jest tell them, 'Meteor hell, Cicero done it'.

"An' I-Gawd, if they don't believe you, take 'em out there an' show them th' Hole, its still there ain't it? They can see for themselves th' damned thing's there—An' that ought to be proof enough for anybody."

THE COYOTE AND THE WOODPECKER

Tradition Bearer: Unavailable

Source: Lummis, Charles. "The Coyote and the Woodpecker." Pages 49–52 in *Pueblo Indian Folk-Stories*. New York: Century, 1910.

Date: 1910.

Original Source: Isleta Pueblo (New Mexico)

National Origin: Native American

This story of the **trickster** trying to imitate another occurs in other **variants** in the Southwest (See, for example, the Jicarilla Apache, "Tales of Fox: Fox and Kingfisher," p. 116). As in the tale types designated by folklorist Stith Thompson as **animal tales**, "The Coyote and the Woodpecker" offers a moral lesson. The philosophy of acceptance and noncompetitiveness is consistent with general Pueblo worldview and morality.

Well, once upon a time a Coyote and his family lived near the edge of a wood. There was a big hollow tree there, and in it lived an old Woodpecker and his wife and children. One day as the Coyote-father was strolling along the edge of the forest he met the Woodpecker-father.

"Good evening," said the Coyote; how do you do today, friend?"

"Very well, thank you; and how are you, friend?"

So they stopped and talked together awhile; and when they were about to go apart the Coyote said: "Friend Woodpecker, why do you not come as friends to see us? Come to our house to supper this evening, and bring your family."

"Thank you, friend Coyote," said the Woodpecker; "we will come with joy."

So that evening, when the Coyote-mother had made supper ready, there came the Woodpecker-father and the Woodpecker-mother with their three children. When they had come in, all five of the Woodpeckers stretched themselves as they do after flying, and by that showed their pretty feathers—for the Woodpecker has yellow and red marks under its wings. While, they were eating supper, too, they sometimes spread their wings, and displayed their bright underside. They praised the supper highly, and said the Coyote-mother was a perfect housekeeper.

When it was time to go, they thanked the Coyotes very kindly and invited them to come to supper at their house the following evening. But when they were gone, the Coyote-father could hold himself no longer, and he said: "Did you see what airs those Woodpeckers put on? Always showing off their bright feathers? But I want them to know that the Coyotes are equal to them. I'll show them!"

Next day, the Coyote-father had all his family at work bringing wood, and built a great fire in front of his house. When it was time to go to the house of the Woodpeckers he called his wife and children to the fire, and lashed a burning stick under each of their arms, with the burning end pointing forward; and then he fixed himself in the same way.

"Now," said he, "we will show them! When we get there, you must lift up your arms now and then, to show them that we are as good as the Woodpeckers."

When they came to the house of the Woodpeckers and went in, all the Coyotes kept lifting their arms often, to show the bright coals underneath. But as they sat down to supper, one Coyote-girl gave a shriek and said:

"Oh, papa! My fire is burning me!"

"Be patient, my daughter," said the Coyote-father, severely, "and do not cry about little things."

"Ow!" cried the other Coyote-girl in a moment, "my fire has gone out!"

This was more than the Coyote-father could stand, and he reproved her angrily.

"But how is it, friend Coyote," said the Woodpecker, politely, "that your colors are so bright at first, but very soon become black?"

"Oh, that is the beauty of our colors," replied the Coyote, smothering his rage; "that they are not always the same—like other people's—but turn all shades."

But the Coyotes were very uncomfortable, and made an excuse to hurry home as soon as they could. When they got there, the Coyote-father whipped them all for exposing him to be laughed at.

But the Woodpecker-father gathered his children around him, and said: "Now, my children, you see what the Coyotes have done. Never in your life try to appear what you are not. Be just what you really are, and put on no false colors."

SOME OF COYOTE'S ADVENTURES

Tradition Bearer: Juan Dolores

Source: Kroeber, Henriette Rothschild. "Papago Coyote Tales." *Journal of American Folklore* 22 (1909): 340–42.

Date: ca. 1909

Original Source: Papago (Arizona)

National Origin: Native American

The Papago are members of a desert culture, different branches of which maintain two different means of subsistence: either they practice hunting and gathering in the harsh environment, or they practice agriculture using irrigation or flood-farming depending on the availability of the water supply. The following tale shows the **trickster**, Coyote, at his worst. He will not provide for his family, preferring to be a nuisance and a drain on limited community resources until his wife strikes at his pride. Coyote demonstrates supernatural power by bewitching small animals through song, but, in an ironic reversal, he is enthralled in the same fashion by even smaller and weaker animals. Throughout the narrative, Coyote is manipulated by these smaller, weaker creatures that exploit his character flaws. Overall, the tale is a portrait of **trickster** at his least admirable and most deceitful.

A short time after Coyote married, he became careless about his appearance, and grew sleepy, lazy, and indifferent. There came a time when he had to provide for four children.

To hunt deer was hard work, so he and his wife went about visiting relatives. When they were given food, they always called the children, so that they could eat too. The women said many ugly things about them, and these finally reached the ears of his wife. One night she became enraged at what was told her. She ordered Coyote to hunt. She refused to continue begging, and said, unless he decided to provide for her and the children, she would return to her father. Coyote's pride was touched at being ordered about by a woman, and being spoken to in such harsh terms.

In the morning he went out. He said, "I will not chase deer all day. I will kill birds or little beasts, for any meat is sweet when one is hungry. I will play my tricks and catch game."

He walked along and soon came within sight of a flock of quail. He commenced singing a song, something like—

"Little quail, what are you thinking about, flying away so quickly?"

This song he repeated until all but one quail had flown. He stopped singing then, and said,—

"That is good, one is left. I shall catch it and make a meal of it."

He set about his self-imposed task, caught and devoured the bird, well satisfied with a good meal.

For a time he rested, and then went leisurely along until he came to a grassy valley. There he came on a gathering, and sang a song, as follows:—

> "Little rats, little rats,
> There you are running,
> One stumbles and falls,
> It is crippled and cannot run."

In this way Coyote is enabled to catch a rat. But not satisfied with one as a meal, he repeats the luring chant three times more, and each time successfully catches food. On four rats he has fed this time, satisfied his hunger, and goes on.

He leaves the valley and climbs the mountain. There he comes to a cave, which is full of flies. He tells them, "Flies, you are making fun of me."

They answer, "No, uncle, we are singing because we are glad to see you. We need some help. Panther comes here to sleep. When he goes to sleep, if anyone by accident touches his whiskers, he wakes up, growls, paws over the cave, and kills many of us."

The flies, knowing Coyote, are ready to trick him, and instead of a song of welcome, they hum, and ask Coyote to dance. The dance excites Coyote and makes him dizzy. During the singing and dancing, Coyote is asked continually not to forget to lend his aid in killing Panther. The words fascinate him, and he helps chant the verses.

"Flies, flies,
Are closing up the cave,
Closing up the cave.
Whoever flies out
Must keep a straight path,
For the opening is narrowing."

He is unable to distinguish how their numbers lessen, and how, at the end of each rhythmic bar, several flies escape through the narrow opening, until the last one wings his way out, leaving only a little air hole.

Only when the last fly is gone, and the victim is left alone, does he come face to face with the fact that he has been unaware of all that transpired about him, and that he is enclosed in the cave. He is compelled to wait for Panther, and hopes to be released unharmed on the plea of relationship.

Panther comes. Seeing the cave closed up except for a little air hole, he looks in and sees Coyote, his uncle, his mother's brother. Anger overcomes him, and he accuses Coyote of having closed the cave. He roars and paws the ground, and in his rage breaks into the cave, catches Coyote, and is about to kill him. Coyote begs to live a moment longer. He wants to pray to Tsi'iho to care for his wife and his children. He tells his nephew,—

"Listen until you hear a whistle. Then rush behind the brush and kill me quickly."

Coyote then goes behind a bush, making a pretence of prayer. On his way he catches a ground squirrel, and carries him to a safe hiding-place. After some moments he buries the squirrel upright in the ground. Coyote then says, "Be quiet, I will return." He runs off, and escapes. The little squirrel remains quiet for some time, then becomes restless and wishes to free himself from the ground. He is unable to effect it himself. In ground-squirrel fashion, he emits his call, which is like a low whistle. This attracts Panther, who follows the sound, and to his astonishment sees the embedded squirrel. He roars, "What are you doing here?" In a feeble trembling voice the squirrel explains. Panther is satisfied, and the squirrel is turned loose.

After all this escapade, Coyote gets thirsty. He looks for water. He comes to a dried-up pond. In a crack in the mud is a cricket singing a song. Coyote thinks the cricket is making fun of him, and decides to look for the little chirper, but it is a vain endeavor. He is about to turn away. This encourages the cricket, which again sings, this time in truth making fun of the trickster.

113

In one verse he ridicules his eyes because they are all tear-stained. In the second he makes fun of his tail, which is scraggy and turned downward, instead of as in early youth, thick, bushy, and carried erect. Gleefully the cricket continues his song. Coyote, not able to resist the temptation, returns to seek the mocker anew. Again thwarted, he determines not to turn again, but to continue his way into the valley.

He walks along listlessly, and unobservant that it has rained and snowed in the high mountains, and that the water is rushing down into the valley. He walks along drowsily and tired, heedless of the fact that the water is about to overtake him. Suddenly he looks around, and to his consternation sees what is happening. In haste he climbs a tree and sits waiting for the waters to recede. While he is perched there, a Crane flies into a neighboring tree. Gleefully the bird sings,—

> "It is going down,
> It is going down,
> It is getting less,
> It is getting less,
> It has gone down."

To prove that such is the fact, each time that he comes to the word "down," he stretches out his foot and brings up some mud to show that the water is receding. Coyote repeats the bird's song, and imitates the action. Having shorter legs, and being in a higher tree, his efforts are of no avail, and he remains treed.

When the water is low enough, the Crane steps down and invites his neighbor to do likewise. Unwilling to be taunted, Coyote accepts the invitation. But the water is still high and the current strong, and he is carried along with the stream. He is almost drowned. He calls for help. Out of sheer pity the Crane comes to his rescue and carries him ashore. Coyote thanks him, and explains that the accident is due to the Crane's having longer legs than he.

Many insincere thanks are spoken by Coyote to his rescuer, and he says, "Since you have saved my life, I will try to do something good for you some of these days."

TALES OF FOX

Tradition Bearer: Laforia

Source: Russell, Frank. "Myths of the Jicarilla Apaches." *Journal of American Folklore* 11 (1898): 265–68.

Date: ca. 1898

Original Source: Jicarilla Apache (New Mexico)
National Origin: Native American

Fox is the Jicarilla **trickster**. His reputation as a **trickster** with potentially weaknesses precedes him, leading both Deer and Rabbit to exploit his foolish nature. The cruel results of their pranks may seem unmotivated, but practical jokes with sadistic results are common in **trickster** tales. Also common is the explanation of features such as the Fox's characteristic cry and eye color. "Fox and Kingfisher" portrays Coyote trying to play the host in an episode reminiscent of "The Coyote and the Woodpecker" (p. 109). Fox's invitations and imitations, in "Fox and Kingfisher" and in "Fox and Mountain Lion," are motivated more by the desire to impress than to be hospitable. The final "tar baby" episode is only the most obvious of many borrowed features in the tale.

Fox and Deer

As Fox was going along he met a Deer with two spotted fawns beside her. "What have you done," said he, "to make your children spotted like that?"

"I made a big fire of cedar wood and placed them before it. The sparks thrown off burned the spots which you see," answered the Deer.

Fox was pleased with the color of the fawns, so he went home and told his children to gather cedar wood for a large fire. When the fire was burning well, he put the young foxes in a row before the fire, as he supposed the Deer had done. When he found that they did not change color, he pushed them into the fire and covered them with ashes, thinking he had not applied sufficient heat at first.

As the fire went out, he saw their white teeth gleaming where the skin had shriveled away and exposed them. "Ah, you will be very pretty now," said he. Fox pulled his offspring from the ashes, expecting to find them much changed in color, and so they were—black, shrivelled, and dead.

Fox next thought of revenge upon the Deer, which he found in a grove of cottonwoods. He built a fire around them, but they ran through it and escaped.

Fox was so disappointed that he set up a cry of woe, a means of expression, which he has retained from that day to this.

Fox and Kingfisher

As Fox went on his way he met Kingfisher, whom he accompanied to his home. Kingfisher said that he had no food to offer his visitor, so he would go and catch some fish for Fox. He broke through six inches of ice on the river and caught two fish, which he cooked and set before his guest. Fox was pleased with his entertainment, and invited the Kingfisher to return the call.

In due time the Kingfisher came to the home of the Fox, who said, "I have no food to offer you;" then he went down to the river, thinking to secure fish in the same manner as the Kingfisher had done.

Fox leaped from the high bank, but instead of breaking through the ice he broke his head and killed himself. Kingfisher went to him, caught him up by the tail, and swung Fox around to the right four times, thereby restoring him to life. Kingfisher caught some fish, and they ate together. "I am a medicine-man," said Kingfisher; "that is why I can do these things. You must never try to catch fish in that way again."

After the departure of Kingfisher, Fox paid a visit to the home of Prairie-dog, where he was cordially received. Prairie-dog put four sticks, each about a foot in length, in the ashes of the camp-fire; when these were removed, they proved to be four nicely roasted prairie-dogs, which were served for Fox's dinner. Fox invited the Prairie-dog to return the visit, which in a short time the latter did. Fox placed four sticks in the fire to roast, but they were consumed by it, and instead of palatable food to set before his guest he had nothing but ashes.

Prairie-dog said to Fox, "You must not attempt to do that. I am a medicine-man; that is why I can transform the wood to flesh." Prairie-dog then prepared a meal as he done before, and they dined.

Fox went to visit Buffalo, who exclaimed, "What shall I do? I have no food to offer you." Buffalo was equal to the emergency, however; he shot an arrow upward, which struck in his own back as it returned. When he pulled this out, a kidney and the fat surrounding it came out also. This he cooked for Fox, and added a choice morsel from his own nose. As usual, Fox extended an invitation to his host to return the visit.

When Buffalo came to call upon Fox, the latter covered his head with weeds in imitation of the head of the Buffalo. Fox thought he could provide food for their dinner as the Buffalo had done, so fired an arrow into the air; but when it came close to him on its return flight, he became frightened and ran away. Buffalo then furnished meat for their meal as on the previous occasion. "You must not try this," said he; "I am a medicine-man; that is why I have the power."

Some time afterward, as Fox was journeying along, he met an Elk, lying beside the trail. He was frightened when he saw the antlers of the Elk moving, and jumped to avoid what seemed to be a falling tree. "Sit down beside me," said the Elk. "Don't be afraid."

"The tree will fall on us," replied Fox. "Oh, sit down; it won't fall. I have no food to offer you, but I will provide some." The Elk cut steaks from his own quarter, which the Fox ate, and before leaving Fox invited the Elk to return the visit.

When Elk came to see Fox, the latter tried unsuccessfully to cut flesh from his own meagre flanks; then he drove sharpened sticks into his nose, and allowed the blood to run out upon the grass. This he tried in vain to transform into meat, and again he was indebted to his guest for a meal.

"I am a medicine-man; that is why I can do this," said Elk.

Fox and Mountain Lion

Fox could find nothing to eat for a long time, so that he grew weak and thin. While on a journey in search of food he met the Mountain Lion, who, taking pity upon his unhappy condition, said, "I will hunt for you, and you shall grow fat again."

The Fox agreed to this, and they went on together to a much frequented spring. Mountain Lion told Fox to keep watch while he slept if a cloud of dust was to be seen arising from the approach of animals Fox was to waken him. Fox presently beheld the dust caused by the approach of a drove of horses.

Fox wakened Mountain Lion, who said, "Just observe how I catch horses." As one of the animals went down to the spring to drink, he sprang upon it, and fastened his fangs in its throat, clawing its legs and shoulders until it fell dying at the water's edge. Mountain Lion brought the horse up to the rock, and laid it before the Fox. Stay here, eat, drink, and grow fat," said he.

Fox thought he had learned how to kill horses, so when the Coyote came along he volunteered to secure one for him. Fox jumped upon the neck of the horse, as Mountain Lion had done, but became entangled in its mane and was killed.

117

Fox and Rabbit

Fox one day met a Rabbit who was sewing a sack. "What do you intend to do with that sack?" asked he.

"I am making this coat to protect myself from being killed by the hard hail which we are going to have today," replied Rabbit.

"My friend, you know how to make them; give me this coat and make another for your-self." Rabbit agreed to this, and Fox put on the sack over his head.

Rabbit then hung him on a limb and pelted him with stones, while Fox, thinking it was hail striking him, endured the punishment as long as he could, but finally fell nearly dead from the tree, and looked out, to see no signs of hail, but discovered the Rabbit running away.

Fox wished to avenge himself by killing Rabbit, and set off in pursuit of him. When overtaken Rabbit was chewing soft gum with which to make spectacles.

Fox's curiosity was stronger than his passion for revenge. "What are you making those for?" said he.

"It is going to be very hot, and I am making them to protect my eyes," answered Rabbit.

"Let me have this pair; you know how to make them and can make yourself another pair."

"Very well," said Rabbit, and he put the eye-shields on Fox, who could then see nothing, as the gum was soft and filled his eyes. Rabbit set fire to the brush all around Fox, who was badly singed in running through it. The gum melted in the fire, and yet remains as the dark rings around his eyes.

Fox again started on the trail of Rabbit, with the determination of eating him as soon as he saw him. He found Rabbit sitting beside the opening of a bee-hive. "I am going to eat you," said Fox; "you have tried to kill me."

"You must not kill me," replied Rabbit. "I am teaching these children," and he closed the opening of the hive, so that Fox could not see what was inside. Fox desired very much to see what was in the hive making such a noise.

"If you wish to see, stay here and teach them while I rest. When it is dinner time, strike them with a club," said Rabbit, who then ran away.

Fox patiently awaited the dinner hour, and then struck the hive with such force that he broke into it. The bees poured out and stung him until he rolled in agony. "When I see you again, I will kill you before you can say a word," declared he, as he started after Rabbit again.

Fox tracked the Rabbit to a small hole in the fence around a field of watermelons belonging to a Mexican. The Rabbit had entered to steal, and was angered at sight of the gum figure of a man which the owner of the field had placed beside the path. "What do you desire from me?" he cried, as he struck at the figure with his fore-foot, which stuck fast in the soft gum. He struck at the gum with every foot, and even his head was soon stuck in the gum.

Thus Fox found him. "What are you doing here?" he asked.

"They put me in here because I would not eat chicken for them," said Rabbit.

"I will take your place," said Fox; "I know how to eat chicken."

The Mexican found him in the morning and skinned him, and then let him go, still on the trail of the Rabbit, who had so frequently outwitted him.

THE POWERS THAT BE: SACRED TALES

WITCH FLIGHTS

Tradition Bearer: Unavailable

Source: "Witchcraft in New Mexico." *Journal of American Folklore* 1 (1888): 167–68.

Date: 1888

Original Source: New Mexico

National Origin: Mexican American

This series of **legends** gives the general outlines of *brujeria* (often translated as "witchcraft"), a practice that embodies elements of both indigenous and Christian belief. The *bruja* (female) or *brujo* (male) is generally considered to constitute the opposite end of the spectrum of Hispanic magical-religious practice from the *curandero* (male healer) or *curandera* (female healer).

Every *paisano* in New Mexico can tell you the witches' strange habits, their marvelous powers, and their baleful deeds. They never injure the dumb animals, but woe to the human being who incurs their displeasure. Few, indeed, are bold enough to brave their wrath. If a witch asks for food, wood, clothing, or anything else, none dare say her nay. Nor dare anyone eat what a witch proffers; for, if he does, some animal, alive and gnawing, will form in his stomach.

By day the witches wear their familiar human form; but at night, dressed in strange animal shapes, they fly abroad to hold witch meetings in the mountains, or to wreak their evil wills. In a dark night you may see them flying through the sky like so many balls of fire, and there are comparatively few Mexicans in the territory who have not seen this weird sight!

For these nocturnal sallies the witches wear their own bodies, but take the legs and eyes of a coyote or other animal, leaving their own at home. Juan Perea, a male witch, who died here in San Mateo some months ago, met with a strange misfortune in this wise: He had gone off with the eyes of a cat, and during his absence a dog knocked over the table and ate up Juan's own eyes; so the unfortunate witch had to wear cat's eyes all the rest of his life.

Before they can fly, witches are obliged to cry out, "Sin Dios, sin Santa Maria!" (Without God and without the Holy Virgin) whereupon they mount up into the air without difficulty. If you are on good terms with a witch you may persuade her to carry you on her back from here to New York in a second. She blindfolds you and enjoins strict silence. If you utter a word you find yourself alone in some vast wilderness, and if you cry, "God, save me!" you fall from a fearful height to the ground, but are luckily never killed by the fall. There are several courageous people in the territory who have made journeys thus upon the backs of witches.

Lorenzo Labadie, a man of prominence in New Mexico, once unknowingly hired a witch as nurse for his baby. He lived in Las Vegas. Some months afterward there was a ball at Puerta de Luna, a couple of hundred miles south, and friends of the family were astonished to see the nurse and baby there. "Where is Senor Labadie and his family?" they asked. The nurse replied that they were at a house a few miles distant, but too tired to come to the ball. The friends went there next day and found the Labadies had not been there. Suspecting the nurse to be a witch, they wrote to Don Lorenzo, who only knew that the nurse and baby were in his house when he went to bed, and there also when he woke up. It being plain, therefore, to the most casual observer, that the woman was a witch, he promptly discharged her.

WITCHES DISCOVERED

Tradition Bearer: Unavailable

Source: Espinosa, Aurelio M. "New Mexican Spanish Folklore." *Journal of American Folklore* 223 (1910): 397–98.

Date: 1910

Original Source: New Mexico

National Origin: Spanish American

In the Southwest, witches were traditionally believed to take on the shapes of owls, foxes, and coyotes to work their evil deeds. As seen in other **belief tales** in this collection, when a human suspect shows wounds similar to those of a witch in animal form, guilt is assumed. See, for example, "The Doe with a Ring" (Vol. I, p. 337), "Woman Cat" (Vol. I, p. 338), and "The Miller's Witch Wife" (Vol. II, p. 171).

In a certain village in northern New Mexico, which was considered a favorite rendezvous for witches, a certain house had been surrounded for various nights by owls and foxes (the fox is another animal whose form witches like to take). Fearing harm from witches, since the hooting of the owls and the howling of the foxes had become almost insufferable, men went out to meet them with bows and arrows. The owls and foxes disappeared in all directions, with the exception of one old fox, which had been wounded near the heart by an arrow. No one dared to approach the wounded fox, however; and the next morning it was discovered that an old lady, a witch, living nearby, was in her death-bed, with an arrow-wound near the heart.

On another occasion a man was riding on a fast horse and saw a fox. He started in pursuit; and after a long chase, when the fox was very tired and was already dragging its tongue along the ground, a sudden transformation took place. At a sharp turn of the road the fox stopped, and the rider did the same. To his amazement, he at once perceived a gray-haired woman sitting on a stone and panting in a terrible manner. Recognizing in her an old woman who was his neighbor, and whom he had suspected of being a witch, he went his way and troubled her no more.

The *brujas* (generally women) are women who are wicked (*pautadas con el diablo*) and non-Christian. By confessing their sins to a priest, repenting, and abandoning their devilish ways, they may become good Christian women.

A certain witch desired to forsake her evil ways and save her soul, since those who die witches cannot expect salvation. She confessed to a priest, and gave him a large bundle in the shape of a ball, which consisted largely of old rags, and pins stuck into it, the source and cause of her evil powers.

The priest took the diabolical bundle and threw it into a fire, where, after bounding and rebounding for several minutes in an infernal manner, it was consumed, and the compact with the Devil ceased (*ya no estaba pautada con el diablo*).

CURANDERAS AND BRUJAS I

Tradition Bearer: Maria Antonia

Source: Bourke, John G. "Popular Medicines, Customs and Superstitions of the Rio Grande." *Journal of American Folklore* 7 (1894): 142–43.

Date: ca. 1894

Original Source: Texas

National Origin: Mexican American

John G. Bourke's comments on the following **legends** offer the cultural outsider's perspective on *brujeria* (Spanish for "witchcraft") and *curandismo* (Spanish for "curing") in the Southwest. See "Witch Flights" (p. 121) and "Witches Discovered" (p. 122) for the insider's perspective on these traditions.

Maria Antonia was emphatic in her expression of belief that there were lots of "*brujas*" (witches) around, who took delight in doing harm to you personally, or in spreading sickness among your cattle, blighting your crops, or ruining your fruit-trees.

Everybody believed in witches; there might be some fool "Americanos" who would say they did not, but she was sure that they were only talking for talk's sake.

Once there was a man down here (Rio Grande City, Texas) who owed a washerwoman five dollars and refused to pay her. Now this washerwoman was a witch, and she filled this man full of worms, but Maria Antonia was called in just in time and gave him a strong emetic and a strong purge, and then dosed him with a decoction of Yerba de Cancer, Yerba Gonzalez, and Guayuli, and expelled thirteen worms ("*gusanos*") with green heads and white bodies.

CURANDERAS AND BRUJAS II

Tradition Bearer: Sam Stewart

Source: Bourke, John G. "Popular Medicines, Customs and Superstitions of the Rio Grande." *Journal of American Folklore* 7 (1894): 144–46.

Date: ca. 1894

Original Source: Texas

National Origin: Mexican American

The last punishment inflicted for witchcraft within the limits of the United States was that imposed by Judge Sam Stewart of Rio Grande City (Fort Ringgold), Texas, in 1886.

As nearly as I can arrange the story from my notes and my recollection of the judge's account, it was about like this: A young man of good Mexican family was slowly wasting away under the attack of a disease, the exact nature of which quite baffled the local medical talent. All the medicines on sale in the "Botica del Aguila" (Eagle Drug Store) had been sampled to no purpose, and the sick man's condition had become deplorable. The physicians, who disagreed in everything else, concurred upon the one point that he had but a few days longer to live. At this juncture, a friend suggested to the mother that she call in one of the numerous old hags, who, under the name of "curanderas," combine in equal portions a knowledge of kitchen botany, the black art, humbuggery pure and simple, and a familiarity with just enough prayers and litanies to give a specious varnish to the more objectionable features of their profession. The "curandera" responded promptly, and made her diagnosis almost with a glance of the eye.

"Your son," she said to the grief-stricken mother, "has neither consumption nor paralysis. The doctors can't tell what ails him, but I can see it all, and with the power of God can soon make him well again."

"What is the matter with him, then, my dear little friend?"

"Black Thomas cats. When I came into the room, the floor was a foot deep with Thomas cats, which had jumped out of your son's throat, but they became frightened when they saw me and scampered back again. I'll soon get rid of them all."

Her intentions may have been good, but she got rid of nothing. Her "remedies" produced no effect, and the patient kept on sinking.

Just then a rival "curandera" came up to the mother and said: "That woman is deceiving you. She don't know what she's talking about. Why your son never has been troubled by Thomas cats, but I can tell you at once what ails him."

"Tell me, then, in the name of God."

"It is bull-frogs. I can see them jumping over each other and running into and out from his mouth."

To make a long story short, the first "curandera" would not give up the case, but insisted on holding on to what, in the language of today, would be called a decidedly soft snap, and the town, as is usual in such cases, taking up a quarrel in which it didn't have the slightest interest, became divided into the two bitterly hostile factions of the "bull-froggers" and the "Thomas-catters." The street became blocked with a crowd of partisans and excitement ran high. Judge Stewart surrounded the whole gang and had them run down to court, where he dismissed all but the ten "curanderas" (for there were ten altogether), who were loudly proclaiming their influence with witches.

"Have you ever seen any witches?" he asked of the first.

"Oh yes, indeed, many times. Why only last Wednesday, the witches picked me up at midnight and took me out on the Corpus Christi road, and up above the clouds, where they played *pelota* (foot-ball) with me, and when they got tired of that, they dropped me into a mesquite thicket, and here you see my clothes all torn to rags to prove that I am telling the truth."

The next one said she could get into any house, no matter whether the doors were open or shut.

The third could tell where to find hidden money, and so on through the list.

The judge wasted no time on the culprits, but fined them all ten dollars apiece, and sentenced them to a month each in the county jail, and when they begged for clemency and told him that they were poor humble women, he brusquely replied: "That's nothing. You can all get out through the keyholes, and you all know where to find buried money to pay your fines. That is all there is about it."

THE GHOST PENITENTE

Tradition Bearer: Unavailable

Source: Espinosa, Aurelio M. "New Mexican Spanish Folklore." *Journal of American Folklore* 223 (1910): 397–98.

Date: 1910

Original Source: New Mexico

National Origin: Spanish American

Los Hermanos Penitente, the Brotherhood of Penitents, are a religious society operating outside the boundaries of official Roman Catholicism. They demonstrate their piety by acts of self-flagellation, cross-bearing, and on Good Friday by the crucifixion of a member.

A certain evening during holy week the Penitentes entered the church in Taos for the purpose of flogging themselves. After flogging themselves in the usual manner, they left the church. As they departed, however, they heard the floggings of a Penitente who seemed to have remained in the church.

The elder brother (*hermano mayor*) counted his Penitentes, and no one was missing. To the astonishment of the other Penitentes, the one in the church continued his flagellation, and they decided to return. No one dared to re-enter the church, however; and while they disputed in silence and made various conjectures as to what the presence of an unknown Penitente might mean, the floggings became harder and harder.

At last one of the Penitentes volunteered to enter alone; but, as he opened the door, he discovered that the one who was scourging himself mercilessly was high above in the choir, and it was necessary to obtain a lighted candle before venturing to ascend to the choir in the darkness. He procured a lighted candle and attempted to ascend. But, lo! He could not, for every time he reached the top of the stairs, the Penitente whom he plainly saw there, flogging himself, would approach and put out his candle.

After trying for several times, the brave Penitente gave up the attempt, and all decided to leave the unknown and mysterious stranger alone in the church. As they departed, they saw the mysterious Penitente leave the church and turn in an opposite direction. They again consulted one another, and decided to follow him. They did so; and, since the stranger walked slowly, scourging himself continuously and brutally, they were soon at a short distance from him.

The majority of the flagellants followed slowly behind; while the brave one, who had previously attempted to ascend to the choir, advanced to the side of the mysterious stranger and walked slowly by him. He did not cease scourging himself, though his body was visibly becoming very weak, and blood was flowing freely from his mutilated back. Thus the whole procession continued in the silence of the night, the stranger leading the Penitentes through abrupt paths and up a steep and high mountain.

At last, when all were nearly dead with fatigue, the mysterious Penitente suddenly disappeared, leaving his good companion and the other Penitentes in the greatest consternation. The Penitentes later explained that this was doubtless the soul of a dead Penitente who had not done his duty in life, a false Penitente, and God had sent him back to earth to scourge himself properly, before allowing him to enter heaven

THE PLAINS AND PLATEAU

Introduction

Those states in the region classified by *The Greenwood Library of American Folktales*—Kansas, Oklahoma, Colorado, Wyoming, North Dakota, South Dakota, Montana, and Utah—are the states most people associate with the Western frontier and the culture of the covered wagon, the cattle drive, and the nomadic Native American Plains cultures. Most of the area, in fact, is referred to as the Great Plains.

Once referred to as the Great American Desert, the Plains continue through these states with little interruption until they reach the Rocky Mountains, which extend from Canada into Colorado and northern New Mexico. Some parts of the region exhibit extreme variations in terrain, rainfall, vegetation, and temperature. Utah, for example, is home to both the Mojave Desert and also the Wasatch Mountains, which remain covered in snow for most of the year.

The earliest Native American inhabitants of the Great Plains and the plateau region were sedentary horticulturists or hunters and gatherers. Some groups had migrated into the area of their own volition; others were driven west by pressures generated by the increasing settlement to the east by Americans of European descent.

The Wichita were representative of the farming cultures on the southern fringes of the region. The Wichita grew the staple of Native American farmers, corn. In addition, they grew tobacco as a sacred plant used for ritual purposes and other food crops such as squash, beans, pumpkins, and melons. Even the sedentary cultures in the region engaged in a seasonal buffalo hunt. Although the Wichita villages of grass-covered pole huts do not suggest a high level of cultural development, their cosmology was sophisticated and, as one of their myths—"Origin of the Universe" (p. 135)—demonstrates, accounted for both the natural and the social order.

At the northern extreme of the Great Plains, the Arikaras, Mandans, and Hidatsas enjoyed a settled lifestyle as well, living in well-protected villages of earth-lodge dwellings. They developed a rich mythological repertoire and ceremonial life as they tended fields of corn, beans, and squash, and—like the other sedentary Plains cultures—engaged in seasonal buffalo hunts. Even before Europeans themselves became a significant factor in the lives of the indigenous Great Plains cultures, the horses that Europeans introduced made their way from the Spanish incursions and from the southern Great Plains northward to the Canadian border. The horses radically changed the lifestyles of both the Southern Plains cultures—such as the Comanches of Kansas, Oklahoma, and the Texas Panhandle—and also, later, the Northern Plains Classic cultures including the Cheyenne, Blackfoot, Dakota, and Lakota. All became master equestrians and came to rely on the horse for mobility and the buffalo for subsistence. "Young Men Who Killed the Horned Serpent and Released the Buffalo" (p. 185), "Coyote and the Buffalo" (p. 228), and "Legend of the Teton Sioux Medicine Pipe" (p. 251) are among the folktales that draw on this way of life for their themes and characters. To the western extremes of the region, in Utah and Colorado, the Utes pursued an equestrian nomadic lifestyle and expressed their worldview through stories of their **culture hero** and **trickster**, Coyote (see, for example, "Coyote's Theft of Fire," p. 164).

Hispanic influence persisted in the Great Plains and the plateau region, especially in the states that, until the conclusion of the Mexican War in 1848, had been first Spanish, then Mexican, territory. The relevant states in this category include Utah and parts of Colorado, Arizona, New Mexico, and Wyoming.

With the opening of these territories for settlement, Americans ultimately discovered the farming potential of the Great Plains. Even those who merely passed across them left their narrative records of hardships and encounters with the Great Plains cultures, as in the **family saga** "Crossing the Plains from Kentucky" (p. 181). Many were induced to stay on the Great Plains and the plateau region for a variety of reasons, however. Even Oklahoma, which—until the great westward migrations following the Civil War—had been a dumping ground for dispossessed Native Americans, became prime territory for those Americans and a good number of immigrants looking for a fresh start. A variety of occupations drew them on. Some immigrated to become small-town businessmen, as in "Joke on Jake" (p. 233). Others became cowboys, and some overcame racism in the bargain, in the tradition of "Matthew 'Bones' Hooks,

Cowboy" (p. 224). Still others, like Marshall W. S. Foscett in "Bill Foscett" (p. 220), tried to maintain order among the rest who were busy trying to make a profit through driving cattle to Dodge City, Kansas, through the Colorado Gold Rush, or by robbing those who did succeed.

Yet another significant group among the many who were drawn to the Great Plains and the plateau region were those who sought religious freedom in the Utah desert—the Mormons, members of the Church of Jesus Christ of the Latter Day Saints. This faction first arrived in the Salt Lake Valley in 1847, the year before the Mexican War erupted and eventually led to Utah becoming part of the United States as a result of the Treaty of Guadalupe Hidalgo. Despite a long period of turmoil, the Mormons remained a strong presence in the area as reflected in the **legends** of "The Three Nephites" (p. 241), which is about the supernatural benefactors to the Mormon community.

The Great Plains and the plateau regions were, throughout the nineteenth century, synonymous with the American frontier. With the virtual extinction of the great buffalo herds, the pacification—and in some cases extermination—of the Native American cultures in the heart of the United States, and the crossing of the continent with railroads, by the end of the century the American frontier survived almost exclusively in its folk narratives and the memories of their performers.

SUGGESTED READINGS

Dooling, D. M. *The Sons of the Wind*. San Francisco: HarperCollins, 1992.

Fife, Austin, and Alta Fife. *Saints of Sage and Saddle: Folklore Among the Mormons*. Bloomington, IN: Indiana University Press, 1956.

Koch, William E. *Folklore from Kansas*. Lawrence, KS: University Press of Kansas, 1980.

Marriott, Alice, and Carol K. Rachlin. *Plains Indian Mythology*. New York: Thomas Y. Crowell, 1975.

Smith, Anne M., ed. *Shoshone Tales*. Salt Lake City: University of Utah Press.

ORIGINS

ORIGIN OF THE UNIVERSE

Tradition Bearer: Unavailable

Source: Dorsey, George A. "Wichita Tales. 1. Origin." *Journal of American Folklore* 15 (1902): 215–39.

Date: 1902

Original Source: Wichita

National Origin: Native American

The Wichita proper were one band of the Wichita Confederacy who at various historical periods occupied territory on the Southern Great Plains—modern Kansas, Oklahoma, and northern Texas. They lived in dome-shaped dwellings and built their villages along streams. They grew crops of corn, melons, and tobacco and engaged in a seasonal buffalo hunt. As the following myth of creation demonstrates, the Wichita developed a complex system of sacred narratives that accounted for both the natural and the social order. "The Origin of the Universe" offers a rare example of a myth that describes creation from the first chaotic state of the universe to contemporary times. Appearing in the detailed descriptions of the following narrative are the relationships of humans to both animals and supernatural forms, the flow of power between worlds by means of culture heroes, and the development of cultural institutions such as the healing and religious rituals.

In the times at the beginning, there was no sun, no moon, no stars, nor did the earth exist as it does now. Time passed on and Darkness only lived. With the lapse of time came a woman, Watsikatsia, made after the form of the man Darkness.

The woman found an ear of corn in front of her, while before Darkness was placed an arrow. They did not know what these objects were nor where they came from, but they knew that they were for their use. The woman wondered what the ear of corn was for, and Darkness, by the gift of Man-Never-Known-on-Earth, was able to tell her that the corn was for her to eat. Then Darkness wondered what the arrow was for, and the woman, by aid from the same power, was able to tell him that with the arrow he was to kill game.

The time now arrived when Man-Never-Known-on-Earth promised them that he would make more people. So a village soon sprang into existence with many families. And according to the wish of Man-Never-Known-on-Earth a certain person was to be chief, and his name was to be Boy-Chief. Man-Never-Known-on-Earth also decreed that the name of the village should be Wandering-Village, which meant that the people should not travel on their feet, as people do now, but should wander like spirits, they could think of a distant point and be there at once.

After a while Darkness and the woman (Watsikatsia) began to wonder why so many things had happened, why there were so many people. For there were crowds and crowds of people. There were so many people that Darkness told them to scatter, to divide into parties and go off in different directions. After this, Darkness began to get power to foretell things. Once he told Watsikatsia everything, that he was about to go to a certain being over there, Man-Never-Known-on-Earth.

When he was ready to go he reached down at his left side and with his right hand and brought up a ball. Then he reached down with his left hand at his right side and brought up a belt. Then he reached down in front, touched the ball to the belt and brought up a shinny stick [a curved stick used to play a game similar to field hockey]. He took the ball, tossed it up and struck it with the stick. As the ball flew he went with it. Thus he went on towards the place for which he had set out and where he expected to find Man-Never-Known-on-Earth.

Now Man-Never-Known-on-Earth had great power and knew that this man was coming to pay him a visit. (The object of this man's visit was that power be given him so that there should be light on the face of the earth.) Again he tossed the ball, struck it and traveled through space with it, but he was not there yet. So he knew that he could not depend on the ball.

Then he took his bow and arrow, which he had brought with him, shot the arrow and flew with it. This he did a second, third, and fourth time, but he had not yet arrived. Still he knew that he had to get there. Then he remembered that he could run. So he made one long run and stopped to rest. Then he ran again, and a third and fourth time. He had now made twelve trials and knew that he was near the place of his journey.

Now he came across a grass lodge and he knew that someone lived there. Before he got right at the lodge, he heard somebody speaking to him, telling him the object of his journey: for Man-with-Great-Power-to-Foretell lived there. Darkness at once asked for something to eat.

Man-with-Great-Power-to-Foretell asked him inside the lodge. When Darkness entered he saw light; for the lodge was filled with bright light. As he had come on a long journey he was very tired and hungry, and again asked for food. So Man-with-Great-Power-to-Foretell reached down behind him and brought up four grains of corn. Darkness began eating, and the four grains were more than he could eat, so full did they make him. Then they began to talk and Man-with-Great-Power-to-Foretell said to Darkness: "Man-Never-Known-on-Earth has made me also; the time is coming nearer; it will not be long until we are able to go around everywhere." So after they had stayed there in the grass lodge a long time, they went outside and faced east.

Man-with-Great-Power-to-Foretell then told Darkness to look, and there was water almost as far as they could see. On the opposite bank they saw a man. This man told them to make haste and cut a stick.

Then he said to them, "There are three animals in the water traveling towards you. Do not kill the first or the second, but kill the third, which is half black and half white."

Then Man-with-Great-Power-to-Foretell said: "We are not quite ready;" for he was just making his arrows.

Then the man said: "Hurry and make your arrows!"

Man-with-Great-Power-to-Foretell replied: "We are about ready; we have the bow, arrows, and sinew, but the arrows are not quite dry." Man-with-Great-Power-to-Foretell again cried out, "We are about ready; we have fixed the sinew." Again the man called to them to hurry. Then Man-with-Great-Power-to-Foretell said, "We are about to feather the arrows." The man again called to them to hurry. Man-with-Great-Power-to-Foretell replied. "We are ready now; we are ready to draw the arrows, for we have trimmed the feathers." While they were working they saw the three animals draw closer.

Again the man called out, "Don't shoot the first or the second, but kill the third, which is half black and half white." Then he said, "They are closer to you. I go now. I will never be here any more. When you go back, tell your people that there will be such a word as *Hosaiisida* (Last-Star-after-Light) and that I will appear from time to time." After he had spoken, they looked, but the man was gone; they looked higher and saw him as a star of bright light, for he was Young-Star, or the morning star.

It now grew a little lighter and they saw the three animals still closer to them, and they saw that they were deer and that they were standing on the water. Then Man-with-Great-Power-to-Foretell shouted, and the first deer jumped up on the bank to the south of the place where they stood, and it was black; then the second deer jumped up, it was white; then the half black and half white deer jumped up on the bank, and Man-with-Great-Power-to-Foretell shot it on its side.

Man-with-Great-Power-to-Foretell now told Darkness that that was the power given to man, that when you go after game such weapons would be used. Then he added: "I will not be on earth much longer, but I will be seen at times."

Darkness now looked, but Man-with-Great-Power-to-Foretell was gone; he looked toward the east and there he saw him as the sun; and his name was Sun-God. Then it became light and they knew that the first deer was day, the second night, and the third, which they had killed, was day and night, and that henceforth there was to be day and night. These three deer became the three stars which we see every night in the west.

When these things had happened, Darkness turned and faced the west. All was bright with light now. He began his journey back to the point from which he had set out. As he went he travelled very fast; for he now had power to travel very fast. Indeed, so rapidly did he travel that he arrived home early that day.

When he got home he found all kinds of people, but they did not know him and asked him who he was. As he also knew no one, he asked where he could go for shelter. He was told to go to the west edge of the village, where he would find a large lodge belonging to Boy-Chief.

So Darkness went there for shelter. He asked Boy-Chief how many more villages there were like that one. Boy-Chief replied that in the south there was one with a chief named Wolf-Robe, who had great power like Man-with-Great-Power-to-Foretell.

Then Boy-Chief asked Darkness where he had been, and he replied that he had been to a certain place where he had met Man-with-Great-Power-to-Foretell and Young-Star. Then Darkness asked Boy-Chief to assemble everyone in the village in order that they might hear what he had to say.

Boy-Chief called for all to come, and a great crowd gathered about the lodge. Boy-Chief then announced that all were present and asked him what he had to say. Then Darkness told them that he and his woman were the first beings created and that Man-Never-Known-on-Earth had given them power to carry out his work, and that they were going to do it. "Therefore," added Darkness, "I have come before you again, to tell you that after I have done this work for you I will have to leave you." After he had said this he commanded all the people to return to their homes and tell everything he had said.

Then he started on his journey to the south village and soon arrived. Again he asked where he could find shelter, and was told as before to go to a certain place at the edge of the village, where he would find the headman, who would treat him well. He went to that house and met the chief, who asked him what he had to say. He replied that he had something to say, and asked the chief to assemble all his people. So someone was sent around to tell the people of the village to gather at the chief's place. Now before Darkness had arrived in this village three people had predicted his arrival, for they had great power in those days; so they were not surprised when he came.

The crowd came and he told them they were to have such a game as shinny ball. He reached down with his right hand on his left side and produced a ball, and then reached down on his right side with his left hand and brought up a shinny stick. These he showed the people and told them they were for their use. Then he commanded the people to gather just outside the village at about evening time, and then he set the time for play. They went as he told them.

When they were all there he tossed the ball toward the north and traveled with it. It went a long ways. When it lit he picked it up and struck it with the stick and drove the ball back south, then said that the point where he stood when he struck the ball would be called "flowing water" (the goal). Then he took the ball, tossed it, went with it, and again struck it southward. Where it hit was the second "flowing water," or goal. Between these two goals or bases was level ground, and in both directions as far as you could see.

Then he divided the men into two parties, and placed one at each goal. Between these two parties and in the centre of the field he placed two men, one from each of the two parties. He gave one man the ball and told him to toss it up. As the ball was tossed he told the other man to strike it towards the south. He did so and drove the ball towards his opponents on the south. Now they played, and the north side drove the ball to the south goal and won. They then changed goals and the other side won. Then Darkness said that they had played enough.

Before the shinny ball game began, Darkness had asked that a lodge be emptied and cleaned out. It was now late in the afternoon. He now entered the lodge, but first told the people to go to their homes, that the times were drawing near when things would change, for the powers which had been given to people were increasing, "And now," he said finally, "I go. I am to leave you, but I am also to be seen." He made his final appearance, the people went to their homes and he entered the prepared lodge, and when he appeared again it was to bring light into darkness.

By this time the power which Man-Never-Known-on-Earth had first given people had developed and the people were very powerful, but they used their power for bad purposes.

The first woman, Watsikatsia, now appeared in this village and asked for shelter. She was told to go to a certain place, but she was warned that the chief had greatly changed and that now he was an enemy to his visitors. She replied that she had great powers, given her by Man-Never-Known-on-Earth, that she could do anything. Her informant told her that she would arrive in the morning. She would find someone inquiring for her who wanted her to go on a journey with him.

The next morning she arrived at the lodge of the chief, and shortly after she went after water, when she heard someone inquiring for her. This was a man who was acting for, or the servant of Without-Good-Power, son of Wolf-Robe. Now Without-Good-Power was a very bad man, while his father was just as good as ever, and had never abused the power, which Man-Never-Known-on-Earth had given him. This servant of Without-Good-Power now told her to get ready to travel, as Without-Good-Power was going to war, and she must go along.

Without-Good-Power now started and a great crowd followed. He told his followers that be was not going very far, only to a place called Eyes-like-Mountains, which stood in the water. After they had gone a short way Without-Good-Power ordered the people to stop for a while so that he could make a sacrifice, by offering his pipe to everyone to smoke. While he was doing this, with his followers sitting around him in a circle, there appeared on his right side and on his left side a bow.

All at once these two bows turned into two snakes and began to fight each other. Then Without-Good-Power asked the people to interpret the meaning of this event. A certain man spoke up and said it meant thus and so. Then Without-Good-Power said that his interpretation was wrong and he got up and went where the man was and killed him with a club.

Then the woman spoke up and said that Without-Good-Power's powers were great, but were not all beneficial to the people, for Without-Good-Power had killed people before this time when they had failed to interpret properly. She now said, "The meaning of what has just happened is that the village which we have left is being attacked by a certain kind of enemy." After she had made this interpretation, all the people turned back to go home.

When they had arrived the woman called all the women together and told them that everywhere she went she had certain great powers, and that the last place where she had been was Place-where-Corn-is-Raised. Then she told the women that power would be given to them, so that they could kill many animals for food, that after taking the hide off all they had to do was to take the hide by one side, shake it, and it would be a robe, that they should take the bark from the trees, save it, sprinkle it on the robe from end to end, and that power would be given them to take up anything and pack it on their back. She also said that the time was coming when certain of their powers would be cut off and all would be just ordinary people; also that she would soon no longer appear as she was, but in a different form. Soon after that she was changed into a bird with bright red feathers; for she had had red hair.

It had now come to pass that, after all these things had happened, Wolf-Robe, the chief of the south village, was an old man, and nearly everything went wrong; the people were no longer good. Wolf-Robe had told them to go ahead and do as they pleased.

Now there was a certain wise man living north of Wolf-Robe, who spoke out and said that this condition could not last, and that there would soon appear a man, by the name of Howling-Boy, who would do things. He also said that the people were not living naturally, that they were exercising too much supernatural power, and that there were certain people who considered themselves greater than Man-Never-Known-on-Earth. In addition to Howling-Boy, who was to appear, another man would appear, whose name was to be Heard-Crying-in-His-Mother's-Womb (although people thought that what they heard crying was a knife which the woman carried at her side). Now the wise man advised the chief, Wolf-Robe, to select all his men who were capable of traveling fast to go out to look for these two men who were to appear.

Wolf-Robe selected only four, two of the number being brothers, and they started, one in each direction, to hunt for the two men, and also to tell other people to look for them and to go to the village. People began to come in from far and wide. Finally it was announced that all were in the village. Then a certain man appeared and gave his name as Howling-Boy, and presently the other man, Heard-Crying-in-His-Mother's-Womb, appeared. The latter told the chief that he had great power, and enumerated what he could do. The chief admitted that he was a man of great power.

Heard-Crying-in-His-Mother's-Womb then said, "I always have known what you have in your mind. Now say what you have in your mind, for it is best for the people to hear what you have to say in my presence."

The chief then talked and said that there were too many people who were bad, who used too much unnatural power, that he ordered all such people to be destroyed; and that he left the performance of this task to Howling-Boy and

Heard-Crying-in-His-Mother's-Womb. He also added that his son was a bad man and that he could not account for it, as he himself was a good man and did not practice so much power as did his son.

Howling Boy then announced that he would delegate his share of the killing of bad people to Heard-Crying-in-His-Mother's-Womb. So Heard-Crying-in-His-Mother's-Womb accepted the task in accordance with the chief's orders. Heard-Crying in-His-Mother's-Womb now arose, saying that he would begin his work at once, and that the chief's son would be the first to be destroyed. So he took his bow, found the chief's son and destroyed him, tearing him to pieces. Then he went on with his work of killing the bad people, shouting before he got to each one, so that his victim would get excited and could not move or do anything. As he encountered each, he also would tell what great powers he had, and that the people thought they had greater powers than anybody else. He also would tell them that Man-Never-Known-on-Earth had given them great powers, but that they had not acted as he wanted them to.

Next he went to a lodge where there was a large family, the father of which had a head with two faces; this man he killed, telling him if he ever lived again he would have less power.

Then he went to another man, whose name was Haitskaria, and who was a creature like an alligator and who burnt the ground over which he traveled. He told Haitskaria that he was there to destroy him, and that if he ever lived again he would have less power.

Then he went to another lodge, where he met a family of Mountain-Lions, consisting of father and mother and two children. He told them he had come to destroy them, that they had lived a bad life.

They begged him not to carry out his orders, but to let them live and continue the possession of their power. But he told them he would have to carry out his order, and that if they came to life again they would have less power.

Then he went on to the mountains where there was a cave. As he approached he hallooed and saw a great crowd of Scalped or Bloody-Head people. When he drew near they ran into the cave. He went to the opening and told them that power had been given him to destroy them because they were bad; that he would have to carry out the order which had been given him by the chief; that they thought they had greater powers than any living being, and that they abused them. Finally one of the men came from the cave and asked what right he had to say and do these things. In reply he told him that a Creator had given them this power so that they might be great, but that they had gone beyond this power. Then he began to kill them, and left only two, a man and a woman.

Then, having done his work, he returned to the village, where he told the chief that he had destroyed the meanest and most powerful creatures. He added, "Now I have fulfilled your orders, and now I want to find out what you have in your mind." The chief then announced that everyone would be changed into another form, that there would be many human beings, but he advised that everyone do as he pleased; that is, if any wished to change into animals they might do so. After Wolf-Robe had made this announcement, he told the people that he had made his choice and had decided to become an animal. So he went on his way, taking with him his walking stick and robe and leaving his other possessions behind, and journeyed to the nearest body of water. There he went down into the water, dived, and after coming up he went out on the other side a wolf.

Then Heard-Crying-in-His-Mother's-Womb said that something charmed him to the water, drew him towards it. So he went to the water, although he did not want to go, dived to the bottom and saw a woman whose name was Woman-in-Water-Never-Seen. As he did not want to stay there he came to the surface, spouted water up in the air and went up and away with it, and became Weather (that is, lightning, rain, etc.).

After he had disappeared, all the people got vessels, went to the water, filled them, and carried water home to their families. Then some of them put water on their fires, and as the steam ascended up in the air they went with it and so became birds; other beings went their way to the woods, prairies, and mountains and became various kinds of animals, while the remainder of the people lived on in the same place.

Without-Good-Power was among these people who remained, and he still had great powers. He announced that he would continue to live with the people. His powers were especially great in doctoring, so great that he could by a simple command change any person into another form. Thus if he saw any of his enemies coming around his lodge he would command them to stop and then they would vanish; sometimes he would change them into wood. Then he decided to give a new name to the group of people who lived about and he changed the name from Okaitshideia (Village) to Katskara (Village).

Then Without-Good-Power went on to a place where there was an earth lodge, which he entered. Within he put his hand to the wall of the lodge and it left the imprint of his hand in color, and wherever he touched the wall there was the imprint in a different color. Now the owner of the lodge knew that Without-Good-Power had great powers, among them that of changing people into different forms, so when Without-Good-Power shouted, the man ran out and started north, but he was changed into a bird, Gtataikwa (its name coming from its peculiar cry, just as if someone were going to strike it). Still another

143

man ran out of the lodge and started north, but he was changed into a star (not the morning star).

Time passed on and the people remembered how things used to be. A certain young man, Every-Direction, went out on an expedition with twelve men. Time passed on and they did not return till about spring. The people wondered why they were gone so long.

In the village at the northeast corner lived an old man and an old woman, who had a little orphaned grandson whose name was Of-Unknown-Parents. This boy finally went into the center of the village and told the people that the thirteen who had gone on the expedition were no longer alive, but had gone into the ground, and that no one of them would return. Then Of-Unknown-Parents said that some hunters should go out for two days and look for a certain place where there would be some people coming out of the ground, enough to form a village.

When it was night the boy went to bed, but before he went to sleep he heard someone calling him. He arose and went out on the northwest side of the lodge. There he saw someone standing, who told Of-Unknown-Parents that he was mistaken, that his prophecy would not come true. He also told Of-Unknown-Parents that his father had sent him down to appear before him and tell him this, that a year hence something would happen, which would be done by his father, and that he would appear to him again.

Now at that time the chief's wife, who had a son among the thirteen, which had disappeared, was confined and brought forth four children shaped like dogs. When one day old, they had grown, and when three days old they had grown so fast that they played with the children. But they were mean and ran over the children. When they were grown up, the chief was tired of them and got people to carry them off to the west, as he did not like them. But on the way the dogs, who were now very large, swallowed up the people who were taking them away, and none of the people ever returned.

As time went on, other people would go out where these monstrous creatures lived, but they had such long necks that they would reach out and get them and swallow them. So the people finally got excited and moved the village. The older people talked much and said that although the Creator had made everything it seemed that he had also made monsters to destroy everyone, and that if things went on in this way more bad things would be done. Time passed on and the people would not go to the west for fear of the monsters. So the chief selected four men to visit the place of the old village, but they returned safe.

Now the old man and woman and their grandson, Of-Unknown-Parents, had been left at the old village. One night the person who had formerly appeared to the boy again visited him. He said, "At noon, go to a certain place due north of here, and I will appear to you."

The next day at noon the boy went to a hill in the north where he had been told to go, and there he saw this person. He called the boy to him and told him that his father did not like the way things were going and that he would have to destroy everything. Then he told the boy to return to the village and tell the people that they were to be destroyed, that if they did not believe him, to repeat the message.

Then Of-Unknown-Parents said his father was tired of the monsters and that he wished to destroy them. The person then told the boy he must do certain things: that he must get the twelve longest canes he could find, fasten them together, and give them to a certain woman (Spider-Woman) who lived in the village, that he must tell this woman to get her servant (Mouse-Woman) to go about and get a big lot of corn of all colors and bring it to her master; that when this was done he must put the canes in the ground up to five joints; that after this four days would elapse and at the end of that time to be on the lookout for something to happen, for some-thing would come from the north. He also said that there was a certain thing in the water that would destroy the four monsters, and that now it was time for him to depart.

Now the boy returned to the village and told the chief what was to happen, but the chief would not believe him. Then he went to the Spider-Woman and told her as he had been commanded. She was pleased to hear the story and was willing to do whatever the boy told her to do. After the people had heard the news some would not believe, especially the people who wished to live longer. But many believed the boy's story.

Spider-Woman now got the twelve long canes and sent her servant out to get whatever seeds she could find. She got seeds of corn, beans, pumpkins, watermelons, and seeds of every kind that she could find. Then Spider-Woman first filled some of the joints with corn seed and closed the cane up, then she put in some pumpkin seed and closed it up, and so on, filling the canes with all the seeds.

When night came, Of-Unknown-Parents returned to Spider-Woman and asked her what she had done. She told him that she had done everything except to put the canes in the ground. So Of-Unknown-Parents told her to take the rib of a buffalo and dig a hole in the ground. She did so, and said there was one thing more to be done, and that was to raise the canes and put them in the ground up to the fifth joint. Of-Unknown-Parents said that he would attend to that. So he went away for a little while and returned. Then he commanded a small whirlwind to blow, and it raised the canes right up, and Spider-Woman and Of-Unknown-Parents placed them in the hole up to the fifth joint as they had been commanded.

The time was now come for something to happen. At noon they looked north and saw something like a wind blowing, but it was the fowls of the air all headed south. After they had passed came the animals, the buffalo first, then the deer, and so on. When the people saw these things they were excited. A little later they looked north and saw great floods of water coming very fast, and they saw the thing that was to destroy the four monsters. It was a great turtle, which had broken out of the water and was headed toward the monsters. On it came, and went under their feet, where it stopped. On came the great floods of water. So Spider-Woman, who had helped Of-Unknown-Parents put up the canes, now began climbing at the bottom and soon reached the top of the twelve canes. Then she let down a rope and drew her husband to the top, and then let down the rope and drew up the boy to the top, and then drew up Mouse-Woman. She now made a place on the top with a good shelter, but so made that the water would leak through.

The time was now late in the evening and the water was to the tops of the lodges in the village. The monsters could hardly stand still, it was so slippery. Late in the evening it was more difficult for them to stand still, and one said to the other three, "My brothers, my legs are giving out, and I will have to fall. I will fall that way (north) and when the time comes in later generations that direction will be called 'North.'"

The next day the backs of these monsters could only just be seen, and one of them said to the other two, "Brothers, do the best you can; I have to fall; my legs are giving out; I will fall in that direction (east), and in later times people will call that direction 'Point-Where-Sun-Rises.'"

On the next day the water was higher and the people on the canes were getting uneasy. The water was now up to the necks of the two monsters. The one said to the other: "Brother, you are the youngest of us four; you will have to get along the best you can; I am going to fall; I am giving out; the direction I am going to fall is that way (south), and by later generations it will be called 'South.'"

The fourth day of the flood came. The fourth monster had to hold his head back to keep the water out of his face. He said that he could tell nobody what was going to happen, as his three brothers had perished, but that he would have to fall towards that point where the sun goes down, and it would be called "West."

From that time it was twelve days more before the flood passed on. Nothing could be seen, no village, no people, only some water and a little earth. The ground was all soft. At this time everything was still. There was no wind. But a certain person appeared who came from above, of the name of

Man-Going-All-Around, who had power to dry all slime. He appeared from the northeast direction and was headed southwest. While on his way he saw something like a shadow shining on the ground. He wondered what it was and thought he had better go over to see. When he got over to the place he saw something on the ground, shaped like a human being. Examining it closely he saw that it was molded like a woman.

Man-Going-All-Around went on in another direction. Time passed and he went all around and again came to the same place where he had seen the form of a woman in earth. He now saw that the upper half of the image, as it lay at full length on its back, was alive, and that the lower half was still mud. Then he saw further that the woman had given birth to a child (Standing-Sweet-Grass), which was nursing, on her breast. After seeing this he went on again on his journey. Then came a bird, a dove, and it saw something on the ground; it went to see what was there. When it got near it lighted on the ground and saw the woman sitting up on the ground with the child in her lap. The dove had a piece of grass in its mouth.

In the meantime Man-Going-All-Around had passed on over a place where he thought he heard someone beating a drum. Then he re-turned a third time to the woman, told her to rise and accompany him. He took her to the place where he had heard the noise of drums. He went in with Shadow-Woman and the child and saw that he was in a room shaped like a beaver's lodge, and that it was deep down under the water. The name of the lodge was Place-of-Beavers or Beavers'-Lodge. When he entered the room he saw many people sitting about. He also saw a young man lying on a bed. Then he told the woman that she was to live with this man who was on the bed, and the man accepted the offer.

After Shadow-Woman had lived in the lodge with the man for five days, her child (Standing-Sweet-Grass) had grown rapidly and was now a boy and could talk. The boy said to his mother, "I am going to begin my work. When I begin this work I want you to keep continent till I finish my work." At this time his mother told him that he was the son of no man on earth, but of Man-Above.

The next day Standing-Sweet-Grass went out in a northwest direction. After he had gone on a while, he stopped, facing the north-west. Then he turned towards the east and saw the same man (Man-Going-All-Around) who had taken him and his mother into the lodge. This man now discovered the place where the people were on top of the canes. All this time it had been still and there had been no wind; only where he went was there wind. Having reached the spot where the canes stood, he was told by Spider-Woman, who was on top of the canes, to look out for the boy, Of-Unknown-Parents, who was coming down the rope. So Spider-Woman let down the rope with the boy on the end of it. When Of-Unknown-Parents was down, he was told to command the wind to blow from the north, east, south, and west, into the ground. Then the canes began to go down to-ward the west, and it was found that the water had sunk as far as the fourth joint of the canes, so that they lacked but one more joint of reaching the bottom. When they were all down the boy from the Place-of-Beavers told them to go with him to his home, saying that there were many people there. Then they set out, carrying the canes with them, Spider-Woman holding the canes at the middle, with Mouse-Woman at one end and Of-Unknown-Parents at the other.

When they arrived at the Place-of-Beavers they all went in, except Standing-Sweet-Grass, and saw crowds of people, birds, and animals. Having entered, Shadow-Woman got up and went to the strangers and told them that she was glad to see them. They re-plied that it was a fact that she was glad to see them, for they had some things for her. Then they opened the canes and divided the seeds, the men putting them in wrappers. Then all the seeds were given to Shadow-Woman for her use in beginning her life. Standing-Sweet-Grass, Shadow-Woman's son, now came down into the lodge to see what they had. After he had seen everything he said it was time for everybody to lie down and go to sleep.

Early the next day after all had awoke, Standing-Sweet-Grass got up and had a talk with his mother. He told her that the seeds had been given her by these people for her use, and for the use of all when they should increase in numbers, and that she should distribute them so that they would always be in use. He himself, he said, had to go on with his work.

So he started on a journey, going south. He commanded the trees to grow and they grew; he commanded the water to flow and it flowed, as he had commanded. After the great flood of waters there were many forms left in the mud, these he commanded to change into hills and mountains. He commanded the wild animals to roam over the prairies and through the forests.

When he had done these things he returned to his mother and told her to remember what he had said to her, that everything must be straight with her while he was doing his work. Then he commanded the birds to leave the Beaver-Lodge, saying that hereafter human beings would sometimes need to use them for food and other things. When he had given this command, the birds all left the lodge, saying first they wished to go near him. So when they left they all gathered around him.

The boy told them that his mother had not obeyed him and had therefore done him wrong, hence he would not return to her, but would go to his father, the Man-Above. While the birds were still around him the boy put them in a trance and when they came to they realized that the boy had disappeared, but where he had stood they saw a little bunch of standing sweet-grass.

After all this had happened, Shadow-Woman, the mother of Standing-Sweet-Grass, and her husband moved out of the Place-of-Beavers and erected a lodge of their own. Soon the woman became pregnant and a little later she gave birth to a child, which was a girl. In those times everything grew very rapidly and soon the girl could move about. Time passed on and Shadow-Woman soon gave birth to an-other child, which was a boy, so that they had now a girl and a boy.

Time passed on and the boy asked his mother if they could not put up another and a better lodge, so that they might have more room. The mother said yes; so the boy and his sister went and got some mud, blood, and sand, mixed them and molded them into an axe that was to be used in cutting the timber. Then the husband of Shadow-Woman had killed a buffalo while hunting and had brought in the four shoulder blades. They were to be used in digging. With these tools the boy and girl went to work and built a house, a dug-out.

They all moved in to the new lodge and the boy and girl married and they soon had a girl baby and then again very soon they had a boy baby. In the meantime, Shadow-Woman had given birth to another boy, and the children all grew very fast. Then the first pair of children, which were married, said to their mother that they ought to make another and a larger house. This they did, and they moved into it, and the boy's wife was now pregnant again.

Time passed on and the boy was now a man, but he was mean and abused his father and mother. Finally the mother told him that it was not right for him to act this way. She also said that the time was about come when she (Shadow-Woman) and her husband would have to go to someplace else. By this time the second girl and second boy of Shadow-Woman were married. They decided to build still another house, into which this couple moved. They now had made pottery to boil meat in, while the newly married couple had brought in a stone with which they were to make a corn grinder.

Time passed on and everything grew rapidly, and soon Shadow-Woman gave birth to a third girl, and soon after to a third boy, and then they grew rapidly, were soon married, and the second couple built a lodge for them. The time now came when the old people called all their children and grandchildren to their lodge, saying to them that they had something to say to them. The mother, when they were all together, told her children that there was some person (above) who had made them and who had given them power, that she was the mother of another son (Standing-Sweet-Grass) who had disappeared, that only by believing that the Man-Above had given them these things could they rely on getting everything. Now in those times it was always the case that the oldest children were the meanest and the youngest the smartest, hence the oldest daughter and the oldest son did not seem to pay any attention to what the mother said.

Time passed on and the three families increased and the three lodges became crowded. So the children, as they married, moved out and built new lodges for themselves. The oldest son kept on abusing his mother, and she had grown more and more tired of this treatment, and she decided to move away off. When she had come to this decision, her husband said that he would go with her.

So they started on a journey and went due north. After they had gone a long distance they stopped, and Shadow-Woman asked her husband to what place he wanted to go. He started on alone and went in a northwest direction, where he became Clearness-after-a-Rain. Then Shadow-Woman went alone on her way toward the north, where she disappeared and became Rain-Woman. Time passed on and there was now a large village of the descendants of these people, for they had increased and increased. There were now three head men: the first chief was named Boy-Chief; the second chief was named Coup-Sticks, for he had two red painted sticks which he used after any brave act; the third chief was named Everywhere-Always-Brave, for in attacks on enemies he had been very brave, had done everything, and had gone every place. The village itself where all these people lived was called Village-by-Side-of-Big-Elm-Tree. Now, if since the time of that village seven men had each lived one hundred years and each man had been born on the day of the death of the other, the seventh man would be alive now and if he should live one hundred years, at his death it would be seven hundred years since the time of the Village-by-Side-of-Big-Elm-Tree.

Time passed on, and this village was attacked by enemies (Apache). In the fight, one of the chiefs killed a chief of the enemy. After the fight they found that of their own people no one was killed and that the enemy had lost one. So the chief invited all his people around the big elm-tree, and gave out four drums, two on each side, and they had a Victory dance. When the dance began it happened that there were so many people around the tree and the drums were making so much noise that the elm-tree began to shake and quiver, and the people saw that the tree was enjoying itself and taking part in the dance. As they danced the women would get partners to dance with.

After this dance the chiefs came together in council, and said that they ought to go and look for another place to live in instead of the old place, so they invited everybody to be present, and when the people had all arrived they told them what they had decided to do. This decision was then announced to all the people. Then they moved under the leadership of Boy-Chief. At those times all had to pack their belongings on their back. Thus they journeyed on and came to a place where they built new houses, and the new village they called Perched-upon-a-Mountain. The people would make journeys to their old homes to fetch things they had left behind.

At the time of the new village there was a big band of people living very near them and called Pawnees. Time went on and matters progressed as usual; they raised their crops, and the men hunted game. The men used to go out in a party, and when they came to buffalo or other game they would make a surround, for they had no horses, and their weapons were stone-pointed arrows and stone knives.

Now of the two big bands (Wichita and Pawnee) there were five chiefs, two of them being Pawnee. They all came together in council, and, in talking over matters, they decided that the time had come for the two bands to depart from each other. One band was to travel northward (the Pawnee), while their own band (the Wichita) with three chiefs was to travel southward.

It was spring, and the band (Wichita) kept traveling toward the south. On their way they would stop a little while, but still they went south, looking over the country to spy out the best place for their homes. But they returned to the place where there were some mountains (Perched-Upon-a-Mountain). It was now about the middle of hot weather. They found that the Pawnee chiefs with their band had gone on to the north. Then they invited all the people about them and told them that they had selected a fine place for their new homes and that soon they would move thither. Finally they all began to move, packing things on their backs and on dog travois. It took a long time to get to the place. When they got there they called their village Village-on-North-Slope-with-Wind-from-the-North.

A little while after they had settled here, enemies began to appear: the Apache would come from the southwest, and the Osage from the northeast. Now there was living at the time an old man who was always giving good advice to the men, especially to the young men, telling them what was right, and the best ways to do things. So now he announced to the young men that there would be a race on the following morning. The next morning he started off for the race, in a northeasterly direction, taking with him all the young men who wished to run.

Arriving at the starting-place, the old man told them that the Man-Above had given them all their power; that these races were for exercise, to make them strong, that they were never to eat anything before the race. Then the time came for the start. They all ran a little way, then they turned and went back to the old man. They did this three times and at the fourth time the race began in earnest. At the end of the race all the young men were told by the old man to go to the nearest stream, dive in the water, and drink a lot of water and vomit it all up again. This was the rule of the race.

The village had now been founded about one year, and they raised a crop to sustain them. They now decided to move camp again. So they packed their things on their backs and on the dog travois and set out on a journey, crossing a river, and went on to a place, which the three chiefs had selected for them. They halted at the bend of the river, where the river had a long straight course toward the east. At night it seemed as if the moon were traveling on the water. Sometimes the river was dry and it had a sandy bed, and then it seemed as though the moon were coming along on the sand. So they named the place Moon-Coming-on-Sand. At this place there was good protection from the enemy and they lived there a long time, forgetting their desire to move on to a better place. The old chiefs had ordered the people to make dug-out lodges, and they were secure from the enemy. By this time the three old chiefs bad grown very old, and were so feeble that they had to be led around. Also by this time the chiefs had grown sons who had become head men in their fathers' places. But the tribe had not yet arrived at the place in the high mountains (Wichita Mountains), which the old man had chosen. And now the three old chiefs, Coup-Sticks, Boy-Chief, and Everywhere-Always-Brave, died of old age.

Time passed on, and one of the young chiefs said it was time to continue their journey to the place, which their fathers had selected for their homes. They now set out again toward the south, but on the way, at a certain place on a rocky ford of the river (near Chilocco) the son of old Coup-Sticks separated from the other two young chiefs and with his band drifted toward the east and made a new settlement near the mouth of Black Bear creek. The other two chiefs with their bands continued their journey and stopped at a place known as High-Hills-Extending-into-River (near the Red Hills at Watonga).

They did not stay there long, and soon moved south again. This time they started down in two bands, for there were so many of them. One band settled on top of the hills, and their village was called High-land Village (head of McCusky Canyon), while the other band settled at Lowland Village. When they were all settled, the people used to go out on hunting trips, and often they would look toward the southwest where they could see the mountains (Wichita) and they would often say among themselves, "Those mountains have been selected for our home." So they called the mountains "Our Mountains," and they often wondered what was over there. Now at this time there was a certain woman who had heard much about the mountains and she wanted to move there, but she died of old age.

At that time there was off to the east of the village a lake and in the middle of the lake was an island with large cottonwood trees on it. In a tree was a nest of bald eagles. The men were always going out hunting, and one day a young man went off that way to hunt. He stopped at the edge of the lake and heard some kind of noise up in the air. He looked up and saw an eagle rapidly descending; it lit on a tree on the island. Then the eagle spoke to the young man, telling him not to go back home but to stay there, as he had some power he wanted to give him.

When it was late in the evening the eagle came down from the nest and requested the young man to come up close to where he was, that he must not be afraid, for the water was shallow. So the young man waded over to the island and went up close to the eagle, from which he received power. The eagle asked the young man if he had seen him descend, whereupon the young man replied that he had, and the eagle told him that this was the way he always looked out for his prey and that this was the power that he had given him. He also said that if at any time anyone should kill a bald eagle he should go and take it to the right side of the wind and take out the eagle's wing-bone and make of it a whistle for his use; but he was forbidden to kill the eagle himself.

After saying this, the eagle continued that he was, of course, one of the fowls of the air, but that once he had been a human being having great powers; that he would give him these powers, though less marked in degree than those which he himself possessed; that he would be useful to him during his life. The eagle also told the young man that he could not say that he should live forever, but that someday he would have to die; that these powers were good until death; that they were of use in doctoring. The eagle also told the young man that he would give him power to start up a dance, which would be for the people, to be called the deer dance.

Then the eagle said, "Come closer," whereupon he blew breath in the young man's mouth, giving him power with which to make himself useful while on expeditions and while doctoring or in dancing. The young man now took his quiver and returned home and went to bed.

While sleeping, he dreamed that someone was talking to him; he did not know who it was, or where he was, but he heard a confirmation that the eagle had given to him power, that it was for his own good, and that it would make him a useful man. On awaking, the young man at first thought that someone had actually spoken to him, but it was only a dream.

After this, time passed on, and the head man of Lowland Village sent for some man from Highland Village to come down to his camp, telling them that he wanted to move to the point south and west, which he had selected. Four men were selected to go down to the Lowland Village chief. They were told on arriving that he wanted to go at once to this spot, that if at any time they should get ready, they would find him there, and that as the country was becoming familiar to all hunters they all would know the way.

The time came when this chief set out with his party for the spot which he had chosen, where they finally arrived, finding that a place had been selected for their home, and they named the place Place-of-Rock-Extending-over-Water (at the west end of the Wichita range). Now on the day of the departure of this party, a second party, ignorant of the plans of the first party, set out for the same place. After the first party had arrived in their new home, the man who had received the power from the eagle bade the people to allow him to make his sacrifice to the eagle by taking his pipe, and thus taking possession of the country. The second party now made their appearance, coming to the very same spot selected by the first party.

The time was now come for the young man to make his offering. Calling upon all, men, women, and children, to arrange themselves in a line from north to south, facing the east, and to sit upon the ground; this done, he passed in front of the line and received from them a small buffalo robe which he placed upon the ground. He then took out of his bundle tobacco seeds and filled his pipe. When the first man made his offering to the above, it meant that they asked the Man-Above to let the people have no trouble, and that they might live without experiencing hard times. By puffing smoke to the south he meant to ask of the South star, which has power to care for a person while out on an expedition, that their people, while out on the expedition, might be under his care and always return home safe. By puffing smoke to the north he meant to ask the North star to watch over their children, that they might grow and be without sickness. By puffing smoke to the east he was making an offering to the Sun, that the people whenever traveling might be in his care.

After these things had come to pass, the people announced that they had seen everything that had been done, that now all the people, especially the women, could go out and stake out their homes in security. He also said that in the middle of the projected village there were to be poles put up for a place for their dances. He also told his people that if he had done his duty aright, on the next morning there would be a fog, for a sign thereof. He then selected two of the strongest men to hold the robe down. They also got two pieces of soap weed, with which he made fire.

Then he lighted his pipe, and puffed on it and blew smoke four times to the above, four times to the west, to the south, to the north, and to the east. After he had done this he gave it to the man on the right, who was holding the robe, and he, taking the pipe so that the opening of the bowl pointed toward the northwest, emptied it.

When the next day came there was a dense fog, showing that he had made his offering in the way that power had been given him. Now the time had come to make their village, and by the time they had put their houses up, they began to get things ready to build the dance lodge. First they cut poles. They then hewed them on the sides so that they would bend. This man now selected a certain woman to do this work, telling her how to put the poles up, and told her to send someone after water-moss and bring it there. Then they took the first pole, put it on the east side, dug a hole, put the moss in it and the pole on top of it. Then they put in position poles on the south, west, and north sides. They then took four more poles and put one on the east, one on the south, one on the west, and one on the north side. Then they all went on with the work, all taking part in finishing the lodge. They made the poles meet at the top, and got bark (soap weed), took it on the south-west and put it in hot ashes, which softened it so that they could use it to tie the poles with. They took willows and used them for cross-binders. Then they began to put on the grass covering.

This was easy work, for they used bark and buffalo hides cut in strips to tie the grass in position. This finished the dance lodge. Then the man announced that in the middle of summer, about the time of the gathering of the corn, he would give them a dance, inviting everybody. In some of the houses they had a whole buffalo hide sewed up, full of corn, and in some it seemed as though a live buffalo were standing up. In other houses the corn was piled up on the top of the arbor.

Time passed on, and the moon began to shine in the early part of the night, i. e. the moon was full. He now said that the time was come for a dance; so he called in all the older people, and got the young boys to go toward the west to gather sage, who, when they had brought it, went around, first on the north side, then by the east side, then to the south side, and finally to the lodge, where they entered. They were told to leave the sage by the south door. Then the man took the sage and spread it out around the lodge, beginning on the south side and continuing it on around to the west side of the north door; then he began spreading it on the east side of the north door, continuing around to the east side of the south door. Thus a barren space was left in front of the two doors. Then he took the remainder of the sage and started a fire. All the old people were now asked to enter the lodge and to take with them their rattles. He now sent a man after four bows, which when they had brought them he placed on the west side of the south door, together with four rattles.

155

At the opening of the dance the servant (i. e. the man who had gotten the bows) was selected to pick out the singers, one group of four for the west side, one group of four for the north side, one group of four for the east side, and one group of four for the south side, one of each group being the leader and having power to make the people eat the red berries. Just before they began to sing there came a woman with a boy about fifteen years old, to have some medicine given him by the doctors in order that he might possess the same power that they had. So the mother made the offering to the people that always came first, that is, corn and pumpkin. Then a leader of the dance told the people to get ready; that the singers were getting ready to sing four songs. Then the leader announced that the next day would be the day for the regular ceremony, and that there should be no boy present. Then the four singers began to sing and the boy was placed on the north side of the fire, facing south. A big fire had been started and the people began to dance, including the boy. While the singing was going on the leader announced that the songs would be sung by the four singers sitting on the south side, that four more songs would be sung by the four singers on the west side, four by the four men on the north side, and four by those on the east side that in that way they should sing thereafter. Passing the bows from one singer to another, they danced four days and four nights.

The leader now announced to the people that they should be getting ready to give the boy the red bean. While the dancing was going on the leader asked certain men from the west side if they could not give the boy the bean so that he could make him able to be like themselves. A certain man was selected to attend to this matter, and he sent the boy to a certain man on the east side, who accepted the order, and took charge of the boy, whereupon he arose, took a sage and went around the fire four times, from north to east, then to the south and west. He then passed the sage around the fire four times. Then, holding one end in his mouth and the other in his hand, he gave it a shake, and two beans fell out, which he ground up in his mouth into a dough. He then made four passes toward the boy's mouth, and made him swallow it at once. Then they went on with the dance, all having whistles with breath feathers on the end, some being of the stork and some of the eagle. The leader arose with an eagle-wing fan in his hand and a bone whistle in his mouth. Then he got the stuffed eagle in his arms, which, the people noticed, moved. Then reaching around over the fire with his right hand he produced a bean, put it in his mouth and chewed it. He then put the bean on his whistle, carried it from south to north, passed it over the fire, approached the boy, and put it in his mouth. (These beans should never be chewed, but should be swallowed whole.)

It was now late in the evening, and the boy was no longer able to dance alone. This is the condition one should be in who wished to become a member of this dancing society. The boy had cramps in his arms and legs, and it was apparent that he was no longer able to dance alone, so his mother assisted him. At noon on the following day the boy was unable to move, which was evidently on account of cramps. He was in a bad condition, so they laid him flat upon the ground, face downward, and with head to the west. Now it was the custom when a person during initiation fell into this condition to apply the jaw of the gar pike to any portion of his body to see if the scratching could be felt. If so he was obliged to get up and continue to dance. But in this case they employed a stone, instead of the jaw of the gar pike, to scratch him with. On finding that the scratching produced no sensation, some became fearful and excited, thinking the boy to have been killed. The leader then selected four men to carry him off on a robe to the east of the lodge and lay him upon a slight elevation. After they had obtained a robe they carried the boy as instructed and laid him on the ground, where they left him.

The leader then instructed the dancers to dance until the four days had expired.

At the approach of the third night the boy had a vision. It seemed as though someone had appeared to him, asking him to get up, as that was his grave. The voice also told him that the dance was one of the most powerful that had ever been given, and that the dancers had done right to bring him there, as he (the speaker) would give him great powers. After he awoke, the boy looked around, but saw nobody, though on the ground he saw something that had been dead a long time. He saw the thing move, and it told the boy that it would be seen of him. Finally the dead person arose, and the boy saw that he was very slender.

He said to the boy, "I died as I am."

The boy looked back again and the dead person was changed. From now on, till the daylight came, this man spoke to the boy, saying that he would disappear. Then the man leaned over, and was gone. The boy fell over on the same place and slept. While he was sleeping, the skeleton told him that he was giving him powers.

Day came. The dance continued. The leader forbade the people to go to the place where the boy was lying. Night came again, when the object again appeared to the boy.

He said, "Wake up, you have slept too much."

The boy woke, rose up, and found the man sitting in front of him. After he had appeared, he told the boy that he would tell him who he was. He was once, he said, the head man of the people who had lived there, and that he had died from sickness. He also told him that his name was Bear. Now that he had given the boy powers, he told him that he should never eat the flesh of the bear. While they were talking, day had come. Bear had disappeared, the boy lying in the same way as before and going to sleep.

This was the final day of the dance. Then the people thought that the boy had died and that the leader had obtained certain power from the animals. Night came again, and Bear appeared to the boy the third time and talked as before. The boy now arose, looked at Bear, who was now before him. Bear seemed different. He now saw that it was a man, that he was painted up and had on a necklace of bear claws. The man now spoke and told the boy that he had brought these things to him; if anything should happen, these things would be of use to him. Thus, he was to use the necklace in times of war, and if he went before his enemies he should wear it upside down, but while doctoring he was to wear the necklace with the claws down. The man also said to the boy that he was dead, never to live again, but that the boy would live again, but was at that time in a dead state, and that it would be night before he would come to life again.

The people at the lodge were uneasy, thinking the boy to be dead, but the leader persisted in his statement that the boy would live again at the end of four days.

On the second night the Bear man again appeared and talked with the boy. He told him that he would give him power which would be valuable in doctoring a sick person that when anyone was very sick he should get a feather from the wing of a buzzard and cut the sick man open with it; thus he could cure lung trouble. Then he disappeared as the day drew near. On the third night the Bear man again talked with the boy and disappeared with the coming of morning.

Night came again, and the boy was again awakened by this same man telling him to rise and stand on his feet. He then said to him that when the time came for him to meet his death, it would not be through war, but by sickness. The Bear man also told the boy that he had come to his real life again and would have to return to his home, but that there was one thing that he could not do, viz., live forever, but that he must die some time. He also told him things that he should do that would never fail him, that in his doctoring he should never fail. After these powers had been given him, the boy was told that he had all the powers which the Bear had, and that if he should have any children, as soon as they were old enough, he should tell them what he had told the boy and give them these powers, so that the Bear man's powers might never run out, but be perpetuated by the children. Then he told the boy that he would have to leave him, as he had given him all his powers. All at once the Bear disappeared.

The morning of the fourth day came and the boy rose up. On looking down where this skeleton had lain, he saw nobody there. Then the boy talked to himself, saying, "You have given me powers and I will make use of them all the days of my life. Now I will have to leave this place and return home. I, Broken-Leg-Bear, will go back to my home."

During the day Broken-Leg-Bear went back to his home, entered his house, saw his mother. She was glad to see him and he was glad to see her. Then said the boy to his mother, "I have come back again and I am pleased to be back again."

The next day after his return, he heard that some enemies had attacked one end of the village and were pressing the people hard. Then he went out, painted like a bear, with his bear-claw necklace upside down, and with his bow and arrows, and went on his way to the scene of the fight. When he got there he went into the midst of the enemy, relying on the power which had been given, so that he would never be hit, or, if he should be hit, the arrow would break, and that each one of the bear claws had the power to multiply to twenty, and that that would cause the enemy to see him as though he were twenty men for each claw. After his appearance the fight ended.

Later on, the time came when a person called on this boy doctor, Broken-Leg-Bear, to treat his son. He offered the boy many things, such as food, robes, and lodges if he should save his son, as he thought that the doctor could surely cure his son. So the Broken-Leg-Bear went to see the sickly son, having his buzzard feather at the back of his head.

He came to the place, and there the sick boy lay on the bed, only just alive. He now made every body leave the lodge, while he went through his performances. He took his feather and drew it edgewise over the boy's body, cutting him open. He looked all through the body and saw that there was a certain sickness in there, which he took out, and the boy was cured. Then be took the feather and passed it over the wound and made the boy whole again. Then he said, "Son, arise! You are healed!" The boy lived.

Broken-Leg-Bear performed many other strange things after that, and he was now grown up to be a man. He had a young brother, whose descendants are living today.

ARIKARA CREATION

Tradition Bearer: Peter Burdash

Source: Grinell, George Bird. "Pawnee Mythology." *Journal of American Folklore* 6 (1893):123–27.

Date: ca. 1893

Original Source: Arikara

National Origin: *Native American*

The Arikaras were closely related to the Skidi Pawnee and historically lived in close proximity to the Mandans (both of whom are mentioned in this **myth**) in the Great Plains area. Their villages were composed of earth-lodge dwellings, and they grew corn, beans, and squash, as well as venturing out to engage in seasonal buffalo hunts. The central ritual for the Arikaras was the Mother Corn Ceremony, and each of the bands preserved sacred bundles that were the source of supernatural power and a focus of ritual life.

In the beginning Atiuch created the earth and a people of stone. These people were so strong that they had no need of the Creator, and would not obey him. They even defied him; so he determined to put an end to them. He therefore caused a great rain, which fell continuously for many days, until the land was all covered with water, and the trees were dead and the tops of the hills were submerged. Many of these people being big and heavy, and so able to move only slowly, could not reach the tops of the hills, to which all tried to escape for safety, and even those who did so were drowned by the rising waters, which at last covered the whole land. Everything on the earth was dead. [Today in the washed clay bluffs of the bad lands, the horizontal lines of stratification are shown as marking the level of the waters at various times during this flood, and the hard sandstone pinnacles which cap the bluffs, and which. sometimes present a rude semblance of the human form, are pointed out as the remains of these giants.]

Now when everything was dead, there was left a mosquito flying about over the water and a little duck swimming on it. These two met, and the duck said to the mosquito, "How is it that you are here?"

The mosquito said: "I can live on this foam; how is it with you?"

The duck answered, "When I am hungry I can dive down and eat the green weed that grows under the water."

Then said the mosquito: "I am tired of this foam. If you will take me with you to taste of the things of the earth, I shall know that you are true." So the duck took the mosquito under his wing, where he would keep dry, and dived down with him to the bottom of the water, and as soon as they touched the ground all the water disappeared. There was now nothing living on the earth.

Then Atiuch determined that he would again make men, and he did so. But again he made them too nearly like himself. They were too powerful, and he was afraid of them, and again destroyed them all.

Then he made one man like the men of today. When this man had been created he said to himself, "How is it now? There is still something that does not quite please me." Then Atiuch made a woman, and set her by the man, and the man said, "You knew why I was not pleased. You knew what I wanted. Now I can walk the earth in gladness." Atiuch seems to have made men and the animals up above in the sky where he lives, and when he was satisfied with what he had made, he resolved to place them upon the earth. So he called the lightning to put them on the earth, and the lightning caused a cloud to come, and the cloud received what Atiuch had made. But the lightning, acting as he always does, set them down on the earth with a crash, and as the ground was still wet with the water that had covered it, they all sank into the soft earth. This made the lightning feel very badly and he cried, and to this day whenever he strikes the earth he cries. That is what we bear when it thunders.

Now all living things were under the ground in confusion and asking one another what each was, but one day, as the mole was digging around, he broke a hole through, so that the light streamed in, and he drew back frightened. He has never had any eyes since; the light put them out. The mole did not want to come out, but all the others came out on to the earth through the hole the mole had made.

After they had come out from the ground, the people looked about to see where they should go. They had nothing. They did not know what to do, nor how to support themselves. They began to travel, moving very slowly; but after their third day's camp, a boy, who had been left behind asleep at the first camp that they had made, overtook the company, carrying in his arms a large bundle. The people asked him what this was. He replied that when he woke up and found the people gone, he cried to Father for help, and Father gave him this bundle, which had taught him to find the way to his people. Then the people were glad, and said that now they would find the way, and they went on.

After they had gone a long way, they came to a deep ravine with high steep banks, and they could not cross it. There they had to stop. All came to this place, but they could not get over it. They asked the boy what they should do, and he opened the bundle, and out of it came a bird with a sharp bill, the most sacred of all birds, the bone striker. Wherever this bird strikes its bill it makes a hole. This bird flew over the ravine and began to strike the bank with his bill, and flew against the bank again and again, and at last the dirt fell down and filled up the ravine, and made a road for the people to pass across.

A part of them passed over, but before all had done so the road closed up, and the ravine became as it had been at first. Those who were behind perished. They were changed into badgers, snakes, and animals living in the ground.

They went on farther, and at length came to a thick wood, so thick that they could not pass through it. Here they had to stop, for they did not know how they could pass through this timber. Again they asked the boy what should be done, and he opened the bundle, and an owl came out from it, and went into the wood and made a path through it. A number of the people got through the wood, but some old women and poor children were lagging behind, and the road closed up and caught them, and these were changed to bears, wildcats, elks, and so on.

The people went on farther, and came to a big river that poured down and stopped them, and they waited on the bank. When they went to the bundle, a big hawk came out of it. This bird flew across the river and caused the water to stop flowing. They started across the dry river bed, and when part had gone across and were on this side, and some old women and poor children were still in the stream bed, the water began to flow again and drowned them. These people were turned into fishes, and this is why fishes are related to men.

They went on until they came to some high hills called the Blue Mountains, and from these mountains they saw a beautiful country that they thought would be good to live in, but when they consulted the boy who carried the bundle he said: "No, we shall see life and live in it." So they went on.

Soon after this some people began to gamble, and one party won everything that the others had, and at last they began to quarrel and then to fight, and the people separated and went different ways, and the animals, which had all this time been with them, got frightened and ran away. But some of the people still remained, and they asked the boy what they should do, and he went to the bundle and took from it a pipe, and when he held up the pipe the fighting ceased. With the pipe was a stone arrow-head, and the boy told them they must make others like this, for from now on they would have to fight; but before this there had been no war. In the bundle also they found an ear of corn. The boy said: "We are to live by this. This is our Mother." The corn taught them how to make bows and arrows.

Now the people no longer spoke one language, and the eight tribes who had run away no longer understood each other and lived together, but wandered about, and the Mother (Atina) no longer remained with them, but left them alone. The ninth or remaining band—which included the Rees, Mandans, and Pawnees—now left the Blue Mountains and traveled on until they reached a great river, and then they knew what the boy meant by saying, "We shall see life and live in it."

Life meant the Missouri River, and they said, "This is the place where our Mother means us to live." The first night they stayed by the river, but they went off in the morning and left behind them two dogs asleep. One was black, the other white; one was male, the other female. At the third camp they said, "This is a good place; we will live here." They asked the boy what they should do, and he told them that they should separate into three bands; that he would divide the corn among them, and they could plant it. He broke off the nub and gave it to the Mandans, the big end and gave it to the Pawnees, and the middle of the ear he gave to the Rees. To this day the Mandans have the shortest corn, the Rees next in size, and the Pawnees the best and largest. He also took from the bundle beans, which he divided among the people, and the sack of a buffalo's heart full of tobacco.

Here by the river they first planted and ate, and were well off, while the eight bands that had run away were dying of hunger. When they got here they had no fire. They knew nothing of it. They tried to get it from the sun, and sent the swallow to bring it. He flew toward the sun, but could not get the fire, and came back, saying that the sun had burned him. This is why the swallow's back is black today. The crow was sent. He used to be white, but the sun burned him too. Another kind of bird was sent, and he got the fire.

After this they traveled again, and as they traveled they were followed by two great fires that came up on the hills behind them and shut them in, so that they did not know how to escape. The bundle told them to go to a cedar-tree on a precipice, and that if they held fast to this they would not be hurt by these two great bad things. They did so and escaped, but all cedars have been crooked ever since. These two great fires were the two dogs that had been left behind at their first camp. These dogs then came to them and said, "Our hearts are not all bad. We have bitten you because you left us without waking us up, but now we have had our revenge and we want to live with you." But sickness and death have followed the people ever since they first left these dogs behind.

The dogs were taken back into the company and grew old. The female dog grew old and poor, and died first, and was thrown into the river, and after that the male dog died, but before he died they said to him: "Now you are going to die and be with your wife."

"Yes," he replied. "But you will not hate us. From this time you will eat us, and so you will think well of us. And from the female dog's skin has come the squash, and you will like this, and on this account, also, you will not hate us."

So ever since that day dogs have been raised as friends, and afterwards eaten for revenge, because of their treachery.

After this, they looked out on the prairie and saw some great black animals having horns, and they looked as though they were going to attack them. The people dug a hole, and got in and covered it over, and when the buffalo rushed on them they were safe, though their dwelling trembled and the people thought the roof would fall in. Finally someone looked out and saw the buffalo standing around. They did not look very fierce, so forty men, women, and children ventured out, but the buffalo attacked them, tore off their arms and ate them, and tore off their hair. Ever since that time there has been a lock of Ree's hair in the buffalo's mouth, hanging down from his chin.

One handsome young woman was carried off by the buffalo. They held a council to know what they should do with her. She said she could not travel, and they did not wish to kill her. They did not wish to let her go either. But one night when she was sleeping in the midst of the band, a young bull came to her and pulled her sleeve, and told her to follow him, that he would show her the way back to her people. He did so, and his parting words to her were, "Tell your people that we do not like the bows and arrows that they make, and so we have attacked you."

The young woman was gladly received. They asked the boy with the bundle what should be done with the buffalo. He answered, "The buffalo are to be our food. They ate us first, so now we will always follow them for food. We must make arrows like the one we got with the pipe, and fight the buffalo with them." After making many arrows of the flint they use for striking fires, they all came out of the hole in the earth and lived by planting and hunting.

COYOTE'S THEFT OF FIRE

Tradition Bearer: Unavailable

Source: Kroeber, A. L. "Ute Tales." *Journal of American Folklore* 14 (1901): 252–60.

Date: 1900

Original Source: Ute

National Origin: Native American

The Utes territory lay in northern New Mexico, western Colorado, and central Utah. After the arrival of the Europeans, the Utes acquired horses and lived as nomadic hunters and gatherers. There was no real central tribal organization among the various bands of the Utes. Instead, each band had a headman who was agreed upon because of his personal charisma and abilities. The headman had no authority to issue orders or command people or resources. This pattern of leadership is reflected in the following **myth** of "Coyote's Theft of Fire." In the narrative, Coyote's usual **trickster** qualities are apparent only in his deceitful acquisition of fire from an outsider group. Otherwise he is purely a **culture hero**.

Coyote lived with the people of whom he was chief. They had no fire. They gathered large flat rocks and piled them together. Toward evening the racks used to begin to be hot. In the morning Coyote threw water on them; then they steamed, and that made them still hotter. The other people did the same with their heaps. They all used these rocks instead of fire.

Now Coyote was lying on his bed in his tent looking before him. Something fell down in front of him. It was a small piece of burnt rush that had gone up with the smoke and had been carried by the wind. Coyote picked it up and put it away. Without delay he went outside and called to his head men to come. They gathered in his tent. He told them about what had fallen down; he said, "This is what I mean. This is what I want you to look at. Here it is. Look at it. What do you think? Do you know what it is? Where does it come from? I wish that you all speak."

They did not speak. They thought about it and were silent.

Coyote said, "I do not want that you do that. I want you to talk. In order that we may find this out, I wish you all not to be silent."

Then one of the head chiefs said to him, "We do not know what this is."

They all assented.

"Yes," said Coyote.

Then he pointed to one of his men, the Owl. "I select you; bring very many Owls." He sent another to call the Eagle people; one to bring the Crows; one to the Grouse and the Sage-Hens and the Hummingbird tribe. He also sent to the Hawk-Moths, and to all the kinds of birds. They were to send runners to other tribes, and all were to come to him quickly.

Then he said to one man, "My friend, go to the river and get reeds. Bring them here." His friend went to get the reeds. The others went home. Because Coyote had told him to be quick, the one man soon came back bringing reeds. Then Coyote took a stick and crushed the reeds into shreds. He finished this about sunset.

When it was dark he called to his friends to come to him again. Then they came. They did not know his plan, and they asked each other, "Why does he do that?" He had a heap of the shredded bark of the reeds. His friends watched him. In the night he told them to go home. It was late. When he was alone he took dark blue paint; he rubbed the paint and the bark together, and the bark became blue. When he rubbed a long time the bark finally became black. It was black like human hair. Coyote could hardly sleep.

Now it was morning again. After sunrise he called to his friends to come. He put the shredded bark on his head, and it was like long hair reaching down to the ground. When they came he did not look to them like Coyote, but like another person.

Then he asked them, "Who knows why I am doing this? What do you think?"

No one of his friends answered. They all sat still. They did not know what his purpose was. "We do not know what this is," they said. They thought that he asked them merely to trick them, because he himself must know his purpose. Then he sent them home again. When they had gone out he took off his bark hair, wrapped it up, and put it away. Then he thought that the tribes that he had sent for must be coming near. He sent his friends on the hills to look out for them. He told them to go quickly. Then they went as quickly as possible. Coyote hardly slept. He constantly thought about what he had found.

Now some of his people met the various tribes coming. The different people continued to arrive at short intervals from different directions. They were all able men, not the entire people. They came towards his tent. He ordered the arriving tribes to go to the tents of his own people and not to camp separately. "Eat quickly and come to council with me," he told them. They did so.

Then all the head men came. They sat in circles in several rows to listen to Coyote. It was night. Continually he asked the new people what the thing was. He asked them from what direction it came, or whether it came from above. It was laid on something and handed from one man to another. Nobody knew what it was.

When no one knew it, Coyote said, "I intend to hunt up this thing. I shall find out from where it comes, from what tribe it is, or whether it is from the sky. I want you to search, looking where each of you thinks best. That is why I called you. We will start in the morning."

They all said, "Very well, we follow your advice. We will go behind you; we wish that you lead us. That is why we came here."

Now they were ready to start. "Which way would you go?" they asked each other. "I do not know," they said to each other.

Then Coyote spoke, "There is mostly a considerable wind from the West; it does not come from any other direction. I think that is where this thing came from. That is what I think. Let us go there." Coyote took his bark hair by a carrying-thong. Then they started. Then they camped for the night.

That night Coyote had nothing to say. Before it was daylight they went on again. They camped overnight. Coyote said nothing. They went on again.

The third night they camped at the foot of a mountain. Next day they climbed the mountain. They stopped at the crest of the range. Coyote asked his people which was the way to go; but none knew. Then Coyote himself spoke. He saw a mountain. It was far off, so that he could hardly see it. It appeared like smoke. He saw only its summit. "We will go straight to that mountain there," he said. So they went down from their mountain and camped at its foot.

Coyote spoke to them there. "I think the place is much farther. I think it is near the mountain that we saw from the summit. My friends, I shall ask for scouts to go ahead." Then they traveled on, and next camped in the level plain.

Again they travelled a whole day. They approached mountains, and made a camp. Coyote said, "We will stay here. To-morrow I wish some of you to go away to look searching all over the world."

The next day he sent a large Red-tailed Hawk up to search. The Hawk came down again in another place. They went towards him. Before they quite reached him, Coyote, who was anxious, said to him, "What did you see, my friend?"

The Hawk said, "I saw nothing. I became tired. I could not fly higher. I could not see the edge of the earth. I was not high enough."

"Yes," said Coyote. He thought who was the best man to send up. "You go," he said to the Eagle.

"I do not think I will reach there," said the Eagle. Now he started, going up and around, up and around. They could not see him. He was away longer than the Hawk; then he came back. At once Coyote, without waiting, asked him where he had been.

The Eagle said, "I could not go farther. It was hard to go farther. I was tired. I saw nothing. Only I saw that the earth looked a little smoky."

Then the others thought that the Hummingbird was the best to go, and that Coyote ought to ask him. "He could do better than the Eagle."

So Coyote went to the Hummingbird. "Try what you can do, my friend. I think you can do something." The Hummingbird gave no answer; he continued to sit. Then he began to make a noise and flew off. They looked after him, but lost him. They could see him no more. He was away a longer time than the other two birds.

Coyote asked the rest, "Can you see the Hummingbird returning?"

They said to him, "No."

Again he asked them, "Has he not come back yet? Search about! See what has become of him; perhaps he has gone to sleep."

It began to be afternoon when they went away searching. Coyote thought that they were a long time. When they were tired from looking for him, the Hummingbird at last came back. They could hardly see him coming down. They went to him, and all gathered around him.

Coyote said, "Well, my friend, how far were you?"

For a while the Hummingbird sat still; he said nothing. Then he said, "Very well, I will begin to speak now. At the edge of the earth and the sky, where they are together, I saw something standing. It was very far away. Something was there; I do not think we can reach it. It was a dark thing standing up, and the top was bent over. That was all I saw."

Coyote said, "That is what I thought one of you would see. That is what we are going for. It is from this that the thing came which I found." Coyote liked very much what the Hummingbird had seen. He said, "My friend, what you say makes my heart feel good." He was happy and went about among all his people. He could hardly sit still. He did not stay in that place the rest of the afternoon. "We will start and go a distance, then camp again for the night," he said.

Next morning they started again. They went over the mountain and camped at the foot of it on the other side. Again they traveled on and camped in the plain.

The next day they crossed another ridge and camped at its farther side. Then Coyote sent some of his people up again to see how near they had come. He sent the Eagle, thinking he might see it now. Soon the Eagle came down again. "My friend, what did you see?" asked Coyote.

The Eagle said, "I saw nothing. It is very dangerous to go up. It is very difficult." Coyote said to the Hummingbird, "Go again, my friend, and see how far from it we are now."

The Hummingbird flew up again. Soon he came back. All gathered around him. The Hummingbird said, "I saw three mountain ranges this side of it. We are approaching it."

Coyote wished to go on. He started again with his people. They camped at the foot of a mountain. Crossing it, they camped at its farther side. From there they went faster, Coyote leading. They went over another range. Then Coyote said, "We will go on again to the foot of that mountain. That mountain is the last one. We will stop here and wash and become clean and dress. I think there are people where that is which we saw; therefore wash and decorate yourselves."

Then they did so. Coyote, too, adorned himself. He took the bark and put it into his hair. He spread it all around like hair. He parted it in the middle and wrapped up two long strands of it that reached to his feet; he wrapped them with bark. Before he had finished this he sent the Eagle up again. They were on this side of the third range.

Then the Eagle came down again. He said, "We are not very far away now. I saw that which the Hummingbird saw. We are near."

"Yes," they all said.

Then they went to the top of the range. There they counted their people, and divided them into twenties. Each twenty were to go to one tent. Coyote said that he would go to the tent of the head chief, with twenty of his own head men.

They descended the mountain. They came near a village that was on the top of a flat hill.

Then Coyote spoke to his friends, "We have burned nothing heretofore. Our fire was not fire. We have come to fire now. We will stay here two days. It is the fire for which we have come. We will take it away from them. They will have none left here. Where the origin of the fire is, there they will have no more fire. We will take it to the place where we live, and we will possess it in our own land. I will use this hair of mine to take it away from them. I will deceive these people that have the fire. I will tell them that we wish them to make a large fire. I think that is the best way to do it. What do you think?"

"Yes, that is the right way," they said.

Coyote said, "Before we take the fire away from them I shall whoop twice; keep apart by yourselves, ready to go. Do not tell them why we come here. Keep it to yourselves. All of you take my advice: follow it. Do not forget it. We have not the right kind of fire to use, but after we take this we shall possess fire in our land. We will run away. No one of us will stay. I do not think that they will let us escape easily, but they will pursue us and attack us and try to kill us."

"Very well," they said. Then, Coyote going at the head, they went to the first tent, and he asked where the chief lived.

"That is where our chief lives," they said to him, pointing. "Very well, that is where I will live."

Coyote went there. He shook hands with the chief. "My friend, I became nearly exhausted from traveling," said Coyote.

The chief said to him, "Very well. You have reached my house. It is good." All of Coyote's men arrived. "Here are my people. You can go to their tents. You can divide and stay with them," said the chief that owned the fire.

Coyote was there overnight. Then he called to his friends, the head men, to gather at the lodge of the chief.

Coyote spoke first [to the other chief], "Well, my friend, I traveled. I came here without intending anything. I came only to see you. I desire that you all make a dance for me on the second night. I came very far, and I wish to see a dance; that is what all my people like."

The other chief said, "It is good; I am glad that you came for a, dance. I like it. I will make a big dance for you near where I live." Before sunset this council was over.

After it was dark the chief called out to his people concerning the dance, "Make a dance for these people. They like to see our way of dancing." They all assented.

Coyote said that they were to put out all the large fires when they danced. The fires in the tents were also to have water poured on them. They should have only one large fire. Now they began to assemble. There were very many. They were all [gathered] in one place. All the women and children were there. None were left in the tents.

Coyote said, "Let us keep up this fire all the night." Then he unwrapped the bark and spread it. When he put it on, the people thought he was adorning himself for the dance. He danced all night without resting. He danced continually.

At the beginning of daylight he whooped as a signal. Then he said, "I do not mean anything. I only whooped to show that I like this very well, to show that I like this dance. I never had this kind of dance in my land. It makes my heart good to see all these women and fine girls and your way of dancing. I mean nothing wrong."

"Very well," they said.

Then it began to be a little lighter. Coyote got close to the fire and whooped again. He was very close to the fire, dancing about it. Now his people separated from the others; they got ready to start. Coyote took off his bark hair, and seized it in his hands. With it he hit the fire and put it out. The fine shredded bark took all the fire. Coyote was not slow; it was just as he started to run that he hit the fire. He ran as fast he could.

All Coyote's people ran. They made a noise like many horses. There was nothing left for the other people; all the fire was out.

They said, "That is what he intended to do [when he came]; now let us kill all his people." Then they pursued him.

Coyote was already over the ridge. They could not catch him at once. Then Coyote said to the Eagle, "You can run fast; take this, my friend."

"Yes," said the Eagle. So the Eagle carried the fire for a distance. Then the Eagle said to the Hummingbird, "My friend, I am nearly exhausted. You take this."

"Very well," said the Hummingbird, and took the fire.

Coyote was far at the rear of his tribe talking to them. "If any of you are tired, and are exhausted, hide somewhere; in this way you will save your lives. When we get over this adventure we shall be safe. In this way we shall be saved by hiding." He thought that the pursuers would kill anyone whom they ran down.

They continued to exchange the fire as they became exhausted; different birds took it. The Hummingbird said to the Hawk-Moth, "I am nearly exhausted. Take it, my friend. I think you are good yet."

"Very well," said the Hawk-Moth, and took it. Then the Hawks and the various slow birds became exhausted and hid, but the others continued to go on, and at last only the best and fastest birds were left. Coyote saw the other people coming near. He thought who of his people might be the best yet.

Then he selected the Chicken-Hawk as the swiftest, and gave him the fire to carry. Coyote asked his friends if they were tired. Then he took the fire himself and ran with it, telling all his people to run after him as hard as they could.

Then Coyote held it out, saying, "Someone take it quickly!"

And the Hummingbird took it [again] and flew ahead.

"Stop! The fire is nearly out," said Coyote. Then the Hummingbird was angry and gave the fire back to Coyote, though he was already far in the lead. Hummingbird went aside and hid, because he was angry with Coyote. Only four were left now, Coyote, the Eagle, the Chicken-Hawk, and the Hawk-Moth. The rest had scattered as they became exhausted.

The pursuers were near Coyote. They were intending to kill him. The Eagle and the two others became exhausted and hid, and Coyote alone was left, running, carrying the fire. There was a little hill. Coyote ran over the top and went into a hole and closed it up with a stone, so that it looked like the ground. He was inside, holding the fire. Only a little spark of it remained.

Then he came out again, and, changing his direction somewhat, ran through a ravine that he saw. After a while the other people saw him again. Then they commenced to pursue him once more. At last they said to each other, "Let him go. We will cause rain and then snow. We will make a hard storm and freeze him to death and put the fire out." Coyote continued to go, and it began to rain much, just as if water were being poured on him. It rained still more, and soon the ground was as if covered by water. All the hollows were filled, and the valleys were nearly knee-deep with water. Coyote thought that the fire would soon be gone. He thought, "I am carrying this fire now, and perhaps it will go out soon. I wish I could find someone, some animal living in this land." He saw a small hill with a few cedars on it. He thought he might stand on the hill and be safe under the cedars, as the valleys would all be filled with water. So he went towards the hill.

Before lie reached it, he saw a Black-tailed Rabbit sitting right in the water. Coyote said to him: "Quick, my friend! I have been getting fire from far away. I have it now. It is this fire that has brought me into difficulty, that has caused this rain. This fire will kill me. I am tired. You should know something. You should do something. You should know how to save this fire. Perhaps you do know some way. My friend, you must do it. I think you know something." He gave him the fire, holding his hand over it. [There was only a finger's length left.]

The Rabbit took it and placed it right under himself. "Do not do that. You are in the water. It will go out. You will put the fire out," said Coyote. So the Rabbit handed it back to Coyote. When he handed it back to him, more was burning than before. Then Coyote said, "Well, my friend, take it, keep it."

"No," said the Rabbit [who was offended].

But he told Coyote, "There is a cave in the rock over there; go into it. It will be good." "Yes," said Coyote. When he reached the cave, he found some dry sagebrush and dry cedar lying there. Standing by the brush, he thought, "I will make a fire out of this." So he heaped it, and placed the fire under it, and blew. Then it began to burn.

Then he spoke to the dry cedar, "I shall use you. I shall make a large fire out of you. You will be burned." So he piled the cedar on the sagebrush. He had been shivering, but soon the fire made him feel good. When the rain was over, the snowstorm and West wind were to come, the people had intended, and they should freeze him dead.

Now they began. It became very cold. Coyote was in the cave. There was deep water on the ground. This began to become ice. Coyote felt good from the fire. He did not think that he would freeze to death. He began to sleep. During the night he dreamed that it was clear, that everything was gone from the sky, and that there were no clouds. In the morning he awoke. He looked up and saw that the sky was clear, everywhere was ice. Then the South wind came, and the ice all melted.

Then Coyote looked for the Rabbit. He was sitting where he had sat last. Then Coyote shot him and killed him. Then he went back to the cave. He took a piece of old dry sage-brush; he bored a hole through it. Then he filled it with coals of fire, and closed it up. He thought that he could carry the fire safely thus.

A Rock Squirrel with big ears was there. Coyote said to him, "I have killed your friend [the Rabbit], but you will eat him." Then the Squirrel went away.

Then Coyote put the fire under his belt and went away with it. He went away without looking around, and without watching, just as if he were at home. Then he got back home. He laid down his tube of sagebrush containing the fire. He called together the few men who were left home with the women and children. After they came, he took the fire. It looked only like a stick. He took an arrow point and bored a small hole into the stick. Then he whittled hard greasewood. "Now look, you people," he said. He told two men to hold the sagebrush firmly to the ground. Then he bored it with the greasewood, and picked up the borings, and put them into dry grass. Blowing upon this, he soon had a fire. "This dry pine-nut will be burned hereafter. Dry cedar will also be burned. Take fire into all the tents. I shall throw away the rocks. There will be fire in every house." Thus said Coyote.

Now all the birds that had become tired and had hidden arrived. Then they all flew back to the places from which they had come; and from that time on they were birds.

THE CANNIBAL AND HIS WIVES

Tradition Bearer: Unavailable

Source: Kroeber, A. L. "Ute Tales." *Journal of American Folklore* 14 (1901): 280–85.

Date: 1900

Original Source: Ute

National Origin: Native American

The young man of this Ute **myth**, although he is not a candidate for the classic **culture hero** role, does have at least two of the central characteristics of such a figure. Living alone with his mother outside the protection of the band and the leadership of a headman (see "Coyote's Theft of Fire," p. 164, for a discussion of Ute social organization) makes the protagonist a marginal figure. More important, however, is his role of cleansing the environment of monsters, thus making it safe for humanity (compare "Rabbit Kills Big Man-eater," Vol. II, p. 98). The concluding remarks clarify that this is a mythic act that creates a permanent change in the world. The extermination of cannibals by a **culture hero** is not limited to Native American narrative, but is a cross-culturally distributed **motif**.

There was a very large man. He had a big head, a protruding belly, and long feet. He had two wives. They had nothing to eat but ground grass-seed. They lived alone, where they saw no one. There was not even game to hunt. The man said to his wives, "Let us go Eastward again. I am tired of eating this grass-seed. I am tired of seeing no tracks, and of seeing no game; therefore I wish to go east." The next day they moved away. Seeing a mountain, they went up it, then down the other side. They saw a spring and camped there, staying the next day. The man said, "Stay here. I will go on and hunt."

He found the tracks of a man, a woman, and two children. Coming back he said, "I saw the tracks of four persons. I shall go and look for them; perhaps we shall see them living somewhere." Then he went with his wives to where he had seen the tracks. There they saw two antelopes. "Kill them. I am hungry," said one of the women to him.

"No, they belong to him," said the man. They followed the tracks and again camped at a spring. Then the man left the two women after saying to them, "I will go after that man and kill him. I want to eat him. I shall bring him back, and you also will like to eat him." Then he went, watching closely. He saw the man, and shot him. Then he shot the woman and choked the children.

He returned to his women and said, "Let us go there. I have killed them all. We will go to butcher them." So they skinned the man and woman. Then he told one of his wives to skin the boy neatly and carefully. The meat they dried, hanging it up. They stayed there two days. The man ate all the meat. He ate the bones of the feet and every-thing else, throwing nothing away. Then he said, "Stay here; I will travel about to see if I can find anything. I will take the skin of that boy with me."

He ascended a mountain; he peered over the top, but saw nothing. Then he raised his head higher, and saw a tent, with two women and a man near it. He took the stuffed skin of the boy, held it up, and moved it about.

The second time he did so, the man saw it, and said to the women, "A boy is up there. Did you see him? I will go up to him." The cannibal laid the stuffed skin down and hid in the bushes. The man came up and said to the boy, "Who are you? Get up. Can you not sit up?"

The cannibal drew his bow and shot the man. He ran a short way, fell, and died. Then the cannibal went on another hill, and did the same there. He held the boy in front of a cedar and made him wave his hand.

"Did you see that boy? He is over there," said a young man, who was with the women. He went up the hill. The cannibal laid the boy down, and shot this one, as he had shot the other. Thus he had killed two men. Then he showed the boy in another place; but the women did not come to him.

"We will both stay here and wait until the men come," they said. Then the cannibal made a circuit to the other side of the tent. He approached it and again showed the skin.

One of the women saw the boy, and called to him, "Who are you? What tribe are you?" But the man only lowered the boy out of sight, and then made him appear to look again. But the women did not come to him; therefore, he left the hide lying and approached the tent from another side.

He came up to the women. "Where is your husband?" he asked.

They said to him, "He went there after a boy. A young man also went away after that one and has not come back; perhaps the boy was only playing." Then he shot both of the women, one after the other. Taking the stuffed hide, he went back to his tent. He told his wives, "I have killed four pieces of game. Let us remove there." Then they went there and lived in that tent. He said to his women, "Skin this woman well and tan her hide; make it your dress. After three nights, I will go to hunt again." Then they skinned her. They tanned the skin; they made it stiff and crackling. One of them used it for a dress. The cannibal ate one of the men. He put the head into the fire to roast. "Gather the bones and get the marrow," he said. Soon the women were fat from eating grease and marrow.

After the man had slept three times, he said, "I will kill another one for you now. You stay here and I will go hunting." Then he went away, taking the boy's skin. He saw an old man, a woman, and a girl. On the top of the hill, he showed them the boy.

The old man said, "I see a boy there. I will go to see what kind of a boy is there." So he went up and was shot.

Again the man showed the boy in another place. The old woman said, "Let us go to see who the boy is. Perhaps someone is living on the other side of the hill now." Then they both went there. The man put down the stuffed skin and hid behind some cedars. He shot both of the women. Then he went to their tent, but he found no one else there; he had killed all.

He went home and told his women. They all went there. He said to them, "Skin this woman, and make a dress of her. I will skin this old man. I think I like his skin for my blanket." So they skinned them and dried the meat. "Now tan that skin," he said to one of the women. Then she made it stiff. Then he said, "Remain here. I will hunt again."

Again he went, carrying the boy's skin. He went far and found no one. In the middle of the day he became tired. He went to a spring and drank, and lay down with the stuffed hide beside him. He slept. Two men came to drink. They found

175

him with the stuffed skin of the boy. They spoke to each other, and knew that he was a bad man. They fled. Then he shot at them and killed one. The other one escaped. The cannibal went home and said, "I killed one at the spring; let us go there. One of them escaped." The women cried. "Why do you cry?" he asked.

"They said, "Because you let him escape. I want him."

"Oh!" he said. "I will get him later."

The other man fled. He said to the people, "I saw a bad person. He has a big belly, a big head, and big feet. I saw that he had the skin of a boy. He is bad." Then they removed to another camp and told those persons there. These also were afraid, and removed to another place. Thus all went away, being much afraid.

Only in one camp there remained a young man and his mother. All the others fled. His mother said to him, "Let us flee, my son. He is a bad person; he will kill us." He said to her, "O no, we will stay here. I want to talk to that one; I think he is my friend." His mother was much frightened, and continued to tell him to go away. After a while he said to her, "Now, mother, get water in a large basket."

They lived on a slate hill. On the rock he made a small lake with the water that she brought. Ten times she brought him water, and he poured it in. Then he told his mother to grind a basketful of seeds and to cook them. She did this.

She was much frightened. "I am afraid," she said. "I will run away."

He said to her, "No, my mother, do not fear him. Let him come. He will not hurt you. Go and set fire to that cedar so that he will see the smoke, and come to visit us."

The man saw it and told his wives. "Someone is over there. I saw smoke." They said to him, "Good, you will kill him."

He said to them, "I will go there now; perhaps there are many people. I will stay there one night; perhaps I will kill ten. If I do not come back after one night, you must come after me."

Then he traveled fast. He went on a hill and peered over.

The young man was looking for him and saw him. "Look, mother, there is that man," he said.

"Oh, my son, I will run away," said she.

Then the cannibal raised the stuffed skin. The young man cried out, "Why do you do that? Come here, you." So that one left the skin and went there.

His mother said, "He is coming now. Let us run."

"No," said the young man. She ran a short distance. He called to her, "Come back, my mother. Let him come. Give him this food."

Then she came back to him, shaking. Now the cannibal arrived there.

The young man went to him quickly and said, "Well, my friend," and took his hand. "Sit down there," he said to him; and the man with the large belly sat down there. "Are you hungry?" he asked him.

"Yes," he said.

"What do wish? Do you want meat or something else?" he said to him. "Anything," said the man.

"Very well. Do you like this food? It is already cooked," said the young man. Then he gave him a basketful. That one drank it all. "Have you finished?" he asked the man.

He said, "No." Then he gave him another basketful. Again the man drank this off.

The young man said to him, "Where do you live? Where is your tent? What is your purpose in coming here?"

The man said to him, "I live far away. I came here with no purpose."

The young man said to him, "Stay here one night. We will talk together." But that one wished to go back home. The young man said, "Do you wish to urinate or defecate?"

"No," said the man.

"When you wish it, do so there," said the young man to him.

After a little while the man said, "I am full now. I must defecate."

The young man said to him, "Very well. Come. I made a lake over there by urinating."

The cannibal said, "Where shall I urinate?"

"Here," said the young man. Then he said, "I have a pretty eagle here on this cliff. Do you wish to see it?"

Then the large-bellied one lay down and looked over the jutting cliff to see the eagle. The young man threw him down into the lake. He swam around and around. All about him the rock was steep. He could not get out. The young man watched him. Soon he began to be tired. He went down. Then he came up again; he was nearly dead. At last he drowned.

The next day the young man stayed at home. He said to his mother, "Where is your rope? What did you do with it? I wish to pull that man out."

"No. He is a bad man," she said to him.

But he said, "Give me the rope. I will do what is good." She gave him the rope. He went down to the water and tied the legs and the hands of the man. Then he pulled him up. He butchered him, skinned him, and told his mother to dry the meat.

"Why do you do this?" she said.

He said to her, "I think his women will come. We will give them his meat to eat and go outside. We will watch what they do." Then he put the head under the fire in order to cook it. He laid down two large, fat pieces ready cooked. Then he went away behind a rock and watched. He saw two women come.

They saw the meat hanging to dry, and saw the cooked meat lying there. They sat down and ate it greedily, laughing. One of them said to the other, "Perhaps my husband went to kill the others. He has already killed a fat one." Soon they had finished. One of them saw the head covered up in the fire. She said, "See the head. Let us eat it."

Then they took it out. "I want part of it," said the other. Then they cut it in two. They ate it, laughing.

One said, "My husband cooks well."

Then one said, "I am sleepy."

The other one said she was sleepy; so they went to sleep. The young man watched them. One began to sleep lightly. Then she awoke.

She said, "Get up, my sister! My heart is bad, it hits me hard. I think I ate the flesh of my husband."

The other one said, "Yes, I also feel bad. I do not know what is the trouble. I think the same as you think." Now they both cried.

The young man had been watching them. Now he came and they saw him. He said, "What is the matter with you? Why do you not eat this meat hanging here? Your husband has gone away hunting."

They said to each other, "Perhaps he killed our husband."

Then he said to them, "Yes, I killed your husband. He is a bad man. I will kill you also."

"No, do not kill me," they cried.

He said, "No, I will certainly kill you."

"Do not kill me," they said.

Again he said, "No, I will kill you." Then he shot them. He killed them both. He said, "That one has killed many persons, but now he is gone. He is killed. People will not do thus any more: They will be friends and will not eat each other. That one was insane."

HOW THE WHITES BECAME RICH

Tradition Bearer: Unavailable

Source: Kroeber, A. L. "Cheyenne Tales." *Journal of American Folklore* 13 (1900): 177–79.

Date: 1899

Original Source: Cheyenne

National Origin: Native American

The Cheyenne were a nomadic Northern Plains culture who based their way of life on the horse for mobility (after Europeans introduced the modern horse to the Americas), and the buffalo for subsistence. Originally from the Northeast, this Algonquian nation was pushed west where they settled in the area of the Black Hills in the modern Dakotas and Wyoming. Regarding this narrative, anthropologist A. L. Kroeber notes that it "seems probable that we have not a case of adaptation and corruption of a European original, but a native story which for some reason has attracted European additions, perhaps because exceptionally European in spirit" (177).

There was a great medicine-man, who was powerful and did injury, but who had a good daughter. He lived near a geyser, in an earth-lodge. Several young men lived with him, and went out hunting for him. He had great quantities of dried buffalo meat hanging all around his lodge. When meat was scarce in a village nearby, he sent his young men to summon the people to him, and then he gave a feast to the various companies.

Then this great man told the companies to dress, and dance before him. When the dance was almost over, he announced that he would pick out a young man to be his son-in-law.

So he selected a young man, but after the marriage he sent the village away again. He was malicious and did not treat his son-in-law rightly. Every night he had a fire, and slept close by his son-in-law and daughter. When they moved, he raised his head, and said: "Don't stir! Sleep!" When they talked, or even whispered, he made them be quiet, and ordered them to sleep. Even when they were outside, and spoke against him, he was so powerful that he knew it. The first morning he sent his son-in-law out to cut arrows. He told him that if he brought no smooth, straight sticks, he need not come back.

The young man wandered through the woods, but he found only rough sticks, and he was discouraged, and tired, and cried. A person called to him, and asked him why he wept.

The young man related his trouble, and the person told him to cut bulrushes of the right length. So he got as many bulrushes as he could carry, and they turned to smooth sticks. Then he went on up a mountain, and cried again. The birds heard him, and asked him why he cried. He said that he could not get the eagle-feathers that his father-in-law wanted for feathering the arrows. So the eagle shook himself, and feathers flew out, and he got as many as he could use. Then he returned, carrying the sticks and feathers.

His father-in-law had four men who could make bows and arrows, and they began to make the arrows for him. Then he sent his son-in-law to get plums for the arrow-makers. It was nearly winter, and there was no fruit of any sort left, but he told him to get fresh plums, and bring none that were rotten or dried. He knew this was impossible.

The young man took a bag, and went out, crying. Again a person asked him why he wept. The young man said it was because he was to get plums for the arrow-makers of his father-in-law.

The person told him to go to a plum-bush, and that contains foreign elements, these are not the same in different tribes the tree would shake itself, and only fresh plums would fall from it. All this happened.

When the great medicine-man saw his son-in-law returning well loaded, he was pleased and went to meet him. So they made the arrows, and ate the plums. Next morning the great man wanted to play at throwing arrows at a hoop with his son-in-law. They played near the geyser, and the medicine-man pushed his son-in-law into it. Only his bones came out again.

Three times the great man had selected a son-in-law, and all this had happened. His daughter did not like his acts; but even when she went far off to tell her husband of his danger, the great man could hear by the wind or the earth what she said.

The fourth time he got a very fine young man for son-in-law. He sent him out to drive a buffalo of good age immediately in front of his house, so that he could shoot him with his new arrows. The son-in-law went far off, crying. Seven buffalo were about him, and one asked him what he wanted.

The young man told him, but they said they were power-less against this great man, and told him to go farther south. He went on and met four buffalo, who asked him what he wished. But they also were powerless, and sent him farther south. He went on and came to two buffalo. With them the same happened. As he again went on southward, he was so discouraged that he walked with his head down, and when he met a single buffalo, did not stop even when the bull asked him what he wished. Finally he turned around, and told his story. He was hopeless, for the great man could not be cut or burnt or wounded in any way. "He is like this rock," he said, and pointed to a large black stone.

Then the buffalo said: "I will try on this whether I can do anything to him." He went off east, and charged against the stone, but did not injure it. He charged from the south, from the west, from the north—all vainly. The fifth time he went toward the northeast, and this time he broke a piece out of the rock. Then he told the young man to drive him toward his father-in-law's house. They arrived there, both seeming completely tired out; the buffalo pretended to be trying to escape, while the young man headed him off. At last, after a long chase, he drove him near his father-in-law's door. The medicine-man came out with his new arrows, and shot at the bull. When the arrows neared the buffalo, they turned to reeds again, and did not injure him; but to the medicine-man they appeared to enter the bull, and disappear in him. The bull staggered and seemed nearly dead, and the man approached him. The bull staggered farther and farther away from the house, leading the medicine-man with him, so that he might not escape. Then he turned, charged, and tossed him. As the man fell, he tossed him again and again, so that he never touched the ground. Thus he tossed him until he was completely bruised and unable to move.

Then they put him in his lodge, covered him with brush and wood, and lit it. The flames burnt higher and higher, but they only heard the medicine-man inside the fire cursing and threatening them with death when he should come out. Then suddenly there were poppings, and explosions, and beads, diamonds, and precious stones flew out of the fire.

They were afraid to touch these, for fear the man might then come to life again, and put them back into the fire. But the whites to whom some of them flew kept them, and thus became richer.

CROSSING THE PLAINS FROM KENTUCKY

Tradition Bearer: Annie Cason Lee

Source: Wrenn, Sarah B. "Interview of Annie Cason Lee." American Life Histories: Manuscripts from the Federal Writers' Project, 1936–1940. Manuscript Division, Library of Congress. 12 October 2005. http://memory.loc.gov/ammem/wpaintro/wpahome.html.

Date: 1939

Original Source: Northern Plains

National Origin: European American

The following set of **legends** offers an insight into the crossing of the Plains in the mid-nineteenth century from the perspective of a young woman. The following set of narratives is equally valuable for the insights it provides into the **family saga**.

My parents, who crossed the plains to Oregon in 1853, were originally from Kentucky. They then had five children, of which one was my sister Miranda. She was a very beautiful girl, quite young, I think not more than fifteen. I remember hearing them tell (There were twelve of us and I was one of the younger ones—born in Oregon) of an outstanding incident of their trip, in the Snake river country.

The Indians, while not yet utterly hostile, were not very friendly, with tactics that harassed and worried the emigrants considerably. Every once in a while a bunch of mounted braves would bear down upon the train and demand tribute of anything that took their fancy. It seemed my father had an especially good knife of the hunting or skinning variety. He had this knife in his hands, doing something with it, when one of the Indians, a chief, or at least the leader of his gang, reached down and snatched it out of his hands. Of course there was nothing the white men could do under such circumstances, but, as the saying now is, grin and take it. In that case, however, it was the Indian who took. Then the Indians caught a glimpse of this pretty sister of mine. They decided they wanted her too. They offered to buy her, however, and it took a lot of diplomacy and tact to get out of a most unpleasant situation, and from that time on whenever Indians came in sight, Miranda was hidden down in a little hole they arranged for her, in the bottom of the wagon.

As you can imagine, such a way of hiding was far from comfortable for Miranda at times. It was when they were fording the Snake River that mother and the children had a terrifying experience, which, looking back at it from today, seems strange.

They reached the fording place late in the day, and, owing to the nearby annoying Indians, were anxious to get on the other side without delay. When the wagons crossed—the women and children being floated across in wagon boxes, made water-proof for that purpose—mother and her children were left on the bank, to be carried over later.

In the crossing there was trouble with the stock, and other things of an unforeseen nature happened, and before it was realized darkness had settled down—and there was mother and her little folk, with no food and no protection from the cold, and unfriendly Indians lurking in the background. To attempt to cross the river, cold and swift as it was, in the darkness, was suicide.

There was nothing to do but wait till morning, with what feelings may be imagined. Mother always said it was nothing but her trust in God that helped her live through that awful night, as the children and she crowded close together for warmth and comfort, in a silence that formed their only protection from the redskins. At the break of day, of course, they were rescued.

It was late in the autumn when they arrived in Portland, where they camped on what is now the block just north of the civic auditorium.

Father was a stone mason. He took up a donation land claim in what is now Montavilla, one of his boundary lines running east for a mile along the Base Line, and then one mile north.

Father and mother were both very religious, but they were Southerners and they, or at least father had the fiery southern temper. Mother was a charter member of the Centenary Methodist church on East Stark, which was organized at our home at East Sixth and Pine streets. This recalls a story that father never liked very much being reminded of, but the family always, in after years, got quite a laugh out of it.

The incident occurred sometime after the Stark Street ferry was in operation under Captain Foster, who was quite a friend of father's. Father, with one of my older sisters was going over to the Taylor Street Methodist Church. They were descending the ferry slip, and were all ready to step aboard the ferry, when the boat pulled out suddenly, leaving them standing there—and already late for church. Father was furious. He was short and thick-set, with a bull-like neck, and when he was mad he was awful mad.

He shook his fist at Captain Foster, up in the pilot-house, and, I guess, Captain Foster must have laughed, for when he returned to the east bank, father was madder than ever and didn't hesitate to let the world know. The men exchanged ugly words, and one thing led to another, until finally they were at it, hammer and tongs. Foster tried to stick his thumb in father's eye, in good old frontier-fight fashion, and father grabbed the thumb in his mouth and bit it nearly off. By this time there was a big bunch of spectators, and of course they interfered and separated the two men, and Father, still sputtering, finally returned home, all torn and bloody, and far from looking the respectable, Christian church attendant who had left the house an hour or so earlier. You'd have thought those two men would have been enemies ever after, but they weren't. The next morning, when father boarded the ferry, he said "Hello, Cap," and Captain Foster grinned and responded, "Hello, Cas," and that was the end of it.

Father never drank, but he came of a race of drinking men, and he must have liked the taste of liquor. Anyway he was afraid of it. During his life-time he always kept a diary. There were a lot of these in mother's possession after his death. If I had them I could give you a priceless store of folklore and anecdotes, but mother made me promise to burn them at her death and I did. I think one reason she wanted them destroyed was father's frequent allusion to being tempted of the devil. Over and over again this entry occurred, "Tempted of the devil today." Once, when he was custodian of a warehouse where liquor was stored, the odor was almost too much for him, so I have been told, and he got down on his knees and prayed for strength to resist the temptation. Well, since he did resist, I think those entries, "Tempted of the devil today," are something to be proud of, and I've sometimes been sorry I destroyed the diaries.

HEROES, HEROINES, TRICKSTERS, AND FOOLS

YOUNG MEN WHO KILLED THE HORNED SERPENT
AND RELEASED THE BUFFALO

Tradition Bearer: Unavailable

Source: Kroeber, A. L. "Cheyenne Tales." *Journal of American Folklore* 13 (1900): 179–81.

Date: 1899

Original Source: Cheyenne
National Origin: Native American

The original lifestyle of hunting and gathering cultures on the Great
Plains used dogs for traction. As a result, tipis were small for transport
by dogs because they could not travel far in a day. Therefore, bands had
to remain close to timber and water. There was buffalo hunting on the
Plains before the acquisition of the horse, but in the pre-horse culture
this was a seasonal activity only. This stage of Cheyenne pre-horse culture is described in the following **myth**. The communal hunt required
careful preparation and close supervision in order to insure that as much
meat as possible would be taken. The cautions about controlling dogs

and proper actions and words in the following narrative allude to these precautions.

Far away there was a large camp-circle. Food was very scarce, and some persons had starved. One day one of the old men went about inquiring whether the people wanted to travel to a large lake, where ducks and game abounded. They moved camp, packing their goods on dogs.

Two young men were sent ahead, but they returned with the news that they had found no game whatever. The children were all crying for food, and the misery was extreme. The people selected two strong young men able to travel four days without food, and told them that they must find something for the whole tribe, and bring back good news.

The young men set out and travelled steadily for two days, until they were worn out and slept from the middle of the night until the morning star rose. Then they went on northward again.

Finally they came near a large river, and beyond it they saw a blue mountain. The river was slow, smooth, wide, and sandy on both sides, but beyond it rose bluffs, and close behind these the mountain. The two scouts put their clothes on their heads, and entered the river. In the centre, one of them got stuck fast. He shouted that some powerful thing under water was taking him; and he asked his friend to tell his parents not to weep too much for him. The other man crossed in safety. Then his friend called to him to come back and touch him as a farewell. So the other went back into the river, and touched him.

Then he went out again, and cried all day, wandering about. A person came to the top of the bank above the river, and asked him why he cried, and whether he could do anything for him. The young man replied that a powerful animal was holding fast his friend in the river, and pointed to him.

The person who had come was powerful; he wore a wolf skin, painted red, on his back; it was tied around his neck and waist, so that he looked like a wolf; and he carried a large knife. He dived into the river, and the water moved and waved, and finally an immense snake with black horns came up, and he cut its throat. The man who had been held fast was already cold and stiff in his legs, but the two others dragged him off, and floated him ashore, and laid him in the sun.

The rescuer told the other young man: "Go to the mountain, to its stone door, and tell your grandmother that I have killed the animal that I have been after so long."

The young man ran to the foot of the mountain, stood before a flat stone door, and called as he had been told, telling the woman to bring a rope with her. The old woman was glad that the animal had at last been killed.

The young man ran back, and was told by the man to help him butcher the snake; then they would carry his friend to his house. They dragged the snake on shore by its horns, and cut it in two, and then into many smaller pieces. They made many trips to the mountain, carrying the meat.

Inside, the mountain was like the interior of a tepee, with tent-poles, beds, and so on. Then the young man carried his friend to the mountain, taking him on his back, and holding his hands. The woman made a sweat-house, and he was put into it. The woman told him to try to move. The second time they poured water on the hot rocks he moved a little, the third time more, and after the fourth time he was perfectly well.

Then they went into the mountain, and the man told his daughter to cook food,—corn and buffalo meat. This was the first time the young men had seen the daughter, who was very handsome. They ate all the food given them, and were well satisfied. Then the woman asked them why they had come. They told her that they were looking for game for their starving people.

The woman said: "It is well, you will have something for your tribe." Then she asked them what kin they would be to the girl; whether they would be her brothers. While they conferred, she said that they could marry her. The other young man proposed to the one that had been fast that he should marry her; and the latter agreed. They were then all very grateful to each other, and the young man married the girl.

The woman told her daughter to take the two young men to the herd of buffalo, and the girl showed them large herds of buffalo, and on the other side wide fields of corn. Then the woman told them to cross the river in the same place as before, and not to look backwards, and to rest four times on their way home. So they travelled for four days.

Then an old man cried through the village that they were coming. All their relatives and many others came forward; but when they saw that there were three persons, they held somewhat aloof. They entered a tent, and the new husband told an old man to cry to the people to come to shake hands with his wife and embrace her. This was done, and then the young man said that he brought good news, and that that same night his wife's herd would come from the mountain.

At night long strings of buffalo came, and the people heard them on all sides. Early in the morning they saw the buffalo, as far as they could look. It was announced that the dogs were not to disturb the game. Then the hunt commenced. The buffalo ran when pursued, but always came back. As many were killed as could be used, and there was abundance of meat. The chiefs gathered, and resolved that they were thankful to the girl for her kindness, and every family was to bring her a present, the best that they had; and they asked her to take the presents to her parents. So all gave to her, and she started back to her parents with her husband and his friend.

When they arrived at the mountain, the man stood there, calling to his wife to come out, for their son-in-law had returned. She embraced the two young men from joy and gratitude. When they returned, the tribe was still hunting successfully, and they were again given presents to bring to the girl's parents.

When they brought presents a second time, the man was still more grateful, and asked his daughter to take a few ears of corn to the tribe. But she, thinking that they had enough with the buffalo, was silent. When her parents asked her why she did not answer, she told them the reason. So they returned, after her parents had warned her not to feel sorry for any buffalo killed in her sight. Soon after, the children drove a young calf toward the village, and the boys shot at it, and it died in front of her tent.

As she came out, she said to herself that she pitied the calf. But as she said it, the herd ran back toward the mountain, and nothing could be seen but dust. A crier went about, saying that presents must again be sent to the old man in the mountain. After prayer and with blessings, the two young men and the girl started once more. After four days they arrived.

At once the old man told his daughter that she ought to have been careful. But he would not let them return to the tribe. The parents of the young men and their relatives felt lonely at the long absence, and went out alone to cry. But the young men never returned.

THE STONE BOY

Tradition Bearer: Unavailable

Source: Wissler, Clark. "Some Dakota Myths II." *Journal of American Folklore* 20 (1907): 199–202.

Date: ca. 1900

Original Source: Ogalala Lakota (Sioux)

National Origin: Native American

The sweat lodge used for healing and ritual purification is found throughout Native North America and is likely, according to some sources, to have been brought across the Bering Strait during migrations of the ancestors of the Native Americans into the New World. As described in the **myth** of the **culture hero** Stone Boy, heated stones (regarded as the "bones" of Mother Earth) are piled inside a covered structure and water is poured over them to produce steam. The emergence from the lodge can be symbolically interpreted as a rebirth reflecting the literal birth of Stone Boy and rebirth of three brothers and four uncles in the course of the following narrative.

Four brothers lived together in the same tipi. One day a strange woman came and stood outside. They sent the youngest brother out to see what it was that stood outside. The youngest brother went out to see, and came back with the information that a woman was standing there. Then the eldest brother said to the youngest, "Call her your sister and invite her inside."

When she was invited she hesitated. She kept her face hidden in her robe. The brothers were cooking buffalo tongues for their meal. They gave some of these to the woman, but she turned her back while eating them so as not to show her face.

After a while the three older brothers went out to hunt. The youngest brother was curious to see the face of the woman. So he went to the top of a high hill and sat down. Then he left his robe on the hill and changed himself into a bird. He flew to the tipi and sat upon the poles at the top. He began to sing and to peck upon a pole, looking down at the woman.

Now she had her face exposed, and he saw that it was covered with hair. Spread out before her was a robe with a row of scalps half way around it. The woman heard the bird pecking on the poles above, and looking up said, "You bad bird, go away."

Then she began to count the scalps in the row, and, talking to herself, said, "I will take the scalps of these four brothers and fill out this row with them in the order of their ages, beginning with the oldest."

Now when the little bird heard this he returned to the hill, resumed his former shape, and waited for his three brothers. When he saw them coming he went out to meet them. He related what he had seen. Then they planned to take a pack strap and boil it so as to make it weak and soft. When this was done they gave it to the woman and sent her out for wood. Now when the woman had gone they took up the bundle she had brought with her and in which she kept the robe with the scalps and tossed it into the fire. Then the brothers went away.

The woman gathered together some wood, but every time she tried to tie it up with the pack strap the strap broke. At last she became very angry and said, "I will kill the brothers." So she returned to the tipi, but found the brothers gone and her bundle burned up. She was very angry.

She thrust her hands into the fire and pulled out the robe. Then she took up a large knife, tied an eagle feather on her hair, and started in pursuit of the brothers. As she was very swift, she soon over-took them, and, shaking the knife at them, said, "I will kill you."

All of the brothers shot arrows at her, but could not hit her. She came up, knocked down the oldest, then the second in order, and then the third. The youngest brother stood far off, with a bow and arrows in his hands.

The woman ran at him, but a crow that was flying around over his head said, "Young man shoot her in the head where the feather is."

The young man did as directed, and killed the woman. He beheaded her and buried the body. Then he made a fire, heated some stones, and made a sweat house. When this was done, he dragged his three dead brothers into the sweat house, where he began to sing a song and beat with a rattle. Then he poured water upon the heated stones, and as the steam began to rise one of the brothers began to sigh. Then all of them sighed. When the youngest brother poured more water upon the stones, the three brothers came to life again. They all returned to their tipi.

One day another young woman came and stood outside of the tipi as before. The youngest brother looked out and said, "My sister, come in."

This woman did not hide her face. After a time she said, "Have you any brothers?" The youngest brother told her that he had.

The youngest brother cooked some buffalo tongues and gave one to the woman. She thanked him for this and. they talked pleasantly together.

Now the brothers were out hunting for buffalo as before, and the youngest went out to the top of a high hill and left his robe, became a bird, and sat upon the poles on the top of the tipi. He pecked at the poles.

The woman looked up and said, "Get away from here. You will spoil my brother's poles." Looking down the bird saw a row of moccasins laid out in front of the woman. She put her hand upon one pair saying to herself, "These are for the oldest." Then she took up another pair, saying, "These are for the next of age." So she went on until all were provided for.

Then the bird flew back to the hill and became a boy again. When he met his brothers, he related to them what he had seen. They were all happy. They had as much buffalo meat as they could carry, and when they came into the tipi the woman said, "Oh my, you are good." At once she began to dry and cook meat.

One day the oldest brother went out to hunt, but did not return. The following day the next in order of age went out to search for him, but he never came back. Then the next went out, but he also failed to come back. Then the youngest went out to look for his brothers, and as he did not come back the woman began to cry. She went out to the top of a hill and found a nice smooth round pebble there. So she slept at that place one night and then swallowed the pebble. When she reached the tipi her abdomen had become very much distended. After a little while she gave birth to a child. It was a boy.

As this boy grew up he always wanted a bow and arrows. And when he got them he was always shooting at birds and small animals. At last he became a tall man. Some of his uncles' arrows were still in the tipi, and one day, as he took them down, his mother related the fate of his four uncles. When the young man heard this story he said to his mother, "I shall find them."

"No, you are too young," said his mother.

"No, I am old enough," said the young man.

So the young man started out to search for his uncles. After a time he came to a high hill, from the top of which he saw a little old tipi. He went up to it and looked in at the door. He saw a very old woman in-side.

When the old woman saw him she said, "Come in, my grandchild; come in and break my ribs."

As the young man entered, the old woman stooped over toward the ground, and the young man kicked her with his foot until all her ribs were broken. At last, as he kicked, one of the ribs turned inward and pierced the old woman's heart. This killed her. Looking around inside the tipi, the young man saw the skeletons of many people. These were killed when breaking the old woman's ribs, because the last rib when broken turned outward and pierced the heart of the kicker. But this young man, who was called the Stone Boy, could not be killed in that way.

Among the skeletons in the tipi were those of the four uncles of the Stone Boy. He looked over the bones, then went outside, made a sweat house, and heated some stones. Then he took the bones into the sweat house, sang some songs, and beat with a rattle as his uncle had done. When he poured water on the stones and the steam began to rise, the dead all came to life. The Stone Boy addressed his uncles and said to them, "You are my four uncles who went away and never came back. Now I shall take you home with me."

One day Stone Boy said to his mother, "I am going out in this direction" (pointing to the left).

"No," said she, "you must not go that way, for it is dangerous."

"Yes, but I am going that way," said he. This was in the winter. He came to a very high hill where four girls were sliding down on the snow.

"Come chase us," said they. Stone Boy sat down behind them on the piece of raw hide they were sliding with. At the bottom of the hill they ran against a bank and Stone Boy bumped the girls so hard that they were killed. Then he went home.

After a time he went out on another journey, and saw an old buffalo bull hooking at a rock. Stone Boy stood watching him for a while and then said, "What are you doing there?"

The buffalo replied: "A man named Stone Boy killed four girls. These girls were four white buffalo, and now all the buffalo are hunting for Stone Boy. So I am practicing my horns on this rock, because Stone Boy is very hard to kill. When winter comes, we shall go out to hunt for Stone Boy."

"I am the one you are looking for," said Stone Boy to the buffalo, as he shot an arrow into his heart.

Then Stone Boy went home, and told his four uncles that they should gather together a lot of brush, because the buffalo were coming, and they would cover the earth. With the brush they built four fences around their tipi. Then the buffalo came. Stone Boy and his uncles shot down many of them with their arrows, but the buffalo tore down one fence after the other until just one remained. But so many buffalo had been killed by this time that the leader of the herd called the others away, and Stone Boy and his uncles were left to live in peace.

THE STORY OF NO-TONGUE

Tradition Bearer: James Holding Eagle

Source: Will, George F. "No-Tongue, A Mandan Tale." *Journal of American Folklore* 26 (1913): 331–37.

Date: 1913

Original Source: Mandan

National Origin: Native American

The Mandans were sedentary farmers who depended primarily on vegetable crops and only secondarily on buffalo and other animals. They lived in villages on the northern Great Plains consisting of earth lodges that measured from forty to eighty feet in diameter. They often selected locations protected on two sides by steep river banks, and to protect the open sides they built stockades of upright posts surrounded by a ten to fifteen feet–wide ditch. Care for the members of one's family was especially important to the Mandan, which made the cannibalism with which the following narrative begins particularly offensive to the group's moral codes. In order to gain access to the supernatural power that was necessary for any enterprise, the Mandan, like many other Native American cultures, pursued a personal vision quest. The ordeal of No-Tongue in obtaining the aid of the Sun and the Moon is only slightly more extreme than the reports of the usual quest. According to the commentary of folklorist George F. Will, this type of story is what is called by the Mandans "a 'four-nights' story;' that is, one which takes for the telling four long winter evenings, when the young people gather around the old lady after the evening work is done" (331).

At a certain village headed by a certain chief there once lived a man and his wife and their two children,—the elder a girl; the other one (some two years younger), about seven or eight years old, a boy. The woman used to leave the village and go into the woods to do her work of preparing and dressing hides. One day the man followed her to a lonely spot in the woods, and killed her. He cut off one leg, and hid the rest of the body. The leg he smeared with the hair and blood of a deer, then he built a fire and cooked it.

After a while, the two children came that way, and their father gave them their mother's flesh to eat. Then he left them and went back to the village. After a while, the children also returned to the village. There they found themselves avoided by all. Their father had given out the report that they had killed their mother and eaten her flesh.

The chief soon called a council to decide what should be done with the children. After some debate, it was determined that they should be taken by the police (military society) out into the woods and lost. So the next day the police took the two children a long ways into the woods, and left them there without food. The children wandered around for several days, living on berries and such roots as they could find. Then, finally, they made their way back to the village again. Once more the children were taken far into the woods and abandoned by the police; but after much suffering, they returned once again to the village.

193

Then a council was again called; and it was decided, at their father's urgent plea, to lose the children once more, and then to leave the village, and move inland for a long stay. So once more the children were taken far into the woods and left; and that night all the inhabitants of the village packed up their belongings and went away.

The boy and girl wandered around for many days, barely subsisting on berries and roots. Then, at last, hungry and tired, they got back to the village, only to find it deserted, with no food to be found. They cried about the village for some time, and at last found the trail that their people had left. This trail they followed for several days, and finally, exhausted and almost dead with hunger, came to the tepees of their people. It was evening, and they ventured to enter an old and much worn tepee on the outskirts of the camp. Within was a poor old woman. When she saw them, though she recognized who they were, she felt sorry, and asked them in and gave them food.

Then she told them that she would hide them for a day or so, but that all the people were against them, and they must go away. She told them to go back to the village on the river-bank, and told them how to find her house. In the house, she said, was a cache; and she gave directions for finding it. In the cache were corn, beans, squashes, and fat, with dishes, robes, and such utensils as were needed for sewing and cooking. In some way, however, the presence of the children in the camp was suspected; and the police were sent around to search every tepee. When they came to the old woman's house, she sat by the door. They asked her if the children were inside, and she did not answer. Then they entered, and found them.

The chief and the head men debated for a long time as to what should be done with the boy and girl this time; and finally it was decided to send them back to the old village with the police, and give orders to have them killed there. So, on the following day, the police took the two and went back. But when they came to the village, they felt sorry for them and did not want to kill them. So they rolled the two children tightly in a large heavy hide, and bound it firmly round the middle with a thong. The bundle thus made they placed on the very edge of a high, steep bank, at the base of which were many stones. To the bundle they fastened another cord, which they tied to a stake, so that, if the bundle rolled off, it would hang suspended over the edge of the bank.

Thus they left the children, who could do nothing to help themselves, and who were so placed that the slightest stirring might cause them to go over the edge. The boy and girl cried almost continuously, stopping only now and then to caution each other against struggling or moving. A long time they lay thus, weeping, and wondering what they had done to deserve such a fate. Then by and by they heard a crying from the direction of the village. At first they thought that it was people; but as it came nearer, they recognized it as the howling of a dog.

It was a very old dog, whose teeth were nearly worn out; and she was very weak. The dog came up, and began to chew on the thong that fastened the children to the stake. She chewed for a long time, crying, and resting occasionally; and all the time the children were fearful, lest they be pushed over the edge. Finally the dog began to chew on the thong that bound the hide, and the children were still more fearful. But, as the dog chewed, she pulled on the bundle, and gradually drew it back from the edge of the bluff. At last she broke the thong, and the hide loosened. The little girl was able to get out, and help the little boy out.

Then they started back to the village to look for the old woman's house; and as they went along, the old dog (which they had thankfully petted and caressed) followed them. They had no trouble in finding the old woman's house, and they found the cache just as she had described it. From it they got robes, utensils, and food enough to last them for some time; and the old dog was not forgotten.

For a long time they lived thus in the old woman's house, going out in the daytime to gather roots and berries, and returning at night. After a time, however, the weather began to grow colder; and the girl suggested that they go down into the bottom-land and build them-selves a winter house in the woods. So they went down, and built a very little house,—just big enough for themselves and the dog. They built it just like the earth lodges, with a frame of poles covered with grass and then with earth; and in it they were snug and warm.

By this time, however, their food taken from the cache was gone, and they began to be very hungry. All the berries were dried up; and they could not dig roots, because the ground was frozen and the snow was coming. So they had to live entirely on the berries from the wild roses. They lived thus for some time. Every day, as they went out to gather rose-berries, they noticed how thick the rabbits were: so one day the little boy told his sister to make him a bow. The next day the sister worked at the bow, and finally succeeded in making a small one that he could handle. Then the little boy went out with his bow, and practiced a great deal. Finally, on the first day, he managed to kill one rabbit, which he took home to his sister. She dressed the rabbit, and saved the skin. After this, the boy kept on hunting with his bow, and soon became a good hunter, and would bring in a number of rabbits every day.

Thus they lived along comfortably for some time, together with the old dog. One day the boy got close to a wolf on the edge of the bank, and managed to kill it. He dragged it home, and they made a robe from its hide.

One day, after thinking for a long time, the girl told her brother that she thought he ought to go up on the hill and fast and pray, as the warriors do. In that way, they might get many good things, and good spirits would come to him. The boy did not understand what she meant at first; but she explained it to him, and he agreed to go. They had plenty of rabbits on hand, so that he did not need to hunt.

So the sister took the rabbit-skins and made him warm mittens and other warm things to wear, for it was very cold. Then she told him to remember whatever appeared to him, and, if he was asked for anything, he must at once give it. So, after dressing warm, he went up on a high hill before sunrise, and stood there all day, fasting and praying. Meanwhile the sister sat at home in the house. She was sorry for her brother, all alone and cold on the hill, and he was so little. And she cried all day.

When he came back at night, she asked him if he had seen anything; but he said that he had not. The next day he went again, very early, as before, and stood on the hill all day; and his sister staid at home and cried. That night, when his sister asked him if he had seen anything, he said that he had. He said that two men came to him out of the air, just as the sun was coming up. One of them asked him for something; but he did not just understand him, and, before he could answer, the man said to his companion, "He does not want to give it." And they disappeared before he could answer. As they went away, they sang a song.

The next morning the little boy prepared to go up on the hill again. His sister told him, if the men came again, to quickly give them what they asked for. So he went up on the hill, and again the men came just as the sun was rising. One man asked him for his tongue. The little boy took his knife with one hand, and tried to pull out his tongue with the other. But it always slipped from his fingers, and he could not hold it. And again the two men disappeared. As they went, they sang the same song.

When the boy told his sister what had happened, she got a little stick and made it very sharp. In the morning, when the little boy was ready to go up on the hill, she gave him the stick, and told him to stick it through his tongue when the men came, and then he could pull it out and cut it off easily. So the little boy went up on the hill; and his sister cried and cried at the thought of her poor little brother having to cut off his tongue. The men came once more, just at sunrise; and one of them again asked the little boy for his tongue. He pierced his tongue with the sharp stick, and thus was able to pull it out. He cut it off and handed it to the man. Then the man said, "That is a brave man! No one can get the best of him." And he said to the boy, "I will make you a great hunter and warrior, and *you* will be very powerful." Then the two men went away as before, singing the same song.

The little boy went back to his sister, crying, and with the blood running out of his mouth and over his clothes. His sister cried more than ever when she saw him. But she washed him up, and made him as comfortable as she could. He felt very bad for several days, but after that he was all right again.

One night there came two strange persons to their lodge, and the boy asked his sister to wait on them. After eating, these men went out without saying a word to them. Then the boy began to hunt again, and one day, on the edge of a high bluff, he met two men. They spoke to him, and said that they were the two men who came to his lodge one night, and they said they had a nice meal. They told him that they had been killed under that bluff, and that they made their home there now; that they knew all the hardships that he and his sister had endured; and that they were the ones who helped them get through all this hardship. They continued to talk to the boy, saying they knew that two persons had, come to him when he was on the hill. The one that had promised to make him powerful was the Sun, they said, the other one was the Moon. The Sun would do all that he had promised; but No-Tongue must be very careful, for the Sun wanted him to die young. The Moon, they said, would help him, and keep him from being killed.

Then the two men said they would continue to help No-Tongue (for such he was henceforth called) and his sister. They told him that they would get all the spirits together, and make a big buffalo corral. They said he must go out and pick out a place for the corral on the next day, and then come and show them where it was. After this, the two men went away.

On the following day, No-Tongue went out and picked a place for a corral in a deep coulee, ending in a sort of pocket. Then he took the men to see the place. They told him that he and his sister must stay in the house the next day while the spirits built the corral. So the next day the boy and the girl staid in the house. Toward evening, the two men came to them, and told them that the corral was done. But they said that the scaffolds for the meat were to be built the next day, in the woods around the house, and that they must neither go out nor look out.

On the following day, then, the two remained shut up in the house again. And all day they heard a great clamor, chopping and hammering, and the sound of many voices, laughing, joking, and giving directions to one another. At night they went out, and saw new meat-scaffolds in every direction as far as they could see. Then the two men came again, and told the children that the first drive would be made on the next day, and that a drive would be made on each day for four days. During this time, the children must remain inside; but each night some of the choicest meat would be placed at their door. Also there would be a white buffalo each day in the herd, and the skin would be placed each night at the door. The rest of the meat would be placed on the scaffolds. The two men said that all the birds were going to help them drive the buffalo into the corral.

For the next four days the children remained inside, as they had been told. Each day they heard a great noise of birds and the tramping and bellowing of the trapped herds; and each night choice pieces of meat were placed at the door, where they could reach them from within.

On the fifth day, the children came out of the lodge and found the scaffolds everywhere covered with meat, ready cut up, and hung up out of reach of the wolves. At their door they found the four white buffalo-skins. They talked over for a long time what they should do with these skins. Finally they decided to save three of them to give to the chief of their people. The other one they gave to the old dog who had saved their lives, and had since been so faithful to them. They fixed up a nice soft bed of it for her.

Soon the two men came again to the children. They told No-Tongue that his people were starving, and that they were going to try to come to their old village on the river again. They told the children to prepare everything, and get ready to receive their people and divide the meat among them.

Meanwhile the people out on the prairie broke camp, and started to move back. They were nearly starved, and had to travel very slowly on account of the old people, the women, and the children, who were hardly able to walk. The chief decided to send a party ahead to try and find some food: so nine of the young men were picked, and they went on ahead as fast as they could. The young men came to the village after a long, hard march. The two men had told the children of their coming, and the children had everything ready to receive them. The young men came to the edge of the bank, and saw the smoke from the children's house. They wondered who it could be, living there in the woods. They feared it might be enemies; but they were so hungry that they decided to go and find out anyhow. So they started out, and soon came to the children's house. It was now night. The children invited them in, and gave them the food prepared. The two men had given No-Tongue full instructions as to what he should do and what was going to happen all the time.

On the following day, the children gave the young men what pemmican they could carry to take back to the rest of the people.

They traveled fast, and got the pemmican back to their people as quick as they could. All were nearly starved, yet the pemmican magically increased as it was used up, until everyone was fully fed.

After being thus refreshed, and having heard the young men's story of the abundance of food at the children's camp, the people pressed on rapidly.

The two men kept No-Tongue warned as to the movements of the people, and told him what to do when they came. So the two children, at the suggestion of the men, prepared a great pot of soup, for their father, when he should come to their house. At last the people arrived and the children received them. Then No-Tongue divided the scaffolds of meat, giving an allotted portion to each household. To the chief he also gave the three white-buffalo robes. After this, the father came to the house of the children. To him they gave the soup, and kept urging him to eat, until he had finished it all. In his half-starved condition, the effects were deadly. The father began to be sick before he left their house, and he died before he could get back to the place where the people were camped.

For several days the people were busy taking care of their meat. Then they moved back to the old village on the bluff. The chief was very good to No-Tongue, and wished him to marry his daughter and take his own house, saying that he would build himself a new one. Shortly after the people moved back to the village, No-Tongue and his sister moved back also, taking with them the faithful old dog.

No-Tongue caused it to be announced that he wished to find out to whom the old dog belonged. Then he led her out into the open place in the village, and all the old women assembled there. They each took their turn, calling to the dog and talking to her; but she lay drowsing, and paid no attention to any of them.

Finally all had tried, but one very poor old woman. She declared she did not believe that it could be her dog; for her dog was so old that it must have died long ago. However, her friends persuaded her to try. She went out and spoke to the dog from quite a distance, and the dog paid no attention. Then she approached nearer and called, and the dog roused up. Still nearer she went, and kept calling. The dog stood up, and, as the old woman approached, ran to her with every sign of gladness and recognition. So to this old woman, No-Tongue gave the white-buffalo robe that had been allotted to the old dog.

THE FURTHER ADVENTURES OF NO-TONGUE

Tradition Bearer: James Holding Eagle

Source: Will, George F. "The Story of No-Tongue." *Journal of American Folklore* 29 (1916): 402–6.

Date: ca. 1916

Original Source: Mandan

National Origin: Native American

The following is a continuation of "The Story of No-Tongue" (for background, see p. 192), in which he grows to become a prominent war leader. His supernatural helpers appear again and the two strange men's prophecies about No-Tongue's spirit helpers come to pass. No-Tongue's "spirit father," the Sun, desires to continue the family tradition of cannibalism begun by No-Tongue's human father, but the Moon prevents this treachery.

No-Tongue rested in the village, where he came to be one of the most important men, for some years after his marriage to the daughter of the chief. Then he decided to go on a war-party. He chose only a single friend to accompany him.

The two were gone from home but a short time when they found an enemy, whom they succeeded in killing, and whom No-Tongue was the first to strike. After this adventure they returned to the village, and ran around among the houses, shouting what they had done. Then No-Tongue was greatly honored by all the people with a general celebration.

After a few months No-Tongue again decided to lead a war-party, and this time he took with him two friends. On this occasion the party met and killed two enemies, and returned in triumph to the village, where they dashed about among the houses, proclaiming a great victory. Again all the people rejoiced and honored No-Tongue. Then he invited all the older people to his lodge, and announced to them that thenceforth his name was No-Tongue, and that all the people should call him by that name. Up to that time his name had been known only to his sister.

No-Tongue now rested for some time in the village; then he announced that he would once more lead a war-party. This time he took with him a large company of warriors; and the party was again successful, killing three of the enemy and capturing their horses, which they took back with them. They arrived within sight of the village early in the morning, and all rushed triumphantly in among the lodges, proclaiming their conquest. No-Tongue, who was now one of the chiefs, was accorded even greater honor and praise than before, and the whole village held a great rejoicing.

After this, No-Tongue remained quietly at home until all the talk and praise over the third exploit had died out. Then he announced a fourth war-party; and all the warriors of the village flocked to join him, for they all remembered his great success on former occasions. The party went forth, and met with good fortune, as before. This time they found and killed four enemies, and captured their horses, which were led back in triumph to the village. No-Tongue was once more received with great rejoicing, and was accorded the principal place in the village by all the people.

Now, the Sun and the Moon had been looking down on the village all this time, and had seen the exploits of No-Tongue, and the honors that were heaped upon him. So, after the return from the fourth war-party, the Sun said to the Moon, "That son of mine must be very fat, with all the praise and honor he has received, and I will eat him."

And the Moon asked, "How will you manage to eat him?"

The Sun replied, "That is easy. I have another brave son. Him I shall have come, and he shall defeat and slay this one, whom I shall then eat."

That evening, when it was dark, the Moon came to No-Tongue and informed him of the Sun's plans.

"Now," said the Moon to No-Tongue, "your father, the Sun, wants to eat you, and he is going to have another very brave son of his from the Sioux come and kill you. When the time for the battle arrives, get another warrior to dress exactly like yourself and go forth to meet the Sioux. Then the other warrior will be killed, and the Sun will eat him, thinking that it is you."

Then he told No-Tongue to dress poorly, paint himself white, and follow the disguised warrior into the battle. After the warrior had been slain, No-Tongue was to kill the Sioux and cut his head off at once. Then he must carry the head home to his lodge, and offer it a corn-ball to eat, and a pipe to smoke. After that the head would die, and he might throw it away.

Soon after, the battle took place; and all occurred as the Moon had said, and No-Tongue acted as the Moon had directed. When the battle was over, the Sun and the Moon both went down to hunt among the bodies, where they found both the disguised warrior and the dead Sioux son. The Sun took the dead Mandan to be No-Tongue, but he wondered very much how the brave Sioux had come to be killed. The Moon told the Sun to take No-Tongue and eat him, while the Moon himself took the dead Sioux home. As the Sun picked up the supposed body of No-Tongue, he was greatly surprised. "Oh, say!" he said to the Moon, "this one is too light, this cannot be No-Tongue. He would be fat and heavy."

But the Moon declared that it was No-Tongue. So each went home with his meat, which he cooked and prepared. However, after the Sun had prepared his feast, he found the meat so lean and tough that he could not eat it. Then he went to the Moon's house to get some of his meat; but when he arrived, the Moon had already eaten it all up.

The next morning No-Tongue dressed himself up, and took his place on the roof of his lodge before the Sun was up. So the first thing that his father, the Sun, saw, as he came out of the door of his house, was the figure of No-Tongue.

"It certainly is No-Tongue," he said to the Moon, who had not yet gone down into his own house. As the Sun said this, No-Tongue turned and faced directly toward him, and he cried out, "Yes, it is No-Tongue. I thought he was dead, but here he is, still alive."

"It is all according to your own words," replied the Moon. "You said that nothing could hurt him, so now you see that even you yourself cannot kill him."

"Yes," said the Sun, "but what I said then I did not mean. This time I shall surely eat him."

The Moon inquired how he intended to accomplish the destruction of No-Tongue this time.

"Oh!" answered the Sun, "I have another very brave son among the Cheyennes, and him I shall have come to kill No-Tongue."

That night the Moon once more visited No-Tongue in his lodge, and told him what the Sun was planning. He told No-Tongue that the Sun had decided to have his most beloved Cheyenne son come to kill him; and that this Cheyenne was very powerful, and could not ordinarily be killed, because his father, the Sun, kept him suspended from above by an invisible cord attached to the top of his head. Through this cord, life and strength continually flowed.

"You must be on your guard," the Moon said, "for he is coming tomorrow. He will be dressed exactly like you, and he will motion toward you, urging you to come and meet him. When he does this, you must advance toward him. As you advance, swing and throw your war-club so that it will go just above his head. In that way you will break the invisible cord and can easily kill him."

The battle took place on the next day; and No-Tongue was in the fore-front, dressed in his very best and finest clothing. The Cheyenne appeared on the opposite side, dressed exactly like No-Tongue; and the two at once recognized each other, and advanced to the meeting. No-Tongue followed the Moon's directions, throwing his club as he approached. The aim was true, the cord was broken, and the Cheyenne fell to the ground dead, and was left there, while the rest of the enemy were defeated and dispersed.

On his return from the pursuit, No-Tongue cut off the head of the dead Cheyenne, and took it back with him to his lodge. As he was returning, his father, the Sun, came to him, praising him for his bravery, and asked for the head. No-Tongue did not yield to his pleading, however, but only told him to wait a while, and then he should have the head. So No-Tongue went on to his lodge, where he placed some corn-meal in the mouth of the head, and also made it smoke. Then it was really dead, and he took it out and gave it to the Sun.

On receiving the head, the Sun thought that he would bring back his beloved Cheyenne son to life. So he wrapped it up with sage, and worked a long time with it, moving it about, but all in vain.

"I wasted time and waited too long," he thought. "It is no use." Then he went to look for the body of the dead Cheyenne, but the Moon had already taken that and made a feast with it.

In the morning No-Tongue again dressed in his best, and placed himself on the top of his lodge before the Sun came out of his house, so that once again he was the first thing to meet the Sun's eyes as he opened his door.

The Sun was now very angry; and once more he talked to the Moon, saying that now he would surely have No-Tongue killed. The Moon asked him how he would attempt it this time.

"I shall have Big-Voice kill him, and he cannot escape," answered the Sun. The Moon inquired who Big-Voice was, and the Sun replied that Big-Voice was the Thunder-Bird.

That night once again the Moon secretly visited No-Tongue, and told him of the Sun's latest plans. He told No-Tongue that he must get another friend to dress in his clothes and sleep in his bed that very night, while he himself must go into some obscure old woman's lodge and conceal himself in a corner under a pile of blankets.

As soon as the Moon had gone, No-Tongue found a friend to dress in his clothes and sleep in his bed, while he himself hid as the Moon had directed. He had been hidden only a little while, when the rain started, and soon after that there was a great clap of thunder. Then No-Tongue knew that the Thunder-Bird had killed his friend.

After the rain was all over, No-Tongue returned to his own lodge, where he found the dead body of his friend. He prepared the body for burial in a very fine way, and dressed it in his own clothes; then he told all the people to go out to the burial-scaffold with it, and make a great mourning.

Soon after, when the Sun came forth from his lodge, he looked toward the village, and saw the finely dressed body on the scaffold, and the great crowd of people about it mourning, and he thought surely that it was No-Tongue. So he came down and took the body, and once more prepared for a feast; but when it was prepared and he started to eat, he found that he had a very lean and tough morsel, and he said to himself that No-Tongue must have changed greatly.

When the Sun came forth again on the following morning, his eyes once more lighted on the figure of No-Tongue, finely dressed, and posed upon the top of his lodge, and he saw that he had once more been tricked.

Toward evening the Sun and the Moon met again, and the Sun related how No-Tongue had fooled him this time. He told the Moon that none of his helpers had succeeded in killing No-Tongue, and that he had finally decided to take the matter into his own hands and dispose of No-Tongue himself.

The Moon argued with the Sun, and told him that the failures had all been the Sun's own fault, that he had promised No-Tongue a long and prosperous life, and that now he was trying to break his own promises. But the Sun remained firm in his decision, and the Moon then asked him how he intended to overcome No-Tongue.

The Sun replied that he would turn himself into a huge buffalo-bull with its sides a solid mass of bone where the ribs usually are, and that he would then go into the village and chase No-Tongue until he caught him.

The Moon again sought out No-Tongue in the night, and told him that the Sun himself would try to kill him on the morrow, and he told No-Tongue what the Sun had said. Then he added that there would be only one way to kill the great bull, and that would be to shoot him in the neck near the collar-bone.

After the Moon left, No-Tongue began to lay his plans for the coming combat, which he knew would be the most severe test of all. A little way outside the village there was a ditch or wash-out just narrow enough for one to jump over it in a very long jump. No-Tongue got the Kill-Deer, who makes the boggy water-holes, to come and make a soft muddy spot just beyond the far side of the ditch, at a spot that No-Tongue had selected.

Early the next morning a huge buffalo-bull wandered into the village, and began running about among the houses. The men swarmed out of the lodges, and commenced to shoot arrows at the bull; but they seemed able neither to harm it nor to drive it away. After a time No-Tongue, for whom, of course, the bull had been searching, appeared, but kept at a distance from the bull. Then the bull pretended to be lame in order to draw No-Tongue closer, but he was not deceived. Gradually No-Tongue worked toward the side of the village near which was the wash-out, allowing the bull slowly to get closer to him. Then he started to run, and the bull followed at full speed. No-Tongue made directly for the ditch at the spot selected, and leaped it, evading by a sudden turn the mud-hole on the farther side.

The bull, in its mad pursuit, leaped the ditch also, but did not see the muddy place, and landed full in the centre of it, where he was soon mired down and helpless. Then No-Tongue came up close and shot the bull in the neck near the collar-bone, one arrow on each side.

When the bull was dead, all the people gathered, and wanted to cut it up and eat it, and No-Tongue had difficulty in persuading them not to do so; but he told them that it was not a real bull, but a great spirit, and that it would be very dangerous for all of them if it were cut up. Then he told them all to bring large bundles of brush and dry sticks, and to heap them upon and around the dead bull.

When a great pile had been built up and the bull was completely hidden, No-Tongue set fire to the brush, which made a big fire and a tremendous smoke, under cover of which the Sun escaped from the body of the bull, and returned to the sky.

That evening the Sun and the Moon met as usual, and the Sun told how he had failed to kill No-Tongue, and what a narrow escape he had had. He added that he had finally decided to let No-Tongue live, and to molest him no further, but to keep his first promise. So now No-Tongue lived a contented and quiet life in the village; for by this time he had grown past the age of a warrior, and was becoming old and losing his strength.

One day a long hunt was decided upon in the village, and all of the people were to go. After careful preparations, they started out, and with them went the old man No-Tongue. No-Tongue, however, was not very strong; and he traveled along slowly, so that he was soon left by himself, walking along far in the rear. After a time the trail came to a high hill; and when No-Tongue reached the foot of this hill, he sat down on a large stone nearby. Then he took out his pipe, filled it, and was ready for a smoke. As he began to puff on his pipe, two men approached, and seated themselves one on either side of him upon the large stone.

No-Tongue recognized the two men as his two fathers, the Sun and the Moon, and he greeted them. Then they all three smoked in turn, and discussed the past life of No-Tongue. The Sun declared that he had fulfilled his promises, and made No-Tongue a great warrior with much honor and glory, and had brought him to a full and prosperous old age. Then the Moon told of all his part in helping No-Tongue toward success and honor, and he told how the Sun had tried to break his promises.

The three sat for a long time, talking and smoking, and then the Sun and Moon prepared to go. Just as the Sun was getting up from his seat at the left side of No-Tongue, he thrust the point of his elbow against No-Tongue's breast, penetrating the ribs and the heart, so that he fell over dead.

"He is dead," said the Sun. "It is better so, for he is now old and losing his strength. It is better not to live too long."

And the Sun and Moon went away.

LONG TAIL AND SPOTTED BODY RESCUE THEIR NEPHEWS WHO BECOME THE TWIN MONSTER KILLERS

Tradition Bearer: Unavailable

Source: Matthews, Washington. "A Folk-tale of the Hidatsa Indians." *The Folklore Record* 1 (1878): 136–43.

Date: 1877

Original Source: Hidatsa

National Origin: Native American

Historically, the Hidatsa were a sedentary Great Plains culture living in North Dakota. They were closely allied to the Mandan, and had a lifestyle virtually identical to them (see "The Story of No-Tongue," p. 192). The Hidatsa Twins cycle—like similar Native American Twin cycles—recounts the exploits of a pair of exceptional brothers who act as **culture heroes** by cleansing the environment of monsters. In some versions of the **myth**, they are the nephews or sons of Charred Body, reputed to be the founder of a major Hidatsa clan. Even in this version, Long Tail is the only uncle who is integral to the plot. Less than halfway through the action, both uncles disappear.

Near the mouth of Burnt Creek, on the east bank of the Missouri, are the vestiges of some large round lodges, which stood there before the Indians came into the land. They were inhabited by several mysterious beings of great power in sorcery. In one of the lodges lived the two great demi-gods Long Tail and Spotted Body; a woman lived with them, who took care of their lodge and who was their wife and sister: and these three were at first the only beings of their kind in the world. In a neighboring lodge lived an evil monster named Big Mouth, "who had a great mouth and no head." He hated the members of Long Tail's lodge, and when he discovered that the woman was about to become a mother, he determined to attempt the destruction of her offspring.

When Long Tail and Spotted Body were absent on a hunt one day, Big Mouth entered their lodge, and, addressing the woman, said he was hungry. The woman was greatly frightened, but did not wish to deny him her hospitality; so she proceeded to broil him some meat on the coals. When the meat was cooked, she offered it to him on a wooden dish. He told her that, from the way his mouth was made, he could not eat out of a dish, and the only way she could serve him the food so that he could eat it, was by lying down and placing it on her side. She did as he intimated, when he immediately devoured the meat, and in doing so tore her in pieces.

She died, or seemed to die; but the children thus rudely brought into the world were immortal. One of these he seized, and throwing him into the bottom of the lodge said, "Stay there for ever among the rubbish, and let your name be Atutish. The other he took out and threw into a neighboring spring, saying to him, "Your name is Mahas; stay there for ever, where you will love the mud and learn to eat nothing but the worms and reptiles of the spring."

When Long Tail and Spotted Body came home, they were horrified to find their sister slaughtered; they mourned her duly, and then placed her body on a scaffold, as these Indians do.

After the funeral they returned hungry to the lodge, and put some meat on the fire to cook. As the pleasant odor of the cooking arose, they heard an infantile voice crying and calling for food. They sought and listened, and sought again, until at length they found Atutish, whom they dragged forth into the light, and knew to be the child, whom they supposed was devoured or lost for ever. Long Tail then placed Atutish on the ground, and, holding his hand some distance above the child's head, made a wish "that he would grow so high," and instantly the child attained the stature, mind, and knowledge of a boy about eight years old. Then Long Tail made many inquiries concerning what had happened to him and the whereabouts of his brother; but the child could give no information of what took place during the visit of Big Mouth.

In a day or two after this transaction, the elders made for the child a little stick and wheel (such as Indian children use in the game called by the Canadians of the Upper Missouri, roulette), and bade him play round in the neighborhood of the lodge, while they went out to hunt again.

While he was playing near the spring, he heard a voice calling to him and saying "miakas" (my elder brother). He looked in the direction from which the voice proceeded, and saw little Mahash looking out of the spring. Wanting a playmate, Atutish invited him to come out and play. So Mahash came out, and the two brothers began to amuse themselves. But when Long Tail and his brother approached the lodge, on their return from the hunt, Mahash smelled them far off, rushed away like a frightened beast, and hid himself in the spring. When the elders returned, Atutish told them all that happened while they were gone. They concluded that he of the spring must be their lost child, and devised a plan to rescue him, which they communicated to Atutish.

Next morning they made another and smaller roulette-stick, for the enchanted child to play with. Then they divested themselves of their odor as much as possible, and hid themselves near the spring and to the leeward of it. When all was ready, Atutish went to the edge of the spring and cried aloud, "Mahash! Do you want to come out?" Soon the latter lifted his head cautiously out of the spring, raised his upper lip, showing his long white fangs, snuffed the air keenly, looked wildly around him, and drew back again into the water.

Atutish then went near where he had seen his brother rise and called again to him, but the child answered from the water that he feared to come out, as he thought he smelt the hunters. "Have no fear," said Atutish; "the old men are gone out hunting and will not be back till night. I am here alone. Come out to the warm sunlight. We will have a good time playing, and I will give you something nice to eat."

Thus coaxed and reassured, the other ventured out, still looking mistrustfully around him. Atutish then gave him a piece of boiled buffalo tongue to eat, which the little boy said was the best thing he had ever tasted. "Very well," said Atutish, "let us play, and I will stake the rest of this tongue against some of your frogs and slugs on the game." Mahash agreed, and soon in the excitement of the play he forgot his fears.

They played along with the roulette some time without much advantage on either side, until at length they threw their sticks so evenly that it was impossible to tell which was the furthest from the wheel. They disputed warmly, until Atutish said, "Stoop down and look close and you will see that I have made the best throw."

The other stooped over to observe; and, while his attention was thus engaged, his brother came behind the little fellow, seized him, and held him fast. Atutish then called to the concealed hunters, who ran up, threw a lariat around the struggling captive, and bound him firmly. Having secured the wild boy, their next task was to break the spell by which his tastes and habits were made so unnatural. To accomplish this, Long Tail and Spotted Body put him in the sweat-house, and there steamed him until he was almost exhausted. They then took him out and began to whip him severely. As they plied the lash they made wishes, that the keen scent would leave his nose, that the taste for reptiles would leave his month, that the fear of his own kind would leave his heart.

As they progressed with this performance, he suddenly cried out to Atutish, "Brother, I remember myself now; I know who I am." When he said this he was released; and his first impulse was to run to the spring. He ran there, but when he reached the edge he stopped, for he found he no longer loved the black mud and the slimy water, and he returned to the lodge.

Long Tail then placed the twins side by side, and holding his extended hand, palm downwards, above their heads, a little further from the ground than on the previous occasion, wished that they would both be "so high"; when at once they grew to the size of boys about fourteen years old, and they grew in wisdom correspondingly.

Then Long Tail made bows and hunting-arrows for the boys, and a pair of medicine-arrows for their protection and for use on extraordinary occasions, and he addressed them saying, "You are now big enough to protect yourselves. Go out on the prairie and hunt, and we will see which one of you will be the best hunter." After that they went out every day and. became expert hunters.

Once, as they were looking for game among the hills, they came to a scaffold on which a corpse was laid. "There," said Atutish, "is the body of our mother. She was murdered, no one knows how."

"Let us try the strength of our medicine arrows upon her," said Mahash, "perhaps we could bring her back to life." So saying he stepped close to the scaffold and shot straight up. As the arrow turned to fall, he cried out, "Take care, mother, or you will get hurt," and, as it descended near the body, the scaffold shook and a low groan was heard.

Then Atutish stepped nearly under the scaffold and shot up in the air. As his arrow turned to fall he cried out, "Mother! Mother! Jump quick or the arrow will strike you." At once she arose, jumped down from the scaffold, and, recognizing her children, embraced them.

The boys then asked her who was the author of their calamities, and how it all happened. She pointed to the lodge of Big Mouth, and related all the circumstances of her death. Upon hearing this, the boys swore they would be revenged. Their mother endeavored to dissuade them, describing Big Mouth to them, assuring them that his medicine was potent, and that he certainly would destroy them if they went near him. They paid no attention to her remonstrances, but proceeded to plot the destruction of the monster.

Now this Big Month had a very easy way of making a living. He neither trapped nor hunted, nor took pains to cook his food. He simply lay on his back, and when a herd of deer came within sight of his lodge, or a flock of birds flew overhead, no matter how far distant, he turned towards them, opened his great mouth, and drew in a big breath, when instantly they fell into his mouth and were swallowed.

In a little while the boys had their plans arranged. They built a large fire, and heated some small boulders in it. Then they carried the stones to the top of his lodge, put them near the smoke-hole, and began to imitate a flock of black-birds. "Go away, little birds," said Big Mouth, "you are not fit to eat, and I am not hungry, but go away and let me sleep, or I will swallow you."

"We are not afraid of you," said the boys, and they began to chirp again. At length Big Mouth got angry. He turned up his mouth, opened it wide, and, just as he began to draw his breath to suck them in, the boys stepped aside, and hurled the stones down into the lodge.

"Oh, what sharp claws those birds have! They are tearing my throat!" exclaimed the monster, as he swallowed the red-hot rocks. The next moment he roared with pain and rushed for his water jars, drinking immense draughts; but the steam made by the water on the rocks swelled him up, and the more he drank the worse he swelled, until he burst and died.

The boys brought the body home, and, after they bad danced sufficiently around it, their mother praised them for what they had done; but she said, "You must not be too venturesome. All these lodges around are inhabited by beings whose power in sorcery is great. You cannot always do as well as you have done this time. You should keep away from the rest of them. There is an old woman in particular whom you must avoid. She is as powerful as Big Mouth; but you cannot kill her in the same way as you killed him, for she catches her food, not in her mouth, but in a basket. Whenever she sees anything that she wants to eat she turns her basket towards it, and it drops in dead. If she sees a flock of wild geese among the clouds, no matter how high they fly, she can bring them down." When the boys heard this, they said nothing in reply to their mother, but set off secretly to compass the death of the witch. They went to the lodge of the latter, and standing near the door, cried, "Grand-mother, we have come to see you."

"Go away, children, and don't annoy me," she replied.

"Grandmother, you are very nice and good, and we like you. Won't you let us in?" continued the boys.

"Oh, no," said she, "I don't want to hurt you; but be gone, or I will kill you."

Despite this threat, they remained, and again spoke to her, saying, "Grandmother, we have heard that you are very strong medicine, and that you have a wonderful basket that can kill anything. We can scarcely believe this. Won't you lend us the basket a little while until we see if we can catch some birds with it?" She refused the basket at first, but, after much coaxing and flattering, she handed it to them. No sooner were they in possession of the basket, than they turned it upon the witch herself, and she dropped into it dead.

After this exploit the mother again praised the boys, but again warned them to beware of the evil genii of the place that she described. One of these was a man with a pair of wonderful moccasins, with which be had only to walk round anything he wanted to kill. Another was a man with a magic knife, with which he could either cut or kill anything that he threw the knife at. These individuals they destroyed in the same manner that they overcame the basket-woman, by coaxing them to lend their magic property, and then slaying the owners with their own weapons. On each occasion the boys retained the charmed articles for their future use.

When all this was done, the old mother called her boys and told them there was but one more dangerous being that they had to guard themselves against. She said, "He lives in the sky where you cannot get at him, but he can hurt you, for his arm is so long that it reaches from the heavens to the earth. His name is Long Arm."

"Very well," said the boys, "we will beware of him." One morning, soon after receiving this advice, they went out very early to hunt, but could find nothing to kill. They walked and ran many miles, until late in the day, when they became very tired and lay down to sleep on the prairie.

As was their custom, they stuck their medicine arrows in the ground, close beside them. The arrows possessed such a charm, that if any danger threatened the boys, they would fall to waken them.

While the brothers lay asleep, Long Arm looked down from the clouds, and, beholding them, stretched his great arm down towards them. As the arm descended, the arrows fell hard upon the boys, but the latter were so tired and sleepy that they did not waken, and Long Arm grasped Atutish and bore him to the sky. In a little while Mahash woke up and discovered, to his horror, that the warning arrows had fallen, and that his brother was gone. He looked round carefully on the prairie for the departing tracks of his brother, or for the tracks of the man or the beast that had captured him, but in vain.

When at his wits' end, and almost in despair, he chanced to glance towards the sky, and there, on the face of a high white summer cloud, he saw the doubled track of Long Arm, where he came near the earth and went back. Mahash laid down his bow and arrow and other accoutrements, retaining only his medicine knife, which he concealed in his shirt. He next stuck his magic arrows into the ground and got on top of them, and then he crouched low, strained every muscle, and sprang upwards with all his might. He jumped high enough to catch hold of the ragged edge of the cloud. From that time he scrambled higher, until he at last got on Long Arm's trail, which he followed.

For fear of recognition he wished himself smaller, and, becoming a little toddling child, moved on till he came to a great crowd, moving in one direction, with much talk and excitement. He ran up to an old woman who walked a little apart, and asked her what was the matter. She informed him that they had just captured one of the children of the new race which was growing on the earth, a boy who had destroyed many favored genii, and that they were about to kill and burn him. "Grandmother," said Mahash, "I would like to see this, but I am too little to walk there. Will you carry me?" She took him on her back and brought him to the place where the crowd had gathered.

There he saw his brother tied to a stake, and a number of people dancing round him. He thought if he could only reach the post unobserved, and touch the cords with his medicine-knife, he could release his brother, but for some time he was puzzled how to do it. At length he slid down from the old woman's back, and wished that for a little time he might turn to an ant.

He became one, and, as such, crawled through the feet of the crowd and up to the post, where he cut the cords that bound Atutish. When the latter was free, Mahash resumed his proper shape, and they both ran as hard as they could for the edge of the clouds.

The crowd pursued them; but, as each foremost runner approached, Mahash threw his knife and disabled him. At last Long Arm started after the brothers, running very fast. As he came within his arm's length of them, he reached out to grasp one of them. As he did so, Mahash again threw his knife, and severed the great arm from the shoulder. The boys got back safely to the earth. They, having ridded themselves of all their enemies, lived in peace, and in time they moved away from that locality.

THE TWO BOYS WHO SLEW THE MONSTERS AND BECAME STARS

Author: Ahahe

Source: Dorsey, George A. "The Two Boys Who Slew the Monsters and Became Stars." *Journal of American Folklore* 17 (1904): 153–60.

Date: 1904

Original Source: Wichita

National Origin: Native American

The Wichita, as discussed in the introduction to "Origin of the Universe" (p. 135), were sedentary farmers and hunters living on the southern areas of the Great Plains and plateau region. The village divided by a street and governed by two different chiefs is a common **motif** in Wichita **myth**. The narrative falls into the "twin hero" category, and—as is the case in many similar tales—the more extraordinary and marginal of the two brothers has gifts that allow the boys to accomplish their marvelous deeds of cleansing the world by killing the monsters that reside in each of the cardinal directions (that is, the entire universe is dangerous and in need of taming). The **motif** of the protagonist's transformation into a star is common not only in Native American **myth**, but also worldwide, as in the Greek Heracles cycle, for example.

There was once a village where there were two chiefs. The village was divided by a street, so that each chief had his part of the village. Each chief had a child. The child of the chief living in the west village was a boy; the child of the chief living in the east village was a girl. The boy and the girl remained single and were not acquainted with each other. In these times, children of prominent families were shown the same respect as was shown to their parents, and they were protected from danger. The chief's son had a sort of scaffold fixed up for his bed, which was so high that he had to use a ladder to get upon it. When he came down from the bed the ladder was taken away.

Once upon a time the young man set out to visit the young woman, to find out what sort of a looking woman she was. He started in the night. At the very same time, the girl set out to visit the young man, to see what sort of looking man he was. They both came into the street-like place, and when they saw one another the girl asked the young man where he was going. The young man replied that he was going to see the chief's daughter, and he asked her where she was going. She replied that she was going to see the chief's son, The young man said that he was the chief's son, and the girl said that she was the chief's daughter. They were undecided whether to go to the young man's home or to the girl's home. They finally decided to go to the young man's home.

The next morning, the young man's people wondered why he was not up as early as usual. It was the custom of all the family to rise early and sit up late, for the people of the village came around to the chief's place at all times. They generally woke the young man by tapping on the ladder, so they tapped on the ladder to have him come down. When they could not arouse the young man they sent the old mother up to wake him. When she got there she found her son sleeping with another person. She came down and told the others about it. She was sent back to ask them to come down from the bed and have breakfast. When they came down it was found that the son's companion was the other chief's daughter.

Meanwhile, the other chief wondered why his daughter did not rise as early as usual. It was her custom to rise early and do work inside the lodge. In the village where the girl was from, there lived the Coyote. Since the girl was not to be found, the chief called the men and sent them out to find her. The Coyote was there when the father sent the men in search of his daughter. The Coyote went all through his own side of the village, and then went to the side of the other chief, where he found the girl living with the chief's son. He went back immediately to the girl's father and told where he had found her. After she was found, the chief was angry and sent word that she was never to come back to her home; and the young man's father did not like the way his son had acted.

The time came when the young man decided to leave the village. He told his wife to get what she needed to take along for the journey. They started at midnight, and went towards the south. They went a long way and then stopped for rest and fell asleep. On the next day they continued their journey in search of a new home. They traveled for three days, then they found a good place where there was timber and water, and there they made their home. The man went out daily to hunt, so that they might have all the meat they wanted. The woman fixed up a home, building a grass-lodge, and there they resided for a long while.

One time, when the man was about to go out hunting, he cut a stick and put some meat on it and set it by the fire to cook. He told his wife that the meat was for someone who would come to visit the place; and that she must not look at him; that when she should hear him talking she should get up in bed and cover her head with a robe. The man left to go hunting that day, and the woman stayed and remembered what she had been told. After her husband had gone the woman heard someone talking, saying that he was coming to get something to eat. When she heard him she went to her bed and covered her head. The visitor came in, took down the meat that the woman's husband had placed by the fire, and ate it.

Before leaving, he spoke and said, "I have eaten the meat and will go back home." When the visitor had gone, the woman got up again, for she had her morning work to do. It was late in the evening when her husband returned from his hunting trip. Every time he went hunting he put the meat up before leaving, and when the visitor came the wife would get in her bed so as not to see who he was. Every time he came in and ate she would listen, and it would sound like two persons eating together.

One morning, after her husband had left, the woman made a hole in her robe and took a piece of straw that had a hole in it. When the visitor came she got in her bed and put the robe over her, with the hole over her eye, having the straw in her hand. As soon as the person came in he commenced to eat. After he had finished eating and was starting out, the woman quickly placed the straw in the hole in the robe, looked through it and saw the person. She saw that he had two faces, one face on the front and one on the back side of his head.

When she looked at him he turned back, telling the woman that she had disobeyed her husband's orders and that she would be killed. Thereupon the Double-Faced-Man (Witschatska) took hold of the woman and cut her open. She was pregnant, so that when the Double-Faced-Man cut her open, he took out a young child, which he wrapped with some pieces of a robe and put on the back of some timber in the grass-lodge, and covered the woman again with her robe. Then he took the afterbirth and threw it into the water.

When the husband returned, he found that his wife was dead. He was there alone and so he spoke out, saying: "Now you have done wrong, disobeying my orders. I told you never to run any risk, but you made up your mind to look and see what sort of a person that was who came here, and he has killed you." The man took his wife's body to the south, laid her on the ground, and covered her with buffalo robes.

When he came back he heard a baby crying, and he looked around inside of the lodge, then outside, but he could not find the child. He finally heard the baby crying again and the sound came from behind one of the lodge poles. He looked there and found the child. He cooked some rare meat and had the child suck the juice. In this way the man nourished his child. He stayed with it most of the time, and when hunting, he took the child on his back. Whenever he killed any game he would not hunt any more until all of his meat was gone. This child was a boy, and it was not very long before he began to walk, though his father would still take him on his back when he went hunting. When the child was old enough the father made him a bow and arrows, and left him at home when he went hunting.

One day when the boy had been left he heard someone saying, "My brother, come out and let us have an arrow game." When he turned around he saw a boy about his own age standing at the entrance of the grass-lodge. The little boy ran out to see his little visitor, who told him that he was his brother. They fixed up a place and had a game of arrows, which is often played to this day. When Double-Faced-Man had killed the woman, he had taken a stick that she had used for a poker and he thrust it into the afterbirth and threw it in the water. This stick was still fastened in the visiting boy. The boy wondered what this stick was there for. They commenced to play. The visiting boy promised not to tell their father about winning the arrows, and the other boy promised not to tell that he had had company. When the visiting boy left he went towards the river and jumped into the water.

When the father came home he asked his boy what had become of his arrows. The boy replied that he had lost all his arrows shooting at birds. His father tried to get him to go where he had been shooting at birds, to see if he could not find the arrows, but the boy said that he could not find the arrows. Next day, the father made other arrows for the boy and then went out hunting again.

As soon as the father left, the visiting boy came, calling his brother to come and have another game. They played all day, until the visiting boy won all the arrows, then he left the place, going toward the river. When the man came back from his hunting trip he found the boy with no arrows, and he asked him what had become of them. The boy said that he had lost his arrows by shooting birds. His father asked him to go out and look around for the arrows, but the boy refused, and said that the arrows could not be found. Again the father made more arrows for his boy.

After a long time the boy told his father of his brother's visits. The father undertook to capture the visiting boy one day, and so he postponed his hunting trip until another time. About the time the boy was accustomed to make his appearance, the father hid himself and turned himself into a piece of stick that they used for a poker. The father instructed his son to invite his brother to come in and have something to eat before they should play. As soon as the visiting boy came and called his brother, his brother invited him to come in, but he refused, because he was afraid that the old man might be inside. He looked all around, and when he saw the poker he knew at once that it was the old man, and he went off. The father stayed still all that day, intending to capture the boy. On the next day he again postponed and instructed his boy as before about capturing the visiting boy. About the time for the boy to make his appearance the father hid himself behind the side of the entrance and turned into a piece of straw. When the visiting boy arrived, he called, and his brother invited him in again. He looked around in the grass-lodge, but not seeing anything this time, he entered and ate with his brother. The father had told his boy that when his brother came he should get him to look into his hair for lice; then the boy was to look into the visiting boy's hair, and while he was looking he was to tie his hair so that the father could get a good hold on it. Then he was to call his father. After eating, they both went out to begin their game. They played until the visiting boy won all his brother's arrows.

When they stopped, the boy asked his brother if they might not look into each other's hair for lice. The visiting boy agreed and looked into his brother's hair first, then allowed his brother to look into his hair. While the boy was looking into his hair the visiting boy would ask him what he was doing; and he would say that he was having a hard time to part his hair.

When he got a good hold of the visiting boy's hair he called his father. The visiting boy dragged him a good ways before their father reached them. When the old man got hold, the boy was so strong that he dragged both the father and brother toward the river, but the father begged him to stop. They finally released the visiting boy and he jumped in the water and came out again with his arms full of arrows. They started back toward their home. This boy was named Afterbirth-Boy.

After that, Afterbirth-Boy began to dwell with his father and brother. When their father would go out hunting the boys would go out and shoot birds. When the father was home he forbid his boys to go to four certain places: one on the north, where there lived a woman; on the east, where there was the Thunderbird that had a nest up in a high tree; on the south, where there lived the Double-Faced-Man.

The father made his boys a hoop and commanded them not to roll it toward the west. It was a long time before the boys felt inclined to lengthen their journeys; but after a time, during their father's absence, Afterbirth-Boy asked his brother to go with him to visit the place at the north, where they were forbidden to go. The brother agreed, and they at once started for the place. On their way, they shot a good many birds, which they carried along with them.

When they arrived they saw smoke. The woman who lived there was glad to see the little boys and asked them to her place. They gave her their birds, and went in. The old woman was pleased to get the birds, and said that she always liked to eat birds; then she asked the boys to go to the creek and bring her a pot full of water. She told the boys that she must put the birds in the water and boil them before she could eat them, so the boys went to the creek and brought the pot full of water.

When they returned with the pot of water the woman hung it over the fire, snatched the boys and threw them in, instead of the birds. The water began to boil and Afterbirth-Boy got on the side where the water was bubbling. He told his brother to make a quick leap, while he did the same. They at once made a quick jump and poured the boiling water upon the old woman and scalded her to death.

When they had done this they started back home. They reached home before their father. On their father's arrival they told him that they had visited the place he had warned them against, and what dangers they had met while visiting the woman, who was the Little-Spider-Woman.

The next day they started to visit the Thunderbird. When they came to the place they saw a high tree where was the nest of the Thunderbird. Afterbirth-Boy spoke to his brother, saying, "Well, brother, take my arrows and I will climb the tree and see what sort of looking young ones these Thunderbirds have." He began to climb the tree and all at once he heard thundering and saw a streak of lightning, which struck him and took off his left leg. Afterbirth-Boy told his brother to take care of his leg while he kept on climbing. When he began to climb higher the bird came again. The thundering began and the streak of lightning came down and took off his left arm. Still he kept on, for he was anxious to get to the nest. He was near the nest when his right leg was taken off, so that he had just one arm left when he reached the nest.

Now the Thunderbirds did not bother him any more. He picked up one of the young ones and asked whose child he was. The young one replied that he was the child of the Weather-Followed-by-Hard-Winds, and that sometimes he appeared in thunder and lightning. When the boy heard this he threw the bird down, saying that he was not the right kind of a child, and he asked his brother to destroy him.

Afterbirth-Boy took another bird and asked him the same question. The young one replied that he was the child of Clear-Weather-with Sun-Rising-Slowly. He put the bird back in the nest, telling him that he was a pretty good child.

He took up another, asking whose child he was, and the bird said that he was the child of Cold-Weather-Following-Wind-and-Snow. Afterbirth-Boy dropped him down and said that he was the child of a bad being, and he ordered his brother to put the bird to death.

He then picked up the last one and asked whose child he was. The young one answered that he was the child of Foggy-Day-Followed-by-Small-Showers. This child Afterbirth-Boy put back into the nest, telling him that he was the right kind of a child. He then started to climb down with his one arm. When he reached the ground his brother put his right leg on him, and he jumped around to see if it was on all right. His brother then put his left arm on him, and he swung it around to see if it was all right. Then the brother put on the left leg, and he felt just as good as he did when he first began to climb the tree.

The two boys returned home before their father came back from the chase. When their father came back, Afterbirth-Boy began to tell what they had done while visiting the Thunderbirds and how his limbs were taken off, and the boys laughed to think how Afterbirth-Boy looked with one arm and both legs gone. The father began to think that his boy must have great powers, and he did not say much more to the boys about not going to dangerous places.

Some time after, the boys went out again and came to the place where their mother was put after her death. They saw a stone in the shape of a human being, and they both lay on the stone. When they started to get up they found that they were stuck to it, and they both made an effort and got up with the stone. They took it home for their father to use for sharpening his stone knife. When they reached home the old man told them to take the stone back where they had found it. He told them that that was their mother, for she had turned into stone after her death. They took the stone back where they had found it.

Some time after, Afterbirth-Boy and his brother started out to the forbidden place where Double-Faced-Man lived who had killed their mother. These creatures were living in a cave. When the boys arrived at the cave they both went in and the Double-Faced-Man's children came forward and scratched the boys. If there was any blood on their fingers they would put them in their mouths. Afterbirth-Boy took the string of his bow and slew the young ones. He caught the old Double-Faced-Man and tied his bow-string around his neck so that he could take him home to his father to have in the place of a dog. When they returned home the old man walked out, and seeing the old Double-Faced-Man, told his boys to take him off and kill him, and they obeyed.

Every day they played, the same as they had always done before, going out shooting birds and playing with their hoop. Afterbirth-Boy said to his brother, "Let us roll the hoop toward the west and see what will happen."

They rolled it toward the west, and it began going faster and faster. The boys kept running after it until they were going so fast that they could not stop. They kept going faster, until they ran into the water where the hoop rolled. When they went into the water they fell in the mouth of a water-monster called, "Kidiarkat," and he swallowed them.

It appeared to them as though they were in a tipi, for the ribs of the monster reminded them of tipi poles. They wondered how they could get out. Afterbirth-Boy took his bow-string with his right hand, drew it through his left hand to stretch it, then swung it round and round. When he first swung it, the

219

monster moved. He swung the string the second time, and the monster began to move more. He swung it the third time, and the monster began to move still more. At this time Afterbirth-Boy told his brother that their father was getting uneasy about them and that they must get out of the place at once, for they had been away from home a long time. Again he swung his bow-string, and the monster jumped so high that he fell on the dry land. He opened his mouth and the boys quickly stepped out and started for home. When the boys arrived at the lodge they found no one. Their father had gone off somewhere, but they could not find out where he had gone. Afterbirth-Boy looked all around for his trail, but could find no trace of him. At last he grew weary and decided to wait until night to look for their father.

When darkness came, Afterbirth-Boy again looked around to see where his father had gone. He finally found his trail and he followed it with his eye until he found the place where his father had stopped.

He called his brother and told him to bring his arrows and to shoot up right straight overhead. The boy brought his arrows and shot one up into the sky. Then he waited for a while and finally saw a drop of blood come down. It was the blood of their father.

When the boys did not return, he gave up all hope of ever seeing them again, and so he went up into the sky and became a star. They knew that this blood belonged to their father, and in this way they found out where he had gone. They at once shot up two arrows and then caught hold of them and went up in the sky with the arrows. Now the two brothers stand by their father in the sky.

BILL FOSCETT

Tradition Bearer: Robert Lindsey

Source: Phipps, Woody. "Interview of Robert Lindsey." American Life Histories: Manuscripts from the Federal Writers' Project, 1936–1940. Manuscript Division, Library of Congress. 12 October 2005. http://memory.loc.gov/ammem/wpaintro/wpahome.html.

Date: 1938

Original Source: Oklahoma

National Origin: European American

The Dalton Gang mentioned in the following **personal experience narrative** consisted of the Dalton Brothers, Bob, Grat, Emmet—all of whom served as lawmen before turning to crime—Bill Doolin, William St. Power, Charlie Pierce, George Newcomb, Charlie Bryant, and Richard Broadwell. This notorious crew committed bank and train robberies throughout the Kansas and Oklahoma areas in the early 1890s. Members of the Dalton Gang later formed the nucleus of the equally notorious Wild Bunch.

In a pool hall, you have time to sit around and talk about things. In fact, that's almost all you do when you have one. One of my customers was a W. S. "Bill" Foscett. Old Bill didn't talk much to anybody, and it took me several years to break him down to talking. I knew that he'd been somebody because you could tell it in his eyes, and his bearing. He'd look at you, and you'd feel like he knew your very thoughts. That caused me to sort of cater to him, and try to win his confidence without ever letting him know I was a-doing it.

One day, I was talking about the Dalton ranches in Palo Pinto county, and a-wondering if they had any connections with the Dalton outlaws. I was talking about Bob Dalton, and asked Bill if he ever heard of him.

He said, "Yes, I knew him well. Truth of it is, I outlawed with him a little."

Being a pretty fair hand a poker playing, I didn't let my face tell what I felt, and I just let him talk on.

He said, "I rode 75 miles to identify Bob after a couple of little old marshals at Chickasha shot him. The way it happened, Bob and a couple other fellows was a-living out in a cabin out of town. They had a woman with 'em, and since they wasn't a-trying to raise nothing, the marshal decided they was bootlegging and went out to see.

"Now, they was a ditch that run for about 300 yards away from the cabin, and when the marshalls showed, Bob run down that to get away. The marshals saw him, and a lucky shot kilt him. They went on to the cabin and the woman come out a-running and hollering 'Now you've done it! You've kilt my hired man!' You know, them marshals like to a-fought right there, the other two men had got away but they found three or four of those seamless wheat sacks, full of money. Then they like to a-been another fight over who shot Bob. Each one claiming he shot Bob so he could collect the reward. That was when I was a Territory Marshall out of Fort Smith, Arkansas."

Another story he told me was about the first time he went into the Territory as a marshal. I recall that he said it was on one of the first trains to go into the Territory, too. He said, "I was in one of the coaches, and asleep, when all of a sudden, I heard a lot of shots, and felt the train stopping. I got up and ran to the door, which a few of the others did, the most of them trying to hide. Since the shots were spanging against the side of the coaches, I had room a-plenty to see outside. I saw that a band of six men were going to rob the train. You know, I really don't know what fear really is, and never have. I've just felt like all along that when my ticket was punched, I could be doing anything and I'd go anyway, so I jumped down on the ground, filled my fists, and started to shooting away.

"The gunmen were on the ground and in plain sight, so I got two of them before the others run. For three–four minutes there, the shots were hitting all around me. The other four men run to their hosses on the other side of the hill, mounted, and rode away with their buddy's hosses. You see what partners they were. Suppose now that one of those that were shot down happened to get a chance to get away. He couldn't get away because his hoss was gone, and his partner had took it.

"They'd draped a coupla sacks on the ground, and one of 'em had a patch on it that was off of a shirt. I cut that patch out, thinking that it might come in handy someday. About a month later, I was in a cafe, eating breakfast, when four men rode up in a cloud of dust, their hosses all lathered. Well, that was a give away that they were in a hurry to get somewhere. I watched 'em as they eat, and noticed that one of 'em had a shirt just like the patch I was carrying around. I went over to him, matched the patch with a hole in one of 'em's shirt, throwed down on the whole gang, and marched 'em right out to their hosses where I made 'em ride in fron' of me to the sheriff's office.

"Another experience I had was once when I was visiting a friend of mine, that was a sheriff in a Kansas town. I found him in a pool room, and as I stood there talking to him, I watched the operator, and thought he acted suspicious. I said to the sheriff, 'Let's arrest him.'

"He said, 'No, that's a good man.'

"We talked it over, and he gave in, arresting the man. On the way to the jail, we passed a drug store and the man asked to go in and get some smoking. Well, since we really didn't have nothing on him, the sheriff let him go but we followed him on in. He went to the end of the counter, and on around behind it. I saw him bend over like he was picking up something, and I jerked my six out. He come out with a box, and had his hand on a '45. I let him get the gun out of the box, then shot his wrist almost in two.

"He held his wrist and hollered, 'I'd have got both of you if it hadn't of been for that red headed gun slinger there.' Well, you now, they sent me an invitation to his hanging out in Arizona two months later. He'd been wanted out there for years.

"There was one thing that happened to me though, where I really should have lost my life. If it hadn't been for my early training on my dad's ranch in Kansas when Kansas was the wildest place in the world, with a good many desperadoes running around, I'd never have been able to stand up to this experience. My dad had a saying, 'That a man can only die once, and he might's well die a man.' That's the way I felt.

"This time come about when I decide to visit a friend of mine, that was sheriff in a town after Oklahoma was a State. I'll send you a clipping from the Kansas City Star that tells a heap of it, but I'll tell you right now how I recall it. You know, in fast gun action, with your life in danger every minute, a lot goes on that you just nacherly don't recall.

"Well, when I reached the outskirts of this little town, I heard a lot of shooting start. I whipped my hoss up, and saw a gang of men split up, and go in three bunches to'ards some buildings. As I rode in, I saw two or three men on the ground, and I figured it was a holdup. Since I didn't see my friend anywhere, I figured that they'd already got him. I filled both fist with six shooters, and rode to the center of the town, where I could shoot at all three gangs at the same time when they showed.

"What they was really doing, was robbing three places. Two banks, and a big store. Well, I stood in the middle of the street, and every time one of 'em showed, I cut down on him. I was so bust that I never noticed what I was doing, but I did feel queer that I hadn't felt a shot yet. They were shooting at me from both ends of the street and the store in the middle. After about 15 minutes, which seemed like a month, the shooting stopped and the rest of the men came out with their hands in the air. When the count was taken, I'd accounted for thirteen of 'em. Thirteen of 'em dead, and me without a scratch. I tell you Bob, I've really got no claim on my life because the law of averages ought to have taken it then."

Well, old Bill sent me a clipping with a request to send it back when I was done with it. If you went to prove this, I'd suggest you get in touch with the Kansas City Star in Kansas City. They're bound to have this and you can get the paper's account of it.

MATTHEW "BONES" HOOKS, COWBOY

Tradition Bearer: Matthew ("Bones") Hooks

Source: "Interview of Bones Hooks." American Life Histories: Manuscripts from the Federal Writers' Project, 1936–1940. Manuscript Division, Library of Congress. 12 October 2005. http://memory.loc.gov/ammem/wpaintro/wpahome.html.

Date: 1940

Original Source: Oklahoma—Texas Panhandle

National Origin: African American

Despite their contributions, few contemporary Americans—outside the occasional history buff—know the particulars about the lives of African–American cowboys. Probably two of the most prominent names that made it into the written record include Nate "Deadwood Dick" Lovewinner of an impromptu Fourth of July celebration in Deadwood City, Dakota Territory, in 1876 that captured the popular imagination of the time. Another is William "Bill" Pickett (1870–1932), inventor of the rodeo sport of bulldogging. The many other AfricanAmerican cowboys contended not only with the grueling labor and deprivation of their occupations, but also with racism, as Bones Hooks's **personal experience narratives** recount.

Matthew (Bones) Hooks, who for years worked on Panhandle ranches as a horse wrangler and "bronc-buster," knows many tales of cowboy life in the early days, but he refuses to tell the most interesting ones "because it would rattle skeletons in the closets of prominent families"—old-timers who are still living or their descendants.

Bones, without calling embarrassing names, recites a case in point. Called as a witness before a grand jury recently, he recognized in the judge a pioneer cattleman.

"Bones, do you know anyone who has stolen cattle"—the judge caught the glint of memory in the piercing black eyes and hastily added—"now?" And Bones, whose lips had been forming the question, "What time are you talking about, Judge?" could honestly answer, "No."

Both of them were recalling a certain day in the past when the judge, then a young man just starting out in the cattle business, and a young Negro cowboy drove a fine young male calf from the pastures of the Capitol Syndicate (XIT Ranch) to the white man's ranch.

The embryo cattleman could not afford to buy a good bull—Bones said "surly"; he would not use the word "bull" before a lady interviewer—which he needed for breeding purposes. He went to the Negro cowboy, who was working at the XIT at the time, and asked him if he knew where he could get one. Bones looked over the range and, seeing no one near, selected a fine-looking calf, which they drove toward the home ranch of the judge-to-be. Coming upon a still better animal, Bones exchanged the tired calf for the other, and proceeded on his way.

The young rancher tied up the calf until it was weaned to keep it from getting back with the mother cow. "It took about four days to wean a calf," said Bones. "After that time he would go down to the water hole and drink and then mosey out on the range and eating grass and forget all about his mamma."

Bones, who was very young when he was working on Panhandle ranches in the days before law and order came, has good reason to remember the Vigilantes who took the place of the "law" in those days. The Negro cowboy, since the death of "Skillety Bill" Johnson of Canadian, is the last person to know the password of the Vigilantes.

When Skillety Bill died, persons interested in the history of the Panhandle went through his personal effects. Among his papers they found the notation that Bones was the only person left knowing the password. These same persons went to Bones and asked for the password, but he refused. "I am going to keep my word until I die," he said, "and then my papers will be left to the museum. The password will be among them."

According to Bones, Skillety Bill got his name because he worked on the Frying Pan Ranch. Cowboys from the Panhandle ranches in the early days went to Mobeetie (early Sweetwater), adjacent to Fort Elliott, to "celebrate." Negro women in the families of colored troops stationed at the army post would see Bill Johnson coming and say "There comes that Skillety (their version of Frying Pan) Bill fellow."

Skillety Bill figured in one of the most important episodes in Bones' life. The Negro boy was working at the time in old Greer County, which was a part of the "neutral Strip," locally called a second "No Man's Land." Bones, young and inexperienced, had hired out to wrangle horses for a certain cattleman.

One day, while he was tending the horses and minding his own business, Vigilantes rode up and asked him, "Are you working for those cattlemen down the creek?" Bones admitted that he was. Before he could says "Jack Robinson," the Vigilantes jerked him up and started to hang him on the nearest tree. They had already hanged the two white men mentioned to other convenient trees.

One of them Bones knew to be innocent. He was only a young boy who had come into the country looking for work two or three days before, who like himself, had hired out to the first men that offered him a job. But the Vigilantes, catching both of the white men with a herd of stolen cattle, took only circumstantial evidence into consideration and hanged them both.

Bones was certain that they were going to add him to their victims, when Skillety Bill spoke up in behalf of the colored lad, saying that he was a mere boy, wrangling horses for the boss and only carrying out orders of the cattle thief, whom he had taken to be a *bona fide* cattleman.

"A red-haired man astride a limb of the tree gave the rope around my neck a rough jerk," Bones vividly recalled; and said, 'Aw, come on, let's got it over with'; but Skillety Bill saved my life."

After this narrow escape, Bones went into Oklahoma (then the Indian Territory) and so successfully "lost" himself that his own family and others thought him dead. At last he ventured back into Greer County. Walking through the streets of a Panhandle town, which he refuses to name, he came face to face with the sheriff (Skillety Bill).

The sheriff looked at him closely and finally said, "I thought you were dead. How long are you going to be here?"

"Only a little bit—a few days," Bones replied.

The sheriff started off down the street, turned back, and said, "How long did you say you were going to be in town? Did you say 'a little bit'?"

Bones, answered quickly, "Yes, sir, a little bit." He knew what would happen to him if he did not get out of town in a "little bit"—and he got.

The pioneer Negro bronco-buster knows cowboy life as few white persons now living. He was an interested listener around the campfires of nearly every ranch in the Panhandle. He heard many a lurid tale around a cow-chip blaze—words that can not be repeated in the hearing of ladies or in polite society. "Every horse, every man, bread and other articles of the camp, had a nickname, often unmentionable in mixed groups," he said.

Bones recalls an incident that occurred during a visit of Mrs. Charles Goodnight to a camp one day. One of the cowboys, who did not know of the lady's presence, said, "Bones, bring me up a horse."

"Which one?"

"That old—," the cowboy stopped suddenly and clapped his hand over his mouth, preventing the escape of the horse's unmentionable name when he saw Mrs. Goodnight standing there. "You know which one I want, "he added significantly.

Bones honors and reveres the pioneer women of his beloved Panhandle, because they helped him as they helped so many others. When the cowboys tormented him—as they were always doing in some fashion—they took his part and made the white boys stop shooting blank cartridges at his feet or whatever they were doing to him at the moment.

It was one of those pioneer women who taught Bones not to "cuss." His favorite byword was "I' God"—a corruption of "by God." This pioneer mother came to him one day and said, "Bones, young Bob is taking up your speech and I don't want him to say 'I' God.' I can't keep his from saying it as long as he hears you, so I'm going to have to break you of the habit. If you'll quit, I'll buy you a Sunday suit."

Bones wanted that suit. When Bob repeated the byword, the Negro boy would say, "Bob, white boys can get suits any time, but this the only way that I can get one. You mustn't say 'I' God,' or I won't get that suit."

Bones, who attends every celebration of old-timers, at one of these recent gatherings met the daughter of one of the pioneer families for whom he used to work—he frequently associated with the children of the early settlers, especially the boys. He reminded her of the time when she was a very young lady indeed. At that time she had never seen a colored person.

"Remember when you first saw me eating with the other cowboys?" he said. "You peeked out from behind your mother's skirt and said, 'Mamma, one of them didn't wash his face.'"

Bones said that he usually ate with the other cow hands. Once, when someone objected to the presence of the Negro boy at the same table, a pioneer housewife told the objector, "Everyone is treated alike at my table."

"In the early days," Bones said in answer to a question, "when a cowboy died on the trail, accidentally or otherwise, he was buried in a hole dug in the sod without loss of time and without much ceremony. The name of the dead man was sent to his family if anyone knew his real name or who his people were.

"Later, coffins were made of pine boards. Those who died were buried as soon as possible in those days, for obvious reasons. Relatives and friends sat up with the dead to keep the cats and dogs away.

"Services for the dead were held by a friend or someone who was qualified—later by traveling preachers. Towns were far apart, and preachers and doctors had to go miles and miles to serve these communities.

"Meetings"—church services—"were held in the homes of pioneers until churches were built," he concluded.

COYOTE AND THE BUFFALO

Tradition Bearer: Unavailable

Source: Wissler, Clark. "Some Dakota Myths I." *Journal of American Folklore* 20 (1907): 124–26.

Date: ca. 1900

Original Source: Ogalala Lakota (Sioux)

National Origin: Native American

The following **myth** illustrates a typical introduction of Coyote tales, "Once Coyote was walking along." Coyote's behavior throughout the narrative is also typical of this **trickster**. He is motivated by hunger, fear, and curiosity. He attempts to use objects and powers that he does not comprehend and, as a result, ends up in no better condition than he was at the beginning of the adventure.

Once Coyote was walking along. He had nothing to eat for a long time and was thin and weak. Finally he came to a deserted camp, but could find nothing save the remains of the fire. While he was looking around for food, he came upon a knife and an arrow. He carried them away with him, and when he came to the top of a high hill he saw many buffalo grazing in the valley below. He crept up close to the crest of the hill and looked over. Then he said to himself as he looked at the arrow and the knife, "Now those people kill buffalo with these things." So he took up the arrow and threw it toward the buffalo, saying, "Now, go and kill the buffalo. Go, hit that one."

The arrow fell down upon the ground and said, "You must take a piece of wood and a string before I can go and kill the buffalo."

Then Coyote went up to a tree, took the knife and cut off one of the branches, trimmed it and peeled off the bark. He twisted the bark into a cord and tied it to the stick. Then he went back, laid the bow on the ground, picked up the arrow, put it on the stick, and said, "Now, go."

The arrow said to him, "No, that is not the way. You must pull on the string."

Then Coyote put the arrow down, took hold of the string, and dragged the bow along the ground.

"No, no!" said the arrow, "that is not the way. You must hold me against the stick with one hand and hold the string with the other." Coyote did so.

"Now," said the arrow, "pull with all your might and then let loose."

The arrow flew towards the buffalo, struck one of them in the side, but did not bring it down. Coyote picked up the knife and ran after the wounded buffalo as fast as he could. He shouted so loud that the wounded buffalo soon fell over from fright. Coyote stopped at once to lick up the blood from his wounds. Then he took up the knife and got ready to butcher the buffalo. Just then he looked up and saw a bear sitting on the other side.

"Come on," said Coyote, "I will give you some." But the bear did not move.

Coyote invited him again. Then he came over and helped Coyote to butcher. Now, Coyote was afraid of the bear and so kept on the other side of the buffalo from him. After a while the blood in Coyote's stomach began to roll. The bear heard the noise. He stopped and said, "What's that?"

Then Coyote struck his stomach, and said in a loud voice, "Keep quiet, my brother."

"What did your brother say?" said the bear.

"Well," said Coyote, "my brother just said that he eats bear."

The bear was puzzled by this, and started to go away.

"Where are you going?" said Coyote.

"Oh," said the bear, "I am just going over the hill."

As soon as the bear was out of sight, Coyote went up on the hill to look, and saw the bear running off as fast as he could. So he called out to the bear, "Come back, come back. I thought you were going to help me with my butchering."

Then Coyote went back to the buffalo, and as there were many leaves upon the ground he covered the meat up with them. Then he went on with his butchering and a magpie flew by. Coyote threw a piece of fat to the bird, saying, "Eat this, and then fly all around the world and tell the people to come here (all the birds and animals). There will be a great feast."

The magpie went out and flew all around the country, inviting all the animals to come to the feast. They soon arrived, and gathered around in a circle. Then Coyote sat down to have a talk with them. As soon as he sat down the night hawk began to fly around over his head and make a noise.

"Oh, you get away, you jealous woman," said Coyote. "I am going to talk now." Then he tried to get up to begin his speech, but he could not rise. The night hawk had defecated around him, causing him to stick fast to his seat. Then all of the animals sprang up, ran to the carcass, and began to eat. Some of them soon found the meat hidden in the leaves, scratched it out, and ate it. Just as the meat was gone, Coyote got loose, but the animals ran away and left him. Then he sat down and cried.

After a time he started on his journey again and saw four buffalo. Now he had lost his knife and the arrow. The buffalo were in a hole among some tall grass. "Now, how can I get them," said Coyote to himself. He went close up to them, and, when the buffalo looked at him, he said, "Brothers, turn me into a buffalo so that I can eat grass."

"Well," said a bull, "you stand over to one side and do not move."

"Now," said the buffalo, "get down and roll in the dust."

When Coyote arose, the buffalo charged upon him, but Coyote was afraid and stepped to one side. The buffalo reproved him for this, and reminded him of the injunction to stand still. So they tried it again, but when the buffalo charged, Coyote stepped to one side as before. The buffalo reproved him, but said he would try again. The third time Coyote stepped aside as before. Now the buffalo was very angry, and he told Coyote he would try once more, and that, if he did not stand still, he would kill him.

This time Coyote stood still when the buffalo charged. The buffalo tossed him up into the air and as he came down he became a buffalo. At once Coyote began to eat grass. He was very hungry. The buffalo started to go, but Coyote lingered behind eating grass. Finally, he refused to follow altogether, and the herd left him.

Coyote saw a wolf, and called out to him, "Here, brother, let me turn you into a buffalo." Then Coyote instructed the wolf to stand to one side and not to move. Then he told the wolf to roll in the dust as before. When Coyote charged upon the wolf, the latter stepped to one side. This he did three times, but the fourth time he stood still. Coyote said, "Now, I will make you eat grass."

Then he tossed the wolf into the air, but he did not change. Coyote, himself, became a coyote again. Then the wolf began to fight him. Coyote was angry and said, "Now, you have spoiled all my fun, and I will punish you." So Coyote bit the wolf.

THE EYE-JUGGLER

Tradition Bearer: Unavailable

Source: St. Clair, H. H., and R. H. Lowie. "Shoshone and Comanche Tales." *The Journal of American Folklore* 22 (1909): 278–79.

Date: 1909

Original Source: Comanche

National Origin: Native American

The Comanches were a nomadic culture of the southern Plains (Kansas, Oklahoma, and the Texas Panhandle) who, after the acquisition of the horse, became regarded as master equestrians. Their Coyote narratives more often portray him as a **trickster** rather than a **culture hero**. His restless wandering, curiosity, and vanity inevitably leads him into trouble as seen in the widely distributed **myth** "The Eye Juggler."

Coyote was always knocking about hunting for something. He came to a creek, where there was nothing but green willows. Two little yellow-birds were playing there. He came up to them. Laughing, they pulled out their eyes and threw them on the trees, while they stood below. "Eyes, fall!" they said. Then their eyes fell back into their sockets.

Coyote went to them. He greatly admired their trick. "O brothers! I wish to play that way, too." "Oh, we won't show you, you are too mean. You would throw your eyes into any kind of a tree and lose them."

"Oh, no! I would do it just like you." At last the birds agreed to show him.

They pulled out his eyes, threw them up, and said, "Eyes, fall!" Then his eyes fell back again. Coyote was well pleased.

He pulled out his eyes himself, threw them up, and said, "Eyes, fall!" They returned to their places.

"Let us all go along this creek!" said the birds. "Other people will see us and take a fancy to us." They went along playing.

Coyote said, "I am going over there. I know the trick well now." He left them. He got to another creek. A common willow-tree was standing there. "There is no need to be afraid of this tree. I'll try it first."

He pulled out his eyes, and threw them at the tree. "Eyes, fall!" he shouted. His eyes did not fall. He thus became blind. He tied something around his eyes, and left.

Walking along the creek, he met two young girls. "What kind of girls are you?" "We are Ya'yaru girls."

"We all belong to the same people, then; I am a Ya'yaru young man." The two girls did not know he was blind. He asked them, "Where are you going?"

"We are going over there."

231

"Well, we will all go together." They debated the matter, then all went together.

One girl said, "Just look at the buffaloes there!"

Coyote laughed. "I was wondering how soon you would catch sight of them, that's why I would not tell you about them." When they had gone a little farther, one of the girls asked the other, "Why does he not kill one of those buffaloes for us?" Coyote laughed, "I was wondering how long it would take you to think of that, that's why I would not tell you before. Go around that way to the other side of the buffalo, then they won't see you. Then they will run here, and I will kill one for us."

They followed his directions. The buffaloes, seeing them, ran towards Coyote. When they came nearer, he shot at them and killed one by chance.

When the girls ran up, they said, "He has really killed one."

Coyote laughed. "I was wondering how soon they would see it, that's what I was thinking about you."

They were skinning and cutting up the buffalo. One of the girls exclaimed, "Oh, isn't he fat!"

Coyote said, "Why, certainly, I was looking for a fat one. I strained my eyes mightily hunting for a fat one."

The two girls said, "Doesn't he know well how to look for a fat one?"

Coyote said, "Do you two cut it up, I will build us a house by the creek." He went off to make them a lodge. There were big holes in it everywhere, because he was blind. He made it of brush.

The two girls came with the meat. They said, "This must be a house built by a blind man, there are holes all over."

Coyote laughed. "Oh, you two don't understand. Why, I built it this way so that if lots of enemies charge on us, we might go out in any direction. There is no danger here of our being hemmed in."

The girls said, "We did not think of that." They made their home there, both becoming Coyote's wives.

Once Coyote said to them, "Louse me." The women sat down, and Coyote placed his head on one, and his feet on the other. For a while they loused him, then he fell asleep.

One of the women said, "Let us pull off this rag from his head! He won't know anything about it, he's asleep. Let us look at his eyes." She raised the cover. "Why, he is blind! There are lots of worms in his eyes."

The one on whose lap his head was resting bade her companion bring a stump with lots of ants on it. "Put it under his head, and fetch another one without ants for his feet."

After they had fixed the stumps, one of them said, "Let us go now!"

The older sister said, "Take hold of those bells!" They got some distance away from Coyote. Shortly after they had left, the ants began to, bite him.

He began butting with his head. "Oh, be easy, you two, louse me!" He tried to butt them, but only struck the ground. He woke up, and looked for their trail. Looking back, the women saw him coming.

They began to run. "That is surely Coyote there. Let us beat him by that big red bluff."

The older sister said, "Tear off those bells of yours."

She pulled them off. "He can't see us, he is just following the bells. When we get to the red bluff, drop your bells, and he will fall over it."

Coyote was pursuing them. The woman's bells were jingling as they ran along. When they got to the cliff, she dropped them. Coyote, hearing the bells, followed after them, and was crushed to pieces.

The women went home.

JOKE ON JAKE

Tradition Bearer: Annette Hamilton

Source: Walden, Wayne. "Interview of Annette Hamilton." *American Life Histories:* Manuscripts from the Federal Writers' Project, 1936–1940. Manuscript Division, Library of Congress. 16 October 2005. http://memory.loc.gov/ammem/wpaintro/ wpahome.html.

Date: 1938

Original Source: Colorado

National Origin: European American

The following narrative displays qualities of several common **genres**. The first person rendition qualifies it as a **personal experience narrative**. In focusing on a practical joke on a well-known citizen of Eton, Colorado, it can be classified as a **local legend**, and the feature of Jake's heavy German accent is a characteristic of the ethnic joke.

I guess it was about two months ago a knock caused me to answer the door, and when I looked out I see a tall, lean and rather ragged old fellow. I knew right away he wasn't a salesman. For one thing he didn't spring at me with his sales baloney, nor try to get his foot in the door. He just took off his hat and seemed kind of uncertain how to begin his spiel. Most of 'em have some sort of spiel. He didn't look so very old—about seventy maybe—and he seemed fairly clean, at least not lousy. And the more I looked at him the more he struck me as someone not of these parts, and possibly not a bum at all.

Well, since he didn't seem to know how to speak up for himself, I finally says, "What is it you want?" and, thinking maybe the man is hungry and a bit embarrassed about asking, I finally says, "Are you hungry?" He was, of course, but I guess he hadn't planned on negotiating a feed quite so easy as all that. So I says, "Come on in" and so he comes in and I sets him up to the table. I put out some grub before him and made him a pot of coffee—if there was one thing he fell for, it was coffee.

After awhile he mentions Colorado. "I've been in that state myself," I says. "I know that old state like a book myself," I says. I guess that remark jerked the old man out of himself more than anything else I'd said before. He looked at me then with real interest. "Do you really?" he says. "Do you know the Lone Cone country? I used to punch cattle all around that part," he says. "I've rode the range from hell to breakfast all over that district." From his talk and looks, I guess he wasn't kiddin' either. He looked like that was what he'd been.

"I did some prospecting up in the hills of Boulder County and I used to work around the northern part of the state quite a bit. Do you know where Eton is?" he asked me. I didn't remember that town, but when he told me it was near Greeley, not so far south of the Wyoming line, I had an idea. "I had some mighty fine times up in that part of the state," he said, "but I guess now it's not the same as it used to be, with the automobile and everything. The open range is about gone," he says, "a lot of it become fenced in and made farms of. It can't be the cow country that it used to be."

"I wasn't around there during the dry spell, when Prohibition hit the country, but I bet it was hell then. It sure must have been dreary. As I recollect the old place, and the fellows I used to know, I don't see how they put it over," he says. "Well, thank you, ma'am, for the meal," he says, "I appreciate it very kindly," he says, "and I sure was glad to find someone from the old country," he says as he gets up to go.

"That's all right, if you happen around again, drop in," I says. "I haven't much, but a little something to eat won't break me nor make me, so don't go hungry," I tells him. He would have done the dishes, if I'd wanted him, but I didn't care to have him messing around with 'em, probably making the joint worse looking than it was. So he beats it.

Well, that visit was, as I said, a couple of months ago, and I'd about forgotten all about it. But, lo and behold! my Mister Man shows up again. I'm going back," he says, "I'm going back to the old stamping grounds. And being in the neighborhood, I thought I'd call on you again," he says, "and see if you had any message you wanted me to take along to anyone out there," he says.

"I just can't think of anybody I might know that you might know, I says, "If I did know anybody you might have known, it would probably be since your day," I told him, "but thanks, just the same."

But, as he was eating, he gets to telling me about certain people and asking if I knew any of them. It seemed that I didn't, though.

"I bet you know old Jake Snyder, or heard of him anyway. Everybody knew old Jake." I had to admit that old Jake was not on my calling list, and shameful as it was, I'd never heard tell of him. For a moment I imagined the old man doubted that I'd ever been west of Hoboken, that maybe I was stringing him about being once in Colorado. Anyhow, pretty soon he goes on, evidently giving me the benefit of the doubt.

"Old Jake, he says, "was a saloon keeper, and a man that weighed well over three hundred pounds—three twenty seven so he told everybody, and he looked it. And so far as anyone knew he had always been a bachelor. It's too bad you didn't know Jake; it would be easier to describe him if you'd a known him."

The old man poured himself another cup of coffee and rolled a cigarette. "Poor old Jake," the old man sort of chuckled, "about as mean and low-down a trick as the boys could play on him happened one night when the Duke came to town. And gosh, how Jake liked to eat! One reason he bached (remained a bachelor) I guess, was 'cause he didn't have a woman. They wasn't many women out there anyway, and what there was didn't seem to hanker much for Jake. He was too heavy to be in the running, I s'pose. But he wasn't all fat. He was stout as a bull, and in a rough and tumble fight it would take a darned good man to go up against him."

"But what was the joke they played on him when the Duke came to town?" I asked.

"I was comin' to that," says the old man, "but I'm glad you reminded me, or I might have strayed off the trail. I was thinking of another time, but I'll tell you that later.

"You see Jake did his batchen in the rear part of the house. The saloon, naturally, was in the front part. So when he wasn't too busy at the bar, he'd be in the back a cookin'. He was great for dumplings, and bragged that he could make as good dumplings as any woman in the country. Well, it happened that several times when Jake cooked a stew with dumplings in it, he'd invite one or two of the boys back to eat with him, and see for themselves how good them dumplings were. But the trouble with Jake was, that when he'd go to test the dumplings, to see if they was done, his test wouldn't be just a taste, but a whole darned dumpling. And he'd do this testing so often, that by the time the dumplings ought to of been done, they'd all be et up.

"It wasn't that he was greedy or selfish. He'd just kinda forget about his having company for dinner. He was always sorry of course, and would try to fill them up with something else. So whether the dumplings was as good as Jake said they was, no one ever knew.

"Jake was so good-natured that even when the boys got stung on his dumplings they didn't hardly get mad at him. But while they wasn't mad, some of the boys thought the joke had gone far enough, and it was time to play a joke on Jake.

"So they lays their heads together and figures out a plan. There was a fellow around town good on doing ventriloquism—talkin' down his throat. He might not a been quite what this Charley McCarthy is, but he was so good at it that he had a lot of 'em fooled, includin' me the first time I heard him. So they gets him as the first move.

"Then they borrow a clothes store dummy from Greeley (Colorado). The next thing was to get the dummy trimmed right. After some argument they decides to fix him up like a real dude; as right fresh from England, a member of the House of Lords. Where the Sam Hill they ever got all the duds and trappings they finally dolled him out in, I never heard.

"The next thing they does, is to lug this dummy into ol' Jake's place and to interduce him as a Duke with plenty of money, and out for a good time. They explains that His Highness was purty drunk as he was, but the rest of 'em wasn't, and that the Duke wanted his guests to have service and lots of it. What's more the Duke is sensitive to a slight, but there is one thing he has, besides a bun on, and that was a big wad of good United States money.

"'Glad to meet you,' says Jake, to the Duke, not noticing that the hand he shook belonged to one of the bunch standing 'round the Duke.

"'What'll you have to drink, Mister Duke,' he says. 'Set 'em up to the boys,' the ventriloquist makes the Duke answer.

"So old Jake puts out the drinks to the whole caboodle except the Duke. As he went to serve him, one of the fellows winks and tells Jake to let the Duke sober up a bit. So they lays the Duke out on a table where he could sleep it off, and the rest of the bunch begins to injoy themselves.

"But every so often the Duke would rouse from his drunken slumber enough to holler out, 'set 'em up to the boys.' And it went on that way, round after round, way into the night.

"Course, ol' Jake was happy as a lark, thinkin' of his profits rolling in. It wasn't within Jake's memory that so rich and wonderful a customer had ever patronized his saloon. Of course His Grace had spent most of the time sloopin' on the table. But his frequent orders kept Jake jumping and sweatin' a servin' the rest of the crowd.

"No wonder ol' Jake was pleased. No other bar was as busy as his that night, and by cheese and crackers, no other saloon had a real live Duke as its customer. 'Dose boys who brung him in,' I guess ol' Jake was thinkin', 'I will gif dem a goot meal of dumblings.'

"Finally, Jake began to notice that the crowd had thinned out somewhat. Some of them still stuck around singin' songs, and the Duke still lay on the table. After awhile the gang grew scarcer yet, and purty soon they'd all cleared out, 'cepting Jake and the Duke.

"'Golly,' thinks Jake, 'that darned Duke didn't do any drinking, and he ought to be comin' out of it by now.'

"So Jake does some tidying up of the place; kicks the spitoons back where they belonged; picks up after the crowd; and to kill a little more time, he swabs the bar. All the while he keeps lookin' at the clock and hoping the Duke will wake up. It was long past closing time, and Jake too was getting all in and sleepy.

"Well, to make a long story short; Jake at last goes over to the Duke and speaks to him. 'Mister Duke,' he says, 'Mister Duke, vill you blease vake op.'

"No answer, of course, from the Duke. 'Hey Mister Duke, I wish to glose up now, and vill you blease bay your bill.' Still the Duke slept on, and Jake was beginning to lose his good nature.

"'Mister Duke,' Jake shouts, 'py golly, I vant you to bay up your bill. I vant to glose up, d'ye hear?' But the Duke remains dead to the world.

"'Maybe,' thinks Jake, 'that damned Duke is trying to get out of paying him.' That was something he hadn't thought of, and, horrified by the awful suspicion, he makes another try at getting the Duke to sit up and take notice. He shakes the Duke, and then he tumbles him off the table and lets him fall on the floor. By now with his Dutch temper up, he was just on the point of cuffing the Duke into sobriety, and collecting his account when some of the gang rushed in. They'd been watching all the time through a window. Seeing the Duke stretched out on the floor, and seeming to be plumb dead, they says: 'My God, Jake whatcha done! Oh! Jake it looks as if you've killed the Duke. Bet you that's just what you done!'

"Old Jake had been purty mad a moment before, but now he gets purty darned scared. He tries to do some swift thinkin'.

"'Boys,' he said, 'py Golly I had to do it. I didn't vant to hit him, but that son-of-a-gun of a Duke drew a knife on me.'

"Then, of course the bunch begin to laugh and, picking the Duke up, they exposes him to Jake for the wooden dummy he was.

"'Boys,' said Jake, forgetting entirely the Duke's bill, and tickled to death that he wasn't goin' to be hung for murder, 'boys gome cop and haf a drink. Py Golly dat vas a goot joke on me!'"

HE-MAN FROM THE WEST

Tradition Bearer: Mrs. R. Ivanoff

Source: Walden, Wayne. "Interview of Mrs. R. Ivanoff." *American Life Histories: Manuscripts from the Federal Writers' Project, 1936–1940.* Manuscript Division, Library of Congress. 12 October 2005. http://memory.loc.gov/ammem/wpaintro/wpahome.html.

Date: 1938

Original Source: Colorado

National Origin: European American

The following **tall tale** alludes to former heavyweight boxing champions: James Jackson "Jim" Jeffries (1875–1953), Arthur John "Jack" Johnson (1878–1946), James John "Gentleman Jim" Corbett (1866–1933), Robert James "Bob" Fitzsimmons (1863–1917) and John L. Sullivan (1858–1918).

I'll give you this as I heard it told years ago by my brother-in-law.

He had come from the West and was therefore regarded by an eight year old boy in the family as a hero, a he-man who had fought many battles with wild Indians and desperadoes. One day, when the kid kept urging him to tell about some of the great fights that he'd been in out West, this is what he told:

"Well, I dunno—I ain't never been the kind that went 'round looking for scraps, but I've been in a few. One that comes to mind, hardly seems worth the tellin', but it happened so quick and was finished so soon, that I almost forgot about it until you reminded me of it.

"It was out in Denver, when one day I walked into a saloon to get a drink. I noticed that there was a long line-up at the bar, but didn't notice till I bellied up that it was a bunch of old-time heavyweights. There was Jim Jeffries and Jack Johnson and Jim Corbett and Bob Fitzsimmons and John L. Sullivan and a lot of others includin' a bunch of lighter weights, all tuff guys too.

"Well, that was alright. I wasn't mad at nobody, so I just stood there friendly like, waitin' for my beer, while the barkeep was tendin' to these other guys. Finally, when he did get around to me and starts to hand me my schooner, one of these here blokes—Sullivan or Jeffries—I forget just which of 'em it was—reaches out to grab it away from me.

"I was kinda hot-tempered in those days, so with that I lets loose and pops him one. Well he, of course, falls back and knocks against the guy next to him, and that one falls over spilling the guy next to him. Anyhow they all went tumbling down like a bunch of stood-up dominoes.

"By that time I had finished the beer and I walked out of the place. There was a mule hitched just outside the door and he happened to be one of them kicking kind. He figured, I guess, that he might as well take a kick at me as anybody so, sure enough, he started in. But me being still kind of sore about what happened inside the saloon, I caught that mule's foot, when he kicked out at me, and bit the darned thing plumb off."

But that was a bit too tall a one for the kid. It probably should have been toned down a bit, because even he half-suspected it was a lie.

THE POWERS THAT BE: SACRED TALES

THE THREE NEPHITES

A Messenger to the Indians

Tradition Bearer: Sextus E. Johnson

Source: Fife, Austin E. "The Legend of the Three Nephites Among the Mormons." *Journal of American Folklore* 53 (1940): 10–11.

Date: 1911

Original Source: Utah

National Origin: European American

According to the teachings of the Church of Jesus Christ of Latter-Day Saints as recorded in the Book of Mormon, Jesus visited the Western Hemisphere after his crucifixion. He promised three of his New World believers, the Three Nephites, immortality. The Three Nephites appear in **legend**, usually alone, often in the guise of beggars or homeless wanderers. They offer assistance in times of trouble, cure the sick, bring enlightenment, or perform other benevolent acts. The tales of the Three Nephites serve to reinforce the teachings of the Book of Mormon and to confirm God's concern for the faithful.

During the summer of 1876 a stranger is said to have appeared to the Indians west of St. George, Utah, at a place called Duck Creek. He told the Indians that he was one of their forefathers and that he had many things to tell them because he had lived for a long time upon the earth. At his request runners were sent out to call in all the bands of Indians who dwelt nearby. The stranger was described by the Indians as a man having a long white beard who was entirely dressed in white. He stayed with them for several months and during the whole of his stay with them not an Indian was seen along the Virgin River or its tributaries.

When the Indians had returned to their homes, Sextus E. Johnson, who is the writer of the account which we are telling, and his brother, Nephi Johnson, called the Indians together and questioned them about the man who had appeared to them out of the west. They were informed that his name was Nephi and that he told them that the Mormons were their friends and that they should listen to their advice, assuring them that in due time prophets would come among the Indians and teach them how to live a better life. When they inquired how long he had lived upon the earth he answered them, but it was so many moons that they could not enumerate them, the number being so far beyond their comprehension.

Mr. Johnson, addressing Joseph F. Smith, who was then President of the Mormon Church, assured him that he and his brother were convinced that this stranger really had visited the Indians from out of the west, that his name was indeed Nephi, and that he was one of those ancient American apostles to whom Christ had given the mission to remain upon this earth as His special witnesses until He should come again in His glory.

A Wonderful Testimony

Tradition Bearer: Maud May Babcock

Source: Fife, Austin E. "The Legend of the Three Nephites Among the Mormons." *Journal of American Folklore* 53 (1940): 13–15.

Date: 1911

Original Source: Utah

National Origin: European American

During the summer of 1900 the writer, Miss Maud May Babcock, was at Brighton, which is in the mountains southeast of Salt Lake City. Since it was her first vacation in the mountains she spent all her time eagerly climbing the various neighboring peaks, on foot and on horseback, in the company of a school teacher, Carrie Helen Lamson, a woman some years her elder. On each of their excursions they grew more venturesome and wandered farther from camp.

On one occasion they explored the canyon beyond Alta, which is in the Little Cottonwood. When they arrived at the pass between that river and American Fork canyon they continued with the intention of climbing the peak beyond. However, when they suddenly discovered that the day was advancing and that they could not hope to climb that distant peak and return before dark, they changed directions and climbed a mountain that was not so far away and which miners of the region call North Pole Peak. They found this mountain much higher than they had expected, and after ascending ridge after ridge, each time expecting to arrive at the summit, they finally reached the top, which dominated the entire valley and neighboring mountains. Having admired the exquisite view, which they had from this summit, they determined to return to this peak when they could make a more extensive excursion and spend two days before returning to camp. This decision made, they returned to camp and made arrangements for their more extensive trip, which was to take place a week later.

When they were ready to leave they were advised to take a shorter trail than the one over which they had traveled previously, going above Dog Lake to Lake Catherine and thence to the divide. By about seven o'clock in the morning they had reached what appeared to be the right trail, which they came upon near a deserted mine camp above Dog Lake. Beyond this point they soon found that they could go no further, nor yet get back without crossing a crevice that was filled with shale. The writer tried to force her horse to cross the shale, but as soon as the shale began to slide the horse refused to move. Meanwhile the other woman had not been able to get her horse to move at all. Finally after leaving her horse the writer succeeded in reaching the top of the mountain where she hoped to be able to find help in the guise of some wandering prospector, but she found no one. She was forced to climb over the jagged peak above her horse, which she then tried to drive across the sliding shale by touching him with a small willow, but he would not move. In this crucial moment when she feared that the shale would begin to slide carrying herself, her companion and both horses to their death, she prayed to her Heavenly Father for help.

As she raised her head a voice above her said, "How did you come here, my daughter?" "I jabbered in my relief and excitement, trying to explain our predicament, and before my explanation was finished I was standing on the top, with Miss Lamson and both our horses in a circle facing the stranger." She affirms that neither she nor her companion have any recollection of how they or their horses got there.

Their mysterious helper had a gray Vandyke beard, a cap on his head, and was dressed in new blue overalls. He was very clean and the women both re-marked that his soft white hands must have been unused to manual labor.

He addressed Miss Babcock as "My daughter," and when Miss Lamson (who was not a Mormon) asked him several questions he directed his answers to Miss Babcock. When the stranger was asked which way they should continue their journey he told them to go right on the way they were going and that everything would be all right.

As they were talking to him they got on their horses and started on their way, but before going twenty feet it occurred to Miss Babcock that she had not thanked him for his great service. When she turned to do so the mysterious stranger was no where to be seen although they had clear vision for at least a mile in every direction—he had vanished. They had seemed dazed from the wonder and marvel of the experience, which up to the mysterious stranger's miraculous disappearance had seemed perfectly natural, but which now made the writer exclaim as if inspired, "He was one of the Three Nephites."

As the two women continued on their way they suddenly became aware of the peculiar hob-nail footprints which the stranger had made as he came toward the point of the hill where he had rescued them. They followed these tracks from about seven in the morning until they had reached the American Fork canyon, about one in the afternoon. At times they left these tracks to make a short-cut, but on each of these occasions they were forced to return and follow the footprints, because the short-cut was impossible. When they had come down the mountain into the canyon they met some miners who advised them to go through Deer Creek into Provo canyon instead of through the South Fork, and thence into the North Fork of the Provo because of the heavy snow. They did as the miners had advised them. The way was long and tiresome, and they were not able to reach camp until after midnight. The writer says she has always believed that if she had continued following the stranger's foot-prints through the South Fork, she would have found the way passable and in addition would have been able to see the glacier behind Timpanogos Mountain as they had planned.

On the following morning the two women started up the Provo River toward the Hot Pots. Because they were not dressed in the conventional feminine dress, they decided to take the north side of the Provo valley and thus avoid the towns located on the south side. They followed a road along this side of the canyon until it suddenly ran out into an irrigation ditch which had on either side large willow trees with foliage so thick that they had to lie flat on their horses to avoid the branches.

After going a half a mile or more the writer's horse suddenly wheeled about almost tearing her clothes off on the overhanging branches. Getting off and looking around, she found a large rattlesnake coiled and ready to strike. Upon consideration the women decided that it would be better to brave the rattler than to go back through all the willows so they forced the horses through, throwing stones at the snake as they passed.

When they had succeeded in getting through the willows and past the snake, the writer discovered that she had lost a watch and chain which was a treasured gift from a dear friend and which she had promised to keep always. Feeling sure that she had lost the watch in the mud of the stream at the point where she had passed the rattlesnake, she prayed for strength and went back to look for it, fearing at every moment to come upon the rattlesnake. She found the water of the ditch muddied from the horses' hoofs and, after poking around for some minutes in the roily water, she again prayed for assistance. Opening her eyes, she saw her watch, all muddy from having dropped into the bed of the ditch and with the case open; yet it was hanging on a low bush a foot or two above the water. When the mud had been cleaned from the case it started to go and has kept good time ever since.

The result of all these experiences was that the companion of Miss Babcock, who was both a non-Mormon and an atheist, received thereby a proof that God answers prayer, and that Mormonism is the true church of Christ.

Ziegler's Conversion

Tradition Bearer: Wesley Ziegler

Source: Fife, Austin E. "The Legend of the Three Nephites Among the Mormons." *Journal of American Folklore* 53 (1940): 17–19.

Date: 1931

Original Source: Utah
National Origin: European American

The experiences reported in this summary took place, according to the writer, when he was between twelve and fifteen years of age.

Wesley Ziegler says that he was born of parents who had left the ministry and who had taught him to believe in Christ without sending him to any particular church. When he was about twelve years old he states that the Lord spoke to him in a dream. He saw an old man coming towards him who was dressed in a long sack-cloth robe and who carried a staff in his hand. Calling the young man by his first name, he told him that he was Peter, and then led him away to the city of Rome and showed him the Emperor Nero who, he states, was a very corrupt man. And he saw the family tree of Nero with its five branches and the three children of this Emperor: the firstborn without a face, the second without a head, and the third born with two heads. This dream frightened the boy very much for he could not make out what it meant.

The young man states that he continued to receive visions and revelations until eventually he came to understand his original dream and many other spiritual things. The city of Rome, he says, represents the Catholic Church, and the corrupt Emperor its corruption. The five branches of his family tree represent the five branches into which that church has been split, i.e., Roman Catholic, Greek Catholic, etc. The children represented the Protestant churches, some of which lack a face, some a head, and others of which have two heads. Some lack this truth, some that, and some of them lay too much stress on certain things. He had received a testimony of the great apostasy although he says that he had never known that such an apostasy had ever taken place.

The young man states that it was through these wonderful experiences that he was brought to the Church of Jesus Christ of Latter Day Saints, long before he had had any contact with this church, and long before he had heard anything more than passing mention of it. He had not even known that the Mormons were Christians. Being thus converted, he went over to the public library to learn something about the Mormons. He found nothing but bitter and prejudiced books, which told mostly lies about the Mormons, but in which he eagerly searched for the truth. At first he conducted this investigation without the knowledge of his parents. He had been told that the library did not contain a copy of the *Book of Mormon* but after about a year's study in this library he ran across a copy and took it home and read it to his parents, who by this time were aware of their son's interest in Mormonism.

Having finished reading the *Book of Mormon*, he returned it to the library but could not bear to leave it there. He went over and got it a second time, and as he was walking home with the book under his arm, he was suddenly accosted by one of the most distressed of men he had ever seen. He was clothed in rags, held together with big safety pins. His beard was grizzled; he was poverty personified. When he asked the youth for charity and was offered the only penny that the boy had, he refused to take it. He wanted not money, he said, so much as a place to sleep. When he was asked if he had a home, he replied that he had no definite one, that he was just a tramp, he guessed. Then he corrected himself and said that he was not exactly a tramp either, but rather a wanderer. The boy told him that he might go to the Salvation Army or to the City Welfare Department. He asked where the Salvation Army was. When the boy tried to explain its approximate location, the wanderer asked him if he really knew where it was and the boy was forced to admit that he did not. Then the wanderer told him that he should always remember never to give directions to anyone on any matter unless he was certain that those directions were correct.

Then he reached down and took the *Book of Mormon* from under the boy's arm, opened it, and started a sermon. The things that he explained were most wonderful, and many of them were beyond the boy's comprehension. As he spoke he would leaf through the *Book,* turning over whole groups of pages at a time, and always he would turn to the very words he wanted to illustrate what he was saying.

"My," he said, "isn't this a wonderful book! If people would only read it, it would do them so much good." For a long time he talked and explained wonderful things and finally he concluded by saying, "Yes, my boy, you are undertaking a very deep study." Next he looked at the boy's identification card and read his name and address aloud. Then he closed the *Book of Mormon,* gave it back to the boy, and extended his hand saying, "Well, goodbye, my friend. You are my friend, aren't you?" The boy took his hand and said that he was.

As the stranger started to walk away the boy turned to watch him. He could have gone only a few steps when he suddenly disappeared.

The boy was bewildered by the situation and looked for him in every direction, but there was no mistaking it, he was gone. Having read the *Book of Mormon,* the boy quite naturally thought of the Three Nephites who were to tarry until Jesus came. Since that time, he says, he has heard the testimonies of other people who have seen one of them, and he finds that his experience corresponds closely to theirs. He says he has no doubt that this man was one of them, although he could have been St. John. This wanderer was the first Mormon that he had ever seen.

One of the Three Nephites Brings a Special Spiritual Message

Tradition Bearer: Joseph Wood

Source: Fife, Austin E. "The Legend of the Three Nephites Among the Mormons." *Journal of American Folklore* 53 (1940): 23–25.

Date: 1939

Original Source: Utah

National Origin: European American

I prayed for six years that I might have the privilege of a visit with one of those men (i.e., one of the Three Nephites), if not more. That's a long time, isn't it? We usually get pretty tired and give up before then. But my faith was that strong that that was possible.

On one winter evening just forty-nine years ago this winter (i.e., 1890) I was chopping wood out in the snow, snow about eighteen or twenty inches deep, and I saw that man coming up the street, and the impression come to me that that's one of the Three Nephites, so I watched him all up the street, kept on chopping but kept watching him.

He come on up and come up to me and said, "Young man, I've come to have a talk with you. Come on in the house. I've got something to show you, and to have a talk with you." I didn't invite him in at all; he come right in my own home and opened the door for me. The house has been torn down, but that's a picture of it. (He showed us a picture of the house, and pointed out the room where he sat with the Nephite).

I mustn't tell you all he told me; it would hit you too hard. I had around half an hour's conversation with that man. He talked about our temples. He talked about the disturbances that've come up in the Church, and he give me to understand that fact that the Almighty God, the Eternal Father, would never give us anything any more that surpassed or excelled that *Book of Mormon*. That was the greatest thing ever come to the people of this dispensation for our guide.

I pressed him hard to know what his name was. I didn't know then that prediction in the *Book of Mormon* that their names would never be known. So when I asked him what his name was so I'd know which one he was he didn't tell me.

He was a fine looking man, the set of his eyes, so sweet and pretty—a fine head of hair—his nose, even and perfect. The finest complexion I ever saw on a human being. No child ever born had as fine a complexion as that man.

It wouldn't do for me to give you all our conversation. It would be too hard for you. I was never asked to make it known. Strange to say, you are the only people ever asked me that question (meaning, if he had ever seen one of the Three Nephites).

The disturbances I went through was outlined, the troubles that we went through. It wasn't long before this people was confronted with this question: "What shall we do about polygamy?" He outlined those troubles then, the troubles coming to this people. I was wonderfully disturbed at that time. Things had taken place in this ward because I stood on an injustice when I was in the bishopric—I was out then—and consolation came through which I was reconciled fully, and also confirmed my conviction that I already had, that *the Book of Mormon* came actually from the only God and was a guide to these people.

When that man left me I questioned him hard where he was from. He was very pointed in not answering me or my questions. He didn't tell me his name, he didn't tell me just where he was going. He give me to understand he was from the north. When he left me he left me as sudden. He opened the door and shut it, and that's all. I opened the door but could not see my visitor. How he went and where he went I don't know. Perhaps he moved quicker than my eye; I couldn't say. It could be compared to sleight of hand.

He was the finest looking character there could possibly be. He was dressed like an ordinary man. Clothes of dark nature. His beard was just as white as the driven snow. And his hair, just as white as it could be. I said to him, "You have the appearance actually of being a young person, but your hair says that you are aged." All I got was a good big smile from that; he didn't say nothing at all. I can't give you all that conversation because I feel that it shouldn't go out. I witnessed it and I saw it all the way through, all he said about the troubles to come to us, and disturbances. He didn't give me any time for certain changes to take place.

He was well proportioned. He stood as straight as an Indian. In all his actions he was so pleasant, so nice looking, so young, in every way just as white as could be, his beard and hair. The prettiest hair I ever saw in my life was on that man's head. Such a lovely complexion. He fulfilled the "white and delightsome people" in every way. He told me of things relative to my own home.

Miraculous Healing by One of the Three Nephites

Tradition Bearer: Larene K. Bleeker

Source: Fife, Austin E. "The Legend of the Three Nephites Among the Mormons." *Journal of American Folklore* 53 (1940): 35.

Date: 1939

Original Source: Utah

National Origin: European American

This was in Provo. Old David John was Stake President there one time, lived in a big two story house on Third South. It happened in the winter time.

The snow was very deep on the ground, especially so, and for days the family hadn't gone outside for anything. It was in the—I don't know just why they were so isolated, think they were quarantined for a contagious disease, one of the children was very ill. They didn't have telephones, and the mother had no way of summoning help. In the night a knock came on the door and she went to the door, and a very benevolent-looking man was standing there. She described him as kind-looking with a snow-white beard. He said he had been sent and he understood there was sickness and they needed help. Her first thought was that he was one of the brethren in the ward. Then a little later she thought, "He isn't anyone I know, he isn't anyone that lives in Provo." He placed his hands on the child's head and blessed the child, and she immediately went to sleep.

It was so cold and the snow was so deep that she asked him to set up to the fire and dry his feet, and then she looked at his feet and there was no snow on them and they were dry. She immediately thought he had left his over-shoes outside by the door, and she asked him if he had. He looked at her and smiled. When he did speak his voice was very mellow and musical.

He said he must go. She tried to prevail on him to stay, but he said he must go. She went out with him to the door, and then came in. Then she thought how strange it was how he got to the door, there was such a narrow space between the house and fence. It seemed to her that it would be impossible for him to walk around, the snow was so deep. The door was one that they didn't use at all. Out of curiosity she took a lantern, but she couldn't see any tracks in the snow, either coming or going. Only then it flashed across her that he was one of the Three Nephites.

LEGEND OF THE TETON SIOUX MEDICINE PIPE

Tradition Bearer: Percy Phillips

Source: Dorsey, George A. "Legend of the Teton Sioux Medicine Pipe." *Journal of American Folklore* 19 (1906): 326–29.

Date: ca. 1906

Original Source: Teton

National Origin: Native American

The Teton were the major division of the Dakota (Sioux) residing in the Dakotas, but originally with bands ranging much of the area west of the Missouri River in pursuit of the buffalo herds that provided their major source of subsistence. The following narrative is a composite of **myth** and, in the final three paragraphs, **legend**. The **myth** couples the pipe as a symbol of spiritual sustenance for the Northern Plains Classic cultures, with the buffalo as the symbol of physical sustenance. Folklorist George A. Dorsey's introductory comments to the tale are worth quoting at length. Dorsey writes, "The following account of what seems to have been an important tribal ceremony was obtained from Percy Phillips, a young full-blood educated Sioux, living on the Cheyenne Reservation, South Dakota. The pipe referred to in the account is said to belong to the Sans Arcs division of the Teton Sioux, and is in the possession of Red-Hair, the keeper. The ceremony lasts about half a day and the singing of the ritual is of about one hour's duration. The ritual is preceded by songs from the medicine-men. The pipe when not in use is kept in a bundle, which is about three feet long; the pipe itself being protected by gifts or offerings which have been made to it, then wrapped with buckskin and placed in a bag of woven buffalo hair. The outer wrapper of buffalo hide has been replaced by one of canvas. The ceremony is said to be performed in influential families when a girl first attains the age of womanhood and also when a period of mourning is stopped by a formal feast" (326).

When the Indians were all living together in the east, near a great lake, they were encamped in a large circle. At that time there was supposed to be but one language spoken; and there were chiefs for every tribe, one chief to every band.

One day two young men went out hunting in a mountainous country. At the top of a high tableland they found game.

On their way down the hill they saw a woman coming towards them. As they came near to the woman they noticed that she had something in her arms. On approaching still nearer they discovered that she was a fine-looking young woman, carrying a pipe on her left arm. Suddenly one of the young men said: "Let us outrage her."

He tempted the other man, who said: "No, it is not well that you should do anything of the sort, for she is of mysterious appearance." When they came closer, both men stopped and obstructed her way.

The woman stopped and said: "I heard what you were saying."

The tempter urged his fellow, and said: "Let us leap upon her."

The other man answered: "No, you must not harm her."

The tempter said: "Yes, I will attack her, for there is no one around."

The other man said: "You may, but I will stand aside."

The woman said: "I do not wish to stir up any strife, since I am on a special errand from the Great Medicine." With this she stepped aside, took the pipe, which was seen to be filled, from her left arm and laid it down upon a buffalo chip, with the stem directly toward the east. Then she laughed and sat down.

The tempter approached her abruptly, threw her prostrate, and as he was on the verge of outraging her there seemed to be a very great rumbling in the heavens, and there came forth from the heavens, as it were, mist which enveloped the place where they lay so that they could not be seen. There they remained for a time, and when the mist lifted there was to be seen only the skeleton of the man, but the woman came away unchanged. The young man who had stood at one side watching was frightened and started to run away, but the woman called him back. As he looked back the woman told him to go to the camp where all the people were and say: "A sacred pipe is coming to you, which will furnish you abundance in the Spirit Land."

The young man went away as fast as he could, and when he came to the place of the chief he delivered his message. Immediately all the chiefs were gathered together, and they erected a tipi large enough to contain a great many people, and they made ready for the coming of the woman with the pipe.

As she appeared on the hill-top on her way to the camp, the lightning flashed in every direction about her. So mysterious was her coming that even the dogs were afraid to bark. As the woman drew near, the chiefs gathered in a circle, holding in their midst a red blanket, with a white border and thus they went forth to meet her. A little distance from the camp the woman stopped, and when the priests came to her they threw down the blanket for her to stand upon. All of the chiefs took hold of the blanket and carried her to the center of the large tipi especially prepared for her coming.

The woman had with her the large pipe, and when she was set down, she spoke as follows: "This pipe is to be transmitted from generation to generation, and thus it shall be handed down to the end of time." The woman laid the pipe on a buffalo chip. Again she spoke, and said: "There shall be but one nation, and by that nation this pipe must be kept sacred; it must be used in time of war, in time of famine, in time of sickness, in time of need of any sort, as an instrument for preservation. This pipe will be your chief deity. It must be kept by the best chief of the tribe, and must be attended to once a year, by the assemblage of the most upright chiefs. Whenever they open the pipe there must be made tools expressly for handling the fire, a certain stick must be trimmed and handled by virgins or by young men of chastity, expressly for the pipe, a tamper, and a little spoon must be made to take up the fire. The pipe must have a wrapping of wool of the buffalo only. From the first enemy that shall be killed through the power of the pipe an ear shall be cut off and tied to the pipe-stem. The first scalp to be taken shall be treated in the same way. Whenever you are hungry my instructions must be followed. Ten men shall open the pipe, to plead to the Great Owner of the pipe. Should the man holding the pipe do any wrong there would be a demolition of his whole family. Through the advice of your ten best chiefs the pipe shall be kept by the very best chief of all. As long as the holder shall walk reverently and keep himself in order, the keeping of the pipe shall be hereditary."

As the woman was leaving the tipi she said that she was going to stop four times on the way to the hill, and the priests should smoke the pipe as she was leaving; that the fourth time she should stop she would transform herself. The ten chiefs lighted the pipe, and as they were smoking the woman went away, then stopped and looked back. Again she went on, and looked back. Again she stopped and looked back, and the fourth time she stopped and looked back she turned toward the hill and ran, and she transformed herself into a splendid five-year-old buffalo, then disappeared in the hills.

Now the chiefs assembled and held a council, so as to establish rules regulating the keeping of the pipe. They selected the best chief to hold the pipe. During the ceremony of the pipe he was to relate exactly the story that the woman had told when she brought the pipe to the camp, nor might he deviate from or leave out any of her words. While the chiefs were still in council they secured a wrapper for the pipe, also all the sticks that were necessary for use with the pipe, all made by maidens. The pipe was then raised high aloft in the midst of the council lodge. The pipe was cared for with great reverence. No unclean woman might approach it.

A few days after the pipe had been brought, there was a quarrel within the camp in which two people were killed. In accordance with the woman's command, they cut the ear from one and tied it on the pipe-stem, together with the scalp, and that ear and that scalp are on the pipe to this day. The same sticks that were made by the ancient people, as also the covering of buffalo hair, are still with the ancient pipe, which is said to be nine hundred years old.

This pipe is now kept by an old Sioux chief who lives at the Cheyenne Agency, South Dakota, and who is about ninety-three years old. They say that when he dies he will have been the last man to hold the pipe; that he is to go to the grave with the pipe.

There have been offerings made to this pipe by different tribes, such as bracelets, earrings, rings, arrows, brushes, stones, and various other trinkets being given to the pipe alone, all of which are kept with the pipe. They say that whenever in need or hungry, the buffalo gone, they go to work and call the ten best men in, who go and plead to the pipe, having unwrapped it, and that within from one to three days thereafter they receive all that they pray for. Since the scattering of the tribe, in times of peace the pipe is held as peacemaker, and hence is sometimes called the "pipe of peace;" but the people call it the "calf pipe," for the woman who brought it transformed herself into a buffalo, and the pipe coming from her must therefore be a calf.

General Custer swore by this pipe that he was not going to fight the Indians any more. But the very next summer he met death, for he disregarded the oath he had made to the pipe. He who swears by the pipe and breaks oath, comes to destruction, and his whole family dies, or sickness comes upon them.

THE WOMAN WITH A BEAR LOVER

Tradition Bearer: Unavailable

Source: Wissler, Clark. "Some Dakota Myths II." *Journal of American Folklore* 20 (1907): 195–96.

Date: ca. 1900

Original Source: Ogalala Lakota (Sioux)

National Origin: Native American

See the Omaha **myth** "The Rolling Skull" (Vol. I, p. 239) for a similar pursuit by the head of a vengeful relative. The "Obstacle Flight" **tale type** (AT313 and 314)—in which victims throw objects (in this case a whetstone) behind them that are magically transformed into obstacles (here, a mountain)—is cross-culturally distributed.

Once there was a man who lived alone with his three children and his young wife. One day, when the man returned from deer hunting, he found the children cooking bear's flesh. The next day, when·he returned, he found them again cooking bear. Then he thought to him-self, "I wonder how they kill these bears. The next time I shall watch." So the next day he made ready as if to go deer hunting, but as soon as he got into the brush he concealed himself and waited.

In a little while he saw his young wife come out of the tipi with an axe on her back and walk toward the woods. As she went along, she struck the trees with her axe until she came to one that sounded hollow. When she struck on this a bear came out of the top, sprang to the ground, and after caressing the woman had sexual relations with her. Then the woman arose from the ground and killed him with the axe.

After the man saw what had happened, he went on with his hunting. When he returned he found his children cooking bear as before. He told the children not to eat any of the meat. His purpose was to make the woman eat all of it. Then he told his wife to eat.

At last she said, "I have enough now." The man did not listen to her but took up the meat and forced it all down her throat until she died.

Then the man said, "Now children, you are to go back to your father [the bear]."

He gave them the skin of an oriole and a whetstone. Then he sent them out to look for their father. "Go home," he said, "you do not belong here."

So the children started on their way. While they were going they heard a little thing coming after them. They looked around and saw their mother's head rolling along. "Where are you going?" said the head to the children.

The children were afraid and made no reply, but went on as fast as they could. They cried when the head was about to overtake them.

One of the children threw down the whetstone, and it turned into a very high mountain. This mountain separated the children from their mother's head. When the head came to the foot of the mountain, a snake came along and the head said to it, "Grandfather, make a hole through this mountain for me. If you will make a hole through this mountain for me I will give you some scrapings from a buffalo-hide."

So the snake bored a hole through the mountain. When the head had rolled through to the other side, it turned upon the snake and said, "No, I will not give you anything."

Then the head took the snake and pulled it in two. Then the head went on in pursuit of the children, who were very tired. At last they went up into a tree to rest. The head came to the foot of the tree, looked up and saw the children at the top.

The head called to them, "My children, I have very hard times; come down and go home with me." The children did not come down. The head waited a while at the foot of the tree, and then said angrily, "If you do not come down I will punish you. I will crush you, I will pound you up fine."

Then the head began to shake the tree, and when the tree began to tremble a voice from above said to the children, "Take the bird's nest you see near you and sit on it." Just as the children got into the nest, the tree began to fall, but the wind carried the nest far off. At last the nest came to the ground, and the children got out and hurried on their way. Finally they came to a very large river.

They looked back and saw the head still following them. Out in the river they saw something black moving along.

When the head saw the children, it called out, "Now, I shall get you. You will drown."

The black object in the water was a boat with a man in it. When the man saw the children on the shore and the head pursuing, he called out to them, "My children, come here. I will kill your mother."

The children sprang into the water and swam to the boat. When they neared it, the man put out his oar and raised the children into the boat one after the other. The head rolled into the water and swam toward the boat also.

The head said to the man, "Take me, too." So the man put out his oar, and the head rolled up on it, but instead of lifting the head into the boat, the man swung the oar with all his might, and the head fell far out into the stream. Then he rowed out to where the head was floating and beat it under with his oar.

MAGICAL FLIGHT

Tradition Bearer: Walter Mountain Chief

Source: Knox, Robert H. "A Blackfoot Version of the Magical Flight." *Journal of American Folklore* 36 (1923): 401–3.

Date: 1921

Original Source: Blackfoot

National Origin: Native American

The resemblance between this **myth** and the previous narrative ("The Woman with a Bear Lover," p. 254) is obvious. The woman who takes a snake as a lover, like the mother in the previous tale, turns entirely against humankind, including her own family. The escape in the present **myth**, however, does not involve the change of ordinary objects into obstacles; rather, the brothers use supernatural power to transform themselves. The human-to-constellation transformation is a common Native American theme.

Once there was a couple in the camps. The woman used to go after fire-wood and would return late carrying it on her back. Finally her husband discovered that she was accustomed to come back late and thought that he would secretly watch her. Next day when the woman went after wood again, the man followed just far enough behind to watch. After the woman had reached the place where she went to gather wood, she packed up a bundle and went to a standing hollow tree. When she reached it she tapped all around on the bark. The man was watching all the while. Suddenly a large rattle-snake crawled out of the tree and on reaching the ground appeared as a nice looking young man. In this guise it became the woman's lover. When the husband saw this he understood why his wife had been so late in returning. Then he went home unseen and paid no further attention to her. The woman came home late as usual but the husband did not tell her what he had seen.

The next morning the man rose early and went to the hollow tree he had seen in the woods. When he reached it he gave a few taps as a signal as his wife always did and the snake crawled out. When it had come part way out, the man

257

took his knife and cut off its head, thus ending the snake's life. The man then went back to camp, but he did not say that he had killed the snake. His wife asked him why he had gone out so early. He said it was of no importance; he had just gotten up early.

They then ate their breakfast and the woman went out as usual for wood. When she reached the hollow tree and saw that her lover had been killed, she wept bitterly for the snake. She returned to the camp at once and her husband saw that she had been weeping. He then asked her if she had loved this fellow, and she replied, "Yes, certainly I do."

Her husband said, "Then you shall die with him," and took his knife to cut off her head. After he had killed her, he left his camp and all the others left theirs.

This woman had seven brothers who were away on the warpath and knew nothing of these happenings. Their sister's lodge was still standing when they returned. They were tired and hungry when they came to the lodge. It was still in the condition the husband had left it, with provisions and bedding still inside. The brothers thought their sister and her husband had gone away on an errand or for a visit.

Suddenly as they were sitting there, they heard their sister talking outside the tent. She said, "I am not alive now; I have been killed. Help yourselves to the dried bear meat; feed yourselves. Brothers, there is one thing I ask of you; do not watch me to see what I am doing, because I do not look as nice as I used to." These boys did not know of the troubles of their sister.

One day when she was scraping hides outside the tipi, the youngest of the seven brothers told another that he would peep through a hole and see how their sister looked. He peeped through the hole and saw her head flopping about the hide as it worked on it. "Oh, come and see for yourselves how horrible our sister looks," he said to his brothers. So they looked and were all frightened.

One day the seven brothers went hunting and when they had gone some distance, they sent their youngest brother back. His name was Breast-Chief. He went back alone. He was a sort of medicine man himself; when he neared the camp he turned himself into a small black bug. Then he went to the lodge and crawled in.

There he saw his sister working on an elk hide. She was painting seven heads of hair on this hide and was talking to herself, saying, "The eldest boy's head will be here, the second eldest will be here, the third will be here," and so on till she came to Breast-Chief. When she came to him she said, "Breast-Chief's head will be right here on this spot." All the while Breast-Chief was watching and listening to every word his sister said. Then he disappeared. Then his sister said, "Oh, you silly bug. After you heard everything I said, you left. I am pretty sure you are Breast-Chief, Bug."

When he was out of sight he changed to a man again. At this time he met his brothers returning with deer meat. He said to them, "Brothers, our sister is making a robe of elk hide. She will kill all of us; then she will scalp us and put our scalps on the robe she is making." He then told them of what he had seen her doing and what she had said. They all said, "Let us fool our sister. Let us tell her that we have gotten a huge quantity of deer meat and left it packed up far away on the last ridge from camp." When they returned to camp they told her this story.

The sister went after the meat and as soon as she had gone, they all ran away. They were already a long way off when she returned. She knew then that they had run away. Breast-Chief was in disguise at the lodge unseen by her. He heard his sister saying as she came into the lodge, "Oh, my, I miss those boys. I did not think that they would save their lives. Breast-Chief is the one I want to kill most." When he heard this, he followed his brothers and told them what his sister had said.

Before the boys had made their escape they had taken their sister's paint, hide scraper, porcupine quills, and her awl. The woman looked for the boys, finally found their trail and followed them. She overtook them in a short time. The boys were frightened.

Their sister said, "Ha, ha, you boys. Who will save your lives now? I shall kill every one of you." One of the boys had the paint, which he spilled on the ground. When the woman reached the spilled paint, she said, "Well, they stole my paint and I must gather it again." It took her a long time to gather it.

Meanwhile the boys had run on again and had gotten a long way off. Then she started after them and overtook them in a short time. She said to them, "There is no hope that you will save your lives: I shall kill every one of you."

The boy who had the scraper threw it back to his sister, saying, "Here is your scraper, sister." The woman saw where it dropped, but she had a hard time to find it. By this time the boys were a long way off again. Then the woman started after her brothers. In a little while she overtook them.

The boy who had her awl threw it back to her, saying, "Here, sister, is your awl." She stopped to pick it up but had a task to find it, and by that time the boys were far off again.

She then started to pursue them and overtook them again, saying, "Now, brothers, I shall kill everyone of you." One of the boys had her quills, which he scattered all over the ground. When the woman saw them scattered about, she was very angry and began to pick them up. When she had finished gathering them, she started after her brothers again. They were now far away as there had been many quills and it had taken a long time to gather them, but at last she overtook them.

One of the boys said to his brothers, "I will tell you now, Brothers. Let us try to save our lives before she comes."

The eldest said, "All right; what shall we do? "

One of the boys said, "Let us turn ourselves into water." But the others did not agree to this.

They all said, "If we turn into water, people will drink us up."

Then the second brother said, "It would be better to turn ourselves into trees."

But the others did not think so, for they said the people would chop them down. The third said, "Let us turn into grass," but the others did not like that, for they said people would burn them up.

The fourth said, "It would be better to turn into rocks," but the others said, "No, the people will gather us and heat us to use in their sweat houses; the women will also break us to make scrapers out of us."

The fifth said, "Let us turn into animals of some sort. We can then live, eat, walk, and see."

The others objected, "No, the Indians will kill and eat us."

The sixth said, "Let us turn into birds of some sort. Then we can fly about."

The others said, "No, the Indians will kill us just the same."

The seventh said, "I have the best idea. Let us leave the earth completely. We will go up into the sky and remain there for the rest of our lives; there we can show ourselves at night. The people will then see us. Those that now see us and those that see us a thousand years from now may die, but we shall be seen forever. The people will look up at night and say, 'Look in the sky and see the seven,' and we shall be talked about forever." When he said this, the brothers all liked it.

Then they said, "The next thing is, how can we get up to the sky?"

One of these boys had magic power; he said to his brothers, "There is no doubt that we can get up to the sky; we shall be there in a little while." He took out a plume, which he carried and held it up in both hands, telling his brothers to look at the plume. When they did so, he told them to close their eyes. He blew on the plume and it rose through the air. And as it went up, they all went up with it. While they were going up, their sister arrived at the place where they had been.

She said, "It is too bad that Breast-Chief saved his life."

When the brothers arrived in the sky they sat in separate places as you see them now. Breast-Chief, the youngest, sits at the lowest place of the seven stars (the Great Dipper).

GHOST WIFE

Tradition Bearer: George Bushotter

Source: Bushotter, George, and J. Owen Dorsey. "A Teton Dakota Ghost Story." *Journal of American Folklore* 1 (1888): 71–72.

Date: ca. 1888

Original Source: Dakota

National Origin: Native American

This tale is a useful source for Dakota beliefs about the afterlife. The lodge was sealed to prevent the escape of the soul of the dead woman, in response to the concept that the souls of the dead linger in the area of their burials before departing for the world of the dead.

In the olden time there was once a large village. The people were many because they killed the buffalo. When they camped for the night, a man used to go through the camp as a crier, saying, "There will be many buffalo. Be on the alert!" When they had gone in this manner for a long time, there was a young man who wished to marry a beautiful young girl, but as they said that he should not marry her unless he gave her father some horses, he became displeased and abandoned the tribe. Just as they struck the tents the next morning the young man found very fine horses, one of which he mounted, and thus he returned to the deserted camping site. He saw there a solitary lodge and, as night was coming on, he thought, "Well, perhaps I shall lie here, though it is not exactly suitable."

He approached the lodge, but he found that it had no entrance, and it was covered half way up all around with square pieces of sod. By and by, he managed to get inside. Four posts had been driven into the ground. He lighted a fire, and looked up. A burial scaffold was there! On the scaffold was a woman, around whose chest and back were rows of teeth of the female elk. She looked down, and immediately the young man recognized her. He dwelt with her for a long time, as she became his wife. At length, when he had almost starved to death, he thought, "Well, I will go to hunt a buffalo."

He did not speak aloud.

And the ghost said, "You said that you were hungry. Mount your horse and ride back to the bluffs. By and by, when you meet some buffalo, rush in among them and shoot the fattest one. Bring the meat home, roast a piece on a stick, and serve me with my share before you eat."

He departed according to her instructions. He reached a valley, where he met a herd of buffalo. He made his horse run among them, killed one, cut up the body, and carried it home. He roasted the piece, as he had been commanded. Then the woman slipped down from the scaffold, alighting on her feet. Her leggins had rows of beadwork on them. The young man was alarmed, but the ghost said, "Fear me not." The ghost knew what he thought before he could say a word.

Then they said that they would go just as their mothers had gone, but the ghost woman said to him, "Let us pitch the tent during the day, and travel by night." So they traveled at night. The woman walked with her head covered, never saying anything; her legs were invisible, and she made no noise as she walked. When the man thought about anything, the ghost knew all, though he did not speak of it.

Therefore the ghosts know all things. The ghost knows when the wind will blow, and when there will be rain or heavy thunder clouds. The ghost is very glad when there is going to be a wind.

And thus did the man and his ghost wife travel about, but the people did not find them; and finally the man himself became a ghost.

It is said that the ghosts also live (and act) just as we do.

TWO FACES

Tradition Bearer: Unavailable

Source: Kroeber, A. L. "Cheyenne Tales." *Journal of American Folklore* 13 (1900): 177–79.

Date: 1899

Original Source: Cheyenne

National Origin: Native American

The character known by various names such as "Two Faces" or "Double Face" appears among Native American Plains cultures other than the Algonquian Cheyenne—see, for example, the Wichita **myths** "The Two

Boys Who Slew the Monsters and Became Stars" (p. 212), and "Origin of the Universe" (p. 135). The protagonist in this tale uses the cleverness and imitative skills reminiscent of a **trickster** to overcome the monster.

Nearly every night a child disappeared from a camp. A young man wondered who stole the babies. One dark night he said to himself, "I will watch tonight. I will watch every tent where the people are sleeping. If anyone takes a child to-night, I may hear it cry out." So he watched the whole village, and looked outside.

He found that the thief was Two-Faces, who had one face in front and one at the back of his head, so that he could look on both sides of him. The young man found him fast asleep. Near him were many dead babies that he had stolen. Most of them had their ears cut off, and Two-Faces had a long string of ears on a line, for he lived on human ears.

The young man ran to the river and looked for shells. He gathered a great number of shells, which looked almost like human ears, and strung them, and bloodied them. Then he cut a piece of meat, and shaped it like an ear. When Two-Faces awoke, he saw a person sitting near him eating an ear. It was this young man eating the meat. Two-Faces asked him where he learned to eat ears. The man said to him, "I live on ears. I always steal children and cut off their ears. The only thing that I am afraid of is that if I eat salt, it will kill me." Then Two-Faces said, "I should at once die if anyone beat a gourd and fat was thrown in the fire."

When night came, they both went to the camp. The young man then told Two-Faces to wait for him; he would go ahead. Then he went to his friends and told them to prepare. He was bringing Two-Faces, who had stolen all the children.

He directed that a gourd be beaten and fat meat thrown at the fire. So at last they succeeded in killing Two-Faces. Then he was burned.

THE WEST

Introduction

For the purposes of the present collection, that which is designated "the West" will be restricted to California, Nevada, and the islands of Hawaii. The narratives that follow will be grouped according to the same categories established for the other regions of the United States. Although Hawaiian narratives will be presented along with those from continental California and Nevada, the discussion of Hawaiian environmental, historical, and cultural features will be discussed separately. This treatment seems appropriate for several reasons. California and Nevada span the spectrum of geographic and climactic features in the forty-eight contiguous states, while Hawaii is the only state located entirely in the tropics. More importantly, perhaps, the historical events that shaped the forty-eight contiguous states from the fifteenth through the nineteenth centuries—the Civil War and the westward migration, for example—had no impact on the islands.

California and Nevada

Geographically, Nevada encompasses much of the Great Basin and a portion of the Mojave Desert, giving this state the most arid climate in the United States. California has its own arid sections, but extends to the Pacific Ocean and contains rivers, fertile valleys, and forests. The extremes of climate and topography gave rise to an indigenous population that, because of its adaptations to the varied ecological niches, was the most culturally diverse of all Native North America.

At one extreme of the pre-European contact cultures were groups such as the Chumash who took full advantage of the abundant material resources for constructing dwellings, tools, and boats, and who also took full advantage of the maritime and terrestrial food resources provided by the ocean, rivers, meadows, and forests. The Chumash and other groups who followed similar lifestyles relied on a plentiful supply of salmon, other fish, and, on the Pacific coast, sea mammals. Inland, they hunted large mammals and gathered plant foods: berries, nuts, and, like much of native California acorns. This plentiful and easily accessible food supply allowed the Chumash a prosperous existence in permanently settled villages, the accumulation of surplus goods and foodstuffs, and the development of a hierarchical society—a chiefdom—with a lower tier of craftspersons, a second tier of religious specialists and, at the top, a bureaucratic class.

At the other extreme were band-level societies such as the Luiseño who, like other Native Californians that greeted the first Europeans, were thought to have migrated into southern California from the Great Basin. The name Luiseño was imposed on the group by the Spanish. The case of Saboba is representative: they were a band of the Luiseño, nomads who foraged for plants, nuts, small animals, and even insect pupae. Despite a relatively simple lifestyle—compared to the Chumash—they led a rich spiritual life, exercising supernatural power and superhuman feats such as "eating" fire and walking on hot coals (see "How the Saboba People Came to California," p. 289, for insights into their worldview). The Mono, a seasonally nomadic group in central California, reflected a different image of the world via **myths** featuring their **trickster** Coyote in confrontation with their **culture hero** Prairie Falcon (see "Coyote and His Sister Robin," p. 367).

The Spanish were the most important European influence in the region from their establishment of New Spain until the granting of Mexican independence in 1821. For most of this period, there was only minor Spanish interference with Native American culture. In the late 1700s, however, a system of Spanish missions was set up throughout what became the modern state of California. These missions ultimately led to the dissolution of the hundreds of small independent bands in the region. The very diversity and independence that characterized the groups prior to European contact led to their demise in confrontation with programmatic Spanish occupation. Upon gaining independence from Spain in 1821, Mexico abandoned the mission system, but this was too late for the indigenous peoples.

Mexican domination of the area was short-lived, though, as immigration from the East quickly progressed from a trickle to flood-like proportions after gold was discovered at Sutter's Mill in Coloma, California, in 1848, the same year as the signing of the Treaty of Guadalupe Hidalgo surrendered the territory to the United States as one of the terms for the the cessation of the hostilities of the Mexican War.

The West became subjected to many of the same pressures after the Civil War that were noted for the Plains and Plateau and Southwest Regions (see Introductions to these regions, pp. 3 and 131). For purposes of the present folktale collection, the most relevant of these was the increased stress placed on the Native American populations of the Plains who attended to the message of the Paiute prophet Wovoka and his Ghost Dance Religion, which lasted from 1899 to 1891. Included here is a **personal experience narrative** of one of the Plains converts to the religion, "Meeting with Wovoka" (p. 361).

Hawai'i

Hawai'i is a group of islands that comprise the southernmost State in the United States. All of the Hawaiian Islands were formed by volcanoes arising from the sea floor. This geographic feature and the ecology associated with it has had a profound effect on the narrative tradition and on the pantheon of traditional gods and godesses. For example, "Pele's Long Sleep" (p. 353) portrays an episode from the mythology of the deity associated with volcanoes and features of the environment caused by volcanic activity, while "Legend of the Breadfruit Tree" (p. 292) focuses on the deification of a distinctive species of tropical vegetation. Anthropologists speculate that the islands were settled by at least two important waves of Polynesian explorers over the period of 300 CE to 1300 CE.

Politically, the islands were ruled by local chiefs until warfare enlarged the provinces of these local rulers into networks of villages, which became the complex society that British Captain James Cook encountered in 1778. Claims to legitimacy by the various local rulers led to the development of extensive lineages recorded in the oral traditions of the Native Hawai'ians. These oral histories were commonly preserved in chants and dance songs. Elements of these poetic renderings are preserved in the reframed versions of the **myths** and **legends** collected in this volume.

SUGGESTED READINGS

Beckwith, Martha Warren. *Hawaiian Mythology.* New Haven: Yale University Press, 1940.

Dixon, Roland B. *Oceanic Mythology*. Boston: Marshall Jones, 1916.

———. "Some Coyote Stories from the Maidu Indians of California" *Journal of American Folklore* 13 (1900): 270.

Gayton, A. H., and Stanley S. Newman. *Yokuts and Western Mono Myths.* Millwood, NY: Kraus, 1976.

Gibson, Robert O. *The Chumash.* New York: Chelsea House, 1991.

Kawaharada, Dennis. *Ancient Oahu: Stories from Fornander and Thrum.* Honolulu: Kalamaku Press, 2001.

Kroeber, Alfred L. *Handbook of the Indians of California.* Smithsonian Institution Bureau of American Ethnology, Bulletin 78. Washington, DC: U.S. Government Printing Office, 1925.

Stewart, Omer C. *The Northern Paiute Bands.* Millwood, NY: Kraus, 1976.

Strong, William D. *University of California Publications in American Archaeology and Ethnology.* Vol. 26, *Aboriginal Society in Southern California.* Berkeley: University of California Press, 1929.

ORIGINS

SILVER FOX CREATES THE WORLD AND HUMANS

Tradition Bearer: Charley Snook

Source: Dixon, Roland B. "Achomawi and Atsugewi Tales." *Journal of American Folklore* 21 (1908): 159–61.

Date: ca. 1900

Original Source: Achomawi

National Origin: Native American

The Achomawi were hunters and gatherers with territory that stretched from northern California to the Oregon border. In the winter they lived in "pit houses," rectangular excavations topped by rafters and covered in grass. Silver-Fox, as detailed in the following **myth**, was their benevolent creator with the power to bring phenomena into existence by the power of thought. Silver-Fox set the model for proper moral conduct. Despite the use of the sweat lodge, the Achomawi did not have a highly developed ritual cycle.

In the beginning all was water. In all directions the sky was clear and unobstructed. A cloud formed in the sky, grew lumpy, and turned into Coyote. Then a fog arose, grew lumpy, and became Silver-Fox. They became persons.

Then they thought. They thought a canoe, and they said, "Let us stay here, let us make it our home." Then they floated about, for many years they floated; and the canoe became old and mossy, and they grew weary of it.

"Do you go and lie down," said Silver-Fox to Coyote, and he did so. While he slept, Silver-Fox combed his hair, and the combings he saved. When there was much of them, he rolled them in his hands, stretched them out, and flattened them between his hands. When he had done this, he laid them upon the water and spread them out, till they covered all the surface of the water. Then he thought, "There should be a tree," and it was there. And he did the same way with shrubs and with rocks, and weighted the film down with stones, so that the film did not wave and rise in ripples as it floated in the wind.

And thus he made it, that it was just right, this that was to be the world. And then the canoe floated gently up to the edge, and it was the world. Then he cried to Coyote, "Wake up! We are going to sink!"

And Coyote woke, and looked up; and over his head, as he lay, hung cherries and plums; and from the surface of the world he heard crickets chirping. And at once Coyote began to eat the cherries and the plums, and the crickets also.

After a time Coyote said, "Where are we? What place is this that we have come to?"

And Silver-Fox replied, "I do not know. We are just here. We floated up to the shore." Still all the time he knew; but he denied that he had made the world. He did not want Coyote to know that the world was his creation.

Then Silver-Fox said, "What shall we do? Here is solid ground. I am going ashore, and am going to live here." So they landed, and built a sweat-house and lived in it. They thought about making people; and after a time, they made little sticks of service-berry, and they thrust them all about into the roof of the house on the inside. And by and by all became people of different sorts, birds and animals and fish, all but the deer, and he was as the deer are today. And Pine-Marten was the chief of the people; and Eagle was the woman chief, for she was Pine-Marten's sister. And this happened at Ila'texcagewa.

And people went out to hunt from the sweat-house. And they killed deer, and brought them home, and had plenty to eat. Arrows with pine-bark points were what they used then, it is said, for there was no obsidian. And Ground-Squirrel, of all the people, he only knew where obsidian could be found.

So he went to steal it. To Medicine Lake he went, for there Obsidian-Old-Man lived, in a big sweat-house. And Ground-Squirrel went in, taking with him roots in a basket of tules. And he gave the old man some to eat; and he liked them so much, that he sent Ground-Squirrel out to get more.

But while he was digging them Grizzly-Bear came, and said, "Sit down! Let me sit in your lap. Feed me those roots by handfuls." So Ground-Squirrel sat down, and fed Grizzly-Bear as he had asked, for he was afraid. Then Grizzly-Bear said, "Obsidian-Old-Man's mother cleaned roots for someone," and went away.

Ground-Squirrel went back to the sweat-house, but had few roots, for Grizzly-Bear had eaten so many. Then he gave them to the old man, and told him what the bear had said about him, and how he had robbed him of the roots.

Then Obsidian-Old-Man was angry. "Tomorrow we will go," he said. Then they slept. In the morning they ate breakfast early and went off, and the old man said that Ground-Squirrel should go and dig more roots, and that he would wait, and watch for Grizzly-Bear.

So Ground-Squirrel went and dug; and when the basket was filled, Grizzly-Bear came, and said, "You have dug all these for me. Sit down!" So Ground-Squirrel sat down, and fed Grizzly-Bear roots by the handful. But Obsidian-Old-Man had come near.

And Grizzly-Bear got up to fight, and he struck at the old man; but he turned his side to the blow, and Grizzly-Bear merely cut off a great slice of his own flesh. And he kept on fighting, till he was all cut to pieces, and fell dead. Then Ground-Squirrel and Obsidian-Old-Man went home to the sweat-house, and built a fire, and ate the roots, and were happy. Then the old man went to sleep.

In the morning Obsidian-Old-Man woke up, and heard Ground-Squirrel groaning. He said, "I am sick. I am bruised because that great fellow sat upon me. Really, I am sick." Then Obsidian-Old-Man was sorry, but Ground-Squirrel was fooling the old man.

After a while the old man said, "I will go and get wood. I'll watch him, for perhaps he is fooling me. These people are very clever." Then he went for wood; and he thought as he went, "I had better go back and look." So he went back softly, and peeped in; but Ground-Squirrel lay there quiet, and groaned, and now and then he vomited up green substances. Then Obsidian-Old-Man thought, "He is really sick," and he went off to get more wood; but Ground-Squirrel was really fooling, for he wanted to steal obsidian.

When the old man had gotten far away, Ground-Squirrel got up, poured out the finished obsidian points, and pulled out a knife from the wall, did them up in a bundle, and ran off with them. When the old man came back, he carried a heavy load of wood; and as soon as he entered the sweat-house, he missed Ground-Squirrel. So he dropped the wood and ran after him. He almost caught him, when Ground-Squirrel ran into a hole, and, as he went, kicked the earth into the eyes of the old man, who dug fast, trying to catch him. Soon Ground-Squirrel ran out of the other end of the hole; and then the old man gave chase again, but again Ground-Squirrel darted into a hole; and after missing him again, Obsidian-Old-Man gave up, and went home.

Ground-Squirrel crossed the river and left his load of arrow-points, and came back to the house and sat down in his seat. He and Cocoon slept together.

Then his friend said, "Where have you been?"

And Ground-Squirrel replied, "I went to get a knife and to get good arrow-points. We had none." Then the people began to come back with deer. And when they cooked their meat, they put it on the fire in lumps; but Ground-Squirrel and Cocoon cut theirs in thin slices, and so cooked it nicely. And Weasel saw this, and they told him about how the knife had been secured.

In the morning Ground-Squirrel went and brought back the bundle of points he had hidden, and handed it down through the smoke-hole to Wolf. Then he poured out the points on the ground and distributed them to everyone, and all day long people worked, tying them onto arrows. So they threw away all the old arrows with bark points; and when they went hunting, they killed many deer.

CREATION OF MAN

Tradition Bearer: Unavailable

Source: Westervelt, W. D. "Creation of Man." Pages 71–75 in *Hawaiian Legends of Old Honolulu*. Boston: G. H. Ellis Press, 1915.

Date: 1915

Original Source: Hawaii

National Origin: Hawaiian

In her study of Hawaiian mythology, folklorist Martha Warren Beckwith notes that, unlike other Pacific traditions, Hawaiian **myth** does not devote itself to the development of the cosmos prior to the arrival of human beings. Traditional Hawaiian narrative did not make the same sorts of distinctions between **myths** and **legends** or folktales as does contemporary folkloristics. The primary distinctions are *kaao* (fictional) and *moolelo* (historical, true). Therefore, that which contemporary scholars label **myth** is *moolelo*. Myths are distinguished from **legend**, anecdote, and other **personal experience narratives** by the manner of performance. Turning again to Beckwith, "Sacred stories are told only by day and the listeners must not move in front of the speaker; to do so would be highly disrespectful to the gods" (1940: 1) Much Hawaiian **myth** is embodied in long epic poems or shorter chants associated with other activities, such as dance, for example. The collector of the following **myth**, W. D. Westervelt, notes that the first "half" is likely to be an indigenous narrative, while the creation of woman is clearly influenced by Biblical accounts of creation brought to the islands by Europeans.

The sky is established.
The earth is established.
Fastened and fastened,
Always holding together,
Entangled in obscurity,
Near each other a group of islands
Spreads out like a flock of birds.
Leaping up are the divided places.
Lifted far up are the heavens.
Polished by striking,
Lamps rest in the sky.
Presently the clouds move,
The great sun rises in splendor,
Mankind arises to pleasure,
The moving sky is above.

Hawaiian Chant

Ku, Ka-ne, Lono, and Kanaloa were the first gods made.
The gods had come from far-off unknown lands. They brought with them the mysterious people who live in precipices and trees and rocks. These were the invisible spirits of the air.

The earth was a calabash. The gods threw the calabash cover upward and it became the sky. Part of the thick "flesh" became the sun. Another part was the moon. The stars came from the seeds.

The gods went over to a small island called Mokapu, and thought they would make man to be chief over all other things. Mololani was the crater hill that forms the little island. On the sunrise side of this hill, near the sea, was the place where red dirt lay mixed with dark blue and black soil. Here Ka-ne scratched the dirt together and made the form of a man.

Kanaloa ridiculed the mass of dirt and made a better form, but it did not have life. Ka-ne said, "You have made a dirt image; let it become stone."

Then Ka-ne ordered Ku and Lono to carefully obey his directions. They were afraid he would kill them, so at once they caught one of the spirits of the air and pushed it into the image Ka-ne had made.

When the spirit had been pushed into the body, Ka-ne stood by the image and called, "Hiki au-E-ola! E-ola!" ("I come, live! Live!")

Ku and Lono responded "Live! Live!" Then Ka-ne called again, "I come, awake! Awake!" and the other two responded, "Awake! Awake!" and the image became a living man.

Then Ka-ne cried, "I come, arise! Arise!" The other gods repeated, "Arise! Arise!" and the image stood up—a man with a living spirit. They named him Wela-ahi-lani-nui, or "The great heaven burning hot."

They chanted, giving the divine signs attending the birth of a chief:

> "The stars were burning.
> Hot were the months.
> Land rises in islands,
> High surf is like mountains,
> Pele throws out her body (of lava).
> Broken masses of rain from the sky,
> The land is shaken by earthquakes,
> Ikuwa reverberates with thunder."

The gods took this man to their home and nourished him. When he became strong he went out to walk around the home of the gods. Soon he noticed a shadow going around with his body. It walked when he walked, and rested when he rested. He wondered what this thing was, and called it "aka," or "shadow."

When he slept, Ku, Ka-ne and Lono tore open his body, and Ka-ne took out a woman, leaving Kill and Lono to heal the body. Then they put the woman by the side of the man and they were alike.

Wela-ahi-lani-nui woke and found a beautiful one lying by him, and thought: "This is that thing which has been by my side, my aka. The gods have changed it into this beautiful one." So he gave her the name "Ke-aka-huli-lani"

(The-heaven-changed-shadow). These were the ancestors of the Hawaiians and all the peoples of the islands of the great ocean.

THE MAKING OF THE WORLD

Tradition Bearer: Molly Kinsman Pimona

Source: Gifford, Edward Winslow. "Western Mono Myths." *Journal of American Folklore* 36 (1923): 305–6.

Date: 1918

Original Source: Western Mono (California)

National Origin: Native American

The Mono were a hunters and gatherers society that moved throughout the Mono Basin region of California, pursuing the staples of their subsistence, which ranged from fly pupae to pinon nuts to jackrabbits and antelope. The following creation **myth** exemplifies the "Earth-diver" **tale type**. The narrative also suggests the power of dreams, or visions, in this culture.

In the beginning, Prairie Falcon and Crow were sitting on a log which projected above the waters that covered the world. They asked Duck of what number he had dreamed, and he replied, "Two."

Prairie Falcon assigned him the number three, and instructed him to dive into the water and bring up some sand from the bottom. Duck dived to get the sand, but, before he reached the bottom, the three days allotted him expired. He awoke from his dream, died as a result, and floated to the surface.

Prairie Falcon, however, brought him back to life and asked him what the trouble was. Duck replied that he had come out of his dream and had consequently died and floated to the top.

Prairie Falcon now asked Coot of what number he had dreamed. Coot replied, "Four." Then Prairie Falcon assigned him two and ordered him to dive for sand. Before Coot had reached the bottom, however, the two days had elapsed and he came out of his dream. He, too, died in consequence, and his body floated to the surface of the waters.

Prairie Falcon espied the corpse, recovered it, and resuscitated Coot. He inquired of Coot what had been his difficulty. Coot replied that he had passed out of his dream.

Grebe was the next individual whom Prairie Falcon interrogated as to the number he had dreamed of. Grebe replied that he had dreamed of five. Prairie Falcon arbitrarily assigned him four as the number of days that he should take in securing sand from beneath the waters. Prairie Falcon then ordered him to dive. Grebe was successful and secured sand in each hand, having gone clear to the bottom of the waters. As he was returning to the surface, he passed out of his dream state, died, and floated to the surface. Prairie Falcon resuscitated him and inquired if he had secured any sand. Grebe replied that he had and Prairie Falcon inquired what he had done with it. Grebe explained that it had all slipped from his grasp when he died. Prairie Falcon and Crow both laughed at him and said that they did not believe it.

Then they examined his hands and found sand under the finger nails of both. They took that sand and threw it in every direction. That is what made the world.

THE CREATION OF THE INDIANS

Tradition Bearer: Unavailable

Source: Lowie, Robert H. "Shoshonean Tales." *Journal of American Folklore* 37 (1924): 157–59.

Date: 1915

Original Source: Moapa (Southern Paiute)
National Origin: Native American

Historically, the Southern Paiute were divided into small bands that foraged for wild plant foods, such as seeds and pine nuts, and hunted small game in the Nevada area in which they lived. Where water was available, the women cultivated corn, squash, pumpkins, muskmelons, beans, and sunflowers. Brush shelters served as their dwellings. While the disjointed plot (according to European criteria) of this **myth** is not unusual in such traditional narratives, the narrative may have become memory culture as distinct from an active sacred narrative.

Long ago an old woman, named Co'tsi'pama'pot, made the whole country. No one lived here at all anywhere except this old woman, her son, and her daughter. The entire country was flooded with water except one little spot where Co'tsi'pama'pot stayed. At last she scattered earth all over, seed-fashion. Then she sent her daughter to see how much land there was.

When the girl came back, she said, "It is not enough yet." Her mother kept sending her, and the girl always came back reporting that there was not yet enough. At last the girl went a great distance and when she came back she said there was now enough land.

The old woman said, "See whether you can find some people, look everywhere, go up to the mountains, and see." So the girl went and looked everywhere but she saw nothing.

The old woman said to her, "I don't think you looked very much." So she went again and found just one man. She traversed the entire country in a very short time.

She returned and told her mother, "I have found only one man."—"Well, that will be well, get him."

The girl went to the man and said, "My mother wants you to come to where we live." He agreed to come.

Co'tsi'pama'pot lived in the middle of a wide stretch of water. The girl laid a stick across from the shore and walked ahead. When she was nearly across, she tipped the stick so as to topple the man into the water, but he flew up, unseen by her, and reached camp first. When the girl arrived, she told her mother, "I called him and he was drowned." She had one lodge while her mother lived in another.

Her mother said, "That man is in your lodge." The girl did not know that he had flown there.

Co'tsi'pama'pot made deer, cottontail rabbits, bears, antelope, and every kind of animal out of mud, threw them off and bade them take to the mountains. She said to her daughter, "You had better stay with him, you can't find anyone else, keep him for a husband." So the man and the girl lay together, but the man, though eager to possess her, was afraid.

The old woman said to him, "Since you can do nothing with her, you had better go to get some deer; kill it and bring the first vertebra." The man went off, killed a deer, and brought the first, hard vertebra. "Well," said Co'tsi'pama'pot, "you had better use this, don't let her see this. This may fix it, perhaps she will bite it, then you can have your will of her." Night fell. He took the vertebra and put it by his penis. The girl had a toothed vagina, but the teeth could not bite the bone and broke off. Then he had his will of her and she bit no more. He lay with her every night now.

After a while the young woman was big with child. Her mother made a big sack and into this the daughter dropped her children so that the bag was full of them. Co'tsi'pama'pot said to the man, "You had better take this bag to the center of the world. Don't open it till you get there, no matter what noise you may hear from within." So the man set out with the sack and went on. After a while his load grew heavy and he heard a noise inside. He thought he would like to see the inside. He took off the bag, sat down and listened to the noise. He was eager to see what it was. At last he opened the bag and saw nothing. The babies got out and scattered all over the country. Most of them escaped. When he tied up the sack again, there were only a few left.

He sat down and gave tribal names to the different babies. "You go up there, you shall be called by such a name, and so forth. To those few that remained at the bottom he said, "these are my people." All the babies in the sack were Indians.

The man had a long stone knife and an awl of hard bone. He had a rabbit skin blanket wide enough for two to sleep under. He had nothing with which to start fire, except a rock on which he would place his food. After a while he saw ashes falling down. "Where did this come from?" He sent several men far up, but they could see no fire anywhere. Others went higher still, and yet they could find no fire.

Finally one of them went higher still and reported, "It looks like fire over there." "Well, I think we had better all go and get that fire by gambling or some other way." He got all of them to come with him. They went to the people who had fire and gambled with them. Before daylight he took a piece of bark, tied it round his head, stuck it into the fire, and then ran off. The people who owned the fire ran after him, but did not catch him.

Then he took some root and said, "Make fire out of this." So he made fire from it, and after a while he threw away the rock he had used to cook on. He cooked seeds in the fire now.

He named all the hills and waters and rocks and bushes, so that people knew what to call them. He was the first to name them.

After a while the people who had come from the sack fought among themselves.

Co'tsi'pama'pot, the old woman who made the earth, is still living. She made all the tribes speak different languages. She saw what all the people were doing. When Indians died they went to her, and she made new ones. People did not know where the dead went to; we don't know it, but she knows it all.

Cuna'waBi had a brother, ToBa'ts. He thought that somebody should kill him and somebody killed him. ToBa'ts left a small package. Cuna'waBi untied it, and after a while he could see nothing there. It suddenly became dark. He groped about, found some feathers, and threw them up to the sky; then it was daylight and the sun shone. He tried several feathers, and one of them made the Sun. When it was day, he heard his brother crying and started to look for him.

Cuna'waBi made all kinds of sickness by thinking that people should be sick. He called the different mountains and everything else by distinct names.

The Mu'qwits tribe used to live here and moved away a long time ago. After a while the white people came here.

The old woman gave people all kinds of seed to eat. She thought of the seeds and the people went to the place she pointed out and would find the seeds and eat them. "Live on this, boys," she would say; "this is yours to eat."

All the birds, big and small, talked Indian once. Duck was a doctor long ago. When a boy was sick, his relatives sent for Duck and gave him a spoon for fee. Duck said, "I'd better try the spoon for my nose. This is all right." He put it on his nose and so he has it now on his face.

A GIANT'S ROCK-THROWING

Tradition Bearer: Unavailable

Source: Westervelt, W. D. "A Giant's Rock-Throwing." *Hawaiian Legends of Ghosts and Ghost-Gods*. Boston: Ellis Press, 1916.

Date: 1916

Original Source: Hawaii

National Origin: Hawaiian

Both **myth** and **legend** have been used to explain features of the environment. This **legend** of a Hawaiian Hercules explains the origin of a geological feature the Rock of Kauai, while offering a cautionary tale about the discrete use of one's natural gifts.

A long time ago there lived on Kauai a man of wonderful power, Hau-pu. When he was born, the signs of a demigod were over the house of his birth. Lightning flashed through the skies, and thunder reverberated—a rare event in the Hawaiian Islands, and supposed to be connected with the birth or death or some very unusual occurrence in the life of a chief.

Mighty floods of rain fell and poured in torrents down the mountainsides, carrying the red iron soil into the valleys in such quantities that the rapids and the waterfalls became the color of blood, and the natives called this a blood-rain.

During the storm, and even after sunshine filled the valley, a beautiful rainbow rested over the house in which the young chief was born. This rainbow was thought to come from the miraculous powers of the new-born child shining out from him instead of from the sunlight around him. Many chiefs throughout the centuries of Hawaiian legends were said to have had this rainbow around them all their lives.

Hau-pu while a child was very powerful, and after he grew up was widely known as a great warrior. He would attack and defeat armies of his enemies without aid from any person. His spear was like a mighty weapon, sometimes piercing a host of enemies, and sometimes putting aside all opposition when he thrust it into the ranks of his opponents.

If he had thrown his spear and if fighting with his bare hands did not vanquish his foes, he would leap to the hillside, tear up a great tree, and, with it, sweep away all before him as if he were wielding a huge broom. He was known and feared throughout all the Hawaiian Islands. He became angry quickly and used his great powers very rashly.

One night he lay sleeping in his royal rest-house on the side of a mountain, which faced the neighboring island of Oahu. Between the two islands lay a broad channel about thirty miles wide. When clouds were on the face of the sea these islands were hidden from each other; but when they lifted the rugged valleys of the mountains on one island could be clearly seen from the other. Even by moonlight the shadowy lines would appear.

This night the strong man stirred in his sleep. Indistinct noises seemed to surround his house. He turned over and dropped off into slumber again.

Soon he was aroused a second time, and he was awake enough to hear shouts of men far far away. Louder rose the noise mixed with the roar of the great surf waves, so he realized that it came from the sea, and he then forced himself to rise and stumble to the door.

He looked out toward Oahu. A multitude of lights were flashing on the sea before his sleepy eyes. A low murmur of many voices came from the place where the dancing lights seemed to be. His confused thoughts made it appear to him that a great fleet of warriors was coming from Oahu to attack his people.

He blindly rushed out to the edge of a high precipice, which overlooked the channel. Evidently many boats and many people were out in the sea below.

He laughed, and stooped down and tore a huge rock from its place. This he swung back and forth, back and forth, back and forth, until he gave it great impetus, which, added to his own miraculous power, sent it far out over the sea. Like a great cloud it rose in the heavens and, as if blown by swift winds, sped on its way.

Over on the shores of Oahu a chief whose name was Kaena had called his people out for a night's fishing. Canoes large and small came from all along the coast. Torches without number had been made and placed in the canoes. The largest fish-nets had been brought.

There was no need of silence. Nets had been set in the best places. Fish of all kinds were to be aroused and frightened into the nets. Flashing lights, splashing paddles, and clamor from hundreds of voices resounded all around the nets.

Gradually the canoes came nearer and nearer the centre. The shouting increased. Great joy ruled the tumult, which drowned the roar of the waves.

Across the channel and up the mountain-sides of Kauai swept the shouts of the fishing-party. Into the ears of drowsy Hau-pu the noise forced itself. Little dreamed the excited fishermen of the effect of this on far-away Kauai.

Suddenly something like a bird as large as a mountain seemed to be above, and then with a mighty sound like the roar of winds it descended upon them. Smashed and submerged were the canoes when the huge boulder thrown by Hau-pu hurled itself upon them. The chief Kaena and his canoe were in the centre of this terrible mass of wreckage, and he and many of his people lost their lives.

The waves swept sand upon the shore until in time a long point of land was formed. The remaining followers of the dead chief named this cape "Kaena."

The rock thrown by Hau-pu embedded itself in the depths of the ocean, but its head rose far above the water, even when raging storms dashed turbulent waves against it. To this death-dealing rock the natives gave the name "Rock of Kauai."

283

Thus, for generations has the deed of the man of giant force been remembered on Oahu, and so have a cape and a rock received their names.

HOW MILU BECAME THE KING OF GHOSTS

Tradition Bearer: Unavailable

Source: Westervelt, W. D. "How Milu Became the King of Ghosts." *Hawaiian Legends of Ghosts and Ghost-Gods*. Boston: Ellis Press, 1916.

Date: 1916

Original Source: Hawaii

National Origin: Hawaiian

The **myth** of the way in which the healing arts were given to humanity explains many other phenomena as well. The ti plant is a member of the lily family and was considered sacred to both Lono, the healer, and also Laka, a goddess associated with dance. The plant was used as a symbol of high rank and divine power. Its roots were used for making liquor and as dressings for wounds; they were also eaten as a baked dessert and mixed with other herbs to make medicines. In some traditions it is common for one who is healed of serious illness to become healer, as happens in this narrative. In addition, the **myth** details what happens when medicine fails and what one can expect in the afterlife.

Lono was a chief living on the western side of the island Hawai'i. He had a very red skin and strange-looking eyes. His choice of occupation was farming. This man had never been sick.

One time he was digging with a long spade. A man passed and admired him. The people said, "Lono has never been sick."

The man said, "He will be sick."

Lono was talking about that man and at the same time struck his spade down with force and cut his foot. Lono shed much blood, and fainted, falling to the ground. A man took a pig, went after the stranger, and let the pig go, which ran to the stranger.

The stranger was Kamaka, a god of healing. He turned and went back at the call of the messenger, taking some popolo fruit and leaves in his cloak. When he came to the injured man he asked for salt, which he pounded into the fruit and leaves and placed in coco cloth and bound it on the wound, leaving it a long time. Then he went away.

As he journeyed on he heard heavy breathing, and turning saw Lono, who said, "You have helped me, and so I have left my lands in the care of my friends, directing them what to do, and have hastened after you to learn how to heal other people."

The god said, "Lono, open your mouth!" This Lono did, and the god spat in his mouth, so that the saliva could be taken into every part of Lono's body. Thus a part of the god became a part of Lono, and he became very skilful in the use of all healing remedies. He learned about the various diseases and the medicines needed for each. The god and Lono walked together, Lono receiving new lessons along the way, passing through the districts of Kau, Puna, Hilo, and then to Hamakua.

The god said, "It is not right for us to stay together. You can never accomplish anything by staying with me. You must go to a separate place and give yourself up to healing people."

Lono turned aside to dwell in Waimanu and Waipio Valleys and there began to practice healing, becoming very noted, while the god Kamaka made his home at Ku-kui-haele.

This god did not tell the other gods of the Medicines that he had taught Lono. One of the other gods, Kalae, was trying to find some way to kill Milu, and was always making him sick. Milu, chief of Waipio, heard of the skill of Lono. Some had been sick even to death, and Lono had healed them. Therefore Milu sent a messenger to Lono who responded at once, came and slapped Milu all over the body, and said: "You are not ill. Obey me and you shall be well."

Then he healed him from all the sickness inside the body caused by Kalae. But there was danger from outside, so he said: "You must build a ti-leaf house and dwell there quietly for some time, letting your disease rest. If a company should come by the house making sport, with a great noise, do not go out, because when you go they wilt come up and get you for your death. Do not open the ti leaves and look out. The day you do this you shall die."

Some time passed and the chief remained in the house, but one day there was the confused noise of many people talking and shouting around his house.

He did not forget the command of Lono. Two birds were sporting in a wonderful way in the sky above the forest. This continued all day until it was dark.

Then another long time passed and again Waipio was full of resounding noises. A great bird appeared in the sky resplendent in all kinds of feathers, swaying from side to side over the valley, from the top of one precipice across to the top of another, in grand flights passing over the heads of the people, who shouted until the valley re-echoed with the sound.

Milu became tired of that great noise and could not patiently obey his physician, so he pushed aside some of the ti leaves of his house and looked out upon the bird. That was the time when the bird swept down upon the house, thrusting a claw under Milu's arm, tearing out his liver.

Lono saw this and ran after the bird, but it flew swiftly to a deep pit in the lava on one side of the valley and dashed inside, leaving blood spread on the stones. Lono came, saw the blood, took it and wrapped it in a piece of tapa cloth and returned to the place where the chief lay almost dead. He poured some medicine into the wound and pushed the tapa and blood inside. Milu was soon healed.

The place where the bird hid with the liver of Milu is called to this day Ke-ake-o-Milu ("The liver of Milu"). When this death had passed away he felt very well, even as before his trouble.

Then Lono told him that another death threatened him and would soon appear. He must dwell in quietness.

For some time Milu was living in peace and quiet after this trouble. Then one day the surf of Waipio became very high, rushing from far out even to the sand, and the people entered into the sport of surf-riding with great joy and loud shouts. This noise continued day by day, and Milu was impatient of the restraint and forgot the words of Lono. He went out to bathe in the surf.

When he came to the place of the wonderful surf he let the first and second waves go by, and as the third came near he launched himself upon it while the people along the beach shouted uproariously. He went out again into deeper water, and again came in, letting the first and second waves go first. As he came to the shore the first and second waves were hurled back from the shore in a great mass against the wave upon which he was riding. The two great masses of water struck and pounded Milu, whirling and crowding him down, while the surfboard was caught in the raging, struggling waters and thrown out toward the shore. Milu was completely lost in the deep water.

The people cried: "Milu is dead! The chief is dead!" The god Kalae thought he had killed Milu, so he with the other poison-gods went on a journey to Mauna Loa. Kapo and Pua, the poison-gods, or gods of death, of the island

Maui, found them as they passed, and joined the company. They discovered a forest on Molokai, and there as kupua spirits, or ghost bodies, entered into the trees of that forest, so the trees became the kupua bodies. They were the medicinal or poison qualities in the trees.

Lono remained in Waipio Valley, becoming the ancestor and teacher of all the good healing priests of Hawai'i, but Milu became the ruler of the Under-world, the place where the spirits of the dead had their home after they were driven away from the land of the living. Many people came to him from time to time.

He established ghostly sports like those that his subjects had enjoyed before death. They played the game kilu with polished coconut shells, spinning them over a smooth surface to strike a post set up in the centre. He taught konane, a game commonly called "Hawaiian checkers," but more like the Japanese game of "Go." He permitted them to gamble, betting all the kinds of property found in ghost-land. They boxed and wrestled; they leaped from precipices into ghostly swimming-pools; they feasted and fought, sometimes attempting to slay each other. Thus they lived the ghost life as they had lived on earth. Sometimes the ruler was forgotten and the ancient Hawaiians called the Under-world by his name—Milu. The New Zealanders frequently gave their Under-world the name "Miru." They also supposed that the ghosts feasted and sported as they had done while living.

THE THEFT OF FIRE

Tradition Bearer: Tom Austin

Source: Lowie, Robert H. "Shoshonean Tales." *Journal of American Folklore* 37 (1924): 228–29.

Date: 1914

Original Source: Paviotso (Northern Paiute)

National Origin: Native American

The Northern Paiute were hunters and gatherers that historically lived in small bands in Nevada. Women foraged wild plants and seeds, and men hunted for various animals, especially jackrabbits. Job's Peak was regarded by many of the bands as the center of the universe. Other elements of religion that are central to the following **myth** were a belief in the general sacredness of mountains and bodies of water and a belief in the acquisition of supernatural power that could be used for various purposes including the control of the weather.

Long ago the whole world was under water except one mountain south of Walker River. The sage-hens at that time spoke Paviotso. They had fire on that mountain, then the only dry place in the world. When waves came, they would touch the tails of the birds.

Sun (*Taba'*) said, "I don't like to see water around here, I want it to dry up. When it dries up, all kinds of animals shall come to the world and use the Indian language." (One can see where the water once touched the mountain.) Sun said, "I'll send something down to this mountain (Job's Peak)".

He sent a messenger, saying, "Go to the mountain and stay there. Anything that comes to the world after the drying up of the water shall be your relative." He said he would send the antelope with his messenger to serve as his food.

Until then neither birds nor beasts had used fire. Two different kinds of birds saw someone very far off using fire. "Someone there is using fire."

All then talked about it and wanted to get fire. "We must get it somehow." "I wonder who is going to get it."

They asked different ones. Soon Wolf asked everyone who wished to do it. He found Wildcat and Jack-rabbit and sent them out at night. They started towards the fire-user. Smoke was passing out of his wikiup. Rabbit and Wildcat both got on the roof; the wildcat's stripes are due to that fire. Soon some live embers came up from the fire. Wildcat caught them and put them under Jack-rabbit's tail. They caused a cold snowstorm to come from the north, and they started to run. They got some sagebrush bark and put the spark inside. Thus they got fire from the other people for everyone of their own to use.

The fire-owners saw their fire going down. "I wonder what is the matter, perhaps someone has stolen the fire." It continued going down until it finally went out.

One of them said, "Someone has stolen it. I have heard that some people toward the north never use fire, perhaps some of them came here and got it. Try to track them." Then all got out to search for tracks but owing to the snowstorm they could not find them. "I have heard that those northern people now use fire, I think they got our fire. We can get along without fire, we'll stay, we can't find a better place." So they stayed there.

After getting fire, the man from Job's Peak came and raised his four children. Before that, all the wild animals, rocks, greasewood, and so on were like persons and spoke the Indian language. After the Indians had been made, these birds and beasts got wild, while the Indians used language and killed wild animals. They got their language from the animals. The Indians began to hunt game to live on. Rabbits, antelope, and other game of that sort belonged to men; ducks, swans, and geese belonged to the woman with vaginal teeth.

Wolf was chief. He said, "When someone from elsewhere comes and kills you, I am going to make you alive again, you are all mine."

HOW THE SABOBA PEOPLE CAME TO CALIFORNIA

Tradition Bearer: José Pedro Losero

Source: James, George Wharton. "A Saboba Origin Myth." *Journal of American Folklore* 15 (1902): 36–39.

Date: ca. 1899

Original Source: Saboba

National Origin: Native American

The Saboba were a band of the Luiseño of California that shared the same foraging lifestyle as the other Native Americans of Southern California. The name was imposed on the group by the Spanish after their arrival in the area. Uuyot (also known among other bands as Wuyoot), the warrior captain of the following **myth**, was believed to have provided supernatural power to his descendants. This power was demonstrated by extraordinary feats, which included "eating" fire and walking on hot coals. *Siwash*, according to an editorial note, is derived from a slang term for "Indian" that traveled down the Pacific Coast from the Chinook.

Before my people came here they lived far, far away in the land that is in the heart of the Setting Sun. But Siwash, our great God, told Uuyot, the warrior captain of my people, that we must come away from this land and sail away and away in a direction that he would give us. Under Uuyot's orders my people built big boats and then, with Siwash himself leading them and with Uuyot as captain, they launched these into the ocean and rowed away from the shore. There was no light on the ocean. Everything was covered with a dark fog, and it was only by singing as they rowed that the boats were enabled to keep together.

It was still dark and foggy when the boats landed on the shores of this land, and my ancestors groped about in the darkness, wondering why they had been brought hither. Then, suddenly, the heavens opened, and lightnings flashed and thunders roared and rains fell, and a great earthquake shook all the earth. Indeed, all the elements of the earth, ocean, and heaven, seemed to be mixed up together and, with terror in their hearts and silence on their tongues, my people stood still awaiting what would happen further. Though no voice had spoken they knew something was going to happen, and they were breathless in their anxiety to know what it was.

Then they turned to Uuyot and asked him what the raging of the elements meant. Gently he calmed their fears and bade them be silent and wait. As they waited, a terrible clap of thunder rent the very heavens, and the vivid lightnings revealed the frightened people huddling together as a pack of sheep. But Uuyot stood alone, brave and fearless, facing the storm and daring the anger of Those Above. With a loud voice he cried out "Wit-i-a-ko!" which signified "Who's there? What do you want?"

But there was no response. The heavens were silent! The earth was silent! The ocean was silent! All nature was silent!

Then, with a voice full of tremulous sadness and loving yearning for his people, Uuyot said, "My children, my own sons and daughters, something is wanted of us by Those Above. What it is I know not. Let us gather together and bring *pivat*, and with it make the big smoke and then dance and dance until we are told what is wanted." So the people brought pivat, a native tobacco that grows in Southern California, and Uuyot brought the big ceremonial pipe, which he had made out of rock, and he soon made the big smoke and blew the smoke up into the heavens while he urged the people to dance. They danced hour after hour until they grew tired, and Uuyot smoked all the time, but still he urged them to dance.

Then he called out again to Those Above, "Wit-i-a-ko!" but still could obtain no response. This made him sad and disconsolate, and when the people saw Uuyot despondent and downhearted they became panic-stricken, and ceased to dance, and began to cling around him for comfort and protection. But poor Uuyot had none to give. He himself was saddest and most forsaken of all, and he got up and bade the people leave him alone, as he wished to walk to and fro by himself. Then he made the people smoke and dance, and when they rested they knelt in a circle and prayed. But he walked away by himself, feeling keenly the refusal of Those Above to speak to him. His heart was deeply wounded.

But as the people prayed and danced and sang, a gentle light came stealing into the sky from the far, far east. Little by little the darkness was driven away. First the light was gray, then yellow, then white, and at last the glistening brilliancy of the sun filled all the land and covered the sky with glory. The sun had arisen for the first time, and in its light and warmth my people knew they had the favor of Those Above, and they were contented.

But when Siwash, the God of Earth looked round, and saw everything revealed by the sun, he was discontented, for the earth was bare and level and monotonous, and there was nothing to cheer the sight. So he took some of the people and of them he made high mountains, and of some, smaller mountains. Of some he made rivers and creeks, and lakes and waterfalls, and of others, coyotes, foxes, deer, antelopes, bears, squirrels, porcupines, and all the other animals. Then he made out of the other people all the different kinds of snakes and reptiles and insects and birds and fishes. Then he wanted trees and plants and flowers, and he turned some of the people into these things. Of every man or woman that he seized he made something according to its value.

When he was done he had used up so many people he was scared. So he set to work and made a new lot of people, some to live here, some to live there, and some to live everywhere. And he gave to each family its own language and tongue and its own place to live, and he told them where to live and the sad distress that would come upon them if they mixed up their tongues by intermarriage. Each family was to live in its own place, and while all the different families were to be friendly and live as brothers, tied together by kin-ship, amity, and concord, there was to be no mixing of bloods.

Thus were settled the original inhabitants on the coast of southern California by Siwash, the God of the Earth, and under the captaincy of Uuyot.

But at length the time came when Uuyot must die. His work on the earth was ended and Those Above told him he must prepare to leave his earthly friends and children. He was told to go up into the San Bernardino Mountains, into a small valley there, and lie down in a certain spot to await his end. He died peacefully and calmly, as one who went to sleep. He was beloved of the Gods above and Siwash, the God of Earth, so that no pain came to him to make his death distressful.

As soon as he was dead the ants came and ate all the flesh from his bones. But the spirit messengers of Those Above looked after him, and they buried him so that the mark of his burying place could never be wiped out. The powers of evil might strive, but this place would always remain clearly shown. A lake of water soon covered the place of his burial, and it assumed the shape of a colossal human being. It was the shape of Uuyot, and from that day to this it has remained there. It has been seen by all the people of all the ages, and will never be wiped out of existence. The legs and outstretched arms, as well as the great body, are distinctly to be seen, and even now, in the Great Bear Valley Lake, which is the site of Uuyot's burial, the eyes of the clear-seeing man may witness the interesting sight.

But it was not all at once that the people could see that Uuyot was buried in this spot. Before they knew it as a fact they sat in a great circle around the place. They sat and wept and wailed and mourned for Uuyot. They made their faces black and then they cut off their hair to show their deep sorrow, and they sat and waited, and wept and wailed, until Those Above showed them the buried body of their great leader and captain.

And to this day the places where that great circle of people sat may be seen. The marks of their bodies are left in the ground and they will remain there forever, or so long as the body of Uuyot is to be seen.

Ah! My people were strong and powerful then. There were many of them. Uuyot had led them to be a great people. They made a solid ring around the whole earth. Alas! That ring is broken now.

LEGEND OF THE BREADFRUIT TREE

Tradition Bearer: Unavailable

Source: Westervelt, W. D. "Legend of the Breadfruit Tree." Pages 29–37 in *Hawaiian Legends of Old Honolulu*. Boston: G. H. Ellis Press, 1915.

Date: 1915

Original Source: Hawaii

National Origin: Hawaiian

Hawaiians venerated nature gods, or "akua." Potentially, any natural phenomenon may be a god. Moreover, an image made from a natural object (such as the breadfruit tree of the following narrative) may become a god if it is worshipped as such. Papa and Wakea, the central gods of this **myth** are significant not only in Hawaiian tradition, but also elsewhere in the Pacific. Papa is the mother of the gods and associated with the earth and the underworld, while Wakea is a god of the heavens and associated with light. The term "tabu" used below is commonly spelled "taboo" in contemporary English usage. The concept here refers to those things that are so sacred as to be dangerous to all but the most supernaturally powerful individuals. Therefore, when chips or sap from the tabooed tree struck ordinary humans, they fell dead on the spot as punishment for their profane touch.

The wonderful bread-fruit tree was a great tree growing on the eastern bank of the rippling brook Puehuehu. It was a *tabu* tree, set apart for the high chief from Kou and the chiefs from Honolulu to rest under while on their way to bathe in the celebrated diving-pool, Wai-kaha-lulu. That tree became a god, and this is the story of its transformation:

Papa and Wakea were the ancestors of the great, scattered, sea-going and sea-loving people living in all the islands now known as Polynesia. They had their home in every group of islands where their descendants could find room to multiply.

They came to the island of Oahu, and, according to almost all the legends, were the first residents. The story of the magic bread-fruit tree, however, says that Papa sailed from Kahiki (a far-off land) with her husband Wakea, landing on Oahu and finding a home in the mountain upland near the precipice Kilohana.

Papa was a kupua-a woman having many wonderful and miraculous powers. She had also several names. Sometimes she was called Haumea, but at last she left her power and a new name, Ka-meha-i-kana, in the magic bread-fruit tree.

Papa was a beautiful woman, whose skin shone like polished dark ivory through the flowers and vines and leaves that were the only clothes she knew. Where she and her husband had settled down they found a fruitful country—with bananas and sugar-cane and taro. They built a house on the mountain ridge and feasted on the abundance of food around them. Here they rested well protected when rains were falling or the hot sun was shining.

Papa day by day looked over the seacoast, which stretches away in miles of marvelous beauty below the precipices of the northern mountain range of the island Oahu. Clear, deep pools, well filled with most delicate fish, lay restfully among moss-covered projections of the bordering coral reef. The restless murmur of surf waves beating in and out through the broken lines of the reef called to her, so, catching up some long leaves of the hala-tree, she made a light basket and hurried down to the sea. In a little while she had gathered sea-moss and caught all the crabs she wished to take home.

She turned toward the mountain range and carried her burden to Hoakola, where there was a spring of beautiful clear, cold, fresh water. She laid down her moss and crabs to wash them clean.

She looked up, and on the mountain-side discerned there something strange. She saw her husband in the hands of men who had captured and bound him and were compelling him to walk down the opposite side of the range. Her heart leaped with fear and anguish. She forgot her crabs and moss and ran up the steep way to her home. The moss rooted itself by the spring, but the crabs escaped to the sea.

On the Honolulu side of the mountains were many chiefs and their people, living among whom was Lele-hoo-mao, the ruler, whose fields were often despoiled by Papa and her husband. It was his servants who, while searching the country around these fields, had found and captured Wakea. They were forcing him to the temple Pakaka to be there offered in sacrifice. They were shouting, "We have found the mischief-maker and have tied him."

Papa threw around her some of the vines, which she had fashioned into a skirt, and ran over the hills to the edge of Nuuanu Valley. Peering down the valley she saw her husband and his captors, and cautiously she descended.

She found a man by the side of the stream Puehuehu, who said to her: "A man has been carried by who is to be baked in an oven this day. The fire is burning in the valley below."

Papa said, "Give me water to drink."

The man said, "I have none."

Then Papa took a stone and smashed it against the ground. It broke through into a pool of water. She drank and hastened on to the breadfruit tree at Nini, where she overtook her husband and the men who guarded him. He was alive, his hands bound behind him and his leaf clothing torn from his body. Wailing and crying that she must kiss him, she rushed to him and began pushing and pulling him, whirling him around and around.

Suddenly the great bread-fruit tree opened and she leaped with him through the doorway into the heart of the tree. The opening closed in a moment.

Papa, by her miraculous power, opened the tree on the other side. They passed through and went rapidly up the mountain-side to their home, which was near the head of Kalihi Valley. As they ran Papa threw off her vine pa-u, or skirt. The vine became the beautiful morning-glory, delicate in blossom and powerful in medicinal qualities. The astonished men had lost their captive. According to the ancient Hawaiian proverb, "Their fence was around the field of nothingness." They pushed against the tree, but the opening was tightly closed. They ran around under the heavy-leaved branches and found nothing. They believed that the great tree held their captive in its magic power.

Quickly ran the messenger to their high chief, Lele-hoo-mao, to tell him about the trouble at the tabu bread-fruit tree at Nini and that the sacrifice for which the oven was being heated was lost.

The chiefs consulted together and decided to cut down that tree and take the captive out of his hiding-place. They sent tree-cutters with their stone axes. The leader of the tree-cutters struck the tree with his stone axe. A chip leaped from the tree, struck him, and he fell dead. Another caught the axe. Again chips flew and the workman fell dead.

Then all the cutters struck and gashed the tree.

Whenever a chip hit anyone he died, and the sap of the tree flowed out and was spattered under the blows of the stone axes. Whenever a drop touched a workman or a bystander he fell dead.

The people were filled with fear and cried to their priest for help. Wohi, the priest, came to the tree, bowed before it, and remained in silent thought a long time. Then he raised his head and said: "It was not a woman who went into that tree. It was Papa from Kahiki. She is a goddess and has a multitude of bodies. If we treat her well we shall not be destroyed."

Wohi commanded the people to offer sacrifices at the foot of the tree. This was done with prayers and incantations. A black pig, black awa, and red fish were offered to Papa. Then Wohi commanded the wood-cutters to rub themselves bountifully with coconut oil and go fearlessly to their work. Chips struck them and the sap of the tree was spattered over them, but they toiled on unhurt until the great tree fell.

Out of this magic bread-fruit tree a great goddess was made. Papa gave to it one of her names, Ka-meha-i-kana, and endowed it with power so that it was noted from Kauai to Hawai'i. It became one of the great gods of Oahu, but was taken to Maui, where Kamehameha secured it as his god to aid in establishing his rule over all the islands.

The peculiar divine gift supposed to reside in this image made from the wonderful breadfruit tree was the ability to aid worshippers in winning land and power from other people and wisely employing the best means of firmly establishing their own government, thus protecting and preserving the kingdom.

Papa dwelt above the Kalihi Valley and looked down over the plains of Honolulu and Ewa covered with well-watered growing plants, which gave food or shade to the multiplying people.

It is said that after a time she had a daughter, Kapo, who also had kupua, or magic power. Kapo had many names, such as Kapo-ula-kinau and Laka. She was a high tabu goddess of the ancient Hawaiian hulas, or dances. She had also the power of assuming many bodies at will and could appear in any form from the mo-o, or lizard, to a human being.

Kapo was born from the eyes of Haumea, or Papa.

Papa looked away from Kapo and there was born from her head a sharp pali, or precipice, often mist-covered; this was Ka-moho-alii. Then Pele was born. She was the one who had mighty battles with Kamapuaa, the pig-man, who almost destroyed the volcano Kilauea. It was Ka-moho-alii who rubbed sticks and rekindled the volcanic fires for his sister Pele, thus driving Kamapuaa down the sides of Kilauea into the ocean.

These three, according to the Honolulu legends, were the highest-born children of Papa and Wakea.

Down the Kalihi stream below Papa's home were two stones to which the Hawaiians gave eepa, or gnomelike, power. If any traveler passes these stones on his way up to Papa's resting-place, that wayfarer stops by these stones, gathers leaves and makes leis, or garlands, and places them on these stones, that there may be no trouble in all that day's wanderings.

Sometimes mischievous people dip branches from lehua-trees in water and sprinkle the eepa rocks; then woe to the traveller, for piercing rains are supposed to fall. From this comes the proverb belonging to the residents of Kalihi Valley, "Here is the sharp-headed rain Kalihi" ("Ka-ua-poo-lipilipi-o-Kalihi").

HEROES, HEROINES, TRICKSTERS, AND FOOLS

THE BRIDE FROM THE UNDERWORLD

Tradition Bearer: Unavailable

Source: Westervelt, W. D. "The Bride from the Underworld." Pages 225–41 in *Hawaiian Legends of Ghosts and Ghost-Gods.* Boston: Ellis Press, 1916.

Date: 1916

Original Source: Hawaii

National Origin: Hawaiian

In traditional Hawaiian culture, a lineage traceable to the earliest mythic beginnings of the islands was necessary for a family to claim the right of rulership. The following **myth** is of a young hero who traveled to the land of the dead (see, "How Milu Became the King of Ghosts," p. 284, for the origins of the realm of the ghosts). The Underworld journey was the last of the tests Hiku passed to demonstrate his right to rule by virtue of his descent from the divine Ku. Earlier tests were his ability to survive the tabooed waters and to ride a surfboard with no prior knowledge of or training in its use.

Ku, one of the most widely known gods of the Pacific Ocean, was thought by the Hawaiians to have dwelt as a mortal for some time on the western side of the island Hawaii. Here he chose a queen by the name of Hina as his wife, and to them were born two children. When he withdrew from his residence among men he left a son on the uplands of the district of North Kona, and a daughter on the seashore of the same district. The son, Hiku-i-kana-hele (Hiku of the forest), lived with his mother. The daughter, Kewalu, dwelt under the care of guardian chiefs and priests by a temple, the ruined walls of which are standing even to the present day. Here she was carefully protected and perfected in all arts pertaining to the very high chiefs.

Hiku-of-the-Forest was not accustomed to go to the sea. His life was developed among the forests along the western slopes of the great mountains of Hawai'i. Here he learned the wisdom of his mother and of the chiefs and priests under whose care he was placed. To him were given many of the supernatural powers of his father. His mother guarded him from the knowledge that he had a sister and kept him from going to the temple by the side of which she had her home.

Hiku was proficient in all the feats of manly strength and skill upon which chiefs of the highest rank prided themselves. None of the chiefs of the inland districts could compare with him in symmetry of form, beauty of countenance, and skill in manly sports.

The young chief noted the sounds of the forest and the rushing winds along the sides of the mountains. Sometimes, like storm voices, he heard from far off the beat of the surf along the coral reef. One day he heard a noise like the flapping of the wings of many birds. He looked toward the mountain, but no multitude of his feathered friends could be found. Again the same sound awakened his curiosity. He now learned that it came from the distant seashore far below his home on the mountain-side.

Hiku-of-the-Forest called his mother and together they listened as again the strange sound from the beach rose along the mountain gulches and was echoed among the cliffs.

"Hiku," said the mother, "that is the clapping of the hands of a large number of men and women. The people who live by the sea are very much pleased and are expressing their great delight in some wonderful deed of a great chief."

Day after day the rejoicing of the people was heard by the young chief. At last he sent a trusty retainer to learn the cause of the tumult. The messenger reported that he had found certain tabu surf waters of the Kona beach and had seen a very high queen who alone played with her surf-board on the incoming waves. Her beauty surpassed that of any other among all the people, and her skill in riding the surf was wonderful, exceeding that of anyone whom the people had ever seen; therefore, the multitude gathered from near and far to watch the marvelous deeds of the beautiful woman. Their pleasure was so great that when they clapped their hands the sound was like the voices of many thunder-storms.

The young chief said he must go down and see this beautiful maiden. The mother knew that this young woman of such great beauty must be Kewalu, the sister of Hiku. She feared that trouble would come to Kewalu if her more powerful brother should find her and take her in marriage, as was the custom among the people. The omens that had been watched concerning the children in their infancy had predicted many serious troubles. But the young man could not be restrained. He was determined to see the wonderful woman.

He sent his people to gather the nuts of the kukui, or candlenut-tree, and crush out the oil and prepare it for anointing his body. He had never used a surf-board, but he commanded his servants to prepare the best one that could be made. Down to the seashore Hiku went with his retainers, down to the tabu place of the beautiful Kewalu.

He anointed his body with the kukui oil until it glistened like the polished leaves of trees; then, taking his surf-board, he went boldly to the tabu surf waters of his sister. The people stood in amazed silence, expecting to see speedy punishment meted out to the daring stranger. But the gods of the sea favored Hiku. Hiku had never been to the seaside and had never learned the arts of those who were skilful in the waters. Nevertheless, as he entered the water, he carried the surf-board more royally than any chief the people had ever known. The sunlight shone in splendor upon his polished body when he stood on the board and rode to the shore on the crests of the highest surf waves, performing wonderful feats by his magic power. The joy of the multitude was unbounded, and a mighty storm of noise was made by the clapping of their hands. Kewalu and her maidens had left the beach before the coming of Hiku and were resting in their grass houses in a grove of coconut-trees near the heiau. When the great noise made by the people aroused her, she sent one of her friends to learn the cause of such rejoicing. When she learned that an exceedingly handsome chief of the highest rank was sporting among her tabu waters, she determined to see him.

So, calling her maidens, she went down to the seashore and first saw Hiku on the highest crest of the rolling surf. She decided at once that she had never seen a man so comely, and Hiku, surf-riding to the shore, felt that he had never dreamed of such grace and beauty as marked the maiden who was coming to welcome him.

When Kewalu came near she took the wreath of rare and fragrant flowers that she wore and, coming close to him, threw it around his shoulders as a token to all the people that she had taken him to be her husband.

Then the joy of the people surpassed all the pleasure of all the days before, for they looked upon the two most beautiful beings they had ever seen and believed that these two would make glad each other's lives.

Thus Hiku married his sister, Kewalu, according to the custom of that time, because she was the only one of all the people equal to him in rank and beauty, and he alone was fitted to stand in her presence.

For a long time they lived together, sometimes sporting among the highest white crests of storm-tossed surf waves, sometimes enjoying the guessing and gambling games in which the Hawaiians of all times have been very expert, sometimes chanting meles and genealogies and telling marvelous stories of sea and forest, and sometimes feasting and resting under the trees surrounding their grass houses.

Hiku at last grew weary of the life by the sea. He wanted the forest on the mountain and the cold, stimulating air of the uplands. But he did not wish to take his sister-wife with him. Perhaps the omens of their childhood had revealed danger to Kewalu if she left her home by the sea. Whenever he tried to steal away from her she would rush to him and cling to him, persuading him to wait for new sports and joys.

One night Hiku rose up very quietly and passed out into the darkness. As he began to climb toward the uplands the leaves of the trees rustled loudly in welcome. The night birds circled around him and hastened him on his way, but Kewalu was awakened. She called for Hiku. Again and again she called, but Hiku had gone. She heard his footsteps as his eager tread shook the ground. She heard the branches breaking as he forced his way through the forests. Then she hastened after him and her plaintive cry was louder and clearer than the voices of the night birds.

> "E Hiku, return! E Hiku, return!
> O my love, wait for Kewalu!
> Hiku goes up the hills;
> Very hard is this hill,
> O Hiku! O Hiku, my beloved!"

But Hiku by his magic power sent thick fogs and mists around her. She was blinded and chilled, but she heard the crashing of the branches and ferns as Hiku forced his way through them, and she pressed on, still calling:

"E Hiku, beloved, return to Kewalu."

Then the young chief threw the long flexible vines of the ieie down into the path. They twined around her feet and made her stumble as she tried to follow him. The rain was falling all around her, and the way was very rough and hard. She slipped and fell again and again.

The ancient chant connected with the legend says:

"Hiku, is climbing up the hill.
Branches and vines are in the way,
And Kewalu is begging him to stop.
Rain-drops are walking on the leaves.
The flowers are beaten to the ground.
Hopeless the quest, but Kewalu is calling:
'E Hiku, beloved! Let us go back together.'"

Her tears, mingled with the rain, streamed down her cheeks. The storm wet and destroyed the kapa mantle that she had thrown around her as she hurried from her home after Hiku. In rags she tried to force her way through the tangled undergrowth of the uplands, but as she crept forward step by step she stumbled and fell again into the cold wet mass of ferns and grasses. Then the vines crept up around her legs and her arms and held her, but she tore them loose and forced her way upward, still calling. She was bleeding where the rough limbs of the trees had torn her delicate flesh. She was so bruised and sore from the blows of the bending branches that she could scarcely creep along.

At last she could no longer hear the retreating footsteps of Hiku. Then, chilled and desolate and deserted, she gave up in despair and crept back to the village. There she crawled into the grass house where she had been so happy with her brother Hiku, intending to put an end to her life.

The ieie vines held her arms and legs, but she partially disentangled herself and wound them around her head and neck. Soon the tendrils grew tight and slowly but surely choked the beautiful queen to death. This was the first suicide in the records of Hawaiian mythology. As the body gradually became lifeless the spirit crept upward to the lua-uhane, the door by which it passed out of the body into the spirit world. This "spirit-door" is the little hole in the corner of the eye. Out of it the spirit is thought to creep slowly as the body becomes cold in death. The spirit left the cold body a prisoner to the tangled vines, and slowly and sadly journeyed to Milu, the Underworld home of the ghosts of the departed.

The lust of the forest had taken possession of Hiku. He felt the freedom of the swift birds that had been his companions in many an excursion into the heavily shaded depths of the forest jungles. He plunged with abandon into the whirl and rush of the storm winds, which he had called to his aid to check Kewalu. He was drunken with the atmosphere that he had breathed throughout his childhood and young manhood. When he thought of Kewalu he was sure that he had driven her back to her home by the temple where he could find her when once more he should seek the seashore.

He had only purposed to stay a while on the uplands, and then return to his sister-wife. His father, the god Ku, had been watching him and had also seen the suicide of the beautiful Kewalu. He saw the spirit pass down to the kingdom of Milu, the home of the ghosts. Then he called Hiku and told him bow heedless and thoughtless he had been in his treatment of Kewalu, and how in despair she had taken her life, the spirit going to the Underworld.

Hiku, the child of the forest, was overcome with grief. He was ready to do anything to atone for the suffering he had caused Kewalu, and repair the injury.

Ku told him that only by the most daring effort could he hope to regain his loved bride. He could go to the Underworld, meet the ghosts and bring his sister back, but this could only be done at very great risk to himself, for if the ghosts discovered and captured him they would punish him with severest torments and destroy all hope of returning to the Upper-world.

Hiku was determined to search the land of Milu and find his bride and bring her back to his Kona home by the sea. Ku agreed to aid him with the mighty power that he had as a god; nevertheless, it was absolutely necessary that Hiku should descend alone and by his own wit and skill secure the ghost of Kewalu.

Hiku prepared a coconut-shell full of oil made from decayed kukui nuts. This was very vile and foul smelling. Then he made a long stout rope of ieie vines.

Ku knew where the door to the Underworld was, through, which human beings could go down. This was a hole near the seashore in the valley of Waipio on the eastern coast of the island.

Ku and Hiku went to Waipio, descended the precipitous walls of the valley and found the door to the pit of Milu. Milu was the ruler of the Underworld. Hiku rubbed his body all over with the rancid kukui oil and then gave the ieie vine into the keeping of his father to hold fast while he made his descent into the world of the spirits of the dead. Slowly Ku let the vine down until at last Hiku stood in the strange land of Milu.

No one noticed his coming and so for a little while he watched the ghosts, studying his best method of finding Kewalu. Some of the ghosts were sleeping; some were gambling and playing the same games they had loved so well while living in the Upper-world; others were feasting and visiting around the poi bowl as they had formerly been accustomed to do.

Hiku knew that the strong odor of the rotten oil would be his best protection, for none of the spirits would want to touch him and so would not discover that he was flesh and blood. Therefore he rubbed his body once more thoroughly with the oil and disfigured himself with dirt. As he passed from place to place searching for Kewalu, the ghosts said, "What a bad-smelling spirit!" So they turned away from him as if he was one of the most unworthy ghosts dwelling in Milu. In the realm of Milu he saw the people in the game of rolling coconut-shells to hit a post. Kulioe, one of the spirits, had been playing the kilu and had lost all his property to the daughter of Milu and one of her friends. He saw Hiku and said, "If you are a skilful man perhaps you should play with these two girls."

Hiku said: "I have nothing. I have only come this day and am alone." Kulioe bet his bones against some of the property he had lost. The first girl threw her cup at the kilu post. Hiku chanted:

> "Are you known by Papa and Wakea,
> O eyelashes or rays of the sun?
> Mine is the cup of kilu."

Her cup did not touch the kilu post before Hiku. She threw again, but did not touch, while Hiku chanted the same words. They took a new cup, but failed.

Hiku commenced swinging the cup and threw. It glided and twisted around on the floor and struck the post. This counted five and won the first bet. Then he threw the cup numbered twenty, won all the property, and gave it back to Kulioe.

At last he found Kewalu, but she was by the side of the high chief, Milu, who had seen the beautiful princess as she came into the Underworld. More glorious was Kewalu than any other of all those of noble blood whom had ever descended to Milu. The ghosts had welcomed the spirit of the princess with great rejoicing, and the king had called her at once to the highest place in his court.

She had not been long with the chiefs of Milu before they asked her to sing or chant her mele. The mele was the family song by which any chief made known his rank and the family with which he was connected whenever he visited chiefs far away from his own home.

Hiku heard the chant and mingled with the multitude of ghosts gathered around the place where the high chiefs were welcoming the spirit of Kewalu. While Hiku and Kewalu had been living together, one of their pleasures was composing and learning to intone a chant that no other among either mortals or spirits should know besides themselves. While Kewalu was singing she introduced her part of this chant. Suddenly from among the throng of ghosts arose the sound of a clear voice chanting the response, which was known by no other person but Hiku.

Kewalu was overcome by the thought that perhaps Hiku was dead and was now among the ghosts, but did not dare to incur the hatred of King Milu by making himself known; or perhaps Hiku had endured many dangers of the lower world by coming even in human form to find her and therefore must remain concealed. The people around the king, seeing her grief, were not surprised when she threw a mantle around herself and left them to go away alone into the shadows.

She wandered from place to place among the groups of ghosts, looking for Hiku. Sometimes she softly chanted her part of the mele. At last she was again answered and was sure that Hiku was near, but the only one very close was a foul-smelling, dirt-covered ghost from whom she was turning away in despair.

Hiku, in a low tone, warned her to be very careful and not recognize him, but assured her that he had come in person to rescue her and take her back to her old home where her body was then lying. He told her to wander around and yet to follow him until they came to the ieie vine which he had left hanging from the hole that opened to the Upper-world.

When Hiku came to the place where the vine was hanging he took hold to see if Ku, his father, was still carefully guarding the other end to pull him up when the right signal should be given. Having made himself sure of the aid of the god, he tied the end of the vine into a strong loop and seated himself in it. Then he began to swing back and forth, back and forth, sometimes rising high and sometimes checking himself and resting with his feet on the ground.

Kewalu came near and begged to be allowed to swing, but Hiku would only consent on the condition that she would sit in his lap. The ghosts thought that this would be an excellent arrangement and shouted their approval of the new sport. Then Hiku took the spirit of Kewalu in his strong arms and began to swing slowly back and forth, then more and more rapidly, higher and higher, until the people marveled at the wonderful skill. Meanwhile he gave the signal to Ku to pull them up. Almost imperceptibly the swing receded from the spirit world.

All this time Hiku had been gently and lovingly rubbing the spirit of Kewalu and softly uttering charm after charm so that while they were swaying in the air she was growing smaller and smaller. Even the chiefs of Milu had been attracted to this unusual sport, and had drawn near to watch the wonderful skill of the strange foul-smelling ghost.

Suddenly it dawned upon some of the beholders that the vine was being drawn up to the Upper-world. Then the cry arose: "He is stealing the woman!" "He is stealing the woman!"

The Underworld was in a great uproar of noise. Some of the ghosts were leaping as high as they could, others were calling for Hiku to return, and others were uttering charms to cause his downfall. No one could leap high enough to touch Hiku, and the power of all the charms was defeated by the god Ku, who rapidly drew the vine upward.

Hiku succeeded in charming the ghost of Kewalu into the coconut-shell, which he still carried. Then, stopping the opening tight with his fingers so that the spirit could not escape, he brought Kewalu back to the land of mortals.

With the aid of Ku, the steep precipices surrounding Waipio Valley were quickly scaled and the journey made to the temple by the tabu surf waters of Kona. Here the body of Kewalu had been lying in state. Here the auwe, or mourning chant, of the retinue of the dead princess could be heard from afar.

Hiku passed through the throngs of mourners, carefully guarding his precious coconut until he came to the feet, cold and stiff in death. Kneeling down he placed the small hole in the end of the shell against the tender spot in the bottom of one of the cold feet.

The spirits of the dead must find their way back little by little through the body from the feet to the eyes, from which they must depart when they bid final farewell to the world. To try to send the spirit back into the body by placing it in the lua-uhane, or "door of the soul," would be to have it where it had to depart from the body rather than enter it.

Hiku removed his finger from the hole in the coconut and uttered the incantations that would allure the ghost into the body. Little by little the soul of Kewalu came back, and the body grew warm from the feet upward, until at last the eyes opened and the soul looked out upon the blessed life restored to it by the skill and bravery of Hiku.

No more troubles arose to darken the lives of the children of Ku. Whether in the forest or by the sea they made the days pleasant for each other until at the appointed time together they entered the shades of Milu as chief and chiefess who could not be separated. It is said that the generations of their children gave many rulers to the Hawaiians, and that the present royal family, the "House of Kalakaua," is the last of the descendants.

THE ADVENTURES OF HAININU AND BAUMEGWESU

Tradition Bearer: Chipo

Source: Gifford, Edward Winslow. "Western Mono Myths." *Journal of American Folklore* 36 (1923): 333–38.

Date: 1918

Original Source: Western Mono (California)
National Origin: Native American

Western Mono settled on the western slopes of the Sierra Nevada Mountains in California. They were a seminomadic hunting and gathering culture that moved residences to obtain seasonally available food source. While Haininu and Baumegwesu are apparently human characters in the following **myth**, all others are animals, some of whom have significance to the Mono. Rattlesnake and bear were the focus of two of the tribal rituals, and Great Horned Owl served as the messenger of death. Haininu partakes of much of his uncle Coyote's irreverence toward the all species, however. His destruction of dangerous animal species and tempestuous winds suggests the role of **culture hero** as well as, in the end, **trickster**.

Coyote made a fire, a large fire. He sat down by it and cried. Then he sang, "Yo i hini, yo i hini wau!" Said Coyote to himself, "My tears drop down all around my flanks. I wish my sister's sons, Haininu and Baumegwesu, would come. If they would come, I would go with them."

The two nephews appeared close by the fire. "What are you going to do, uncle?" asked Haininu.

Coyote replied, "What do you expect me to do? I am going with you. I am going along when you get that yellow jackets' nest. I will clean it very thoroughly." So they started.

They encountered Roadrunner, who was also Haininu's mother's brother. "What are you going to do?" queried Haininu.

"I am going along too," replied Roadrunner.

Next they came to House Finch's place and Haininu said to House Finch, who was also his mother's brother, "What are you going to do?"

House Finch responded, "I am going along too."

Then they arrived at the camp of Brewer's Blackbird. "What are you going to do, mother's brother?" asked Haininu.

He replied, "I am going along too."

A creek was reached and there Haininu shot a large salmon with his bow and arrow. When he killed it, the water rose and nearly overwhelmed him. It pursued him. He jumped from cliff to cliff far back in the mountains, but the water still followed him. Finally he got out of reach of it, but he was so exhausted that he fainted. When he revived he asked himself, "Who is doing this to me? I am going to see you again," he said, referring to the salmon and the water of the creek that had pursued him. He was all covered with mud when the water receded. He looked over the edge of the cliff on which he was resting, put over his bow and arrow, so they leaned against it, and then slid down to the bottom of the cliff on them.

He returned to the place where he had shot the large salmon. Then out of revenge he shot all of the salmon he could see, a task that was made easy because the water was low. "That is what I can do to you now," he said. He walked around amongst the slaughtered salmon in the now waterless creek bed. All of the water had disappeared when he killed the salmon. "This is what I can do to you," he said.

He took his departure and caught up with his brother Baumegwesu, who had gone on with his uncles. As they proceeded Haininu espied two bears swinging. He said to them, "Friends, you are doing some-thing fine there. Let me swing."

The bears replied, "Yes, Yes, it is nice. You may swing." The bears swung him on the tree and then let go. He was projected upward, but alighted feet first, though buried up to his neck in sand. The bears laughed and went into their house, leaving their cubs outside.

Haininu killed and skinned the cubs and took their flesh in the house. "My father's sisters," he said, "here is some deer meat. Eat it."

The bears remarked, "It smells like our children, and it tastes like them." Then they vomited. The bears pursued Haininu, who called to Baumegwesu, across the creek, to put his leg out so that the bears might cross on it. Baumegwesu did so, but when one bear was half way over, he withdrew his leg and she fell into the water and was drowned. One bear was left and that is why there are still bears in this country today.

The two brothers went on until they neared the home of their father's sisters, the Winds. There Baumegwesu said to Haininu, "You go over there and see our aunts and get a basket from them." This was at a big cave, in the mountains, called Piyau. The Winds lived in the cave. When Haininu entered Piyau cave, the habitation of his aunts, he seized each of the old women by the ears.

They protested, "Ouch! Nephew, do not do that. You are always treating us this way."

"Give me a basket, aunts," he demanded. "I want to put some of my food into it. We are going down to the plains." As soon as they turned their backs, Haininu mischievously made holes in all of their baskets by shooting arrows into them.

When the Winds perceived what he had done, they became whirlwinds and pursued him. They chased him, overtook him, and beat him with large tree limbs. He kept shouting his name as he jumped this way and that to escape their blows. They finally gave up in despair, as he was too agile for them, and went home. Haininu followed them back and shot them and all but two of their children, who escaped. They secreted themselves in crevices in the cliff. Haininu tried to poke them out, but could not. We would not have wind today if these two little ones had not escaped.

Baumegwesu sat singing his own name, while Haininu was having the tussle with the Winds. "I did not send you to murder our aunts," scolded Baumegwesu, "but you are always getting into mischief. We will travel now." They had not gone far before Baumegwesu said, "My younger brother, you go to our father's sisters living over there and try to get a basket from them." These aunts were Rattlesnakes.

To Haininu's request they responded, "Yes, my nephew, we have baskets for you here. Let us enter and seek a good one." They selected their best basket and handed it to Haininu. "This is the best we can do, nephew," they said.

Haininu departed and the aunts sat down to resume work on the baskets they were making. "What is the matter with this basket?" asked one, "it is full of holes." "Mine too," said the other, for Haininu had been up to mischief when their backs were turned. "We will cut across here and get ahead of our nephew before he gets far up the road. Run quickly."

They hastened and hid themselves at a fork of the trail ahead of Haininu. As he passed, each one bit him on the leg, one on the right, one on the left. Haininu sat down on a great rock, where one can still see his blood. He fainted. His legs swelled and rotted.

Baumegwesu came to see what the trouble was. He whipped Haininu's legs with an arrow. The swelling subsided and Haininu awoke. "What are you doing to me?" he asked. "I have been sleeping right here."

"You certainly have not been sleeping here. I told you not to do this thing. You are always bothering our poor aunts," thus Baumegwesu reprimanded him.

Haininu ignored the reproof and said, "You go ahead, brother, and I will follow shortly."

He ran back to his aunts' house and shot both of them. One child escaped. "Well, I do not believe that you amount to anything, so I will let you go," said Haininu to the escaping child. Haininu hastened to over-take his brother. When he caught up with him, Baumegwesu asked, "What have you been doing now?"

"I went back and killed those old women," said Haininu. "They cannot get the best of me."

They camped near Napasiat, where they found a yellow jackets' nest under a stone. Haininu said, "We will leave this one for the Indians in this part of the country. We do not want to dig this one out. We will go down to the plains and get a large one."

They made a bait for the yellow jackets. It consisted of a grass-hopper's leg with a white feather tied to it. The feather was to serve as a guide when the grasshopper leg was being carried away by a yellow jacket to its nest. It was not long before a yellow jacket started to carry it away. Then Haininu saw a yellow jacket with a piece of deer meat, also a giant yellow jacket carrying a deer's antlers.

Haininu left his companions and followed the giant yellow jacket that was carrying the deer's antlers. He followed it to its nest. Then he returned to his companions, singing his name as he went along, "Haina, Haininu."

Coyote heard him singing as he approached and he sang too. "Oh, I am so happy," said Coyote, as he thought about the coming feast.

Haininu tarried with Vulture. "Give me one of your feathers," requested Haininu. "All right," said Vulture, "I will give you one." So saying, he pulled out the largest and handed it to Haininu.

"Yes. This is what I want," said Haininu.

"You may have anything you want," said Vulture. "You know your mother's brother always gives you whatever you wish."

Haininu next visited Great Horned Owl and asked him, "What are you going to do?" "I am going down to eat my fill of yellow jacket grubs," said Great Horned Owl. "Well, come on then," urged Haininu. As they proceeded they encountered Raccoon. "Well, mother's brother, what are you going to do?" queried Haininu.

"I am going down to eat my fill of yellow jacket grubs," replied Raccoon. "Well, come on then," invited Haininu.

Baumegwesu sang when they arrived at the yellow jackets' nest. He instructed Haininu and the uncles to go and gather pine needles for the roasting. After they had secured the pine needles, Baumegwesu changed his mind and said, "This is not the nest we are seeking. We ought to have a larger nest. We will have to seek further. This is a different one." Again they used a grasshopper leg for bait and a yellow jacket took it. Haininu followed him way over to the Coast Range (Panakap), located the nest, and then returned to report to his older brother. "No. That is not the nest, either," said Baumegwesu.

They fixed another bait. It was carried towards Mariposa by a yellow jacket. Coyote, meanwhile, had developed such an appetite that he had eaten all the pine needles that had been collected. He complained, "I am so very hungry. When will that yellow jackets' nest be in sight?" Then Haininu followed the yellow jacket toward Mariposa. When he returned to his companions, he found the deer's antlers again in the same hole where he had first found them.

Baumegwesu now declared that after all this was the nest they were seeking. "That is the one," he said. "Bring the antlers here. That is certainly the nest."

Haininu went out and gathered pine needles, "Are these right, my elder brother?" he asked Baumegwesu.

"No. You have gathered the wrong kind," replied Baumegwesu. So Haininu started again in the morning. Then he came in with a big load of pine needles.

"Are these all right?" he asked.

Baumegwesu said, "Yes. That is the kind I told you to get in the first place."

Haininu protested, "You make so much work for me, elder brother. Why did you bring that old uncle Coyote? He ate all of our pine needles to begin with."

Baumegwesu warned him, "You had better say nothing about him. We have our nest and we do not care." Then Baumegwesu continued, "There are not enough pine needles. You will have to get some more."

"Oh dear," sighed Haininu, "what work!" He went further this time, crossing the mountains and securing needles from the pinion trees. When he returned with his burden Baumegwesu said, "This quantity is going to be sufficient to cook the nest. This is the best thing you could get."

Then Baumegwesu discovered that they had no fire drill. "We have forgotten our fire drill and hearth," he said to Haininu. "Go back to Napasiat and get them." As the yellow jackets' nest they were about to cook was at Yoninau, between Fresno and Coalinga, this order meant another long trip back into the mountains for Haininu. However, he set out on the errand and in due time returned with the implements. "You have brought the wrong ones," said Baumegwesu, when Haininu handed him the sticks. He sent Haininu back again.

Baumegwesu said, "Oh yes, here it is," referring to the first drill that Haininu had brought. "What am I thinking of? This is it, my younger brother. This is what I told you to get."

They now filled the yellow jackets' hole with pine needles. Baumegwesu secured a spark with the fire drill and blew it into flame. When the nest was cooked they took it out, they took it out, they took it all out. They kept digging and the nest seemed to get bigger and bigger, wider and wider. Coyote cried, "I want the bottom one, the last." Then his companions said, "Feed him separately. Do not let him eat with us." This pleased Coyote, for he said, "If I eat separately,

I shall have that much more." Coyote got the best. They finished the feast and prepared to travel the following morning.

"We will divide what is left of the yellow jackets' nest," said Baumegwesu. "You had better all go home now." The division was made and each started for home with a little bundle of yellow jacket grubs.

Different tribes of Indians met Haininu and Baumegwesu when they were returning. The two brothers made a house at Yuninau, a high hill near Friant. They did not like it, however, and Haininu left, but Baumegwesu remained behind singing. Baumegwesu after a bit noticed the absence of Haininu and said to himself, "Where has my younger brother gone?" Then Baumegwesu, from his station on the hill Yuninau, could discern Haininu on the plains below. Different tribes were chasing him, but his vulture feather, which he wore on his head, was still insight. "My brother is yet alive," said Baumegwesu. Haininu and his pursuers, who were shooting at him, drew near. Baumegwesu spread out his bow and arrows to dry and, when the people got close, he shot at them. While Baumegwesu was shooting these people, Haininu went off a short distance and lay down, quite exhausted. His pursuers were very weary, too, as Baumegwesu shot them.

When the slaughter was over, Baumegwesu went to Haininu and kicked him. Then he beat him with an arrow and asked, "What is the matter with you?"

"Do not disturb me," protested Haininu. "I am sound asleep."

Baumegwesu laughed ironically, "Yes, you are!" Then he ordered Haininu to arise and start the fire. When the fire was kindled, Baumegwesu butchered the different tribes of people to eat. He made charqui of some; others he roasted. He put some on the coals, but they disappeared. "I do not think the meat has been consumed by the fire," said Baumegwesu in wonder. "Next time I shall watch it."

Then he put a whole head on the fire to roast and held it by the horns, for these people had horns. He stirred the fire, still holding the head by the horns, but it slipped away from him and turned into Elk. It started to pursue Haininu, but it traveled slowly. Haininu retired into the mountains with Elk after him.

He arrived at a village. "What are you going to do for me?" he asked the people. "Something is after me."

They replied, "We can do nothing for you." He passed on and approached another village. "What are you going to do for me? Something is after me."

"We can do nothing for you," was the reply.

At last he arrived at Skunk's habitation. "What are you going to do for me? Something is after me," pleaded Haininu.

Skunk replied, "We have some soapstone here. We might make some red hot stones. They started a fire as quickly as they could and heated some stones. After a time Elk appeared. "Where is that man I am following?" he asked.

"We have already butchered him," responded Skunk. "Open your mouth wide and we will give you what is left." Elk obeyed and Skunk threw the red hot stones in the gaping mouth. Elk boiled and burst. "That is the way we fix them," boasted Skunk.

KAMPUAA LEGENDS: LEGENDS OF THE HOG GOD

Tradition Bearer: Unavailable

Source: Westervelt, W. D. "Kampuaa Legends." Pages 247–78 in *Hawaiian Legends of Old Honolulu*. Boston, G. H. Ellis Press, 1915.

Date: 1915

Original Source: Hawaii

National Origin: Hawaiian

Abraham Fornander, an early collector and compiler of Hawaiian oral tradition writes, "The Kamapuaa stories ... seem to have no counterpart in any mythology beyond the borders of the Hawaiian Islands." Although W. D. Westervelt does not emphasize the connection, Hina is identified as a god and Kamapuaa is explicitly named as a demigod by folklorist Martha Warren Beckwith. His nature bears all the marks of a "kupua" (the offspring of a god born into a human family): he is a shape-shifter with extraordinary strength; he is extraordinarily ugly and can control nature. The following cycle of tales of Kampuaa has been collated and rewritten with interjections by Westervelt. In spite of this, however, the content remains true to tradition.

Some of the most unique legends of the nations have centered around imagined monsters. Centaurs, half man and half horse, thronged the dreams of Rome. The Hawaiians knew nothing about any animals, save the fish of the seas, the birds of the forests, and the chickens, dogs, and pigs around their homes. From the devouring shark, the Hawaiian imagination conceived the idea of the shark-man who indulged in cannibalistic tendencies.

From the devastations of the hogs, they built up the experiences of a rude vicious chief whom they called Kamapuaa: the principal figure of many rough exploits throughout the islands. Sometimes he had a hog's body with a human head and limbs, sometimes a hog's head rested on a human form, and sometimes he assumed the shape of a hog—quickly reassuming the form of a man. Kalakaua's legends say that he was a hairy man and cultivated the stiff hair by cutting it short so that it stood out like bristles, and that he had his body tattooed so that it would have the appearance of a hog. In place of the ordinary feather cloak worn by chiefs he wore a pigskin with its bristles on the outside and a pigskin girdle around his waist.

The legends say that he was born at Kaluanui, a part of the district of Hauula or Koolau coast of the island Oahu. His reputed father was Olopana, the high chief of that part of the island, and his mother was Hina, the daughter of a chief who had come from a foreign land. Other legends say that his father was Kahikiula (The Red Tahiti), a brother of Olopana. These brothers had come to Oahu from foreign lands some time before. Fornander always speaks of Olopana as Kamapuaa's uncle, although he had taken Hina as his wife.

The Koolauloa coast of Oahu lies as a luxuriant belt of ever-living foliage a mile or so in width between an ocean of many colors and dark beetling precipices of mountain walls rising some thousands of feet among the clouds. From these precipices, which mark the landward side of a mighty extinct crater, come many mountain streams leaping in cascades of spray down into the quiet green valleys, which quickly broaden into the coral-reef-bordered seacoast. From any place by the sea, the outline of several beautiful little valleys can be easily traced.

One morning while the sunlight of May looked into the hidden recesses and crevices of these valleys, bringing into sharp relief of shadow and light the outcropping ledges, a little band of Hawaiians and their white friends lay in the shade of a great kamani tree and talked about the legends which were told of the rugged rock masses of each valley, and the quiet pools of each rivulet. Where the little party lay was one of the sporting-places of Kamapuaa, the "hog-child treated in the legends as a demigod." Not far away, one of the mountain streams had broadened into a quiet bush-shaded lakelet with deep fringes of grass around its borders. Here the legendary hog-man with marvelous powers had bathed from time to time. A narrow gorge deep shadowed by the morning sun was the place that Kamapuaa had miraculously bridged for his followers when an enemy was closely pursuing them. Several large stones on the edges of the valleys were pointed out as the monuments of various adventures. An exquisitely formed little valley ran deep into the mountain almost in front of the legend-tellers. Far away in the upper end where the dark-green foliage blended with still darker shadows the sides of the valley narrowed until they were only from sixty to seventy feet apart, and unscalable precipices bent toward each other, leaving only a narrow strip of sky above. On the right of this valley is a branch-gorge down which fierce storms have hurled torrents of waters and mist. The upper end has been hollowed and polished in the shape of a finely rounded canoe of immense proportions. It was from this that the valley took its name Ka-liu-waa, possibly having the meaning, "the leaky canoe." Some of the legends say that this was Kamapuaa's canoe leaning against the precipice and always leaking out the waters that fell in it.

Lying toward the west was a very fertile and open tract of land, Kaluanui, where Kamapuaa was said to have been born of Hina. After his birth he was thrown away by Kahiki-houna-kele, an older brother, and left to die. After a time Hina, the mother, went to a stream of clear, sweet water near her home to bathe. After bathing she went to the place where she had left her pa-u, or tapa skirt, and found a fine little hog lying on it. She picked it up and found that it was a baby. She was greatly alarmed, and gave the hog-child to another son, Kekelaiaika, that he might care for it, but the older brother stole the hog-child and carried it away to a cave in which Hina's mother lived. Her name was Kamaunuaniho.

The grandmother knew the hog-child at once as her grandson endowed with marvelous powers, and since the gods had given him the form of a hog he should be called kama (child), puaa (hog). Then she gave to the older brother kapa quilts in which to place Kamapuaa. These were made in layers; six sheets of kapa cloth formed the under quilt for a bed and six sheets the upper quilt for a cover. In these Kamapuaa slept while his brother prepared taro and breadfruit for his food. Thus the wonderful hog ate and slept usually in the form of a hog until size and strength came to him.

Then he became mischievous and began to commit depredations at night. He would root up the taro in the fields of his neighbors, and especially in the field of the high chief Olopana. Then he would carry the taro home, root up ferns and grass until he had good land, and then plant the stolen taro. Thus his grandmother and her retainers were provided with growing taro, the source of which they did not understand.

His elder brother prepared an oven in which to cook chickens. Kamapuaa rooted up the oven and stole the chickens. This brother Kahiki-houna-kele caught the hog-child and administered a sound whipping, advising him to go away from home if he wanted to steal, and especially to take what he wanted from Olopana.

Adopting this advice, Kamapuaa extended his raids to the home of the high chief. Here he found many chickens. Kamapuaa quickly killed some, took them in his mouth and threw many more on his back and ran home. The morning came before he had gone far and the people along the way saw the strange sight and pursued him. By the use of charms taught him by his sorceress-grandmother he made himself run faster and faster until he had outstripped his pursuer. Then he carried his load to his grandmother's cave and gave the chickens to the family for a great luau (feast).

Another time he stole the sacred rooster belonging to Olopana, as well as many other fowls. The chief sent a large number of warriors after him. They chased the man who had been seen carrying the chickens. He fled by his grandmother's cave and threw the chickens inside, then fled back up the hillside, revealing himself to his pursuers. They watched him, but he disappeared. He dropped down by the side of a large stone. On this he seated himself and watched the people as they ran through the valley calling to each other. The high grass was around the stone so that for a long time he was concealed. For this reason this stone still bears the name Pohaku-pee-o-Kamapuaa (Kamapuaa's-hiding-stone).

After a time a man who had climbed to the opposite ridge cried out, "E, E, there he is sitting on the great stone!" This man was turned into a stone by the magic of Kamapuaa. The pursuers hastened up the hillside and surrounded the stone, but no man was there. There was a fine black hog, which they recognized as the wonderful one belonging to Kamaunuaniho. So they decided that this was the thief, and seized it and carried it down the bill to give to the high chief Olopana. After getting him down into the valley they tried to drive him, but he would not go. Then they sent into the forest for ohia poles and made a large litter. It required many men to carry this enormous hog who made himself very heavy.

Suddenly Kamapuaa heard his grandmother calling: "Break the cords! Break the poles! Break the strong men! Escape!" Making a sudden turn on the litter, he broke it in pieces and fell with it to the ground. Then he burst the cords that bound him and attacked the band of men whom he had permitted to capture him. Some legends say that he killed and ate many of them. Others say that he killed and tore the people.

The wild life lived by Kamapuaa induced a large band of rough, lawless men to leave the service of the various high chiefs and follow Kamapuaa in his marauding expeditions. They made themselves the terror of the whole Koolau region.

Olopana determined to destroy them, and sent an army of four hundred warriors to uproot Kamapuaa and his robbers. It was necessary for them to hasten to their hiding-places, but they were chased up into the hills until a deep gorge faced them. No way of escape seemed possible, but Kamapuaa, falling on the ground, became a long hog—stretching out he increased his length until he could reach from side to side of the deep ravine—thus, he formed a bridge over which his followers escaped.

Kamapuaa, however, was not able to make himself small quickly enough to escape from his enemies. He tried to hide himself in a hole and pull dead branches and leaves over himself; but they soon found him, bound him securely, and tied him to a great stone, which, with "the stone of hiding" and "the watcher," are monuments of the legends to this day.

The people succeeded in leading the hog-man to Olopana's home, where they fastened him, keeping him for a great feast—which they hoped to have in a few days—but Kamapuaa, Samson-like, broke all his bonds, destroyed many of his captors, wantonly destroyed coconut-trees and taro patches, and then went back to his home.

He knew that Olopana would use every endeavor to compass his destruction. So he called his followers together and led them up Kaliuwaa Valley, stopping to get his grandmother on the way. When he came to the end of the valley, and the steep cliffs up which his people could not possibly climb, he took his grandmother on his neck and leaned back against the great precipice. Stretching himself more and more, and rubbing against the black rocks, at last he lifted his grandmother to the top of the cliffs so that she could step off on the uplands, which sloped down to the Pearl Harbor side of the island. Then the servants and followers climbed up the sides of the great hog by clinging to his bristles and escaped. The hollow worn in the rocks looked like a hewn-out canoe, and was given the name Ka-waa-o-Kamapuaa (The canoe of Kamapuaa). Kamapuaa then dammed up the water of the beautiful stream by throwing his body across it, and awaited the coming of Olopana and his warriors.

An immense force had been sent out to destroy him. In addition to the warriors who came by land, a great fleet of canoes was sent along the seashore to capture any boats in which Kamapuaa and his people might try to escape.

The canoes gathered in and around the mouth of the stream that flowed from Kaliuwaa Valley. The warriors began to march along the stream up toward the deep gorge. Suddenly Kamapuaa broke the dam by leaping away from the waters, and a great flood drowned the warriors and dashed the canoes together, destroying many and driving the rest far out to sea. Uhakohi is said to be the place where this flood occurred.

Then Kamapuaa permitted the people to capture him. They went up the valley after the waters had subsided and found nothing left of Kamapuaa or his people except a small black hog. They searched the valley thoroughly. They found the canoe, turned to stone, leaning against the precipice at the end of the gorge. They said among themselves, "Escaped is Kamapuaa with all his people, and ended are our troubles."

They caught the hog and bound it to carry to Olopana. As they journeyed along the seashore, their burden became marvelously heavy until at last an immense litter was required resting on the shoulders of many men. It was said that he sometimes tossed himself over to one side, breaking it down and killing some of the men who carried him. Then again he rolled to the other side, bringing a like destruction. Thus he brought trouble and death and a long, weary journey to his captors, who soon learned that their captive was the hog-man Kamapuaa. They brought him to their king Olopana and placed him in the temple enclosure where sacrifices to the gods were confined. This heiau was in Kaneohe and was known as the heiau of Kawaewae. It was in the care of a priest known as Lonoaohi.

Long, long before this capture Olopana had discovered Kamapuaa and would not acknowledge him as his son. The destruction of his coconut-trees and taro patches had been the cause of the first violent rupture between the two. Kamapuaa had wantonly broken the walls of Olopana's great fish-pond and set the fish free, and then after three times raiding the fowls around the grass houses had seized, killed, and eaten the sacred rooster, which Olopana considered his household fetish.

When Olopana knew that Kamapuaa had been captured and was lying bound in the temple enclosure he sent orders that great care should be taken lest he escape, and later he should be placed on the altar of sacrifice before the great gods.

Hina, it was said, could not bear the thought that this child of hers, brutal and injurious as he was, should suffer as a sacrifice. She was a very high chiefess, and, like the Hinas throughout Polynesia, was credited with divine powers. She had great influence with the high priest Lonoaohi and persuaded him to give Kamapuaa an opportunity to escape. This was done by killing a black hog and smearing Kamapuaa's body with the blood. Thus bearing the appearance of death, he was laid unbound on the altar. It was certain that unless detected he could easily climb the temple wall and escape.

Olopana, the king, came to offer the chants and prayers that belonged to such a sacrifice. He as well as the high priest had temple duties and the privilege of serving at sacrifices of great importance. As was his custom he came from the altar repeating chants and prayers while Kamapuaa lay before the images of the gods. While he was performing the sacrificial rites, Kamapuaa became angry, leaped from the altar, changed himself into his own form, seized the bone daggers used in dismembering the sacrifices, and attacked Olopana, striking him again and again until he dropped on the floor of the temple dead. The horrified priests had been powerless to prevent the deed, nor did they think of striking Kamapuaa down at once. In the confusion, he rushed from the temple, fled along the coast to his well-known valleys, climbed the steep precipices and rejoined his grandmother and his followers.

Leading his band of rough robbers down through the sandalwood forests of the Wahiawa region, he crossed over the plains to the Waianae Mountains. Here they settled for a time, living in caves. Other lawless spirits joined them, and they passed along the Ewa side of the island, ravaging the land like a herd of swine, a part of the island they conquered, making the inhabitants their serfs.

Here on a spur of the Waianae Mountains they built a residence for Kama-unu-aniho, and established her as their priestess, or kahuna. They levied on the neighboring farmers for whatever taro, sweet-potatoes, and bananas they needed. They compelled the fishermen to bring tribute from the sea. They surrounded their homes with pigs and chickens, and in mere wantonness terrorized that part of Oahu.

"Kamapuaa on Oahu and Kauai"

While he lived on the Koolau coast he was simply a devastating, brutal monster with certain powers belonging to a demigod, which he used as maliciously as possible. After being driven out to the Honolulu side of the mountains, for a time he led his band of robbers in their various expeditions, but after a time his miraculous powers increased and he went forth terrorizing the island from one end to the other. He had the power of changing himself into any kind of a fish. As a shark and as a hog he was represented as sometimes eating those whom he conquered in battle. He ravaged the fields and chicken preserves of the different chiefs, but it is said never stole or ate pigs or fish.

He wandered along the low lands from the taro patches of Ewa to the coconut groves of Waikiki, rooting up and destroying the food of the people.

At Kamoiliili he saw two beautiful women coming from the stream that flows from Manoa Valley. He called to them, but when they saw his tattooed body and rough clothing made from pigskins they recognized him and fled. He pursued them, but they were counted as goddesses, having come from divine foreign families as well as Kamapuaa. They possessed miraculous powers and vanished when he was ready to place his hands upon them. They sank down into the earth. Kamapuaa changed himself into the form of a great hog and began to root up the stones and soil and break his way through the thick layer of petrified coral through which they had disappeared. He first followed the descent of the woman who had been nearest to him. Down he went through soil and stone after her, but suddenly a great flood of water burst upward through the coral almost drowning him. The goddess had stopped his pursuit by turning an underground stream into the entrance that he had made

After this narrow escape, Kamapuaa rushed toward Manoa Valley to the place where he had seen the other beautiful woman disappear. Here also he rooted deep through earth and coral, and here again a new spring of living water was uncovered. He could do nothing against the flood, which threatened his life. The goddesses escaped and the two wells have supplied the people of Kamoiliili for many generations, bearing the name, "The wells, or fountains, of Kamapuaa."

The chief of Waikiki had a fine tract well supplied with bananas and coconuts and taro. Night after night a great black bog rushed through Waikiki destroying all the ripening fruit and even going to the very doors of the grass houses searching out the calabashes filled with poi waiting for fermentation. These calabashes he dashed to the ground, defiling their contents and breaking and unfitting them for further use. A crowd of warriors rushed out to kill this devastating monster. They struck him with clubs and hurled their spears against his bristling sides. The stiff bristles deadened the force of the blows of the clubs and turned the spear-points aside so that he received but little injury. Meanwhile his fierce tusks were destroying the warriors and his cruel jaws were tearing their flesh and breaking their bones. In a short time the few who were able to escape fled from him. The chiefs gathered their warriors again and again, and after many battles drove Kamapuaa from cave to cave and from district to district. Finally he leaped into the sea, changed himself into the form of a fish and passed over the channel to Kauai.

He swam westward along the coast, selecting a convenient place for landing, and when night came, sending the people to their sleep, he went ashore. He had marked the location of taro and sugar-cane patches and could easily find them in the night. Changing himself into a black hog he devoured and trampled the sugar-cane, rooted up taro, and upset calabashes, eating the poi and breaking the wooden bowls. Then he fled to a rough piece of land that he had decided upon as his hiding-place.

The people were astonished at the devastation when they came from their houses the next morning. Only gods who were angry could have wrought such havoc so unexpectedly, therefore they sent sacrifices to the heiaus, that the gods of their homes might protect them. But the next night other fields were made desolate as if a herd of swine had been wantonly at work all through the night. After a time watchmen were set around the fields and the mighty hog was seen. The people were called. They surrounded Kamapuaa, caught him and tied him with strongest cords of olona fibre and pulled him to one side, that on the new day so soon to dawn they might build their oven and roast him for a great feast.

When they thought all was finished the hog suddenly burst his bonds, became invisible and leaped upon them, tore them and killed them as he had done on Oahu, then rushed away in the darkness.

Again some watchers found him lying at the foot of a steep precipice, sleeping in the daytime. On the edge of the precipice were great boulders, which they rolled down upon him, but he was said to have allowed the stones to strike him and fall shattered in pieces while he sustained very little injury.

Then he assumed the form of a man and made his home by a ledge of rock called Kipukai. Here there was a spring of very sweet water, which lay in the form of a placid pool of clear depths, reflecting wonderfully whatever shadows fell upon its surface. To this two beautiful sisters were in the habit of coming with their water-calabashes. While they stooped over the water Kamapuaa came near and cast the shadow as a man before them on the clear waters. They both wanted the man as their husband who could cast such a shadow. He revealed himself to them and took them both to be his wives. They lived with him at Kipukai and made fine sleeping mats for him, cultivated food, and prepared it for him to eat. They pounded kapa that he might be well clothed.

At that time there were factions on the island of Kauai warring against each other. Fierce hand-to-hand battles were waged and rich spoils carried away.

With the coming of Kamapuaa to Kauai, a new and strange appearance wrought terror in the hearts of the warriors whenever a battle occurred. While the conflict was going on and blows were freely given by both club and spear, suddenly a massive war-club would be seen whistling through the air, striking down the chiefs of both parties. Mighty blows were struck by this mysterious club. No hand could be seen holding it, no strong arm swinging it, and no chief near it save those stricken by it. Dead and dying warriors covered the ground in its path. Sometimes when Kamapuaa had been caught in his marauding expedition, he would escape from the ropes tying him, change into a man, seize a club, become invisible, and destroy his captors. He took from the fallen their rich feather war cloaks, carried them to his dwelling-place and concealed them under his mats.

The people of Kauai were terrified by the marvelous and powerful being who dwelt in their midst. They believed in the ability of kahunas, or priests, to work all manner of evil in strange ways and therefore were sure that some priest was working with evil spirits to compass their destruction. They sought the strongest and most sacred of their own kahunas, but were unable to conquer the evil.

Meanwhile Kamapuaa, tired of the two wives, began to make life miserable for them, trying to make them angry, that he might have good excuse for killing them. They knew something of his marvelous powers as a demigod, and watched him when he brought bundles to his house and put them away. The chief's house then as in later years was separated from the houses of the women and was tabu to them, but they waited until they had seen him go far away. Then they searched his house and found the war cloaks of their friends under his mats. They hastened and told their friends, who plotted to take vengeance on their enemy.

The women decided to try to drive the demigod away, so destroyed the spring of water from which they had daily brought water for his need. They also carefully concealed all evidences of other springs. Kamapuaa returned from his adventures and was angry when he found no water waiting for him. He called for the women, but they had hidden themselves. He was very thirsty. He rushed to the place of the spring, but could not find it. He looked for water here and there, but the sisters had woven mighty spells over all the water-holes and he could not see them. In his rage he rushed about like a blind and crazy man. Then the sisters appeared and ridiculed him. They taunted him with his failure to overcome their wiles. They laughed at his suffering. Then in his great anger he leaped upon them, caught them, and threw them over a precipice. As they fell upon the ground he uttered his powerful incantations and changed them into two stones, which for many generations have been guardians of that precipice. Then he assumed the form of a hog and rooted deep in the rocky soil. Soon he uncovered a fountain of water from which he drank deeply, but which he later made bitter and left as a mineral-spring to the present day.

The people of Kauai now knew the secret of the wonderful swinging war club. They knew that a hand held it and an invisible man walked beside it, so they fought against a power that they could not see. They felt their clubs strike some solid body even when they struck at the air. Courage came back to them, and at Hanalei the people forced him into a corner, and, carrying stones, tried to fence him in, but he broke the walls down, tore his way through the people, and fled. The high chief of Hanalei threw his magic spear at him as he rushed past, but missed him. The spear struck the mountain-side near the summit and passed through, leaving a great hole through which the sky on the other side of the mountain can still be seen. Kamapuaa decided that he was tired of Kauai, therefore he ran to the seashore, leaped into the water and, becoming a fish, swam away to Hawai'i.

"Pele and Kamapuaa"

The three great mountains of Hawai'i had been built many centuries before Pele found an abiding home in the pit of Kilauea. Kilauea itself appears rather as a shelter to which she fled than as a house of her own building. The sea waters quenched the fires built by her at lower levels, forcing her up higher and higher toward the mountains until she took refuge in the maelstrom of eternal fire known for centuries among the Hawaiians as Ka-lua-o-Pele (The pit of Pele),—the boiling center of the active pit of fire. Some legends say that Kamapuaa drove Pele from place to place by pouring in water.

The Kalakaua legends probably give the correct idea of the growths of Pele-worship as the goddess of volcanic fires when they say that the Pele family of brave and venturesome high chiefs with their followers settled under the shadows of the smoke-clouds from Kilauea and were finally destroyed by some overwhelming eruption. And yet the destruction was so spectacular, or at least so mysterious, that the idea took firm root that Pele and her brothers and sisters, instead of passing out of existence, entered into the volcano to dwell there as living spirits having the fires of the underworld as their continual heritage. From this home of fire Pele and her sisters could come forth assuming the forms in which they had been seen as human beings. This power has been the cause of many legends about Pele and her adventures with various chiefs whom she at last overwhelmed with boiling floods of lava tossed out of her angry heart. In this way she appeared in different parts of the island of Hawai'i apparently no longer having any fear of danger to her home from incoming seas.

The last great battle between sea and fire was connected with Pele as a fire-goddess and Kamapuaa, the demigod, part hog and part man. It is a curious legend in which human and divine elements mingle like the changing scenes of a dream. This naturally follows the statement in some of the legends that Ku, one of the highest gods among the Polynesians as well as among the Hawaiians, was an ancestor of Kamapuaa, protecting him and giving him the traits of a demigod. Kamapuaa had passed through many adventures on the islands of Oahu and Kauai, and had lived for a time on Maui. He had, according to some of the legends, developed his mysterious powers so that he could become a fish whenever he wished, so sometimes he was represented as leaping into the sea, diving down to great depth, and swimming until he felt the approach of rising land, then he would come to the surface, call out the name of the island and go ashore for a visit with the inhabitants or dive again and pass on to another island. Thus he is represented as passing to Hawaii after his adventures on the islands of Kauai and Oahu.

On Hawaii he entered into the sports of the chiefs, gambling, boxing, surf-riding, rolling the round ulu maika stone and riding the holua (sled). Here he learned about the wonderful princess from the islands of the southern seas who had made her home in the fountains of fire.

Some of the legends say that he returned to Oahu, gathered a company of adherents and then visited the Pele family as a chief of high rank, winning her as his bride and living with her some time, then separating and dividing the island of Hawai'i between them, Pele taking the southern part of the island as the scene for her terrific eruptions, and Kamapuaa ruling over the north, watering the land with gentle showers or with melting snow, or sometimes with fierce storms, until for many centuries fertile fields have rewarded the toil of man.

The better legends send Kamapuaa alone to the contest with the fire-goddess, winning her for a time and then entering into a struggle in which both lives were at stake.

It is said that one morning when the tops of the mountains were painted by the sunlight from the sea, and the shadows in the valley were creeping under the leaves of the trees of the forests, that Pele and her sisters went down toward the hills of Puna. These sisters were known as the Hiiakas, defined by Ellis, who gives the first account of them, as "the cloud-holders." Each one had a descriptive title, thus Hiiaka-noho-lani was "the heaven-dwelling cloud-holder," Hiiaka-i-ka-poli-o-Pele was "cloud-holder in the bosom of Pele." There were at least six Hiiakas, and some legends give many more.

That morning they heard the sound of a drum in the distance. It was the tum-tum-tum of a hula. Filled with curiosity, they turned aside to see what strangers had invaded their territory. One of the sisters, looking over the plain to a hill not far away, called out, "What a handsome man!" and asked her sisters to mark the finely formed athletic stranger who was dancing gloriously outlined in the splendor of the morning light.

Pele scornfully looked and said she saw nothing but a great hog-man whom she would quickly drive from her dominions. Then began the usual war of words with which rival chiefs attacked each other. Pele taunted Kamapuaa, calling him a hog and ascribing to him the characteristics belonging to swine. Kamapuaa became angry and called Pele "the woman with red burning eyes, and an angry heart unfit to be called a chiefess." Then Pele in her wrath stamped on the ground until earthquakes shook the land around Kamapuaa and a boiling stream of lava rolled down from the mountains above. The stranger, throwing around him the finest tapa, stood unmoved until the flood of fire began to roll up the hill on which he stood. Then, raising his hands and uttering the strongest incantations, he called for heavy rains to fall. Soon the lava became powerless in the presence of the stranger. Then Pele tried her magical powers to see if she could subdue this stranger, but his invocations seemed to be stronger than those falling from her lips, and she gave up the attempt to destroy him. Pele was always a cruel, revengeful goddess, sweeping away those against whom her wrath might be kindled, even if they were close friends of her household.

The sisters finally prevailed upon her to send across to the hill inviting the stranger, who was evidently a high chief, to come and visit them. As the messenger started to bring the young man to the sisters he stepped into the shadows, and the messenger found nothing but a small hog rooting among the ferns. This happened day after day until Pele determined to know this stranger chief who always succeeded in thoroughly hiding himself, no matter how carefully the messengers might search. At last the chant of the hula and the dance of the sisters on the smooth pahoehoe of a great extinct lava bed led the young man to approach. Pele revealed herself in her rare and tempting beauty, calling with a sweet voice for the stranger to come and rest by her side while her sisters danced. Soon Pele was overcome by the winning strength of this great chief, and she decided to marry him. So they dwelt together in great happiness for a time, sometimes making their home in one part of Puna and sometimes in another. The places where they dwelt are pointed out even at this day by the natives who know the traditions of Puna.

But Kamapuaa had too many of the habits and instincts of a hog to please Pele, besides she was too quickly angry to suit the overbearing Kamapuaa. Pele was never patient even with her sisters, so with Kamapuaa she would burst into fiery rage, while taunts and bitter words were freely hurled back and forth. Then Pele stamped on the ground, the earth shook, cracks opened in the surface and sometimes clouds of smoke and steam arose around Kamapuaa. He was unterrified and matched his divine powers against hers. It was demigod against demigoddess. It was the goddess of fire of Hawaii against the hog-god of Oahu. Pele's home life was given up. The bitterness of strife swept over the black sands of the seashore. When the earth seemed ready to open its doors and pour out mighty streams of flowing lava in the defense of Pele, Kamapuaa called for the waters of the ocean to rise. Then flood met fire and quenched it. Pele was driven inland. Her former lover, hastening after her and striving to overcome her, followed her upward until at last amid clouds of poisonous gases she went back into her spirit home in the pit of Kilauea.

Then Kamapuaa as a god of the sea gathered the waters together in great masses and hurled them into the fire pit. Violent explosions followed the inrush of waters. The sides of the great crater were torn to pieces by fierce earthquakes. Masses of fire expanded the water into steam, and Pele gathered the forces of the underworld to aid in driving back Kamapuaa. The lavas rose in many lakes and fountains. Rapidly the surface was cooled and the fountains checked, but just as rapidly were new openings made and new streams of fire hurled at the demigod of Oahu. It was a mighty battle of the elements. The legends say that the hog-man, Kamapuaa, poured water into the crater until its fires were driven back to their lowest depths and Pele was almost drowned by the floods. The clouds of the skies had dropped their burden of rain. All the waters of the sea that Kamapuaa could collect had been poured into the crater. Fornander gives a part of the prayer of Kamapuaa against Pele. His appeal was directly to the gods of water for assistance. He cried for ... "The great storm clouds of skies," while Pele prayed for

> "The bright gods of the underworld,
> The gods thick-clustered for Pele."

It was the duty of the Pele family to stir up volcanic action, create explosions, hurl lava into the air, make earthquakes, and blow out clouds of flames and smoke and sulphurous-burdened fumes against all enemies of Pele. Into the conflict against Kamapuaa rushed the gods of Po, the underworld, armed with spears of flashing fire, and hurling sling-stones of lava. The storms of bursting gases and falling lavas were more than Kamapuaa could endure. Gasping for breath and overwhelmed with heat, he found himself driven back. The legends say that Pele and her sisters drank the waters, so that after a time there was no check against the uprising lava. The pit was filled and the streams of fire flowed down upon Kamapuaa. He changed his body into a kind of grass now known as Ku-kae-puaa, and tried to stop the flow of the lava. Apparently the grass represented the bristles covering his body when he changed himself into a hog. Kamapuaa has sometimes been called the Samson of Hawaiian traditions, and it is possible that a Biblical idea has crept into the modern versions of the story. Delilah cut Samson's hair and he became weak. The Hawaiian traditions say that if Kamapuaa's bristles could be burned off he would lose his power to cope with Pele's forces of fire. When the grass lay in the pathway of the fire, the lava was turned aside for a time, but Pele, inspired by the beginning of victory, called anew upon the gods of the underworld for strong reinforcements.

Out from the pits of Kilauea came vast masses of lava piling up against the field of grass in its pathway and soon the grass began to burn; then Kamapuaa assumed again the shape of a man, the hair or bristles on his body were singed and the smart of many burns began to cause agony. Down he rushed to the sea, but the lava spread out on either side, cutting off retreat along the beach. Pele followed close behind, striving to overtake him before he could reach the water. The side streams had reached the sea, and the water was rapidly heated into tossing, boiling waves. Pele threw great masses of lava at Kamapuaa, striking and churning the sea into which he leaped midst the swirling heated mass.

Kamapuaa gave up the battle, and, thoroughly defeated, changed himself into a fish. To that fish he gave the tough pigskin that he assumed when roaming over the islands as the hog-man. It was thick enough to stand the boiling waves through which he swam out into the deep sea. The Hawaiians say that this fish has always been able to make a noise like the grunting of a small pig. To this fish was given the name "humu-humu-nuku-nuku-a-puaa."

It was said that Kamapuaa fled to foreign lands, where he married a high chiefess and lived with his family many years. At last the longing for his home-land came over him irresistibly and he returned, appearing as a humu-humu in his divine place among the Hawaiian fishes, but never again taking to himself the form of a man.

Since this conflict with Kamapuaa, Pele has never feared the powers of the sea. Again and again has she sent her lava streams over the territory surrounding her fire pit in the volcano Kilauea, and has swept the seashore, even pouring her lavas into the deep sea, but the ocean has never retaliated by entering into another conflict to destroy Pele and her servants. Kamapuaa was the last who poured the sea into the deep pit. The friends of Lohiau, a prince from the island of Kauai, waged warfare with Pele, tearing to pieces a part of the crater in which she dwelt; but it was a conflict of land forces, and in its entirety is one of the very interesting tales handed down by Hawaiian tradition.

Kamapuaa figured to the last days of Pele-worship in the sacrifices offered to the fire-goddess. The most acceptable sacrifice to Pele was supposed to be puaa (a hog). If a hog could not be secured when an offering was necessary, the priest would take the fish humu-humu-nuku-nuku-a-puaa and throw it into the pit of fire. If the hog and the fish both failed, the priest would offer any of the things into which, it was said in their traditions, Kamapuaa could turn himself.

CENTIPEDE

Variant A

Tradition Bearer: Annie Lowry

Source: Lowie, Robert H. "Shoshonean Tales." *Journal of American Folklore* 37 (1924): 229–32.

Date: 1914

Original Source: Paviotso (Northern Paiute)
National Origin: Native American

Paiute "football" resembles a particularly aggressive version of soccer, including wrestling and kicking both the opponents and the ball. The hand game requires one player to hide a pair of bones in his or her hands (one bone is marked and the other is plain). Sticks are used as counters to keep track of correct guesses. A player from the opposing side (usually a person believed to have visionary power) tries to guess where the unmarked bone is hidden. The hider's side sings songs that supposedly have the power to block the guesser's power of supernatural sight. Gambling games of all sorts were regarded as opportunities for demonstrating one's supernatural power.

Centipede (A'gonidza'Ba) was a great gambler who played the hand-game and football. A large tribe was living in the valley. Men and women would go thence to play with Centipede, but none came back.

The members of the tribe went, till all were gone except two girls and a baby boy. These cried for their relatives to come back; they climbed a tree, but could see nothing of their people. They nearly starved. The boy grew up so he was big enough to kill small game, so the girls made him a bow and arrows and told him what animals he should kill. He went out, stayed away for a whole day and came with a lizard. "Well, brother, this is not good to eat."

"All right, grind me some seed tomorrow and I'll go again."

The next day he went off and came back with a snake. The sisters told him that was not good to eat either. "Very well, grind me some seed, I'll hunt again."

But every time he brought either a snake or a lizard. One night, at last, he brought a little bird. The girls thought this was fine.

"Oh, that's good, we shall cook it and divide it." So the boy thought he had done a great thing.

He said, "Get up earlier tomorrow, so that I can get another bird."

So the next day he started early and caught sight of a little bird on a bush. It did not try to get away, but when he aimed, it flew to the other side of the bush. At last it spoke to the boy, "Little boy, why do you want to kill me. You should not kill me, I'll tell you something great. Do you know where all your people have gone to?"

Still the boy was going to shoot, but the bird spoke again, "No, don't shoot me, I'll make a great man of you." Then the boy stopped and listened, "Little boy, far across the mountain there lives a very bad man. He has killed all your people, cut out their hearts and dried them in his lodge. He has hung up their hands, all together, and the rest of their bodies he has burnt up. You can bring all your people back to life if you listen and do as I tell you."

The boy went on his knees and said, "Little bird, I'll listen." "I am going to tell you; get up before sunrise and come here to my nest." With this he flew to his two eggs. "Come here before sunrise. These are my eggs. Just as you see the rays of the sun, my eggs will begin to wobble. Then hit my eggs, and then there will be little birds under you, which will take you through the sky above Centipede, and he won't see you. Every morning, when the sun gets high, he's always practicing. When you get above him, spit on his forehead. Then tomorrow morning, come again, I'll tell you more. I wish to tell you what his place looks like. He always spreads a big red robe, but don't sit on it."

The boy came home without any game.

His sisters asked, "Where is your game?" "I haven't any." "What shall we eat?"

"Never mind, we'll soon have our fill." He was asked, when they should get something for him to eat the next day, but he said, "Never mind about food, I'll leave very early."

He went to the nest again. When he got up that day he was a handsome man. The bird said, "When you cross the mountain, you'll be able to see him. If he sees you, he will shake his red robe and spread it, but do not sit on it, sit on the ground. Don't let him touch you, he will try to get his arms under yours. Choose the game you want to play, you'll beat him in the end. Don't play the hand-game, but choose football. You will have to go through a dark place, where it is always night. That is where the Indians lost their ball and thus lost the game, after which he burnt them up. Those two eggs of mine shall go with you, but Centipede will not see them. One will be the Gopher, the other Owl. Owl will sit on the right side in the dark place and blink his eyes, so it will be light for you. Gopher will be on the other side and dig a hole, so that Centipede will lose his ball in it. When you have beaten him, he'll be very apt to want to pay you in hearts and hands, but don't take them. Take him by the arm and burn him up. There is just one of your people left, but he is so burnt that he has turned into the crow."

The boy struck the eggs and went flying through the air. He landed on top of a mountain. He saw Centipede shaking his red blanket. Gopher and Owl were with the boy, but the boy could not see them though he heard them talk-ing. Centipede washed and brushed himself and said, "What a handsome man is coming." When the boy arrived, Centipede asked him to sit down on the blan-ket, but he would not do so, sitting on the ground instead.

Centipede asked, "Why is it you do not want to sit on my blanket but want to soil your clothes?" He went inside his wikiup and got his hand-game sticks, but the boy said, "No, I came to play football."

"All right, whatever you say. "He got ready, went into his lodge and brought two balls. "Choose your ball." The boy chose the right one, and they went to the starting-place. Both began to run. When he got to the dark place the boy did not know where he was, but Owl blinked his eyes, so that he saw his ball, got out, carried it to the goal and was bringing it back while Centipede was still in the dark place, for Gopher had dug a hole and his ball had rolled into it.

The boy returned to the starting place, and when Centipede saw he had lost he went no farther but returned and said, "My boy, you have won, come to my lodge and choose whatever you want for your prize." "No, I don't want to go in there, I want you for my prize."

"Oh, no. I'll give you anything I have."

"No, I want you." The boy took hold of him and seized him, so he could not get away, although Centipede was much bigger. Centipede always had a big fire burning. The boy pulled him toward the fire. Centipede could not get away. Crow recognized the boy, hopped up to him, and said, "I'll help you throw him in, that is what he did to all our people." They threw him in and held him down with the fire-tongs he had used on other people until he was burnt up.

Crow took him to Centipede's lodge, which was full of hearts and hands. The boy did not touch the hands, but he and Crow carried out the hearts, which were so dried up and shrunken that they two could carry them all. As the boy traveled homeward, he buried the hearts in a damp place every night. The third night he was not far away. He went to his sisters.

They asked, "Where have you been?"

"I have been hunting." "We are nearly starved and famished."—"Never mind, you'll forget that when all our people come back."

On the third morning, before sunrise, the sisters woke up, while their brother pretended to be asleep. They heard laughter and conversation. "Wake up brother, hear all the people coming."

They were afraid and were going to run away, but he said, "Those are our parents and relatives." Thus he got them back.

The crow now hops because his legs were burnt in Centipede's fire.

Variant B

Tradition Bearer: Railroad Tom

Centipede was living south in a valley. He was a good ball player. He would play with two balls and those who lost were thrown into the fire.

Chickenhawk (Tu'kiwi'na) was his opponent. He had a wife, two daughters, and a child just old enough to walk. He played against Centipede, lost, and was killed.

The little boy at home tried to get out of his cradle. His sisters stopped all the holes in the house and took him out of his basket. He wished to follow his parents, but his sisters would not let him.

When he was old enough to hunt, they made a bow and arrows for him and he went out and killed birds and fetched them home. Once he was hunting and tried to get close to a bird that began to speak to him as follows, "Boy, you had better not shoot me, let me alone, and I'll tell you something. Your father and mother went to a certain place and never returned. Do you remember that? I'll tell you about that. Boy, lay an egg."

He laid an egg, and the bird told him to use it for a ball. He was going to kick it with his foot but when he did it broke into pieces. Then he laid another egg; when he kicked this he could not break it, it was like a ball. The boy kicked it to the top of a mountain and thence to another mountain. Thus he trained himself.

Woodpecker said he would help the boy. "My sister's son, I will help you."

Another person promised to dig where they were going to play.

Big Owl said he too would help. "When they go along at night, I'll open my eyes and make it light for them." In the night it was dark for playing ball, that was why he said this.

The boy trained, then he went over to Centipede. He spat on him.

Centipede looked at the sky but did not see anything. It was like rain. "I don't know where the rain comes from." There were no clouds. Centipede had killed and beaten many people in the game. He made a fire where the game was played, threw in his defeated opponents and took off their hair. He scattered this all over and when visitors came he told them to sit down on the hair. When the boy arrived, he bade him sit down, but the boy merely stepped on it, then went some distance away and sat down there. He had three comrades who did likewise. Centipede was keeping Crow as a prisoner; Centipede had cut Crow's knees and allowed his children to urinate on Crow.

There were four men to play ball for each side. They started at the same time. They got into a dark place, but Owl opened his eyes and it was like daylight for the boy while Centipede was in the dark. Until they got to this place Centipede had been in the lead, but now the boy overtook and passed him. Woodpecker made a hole for the ball to go into. The boy got out of the cave while Centipede was still in there, then he kicked the ball once and got back to the starting-point and goal. Centipede's sons thought it was their father, but it was his opponents.

When Crow saw who had won, he said, "Get something to cure my leg, so I can help you." The boy got a stick and put it in place of the old leg making it well again.

Long after this Centipede arrived. He had a big forehead. After sitting down he said, "I'll give you beads to ransom myself from the fire."

"No, I will not accept this pay, you have killed many people and I'll do the same to you." Centipede cried when he was thrown into the fire. As leader of his party he was thrown in first, then all his family.

This is what he had done to other people. He had taken out people's eyeballs and hung them up on ropes. The boy took all of these home.

In the evening he placed them into wet earth over-night, then took them out again. Thus he restored to life the people whose eyeballs had been strung up.

THE THEFT OF PINE NUTS

Tradition Bearer: Humboldt Joe

Source: Lowie, Robert H. "Shoshonean Tales." *Journal of American Folklore* 37 (1924): 217–20.

Date: 1914

Original Source: Paviotso (Northern Paiute)

National Origin: Native American

The primary function of the following **myth** is to emphasize the importance of the pine nut as a food source by making it the object of a war among the animals. A second major theme in the narrative is the role of supernatural power in attaining success in any enterprise. Coyote—like all **tricksters**—manifests power, but it is typically limited by his character flaws. Crow wields power that is unlimited by Coyote's weakness and therefore succeeds in overcoming obstacles that have stymied the **trickster**. Wolf, the model of the leader who uses persuasion rather than coercion, proves to be powerful as well by bringing himself and his followers back to life after having been killed and dismembered.

Coyote and Wolf were brothers. They lived in the eastern Pine-Nut Range. Squirrels, cottontails, the crow, and all the four-footed animals lived there.

One day they were playing the hand-game. The crow felt strangled on something that smelled a peculiar way. All of them began to wonder what it could be. Coyote got up to see whence the odor came. First he went south, then west, then east. When turned north, he found where the smell had come from. It was late in the afternoon and he said, "I'll see what it is."

He started out. "Let steps be made into miles, so I can get there quickly." He made the trip in a short time and soon arrived where the other tribe was living. They were the Crane people. He sat down and watched for what it was. When the little ones passed with pine-nuts in their hands, he tried to poke their fingers so as to get one.

Crane was chief. He was suspicious of Coyote, so he made a speech to his people, telling them not to make the pine-nut mush thick as usual, but to make it very thin. They did so and gave Coyote some of it. When they gave him a cupful of the soup, he wanted to take it home but did not know how. He put some into his mouth, but then he swallowed it. Then he tried to put some in his coyote robe, but being so thin it ran through and could not be held.

"I cannot take any home," he thought, "but I'll run home and tell them about it. Let steps be made into miles, so I may get home soon," he said. He got home and told his brother what a fine meal he had had with his brothers from afar and had found the food detected by the Crow. Wolf then made a speech telling the people of Coyote's find and bade all the animals get ready to go for what Coyote had found.

Everyone went with Coyote and Wolf except Hummingbird who said, "I'll stay home and keep the place. I'll watch for you and when I see you returning I'll make a big fire and smoke myself."

While on their way they had to hunt deer to live on. They traveled all day. In the night they stopped and had no water there. All were pretty thirsty and said, "What shall we do without water tonight? Somebody ought to get us some." They talked it over and decided that Coyote should get the water for them. He was to get all the marrow from the deer bones as his reward when he got back.

Coyote took a jug and went for water. While he was gone, the rest said he was getting too much pay for his work and that someone with a sharp bill ought to remove the marrow from some of the bones; that they should pile the good bones on top so that Coyote might not notice the deception at first. Hummingbird said, "I'll do it." So he took out the marrow of about half the bones, then they piled the bad ones under the good bones. When Coyote got back, all hurried to get a drink of water before he should find out. While he was eating the good bones on top, they made haste and drank the water. When he got to the empty ones, he broke one bone after another. He got angry and was going to empty the water, but all the people had had their drink, so only a little was left. The people gave him a little fat then, but Lizard came along and fell into it while it was boiling. Lizard did not get hurt. Coyote was angry and chased Lizard, who ran into the river. There Coyote could not follow, so he said, "Your name will be Fish hereafter, not Lizard any more. The Lizards outside the water shall be black."

Crane's people were suspicious, so they made a canyon on the road close up with slippery ice, so that Coyote's people could not pass. The next morning they reached this canyon. Coyote was going to show the other people what he could do and scratched the ice, but that did not help.

The Crows were there and Coyote said to them, "What do you think will happen to you black things? I am a mighty man, still I cannot pass." Coyote made fun of them. One of the Crows said, "We'll show him that we are mightier than he is. One of us will fly so high and come down so hard as to crack the ice."

Another Crow said, "I'll go up the second time and come down so as to break it in so many pieces that each one will be able to pass." So one crow flew high up and roared like the thunder.

Coyote looked up and said, "There is nothing up there, only a little red cloud." The Crow came down so that the ice cracked with a terrible thud. Then the second Crow went up and came down with still greater force, breaking the ice all up, so that the people could pass through.

Now Coyote said, "It is a very good thing you have done, my sister's son, I'll be the first one to pass." But he had on his back such a load of wild flax for netting that he got caught in the narrow passage and could not get through. So everyone jostled him and got ahead of him, and he was the last to go through.

At last they got to Crane's people. When they got there, the first thing they were going to have a hand-game. They began to play and continued till toward morning. The Cranes were winning, but then Crow got into the game and then his side began to win in turn. Crow was a very handsome man; he wore a pebble necklace, and today his neck is still very pretty.

While this gambling was going on, the Mice were looking for the pine-nuts, which the Cranes had hidden in a tree-trunk, so that none of the large animals could find them. The Mice looked everywhere without finding what they sought. At last one of them ran to the top of a tree, and at the top there was an old bow, and in the middle of the bow there was a pine-nut. Just at daybreak the Mice reported they had found the nut.

When Coyote heard of it he said, "I'll make them all sleep. We'll take the pine-nut home with us" But the nut was so high up that nothing but a bird could get it.

They said to the Wood-peckers, "You go and break the tree in two, and take out the nut."

Woodpecker said, "Our bills are not strong enough."

Another Wood-pecker said, "We'll put our two bills together, then they'll be strong enough." So they put the two bills together and one of them flew up with a long bill and broke the tree. Thus he got the nut out. When he got it he set out straight for home.

Wolf said, "Do you all go first, I'll follow in the rear."

When Crane awoke and found the nuts were taken he made a speech. "We are starving. If there's an orphan here, you had better kill him, feed on him, and then we'll be able to chase those people with the nut." Crane's people did so and then gave chase. They overtook the Wolf's people. First they killed Wolf and cut him all up but could not find the nut in him. They killed one after another and searched for the nuts in their bodies. Coyote was among the foremost and he said to his companions who carried the nut, "Give me the nut, nephew, I can run very fast."

But the others said, "No, don't give it to him, or he'll swallow it." Coyote was killed. Then Crow and Chickenhawk were the only ones left. After a while no one was left but Chickenhawk. He looked back and saw that all the rest were killed, so he said, "May my thigh be inflamed and malodorous, then I'll put the nut in this bad spot and they won't find it."

They caught him and were going to kill him, but his odor was so bad, that they took him by the neck and threw him away thinking, "The nut would not taste well if it were in him."

So they turned back to the rest of his party and examined each one. "Well our nut is gone, I suppose that stinking one has it."

The Chickenhawk by this time was pretty far on his way back. When Wolf saw that the Cranes were gone, he revived and restored all the other people to life. Then they returned to their own country. Wolf and Coyote took the nut, took a bite of it, and sprinkled it allover the mountains, so that pine-nut trees should grow there.

Wolf said to Coyote, "Don't swallow any of it, lest juniper trees be mingled with the nut trees, we want them all to be nut trees."

But Coyote swallowed some, so when he besprinkled the mountains, they were half covered with junipers and half with pine-nuts. Where Wolf sprinkled, there were only pine-nut trees.

When Crane got back, he spoke to his people. "I don't know what we'll do, the trees are here, but there are no cones. I am going to follow, I will not stay here, I'll share my food with those people."

He started and crossed the mountains. Looking this way he saw smoke all along the mountains, where they were cooking nuts. When Crane saw the smoke, he said, I am going right over there."

When they saw him coming, they said, "Place all the rotten ones in one place and tell him to sit there and help himself." He carne, sat down and helped himself, but the food was rotten. They did this because his bill was so long that they were afraid he would not leave anything for the other birds. Blue-jay picked out some good nuts for Crane and gave them to him, but as soon as he touched them they turned into rotten ones.

Crane said, "You live here in the mountains on food taken from us. I'll go to the valley and live on moss and seeds." When he said this, he began to fly. An old woman got a stick and hit him, knocking his tail off. When he saw that he had no tail, he took the ends of his feet and made a little tail for himself. He went to the valley. This is why he never goes to the mountains any more.

PRAIRIE FALCON'S CONTEST WITH MEADOWLARK

Tradition Bearer: Chipo

Source: Gifford, Edward Winslow. "Western Mono Myths." *Journal of American Folklore* 36 (1923): 352–54.

Date: 1918

Original Source: Western Mono (California)

National Origin: Native American

Prairie Falcon as a heroic character is unique to the tales of Native American Central California. Again, Coyote provides a contrast to the more sensible figures in the fact that he misses the opportunity to become an eagle by underestimating his own abilities. This narrative of closely parallels the Northern Paiute "Centipede" (p. 326), which revolves around a ball game in which death awaits the loser. As in the Paiute tale, Prairie Falcon is assisted by his mother's brothers. In many cultures the maternal uncle serves a special role as tutor and patron in a young male's life.

Eagle was chief. He was up on a high smooth rock, looking at the people. "I will take care of you people, now," he said. "I am the chief. I am going to be the greatest chief in the world. I am going to sit here in this bright light and look like the sun all of the time. I will call all of you my children. I will look after you. I will take care of all you children."

Prairie Falcon and Crow came and settled down close to Eagle's place. The two were great friends and they camped together.

Eagle said, "You folks must stay right there. You will have to stay there altogether, now."

Prairie Falcon and Crow practiced shooting each other with bow and arrows. Crow asked Prairie Falcon, "What on earth are you doing?"

"Oh, nothing, nothing at all," responded the latter. Then Prairie Falcon and Crow set out on a journey, but before they started the former sang on the edge of the cliff.

Prairie Falcon made a wooden shinny ball, but every time he tried the ball it broke. He said to himself, "What can I do now? If I cannot get a proper shinny stick, what am I to do?" Every time he struck the ball it broke. He returned home each night and every time he came home, he brought a mountain quail with him. Then he would set out again in the morning for the same place. When he arrived there he made shinny balls.

Two sisters of Prairie Falcon's, both Cormorants, lived with him. These two girls were playing ball one evening when Prairie Falcon brought home a number of mountain quails for supper.

Next morning, when he went back to the place where he was making balls, he found an egg presumably laid by one of his sisters. As soon as he struck the egg it gave evidence of being about to hatch, for a chick made a peeping noise within it. Then he tried the egg with his shinny stick and found that it served admirably as a shinny ball. Moreover, it kept going once he struck it.

"This is just what I want," he said, very much pleased. He took great care of the egg and, taking it with him, set out on a journey down to the plains. He set out to see that place down on the plains where formerly gambling contests were held. Meadowlark lived at that place, and it was he whom Prairie Falcon went to see and with whom he arranged a shinny contest.

Upon returning home, Prairie Falcon said to his two sisters, "We are going to Meadowlark's place down on the plains to gamble. Now we will start." So they set out.

Prairie Falcon's people had been worsted by Meadowlark in an earlier contest. They had all forfeited their lives and been skinned by Meadowlark and his people. A great swarm of flies infested the place where the killing and skinning had taken place. Coyote came to the place. "What is wrong that there are so many flies here?" he thought to himself, as they swarmed about him and hummed in his ears. Just then Coyote heard Prairie Falcon singing as he was passing. "Well," said Coyote, "that must be my sister's son." Then he asked him about the presence of the swarm of flies.

"My people," answered Prairie Falcon, "were all killed here, so I am going again to Meadow-lark's place on the plains for another contest."

"What can I do alone here?" asked Coyote. "I want to go with you."

Prairie Falcon and Coyote travelled until they reached the house of Owl, also the mother's brother of the former. Prairie Falcon said to Owl, "My uncle, I may never return, for I am going down to the plains for another contest with Meadowlark." "I will be in the contest myself," said Owl. "I shall blind your opponent. That is what I will do."

Gopher was the next individual that the travelers encountered; and he said, "I shall go along. I shall make holes for your opponent's ball to roll into."

The party rested for a while and Prairie Falcon sang while they rested. Next they came to Skunk's camp.

Skunk, too, volunteered to go, saying, "I will go along. I shall fix things for you. I will turn loose my scent bag and they will not be able to bear my odor. I will go along."

Swan, another mother's brother of Prairie Falcon's, was the next person whose camp was visited. "My uncle," asked Prairie Falcon, "what are you going to do to help me?"

"I am going along," said Swan, "and I shall trumpet to confuse your opponent." When the party arrived at Meadowlark's place, Prairie Falcon erected his house right beside the ground on which the contest was to take place.

The following morning the game started, Prairie Falcon playing against Meadowlark, a fat man and chief of the plains tribe. Just before the game commenced there was much shouting to the prospective players. "Get ready. Finish your meal. We are going to start now."

Girls of Meadowlark's tribe poked fun at Prairie Falcon's people. "See the gambling. See the gambling," they cried. Prairie Falcon's people did not allow this to perturb them but remained quiet.

"You have a pretty good ball," said Meadowlark as he examined Prairie Falcon's. "Let us trade balls." But Prairie Falcon would not do so. The game started in earnest and the players drove their balls as far as the Coast Range (Panakap); then they turned and drove back.

"Look at them coming," shouted Meadowlark's daughter, and then to Meadowlark's wife she said, "Look at them coming. Your husband is ahead."

Prairie Falcon had been behind him since they had started the game. In fact, he had fallen far behind him. However, when Meadowlark made a turn, Prairie Falcon drove ahead of him. Prairie Falcon looked back and saw Meadowlark behind him.

A crowd of people stood by the hole into which the ball of the winner was to be driven. Prairie Falcon won the game.

"Well, you win already," said Meadowlark. "You had better take my wife. Do not say anything to me any more about playing this game. I will give you my daughter, too. I wish I could give you all of the beads I have."

"You destroyed all of my people, burned them alive," sternly replied Prairie Falcon." Now give me back their skins. Give them back to me."

"All right, I will return them to you," said Meadowlark, and he did so. Meadowlark's people had started a big fire in anticipation of his winning and of again destroying Prairie Falcon's followers by casting them into the flames. The latter's people now turned the tables and cast Meadowlark's people into the flames alive, burning them all.

After the massacre of Meadowlark's people, Prairie Falcon and his followers returned to their hill homes. As they returned Prairie Falcon left each of his uncles at his proper place. Upon arriving home, he buried all of the skins that he had brought with him.

He said to his people, "Lie quiet tonight. I am burying the skins and I want you all to sit still and listen for any sounds that they may make." The skins were then buried where their owners formerly had lived.

Towards morning the listeners heard the skins remark, "Is it not cold? Is it not cold?" The Cormorant girls then set fire all around where the skins were buried. After that all of the people came out of the places where their skins had been buried. Then they began to pound acorns that day.

"I think that we people are going to fly from our nest," said Prairie Falcon.

"All right," the people said. Then Prairie Falcon told Coyote to get a bucket of water, saying, "You go for the water and when you return you will turn into Eagle and fly." Coyote scratched the dirt in happiness over his prospective transformation. They all started to fly and shouted to Coyote as he was getting the water.

Coyote said, "Well, I must climb up the tree. I will get there too just the same. The shadows look pretty close," he continued as he mounted the tree. "I will soon catch up with them, once I have reached the top of this tree." Having reached the top, he tried to fly, but fell to the ground with a thud.

Then he went to the camp, seeking a bow and arrows. He went to where they were cooking acorns. "I can eat acorn bread anyway," he said by way of solace. When he tried to eat the acorn bread it turned into stone. Then he scratched around and saw a gopher at work.

He sneaked up to the gopher and caught him. "Ah!" he cried," I shall live anyhow." Then he smacked his lips and laughed all over.

COYOTE AND THE GRIZZLY BEARS

Tradition Bearer: Unavailable

Source: Dixon, Roland B. "Some Coyote Stories from the Maidu Indians of California." *Journal of American Folklore* 13 (1900): 267–68.

Date: 1899

Original Source: Maidu
National Origin: Native American

Historically, the Maidu inhabited the region of the Sacramento River east of the Crest of the Sierra Nevada mountain range. They gathered plant foods, fished and hunted a wide variety of animals. Coyote was one of the protein sources that was strictly avoided, however. As seen in "Coyote and the Grizzly Bears"(p. 339) and "How the Coyote Married His Daughter" (p. 341), there is little of the **culture hero** in this **trickster**. His cunning allows him to defeat his adversaries, but these confrontations are always to serve his own ends. The Maidu characteristically use some **variant** of the **formulaic** closing "All people can call me Coyote" to signify that this trick was in keeping with his nature.

339

Long ago the Coyote and the Grizzly Bears had a falling out. There were two Bears who had a couple of small birds, called Pitsititi. Whenever the Bears went down to the valley to get berries, they left these two birds at home.

Once, while the Bears were away, the Coyote came to the Bears' camp, and asked the two little birds whether the Bears gave them enough to eat.

Said the little birds, "No, they do not; we are always hungry."

The Coyote then asked whether there was any food in the camp, and the birds told him that there was, the Bears keeping a large supply on hand.

Said the Coyote, "If you will show me the food, I will get up a fine dinner, and then we can all eat."

The little birds agreed, and the Coyote prepared the food, and all had a great feast. When they were all through, the Coyote took up a small stick from the ground, thrust it into his nose to draw blood, and then with the blood marked a red stripe on the heads of the birds, and said, "When the Bears come back and ask you two who did this, say, 'The Coyote did it.'"

Then the Coyote went off down the hill into the valley where the Bears were picking berries, and shouted from the side-hill, "Get out of there! That ground belongs to my grandmother." Then he went back up the hill to his own camp.

The two Bears came home, and when they saw the birds, asked them who had been there, and painted their heads with red. The two little birds answered that it was the Coyote. The Bears were very angry. They wanted to have their revenge, so they set out for the Coyote's camp.

Before they reached it, however, the Coyote had made all his preparations to receive them. He let the fire go out, cluttered up the camp with filth, then lay down beside the fireplace, and blew the ashes up into the air, so that they settled on him as he lay there, and made it appear as if he had not been out of the camp for a long time. He meant to deny everything that the two little birds had said, and claim to have been sick for a long while.

The Bears on their part had made plans also. Said one, "I will go in after him, while you stay by the smoke-hole outside, and catch him if he tries to escape by that way." They both carried sharp-pointed digging-sticks. The first Bear went into the hut, and found the Coyote lying by the fireplace, groaning.

The Bear asked him what the trouble was, and the Coyote replied, "Oh, I'm sick."

To this the Bear said, "I don't believe you. You have been down at my camp, and made trouble there."

"No, I haven't," said the Coyote, "I've been sick up here for a long time."

"But the birds said that you had been down at the camp, and had marked their heads with red, and eaten up all the food," replied the Bear.

The Coyote, however, stoutly denied that he had been to the Bears' camp, and repeated the statement that he had been lying sick in his hut for a long time. "I've been here sick," he said, "and have heard the children playing round outside, but no one has come in to see how I was."

At this moment the Bear made a thrust at the Coyote with the sharp stick. The Coyote dodged, crying, as he did so, "Whee." The Bear struck again, but this time the Coyote jumped up through the smoke-hole, and escaped. The other Bear, who was stationed at the smoke-hole, struck at the Coyote as he passed, but missed him.

As soon as he was clear of the hut, the Coyote ran to a big log, where he had hidden his bow and arrows.

The Bears followed as fast as they could, crying, "Hurry up, there, hurry up! We'll catch him, and make a quiver out of his skin." The Coyote jumped over the log to where his bow was, and got it and his arrows all ready. He waited for the Bears to jump up on the log.

The one that had been at the smoke-hole reached the log first, jumped up on it, and was shot by the Coyote at once. The other Bear came next, and was likewise shot by the Coyote. When he had killed both the Bears, he came out from behind the log, and said, "All people can call me Coyote."

HOW THE COYOTE MARRIED HIS DAUGHTER

Tradition Bearer: Unavailable

Source: Dixon, Roland B. "Some Coyote Stories from the Maidu Indians of California." *Journal of American Folklore* 13 (1900): 270.

Date: 1899

Original Source: Maidu
National Origin: Native American

Again, the Maidu Coyote displays the antisocial aspect of **trickster**. Coyote's sham cremation suggests that the tale originated among the hill-dwelling division of the Maidu; the valley and mountain dwellers buried, rather than cremated, their dead. Even with this more serious social violation, Coyote ends this tale, like "Coyote and the Grizzly Bears" (p. 339), with a flippant "People can call me Coyote."

One of the Coyote's daughters was a very beautiful girl. The Coyote was very fond of her, and was always scheming as to how he might succeed in marrying her. One day a plan occurred to him.

He made believe that he was sick, and lay there, groaning. He told his family that he was going to die, and instructed them to prepare a scaffold three or four feet high of boughs to burn his body on. The Coyote's wife and daughters prepared everything according to directions, and gathered a great quantity of sage-brush to put under the scaffold when the time came to burn the body. The Coyote told them that when they had once started the fire, they were to go away at once, and not look back. Soon after telling them this, the Coyote made believe he was dead.

His family carried out his orders, and, having lit the fire under his body, went away crying. As soon as they were gone, the Coyote jumped down from the scaffold, and went off.

Two or three days after he came back, and meeting his daughter, made love to her. After a while he married her. A week or two after they were married, the old woman who had been the Coyote's wife before suspected that there was something wrong. She suspected that the man who had married her daughter was really her own husband whom they had thought dead.

One day, when the Coyote had gone out hunting, the old woman said to her daughter, "I think that you have married your father." The old woman knew that the Coyote had a scar on the back of his head, which was due to an old wound. So she told her daughter to try to get her husband to let her hunt for lice on his head, when she would have an opportunity to see if he had a scar.

After several days the young girl succeeded in getting her husband to let her hunt for lice on his head, and in a minute she found the scar.

She said, "Now I have found you out; you are my father."

The Coyote jumped up and laughed till his sides ached, then he said, "People can call me Coyote."

COYOTE AND WOLF

Tradition Bearer: Tom Austin

Source: Lowie, Robert H. "Shoshonean Tales." *Journal of American Folklore* 37 (1924): 212–13.

Date: 1914

Original Source: Paviotso (Northern Paiute)

National Origin: Native American

Wolf and Coyote appear in this tale as their usual Northern Paiute role of brothers (see "The Theft of Pine Nuts," p. 331). Again, Wolf is sensible, and Coyote is impulsive but powerful. His curiosity leads to Wolf's death, but Coyote brings him back to life from his scalp.

Coyote and Wolf were living together on the other side of the mountains. They were brothers, Wolf being the elder one. Coyote went a little ways from their home and came upon a great many people coming after Wolf. He went back home and told Wolf: "I found plenty of people coming against you." Wolf sent Coyote for arrows. He brought them all ready for use.

The enemy began to attack Wolf. Wolf said to Coyote, "Stay indoors and don't look at the fight." He fastened all the doors to keep Coyote inside during the battle, then he began to fight the enemy. Coyote was eager to look on, he jumped all over in his attempts to see. At last he made a hole in the top of the lodge. As soon as he saw his brother, Wolf was killed; that is why he had ordered Coyote not to look. Wolf had killed lots of people, and now there are plenty of little rocks where the people were killed; the Paiute can see them even today.

The enemy took off Wolf's hair and went away to their home. Coyote was grieving and followed them. At their home the enemy danced, putting the hair on a long stick. After traveling a long way, Coyote found one of the enemy's old campsites. When he got closer to them he found a campfire still aglow. Then he thought he would soon overtake them.

He caught up with the people and asked for the chief's house; they told him it was where someone's hair was hanging up. So he went there and said, "I want to see what this thing is." The chief gave him the hair. Coyote looked at it and recognized it as his brother's hair. He returned it to the chief who hung it up again.

It was in the evening. People began to dance, and Coyote sang for them.

He sang for them until daylight. Then everyone fell asleep. Coyote alone continued to dance. Two old women who had not danced at all were sitting outside. Coyote took his brothers' hair and ran homeward.

The two old women saw it. They had suspected Coyote of being Wolf's brother even during the dance. Now they roused their people, "Don't sleep any more, he has taken that hair away with him. You had better get up and chase him."

So they pursued him and ran him down, took the hair away and brought it back to the dance ground.

Coyote tried to get the scalp again. He changed himself into a woman. He made lots of people to help him. He went back to the dance ground and being a woman he went among the women. He made a baby and took it over to the women. The baby was crying.

The other women said, "Let us see the baby."

Coyote replied, "No, I don't want to give it to other women."

The others said, "You smell like a man."

He said, "I am married to a man, that is why." He made a great many men and said to the women, "We'll go somewhere and hide. Some time a great many bad persons will come and kill all these people. Let us go somewhere else and hide."

So the other women went off with Coyote. They all went to bed. Coyote said, "I am going to sleep at the end of the line." All the rest went to sleep, but Coyote kept awake. He killed off all the sleeping women.

The men he had created went to the dance ground and killed all the men there. Then Coyote went there and got his brother's hair. He took it home. Every evening, while on the way he soaked the hair in water. Thus he revived him before he got home. Now they were both back home again.

COYOTE AND THE SUN

Tradition Bearer: Mrs. Haydon

Source: Sapir, Jean. "Yurok Tales." *Journal of American Folklore* 41 (1928): 256–57.

Date: 1927

Original Source: Yurok

National Origin: Native American

The Yurok settled at in Northwestern California on the Pacific Coast at the mouth of the Klamath River. Living in villages of plank houses in winter and foraging in the summer, their subsistence was based on acorns and salmon. The "strings" used for payment are likely to be dentalia strings composed of a type of mollusk shell used as currency in the region. The Yurok Coyote shows himself to be as indestructible as the other Native American **variants** of this **trickster**.

Coyote had a wife and children. In the springtime, when there was a great deal of grass, the children once went out picking grass. There was a shower and then snow, and those children were frozen and did not come home. Coyote went looking for his children and found them frozen. He came home and told his wife that he was going away, that he was going to kill the sun because his children had frozen to death.

So Coyote started out with some sharp rocks. He stopped right where he had always seen the sun come out of the mountain in the morning. Next morning he saw the sun come out away over there, so he started out again. He stopped where he had seen the sun come out and waited until morning. Next morning he saw the same thing, the sun came out away over there. He went on a long way and he could not catch him. He went a long way, he went until he saw the ocean, and that sun came out on the other side of the ocean. So he walked around, he could not do anything.

Then he found a man in the sweathouse. He asked him if he knew where he could find that sun. This man said to him, "I'll take you up if you pay me some strings."

"Well," Coyote said, "I have lots of that."

So the man said, "That's all right. You get on my back and shut your eyes. Don't open your eyes if you feel it snowing, if the wind blows, or if you hear a noise somewhere."

So Coyote hung on to that man and got to the sky.

He said to him, "Get off right here."

So he got off. He looked around. It was a nice place; he saw trails. He took one trail and went all around. He saw a big village and at evening he stopped there. It was about supper-time and everyone went into the house to eat, so Coyote went into the sweathouse and sat down behind the ladder.

Late in the evening the men came in to go to sleep. They called the name of everyone there and they called the sun by his name. Coyote thought he was going to catch him, so when everyone was asleep and snoring, he came out and hit that sun on the head and killed him. Everybody woke up and he ran out. They could not catch him. He went to another place that same evening.

He saw seven girls' going along. He asked them, "Where are you going?"

The girls said, "We're going dancing."

"Can I go along with you?"

The girls said, "No, you could not keep up with us. We dance all night long, we never stop anywhere."

"No," said he, "I can keep up, we dance a lot, too." So Coyote went along and danced between those girls.

Soon he said, "Wait," and the girls said, "No, we can't wait."

And he said, "Wait, I lost my pipe."

The girls said, "No, we can't stop." They were just dragging him along after them, he was so worn out. He dropped a leg; then another leg dropped. When that happened, those girls let go of him altogether.

Next morning Coyote woke up and looked around. He went all around and could find no place to get out into this world again. One place looked as though it was open, so he spit on it. He saw his spit lying there and thought it must be just a little way through there to this world.

So he jumped, for this was the only way he could get back to his village. But he died on his way here. He landed near his grandmother's. While that old woman was walking around next day she found some bones. "Diy," she thought, "are those my grandson's bones?"

So she picked them up and put them in the house. Next day his bones rattled and he came alive again.

HELL, BOB AND ME PLANTED 'EM

Tradition Bearer: Harry Reece

Source: Bowman, Earl. "Interview of Harry Reece." *American Life Histories: Manuscripts from the Federal Writers' Project, 1936–1940.* Manuscript Division, Library of Congress. 12 October 2005. http://memory.loc.gov/ammem/wpaintro/wpahome.html.

Date: 1939

Original Source: California

National Origin: European American

The following **tall tale** incorporates the elements usually associated with narratives of this category: a claim of personal experience and expressed disdain for lies and liars, for example. The **motif** of rich soil giving rise to extraordinarily fast and huge plant growth is frequently encountered in tales from the "frontier regions." The source of the soil's fertility also attests to the anti-Native American sentiments that were an unfortunate element of the region's repertoire.

We were camped by a little trout steam that cut its way through the rich mountain soil just off the low divide between Price Valley and Salmon Meadows when my Uncle Steve Robertson told me the "true" story of the "Big Trees" of California, and how they happened to be so big.

All around us was a park-like forest of stately Idaho Yellow Pines, their three, four, even five-foot trunks straight and smooth and limbless for thirty feet or more, their crowns towering into the sky a hundred or a hundred and fifty feet.

"Gee, Uncle Steve, there's sure some wonderful timber in this part of Idaho, isn't there?" I said. "Just look at those tree, why one of 'em must have lumber enough in it to almost build a house—Gosh they're big. But beside some trees I saw in California once, these Idaho pines, big and grand as they are would only be saplin's. 'Sequoias,' they call those big trees in California, and some of them must be thirty-five or forty feet in diameter. They're supposed to be thousands of years old and they probably are because it would take a tree a hell of a long time to grow as big as those California 'sequoias' are. They're 'whoppers,' no doubt about that...."

"Yeah, I-Gawd," my Uncle Steve Robertson said, 'they probably are whoppers by this time, I ain't sayin' they ain't. In fact they couldn't be nothin' else but big, considerin' what they was fertilized with. Yeah, they sure as hell was fertilized an' to such a extent, I-Gawd, they jest couldn't help growin' as big as they be an' more'n likely they'll be a hell of a sight bigger 'fore they quit growin'.

"But when it comes to them California big trees bein' thousands of years old, like you said, or even bein' 'sequoias,' I-Gawd that's jest some smart-aleck's idea.

"Probably some feller that didn't know nothin' about trees an' timber an' things like that wanted to show off an' told people they was 'sequoias' an' they was 'thousands of years old,' an' I-Gawd like damned fools people believe it. But that's th' way people is, most of 'em believe any danged thing they hear without takin' th' trouble to git at th' bottom of things and find out for theirselves whether its so or not.

"An' that's th' way it is with them big trees in Californy! They ain't no thousands of years old an' they ain't no cussed 'sequoias'—They're jest plain damned Arkansas cedar trees, an' they like a hell of a lot of bein' any older probably than these Idaho yaller pines is, an' also they was jest as much saplin's oncet as any other doggone trees ever was.

"Yeah, I-Gawd, I ought to know, 'cause—*Hell, Bob White an' me planted 'em!*

"Course we didn't realize what we was startin' when we planted th' damned things or we never would a-done it in th' first place.

"But us Pioneers of th' Far West in th' early days probably made mistakes oncet in a while like ever'body else does, but one thing about it, when we did make any damned mistake an' found out we'd made one, I-Gawd we didn't keep on makin' it jest for pure contrariness like lots of people does now-a-days.

"Yeah, I-Gawd, Bob an' me made a hell of a mistake when we planted them big Californy trees in th' first place. But, our mistake wasn't in jest planted 'em so much probably as in *where* we planted th' damned things.

"If we'd had any idea what th' damned things was goin' to be fertilized with, we'd never a-planted 'em to start with ... I-Gawd we sure as hell wouldn't have.

"But we planted 'em an' after th' damned things got started to growin' they wasn't no chance on earth to do nothin' about it but jest let 'em grow—an' I-Gawd you see what happened! What we thought was goin' to be jest a nice, comfortable Arkansas cedar grove turned into a regular cussed wilderness of 'big trees' that nobody can do a doggone thing with only jest let 'em grow an' grow until Gawd known how damned big they'll be 'fore they quit growin'—

"Yeah, that's the way it is, an' that's th' way it usually is, people start some damned thing an' then I-Gawd they find out they've made a hell of a mistake but they can't stop it!

"Bob an' me planted them big Californy trees th' time we was gittin' out of th' Arizony country after th' hot spell that petrified all them damned buzzards, et ceterry.

"When we got up in th' Californy country—After we'd stopped that time out in the Mojave desert where we staked down that damn floatin' lake, I told you about oncet, well, we come to that valley where them big trees is an' it looked like it might be a hell of a good place to start a ranch. It was smooth an' nice lookin' land but there wasn't a damned thing growin' on it—jest smooth, rich lookin' soil.

"So, Mam, (she was Bob's wife) said: 'Bob White, an' you too, Steve Robertson, if I know anything about th' looks of land, this would be a hell of a good place to stake out a ranch an' settle down. I Know,' Mam says, 'they's a heck of a lot of Piute Injuns in this section, 'cause we've seen 'em, but in spite of that land looks like things would grow on it an' I'm tired of movin' 'round. So, I'm in favor of stoppin' right here an' startin' a ranch. If I'm any judge of rich land, this land is th' richest danged land I ever seen in my life, even if it is kind of funny lookin',' Mam said.

"Well, Bob an' me'd sort of set our minds on gittin' up into this Idaho country, but Bob always was considerate of Mam an' tried to do whatever she wanted him to do, 'cause he wanted her to be as happy as she could, knowin' like he did that it was hard enough life them women-Pioneers like Mam was, had to live anyhow without contraryin' them any more'n was necessary.

"So, Bob said: 'Far's I'm concerned Mam, I'd jest as soon stop here an' start a ranch as not if you think you'd be contented here, Mam. 'Cause I sure as hell want you to be contented, Mam. But, I-Gawd, they ain't no trees an' you know damned well you was always a great hand for trees—an' what th' hell will we do about that? An' also, th' surroundin' country's full of them cussed Piute Injuns—we know it is 'cause we've seen 'em almost steady ever since we got up into this section, an' Piute Injuns ain't very damned nice neighbors. What'd you think about it, Steve?' Bob said.

"'Personally, it don't make no difference to me,' I said, 'As far as Piute Injuns being plentyful in concerned, I'd jest as soon have Piutes as any other cussed kind of Injuns for neighbors and regardin' startin' a ranch here, I'd jest as soon start it here as anyplace else, so I don't give a damn either direction,' I said.

"'That's perfectly alright, Bob White, an' you too, Steve Robertson,' Mam said, 'I've thought about all that. An' as far as Piute Injuns is concerned, you notice that even if the general country does seem like it's full of 'em, you notice they ain't none of 'em hangin' around this imedjiate neighborhood. So, I calculate they won't bother much. An' regardin' they not bein' no trees growin', that can be fixed danged easy 'cause I got a whole sack full of Arkansas red cedar tree seed I picked offen that cedar tree in our front yard in Arkansas 'fore we started migratin' to th' Far West. All we got to do is plant them Arkansas cedar tree seed an' if that soil's as rich as it 'pears to be we'll soon have a nice grove of cedar trees, which will be a good place for th' chickens I'm aimin' to raise to waller under in th' dust. Th' smell of th' cedar trees will also help keep th' mites an' lice from worryin' th' chickens to death,' Mam said.

"Well, I-Gawd that's th' way it started.

"Jest to please Mam an' keep her contented, Bob an' me took that sack full of Arkansas red cedar tree seed an' planted th' whole cussed works, figgerin' that maybe some of 'em wouldn't grow, but we planted 'em all so Mam would be sure to have a cedar grove for her chickens to waller under in th' dust.

"Yeah, Bob an' me planted ever' cussed cedar tree seed Mam had brought from Arkansas, never realizin' I-Gawd how rich an' fertilized that damned land was, an' th' whole works come up! Ever damned seed! Hell yes, we hadn't hardly got th' last of 'em planted when th' one we planted first was already up an' growln' to beat hell!

"Yes, sir, I-Gawd, you never saw nothing come up as prompt as them damned Arkansas red cedar tree seed done. It seemed like that soil jest squirted 'em right up.

349

"'Gawd-a-mighty,' Bob said, 'I never seen nothin' like it in my life. This whole district must a-been a old sheep corral or somethin' oncet for th' soil to be as fertilized as it is!' Bob said.

"'No damned sheep manure ever made things grow like them cedar tree seed's growin',' I said. 'I-Gawd, no. Sheep manure's a powerful fertilizer but it ain't powerful enough to make things grow that a-way. Whatever this lands fertilized with is a hell of a sight powefuler than any cussed sheep manure.' I said.

"Mam, she was tickled as hell. 'I told you, Bob White, an' you too Steve Robertson, that this was th' richest dang land anybody ever seen, an' now I reckon you'll believe me. It won't be no time now till we'll have a nice cedar tree grove for me to watch th' chickens waller in th' dust under an' to hang my washin' on when wash days comes.' Mam said.

"Well, I-Gawd, Mam was plumb right.

"Yeah, she was right as hell. Bob an' me finished plantin' them damned Arkansas cedar tree seeds on Friday—no, I'Gawd, it was on a Thursday, yeah, Thursday about a hour before sundown, I don't want to stretch things none cause I sure hate a damned liar or 'xaggerater—an' by th' next Monday them cussed cedar trees was up an' jest about tall enough for Mam to spread her washin' on (Monday was always Mam's washday).

"'Its a pleasure to have cedar trees to spread my washin' out on,' Mam said. 'It makes me think of how I used to spread things out on our cedar trees back in Arkansas.'

"Well, Mam didn't git her washin' out till late, plumb near sundown, so they wasn't dry enough to take in that night an' she had to leave 'em out till th' next day. An' I-Gawd, that's where Mam got a surprise: Th' next mornin' them damned cedar tress had growed so fast that Bob's an' my shirts an' drawers an' Mam's 'Mother Hubbards' an' aprons an' night-gowns an' et ceterry was up so cussed high she couldn't reach 'em.

"Bob an' me had a hell of a time climbin' them danged trees fast enough to ketch up with 'em an' git 'em down for her. An' we never did git one of Bob's sox, which Mam had hung plumb on top of one of 'em—

"Gawd, we never did git it an' far as I know th' damned thing's still up there flutterin' from a limb on top of one of then doggone trees. Yeah, it probably is. Bob cussed awful on account of th' blisters he got on his foot that didn't have no sock on it when he had to go around wearin' jest one sock while Mam had his other pair in th' wash.

"Hell, I don't reckon there ever was anything growed faster'n them cussed cedar trees that people that don't know anything about it calls them 'sequoias,' like you said

"Yes, sir, I-Gawd, some of Mam's chickens managed to climb up in one of 'em one night to roost in it an' th' next mornin' them damned chickens was up so high that when they tried to jump down out of it practically ever' one of 'em busted a leg when they hit th' ground—It was pitiful as hell to see them poor doggone chickens tryin' to stand on th' only good leg they had an' scratch with it at th' same time!

"It was plumb unnatcheral how fast an' how cussed big them trees growed.

"'I'd like to know what th' hell this soil's fertilized with,' Bob said. 'I-Gawd, I never seen nothin' like it—for two cents I'd plant some watermelon seeds an' see jest how damned big watermelons this ground would raise anyhow!'

"'You'll do no sech a cussed thing,' Mam said, an' put her foot right down on it, 'if this ground works on watermelons like it does on them cedar trees, I-Gawd, an' th' watermelons growed in proportion, by th' time they was ripe they'd be so cussed big that if th' lightin' struck one an' busted it an' knocked th' water out of it it would flood th' whole danged country! No, sir, Bob White an' you too Steve Robertson, jest keep them watermelon seeds out of this doggone soil, we ain't goin' to take no chances like that,' Mam said.

"'Probably you're right, Mam,' Bob said, 'that's jest about what would happen, but I-Gawd, I'd sure as hell like to know what this damned section of Californy's fertilized with, anyhow,' Bob said.

"'Well, sir, I-Gawd th' very next day I found out what was makin' them doggone Arkansas red cedar trees Bob an' me had started growin' in that Californy soil act th' way they did.

"A old Piute Injun chief I knowed come along an' when he saw all them damned trees growin' where they was he started howlin' an' wailin' like his heart was plumb broke. Natcherally, I asked him what th' hell was th' matter ('cause while I ain't never mentioned it, I can talk Piute jest like a native.) An' besides I'd give th' old chief a sack of smokin' tobacco oncet an' we was good friends, so he told me.

"For millions of years th' damned Piutes had been comin' for miles around an' bringin' any doggone Piute that was dead to bury him in that special part of Californy; from what th' old chief said it was th' only damned spot in Californy that was easy diggin', th' rest of it bein' hard ant gravelly, so for millions an' millions of years they'd been plantin' dead Piutes on that same doggone spot! I-Gawd, th' whole damned country was under-laid with dead Piutes an' anybody that knows anything about dead Piutes knows that a dead Piute is th' strongest cussed fertilizer they is!

"Hell, yes, dead Piutes is richer fertilizer than any damned sheep manure or any other kind of doggone manure they is. Things planted where th' soil is fertilized with dead Piutes jest can't keep from growin' an' I-Gawd when it oncet starts to growin' they ain't nothin' nobody can do about it only jest let it keep on growin'. So that's th' way it was.

"Natcherally, when Mam found out they wasn't no doggone way to keep then damned Arkansas cedar trees from growin' till they'd exhausted all th' Piute Injun fertilizer they was planted in, or till they finally died from old age, or got so big, they covered th' whole danged country, I-Gawd, she saw how foolish it would be to try to start a ranch there, so she said:

"'Bob White, an' you too, Steve Robertson, we'd jest as well hitch th' mules up an' git out of this cussed neighborhood. I can stand 'most ever'thing but I'm drawin' th' line at livin' where th' whole country's saturated with dead Piute Injuns. But they sure as heck are strong fertilizer, ain't they?' Mam said.

"Well, Bob an' me hitched up th' mules an' we headed an up to this Idaho country where th' soil's good an' rich but not too damned rich an' things grow natcheral an' normal an' like Natchure aimed for 'em to grow in th' first place.

"But, I-Gawd that's th' way them 'big trees' (sequoias, some damned fools call 'em) happened to be there in th' first place an' how they happen to be so cussed big—They can't help growin' an' can't help bein' big, fertilized like they be with dead Piute Injuns. An' I-Gawd if anybody don't believe it all they got to do is dig one of 'em up an' see for theirselves if th' cussed thing ain't bein' fertilized with dead Piute Injuns.

"Hell, I ought to know, Bob an' me *planted* 'em!"

PELE'S LONG SLEEP

Tradition Bearer: Unavailable

Source: Westerveldt, W. D. "Pele's Long Sleep." Pages 72–86 in *Hawaiian Legends of Volcanoes*. Boston: G. H. Ellis Press, 1916.

Date: 1916

Original Source: Hawaii

National Origin: Hawaiian

In Hawaiian **myth**, the goddess Pele is associated with the volcano and with unusual geological features of the environment produced by volcanic activity. These formations are attributed to divine conflicts that pit Pele against other mythic figures. In contemporary **belief tales, legends**, and **personal experience narratives**, Pele is credited with taking vengeance on tourists who take away bits of lava rock as souvenirs. Pele's younger sister, Hiiaka, goddess of the dance, remained a favorite of the volcano goddess in spite of Pele's jealousy.

Pele and her family dwelt in the beauty of Puna. On a certain day there was a fine, clear atmosphere and Pele saw the splendid surf with its white crests and proposed to her sisters to go down for bathing and surf-riding. Pele, as the high chiefess of the family, first entered the water and swam far out, then returned, standing on the brink of the curling wave, for the very crest was her surf-board which she rode with great skill. Sometimes her brother, Kamohoalii, the great shark-god, in the form of a shark would be her surf-board. Again and again she went out to the deep pit of the waves, her sisters causing the country inland to resound with their acclamation, for she rode as one born of the sea.

At last she came to the beach and, telling the sisters that the tabu on swimming was lifted and they could enter upon their sport, went inland with her youngest sister, Hiiaka, to watch while she slept. They went to a house thatched with ti leaves, a house built for the goddess.

There Pele lay down, saying to her sister Hiiaka: "I will sleep, giving up to the shadows of the falling evening—dropping into the very depths of slumber. Very hard will be this sleep. I am jealous of it. Therefore it is tabu. This is my command to you, O my little one. Wait you without arousing me nine days and eight nights. Then call me and chant the 'Hulihia'" [a chant supposed to bring life back and revive the body].

Then Pele added: "Perhaps this sleep will be my journey to meet a man—our husband. If I shall meet my lover in my dreams the sleep will be of great value. I will sleep."

Hiiaka moved softly about the head of her sister Pele, swaying a kahili fringed and beautiful. The perfume of the hala, the fragrance of Keaau, clung to the walls of the house. From that time Puna has been famous as the land fragrant with perfume of the leaves and flowers of the hala tree.

Whenever Pele slept she lost the appearance that she usually assumed, of a beautiful and glorious young woman, surpassing all the other women in the islands. Sleep brought out the aged hag that she really was. Always when any worshipper saw the group of sisters and Pele asleep in their midst they saw a weary old woman lying in the fire-bed in the great crater.

While Pele was sleeping her spirit heard the sound of a hula-drum skillfully played, accompanied by a chant sung by a wonderful voice. The spirit of Pele arose from her body and listened to that voice. She thought it was the hula of Laka, who was the goddess of the dance. Then she clearly heard male voices, strong and tender, and a great joy awoke within her, and she listened toward the east, but the hula was not there. Then westward, and there were the rich tones of the beaten drum and the chant. Pele's spirit cried: "The voice of love comes on the wind. I will go and meet it."

Pele then forsook Keaau and went to Hilo, but the drum was not there. She passed from place to place, led by the call of the drum and dance, following it along the palis (precipices) and over the deep ravines, through forest shadows and along rocky beaches until she came to the upper end of Hawai'i. There she heard the call coming across the sea from the island Maui. Her spirit crossed the channel and listened again. The voices of the dance were louder and clearer and more beautiful.

She passed on from island to island until she came to Kauai, and there the drum-beat and the song of the dance (lid not die away or change, so she knew she had found the lover desired in her dream.

Pele's spirit now put on the body of strong healthful youth. Nor was there any blemish in her beauty and symmetry from head to foot. She was anointed with all the fragrant oils of Puna. Her dress was the splendid garland of the red lehua flower and maile leaf and the fern from the dwelling-places of the gods. The tender vines of the deep woods veiled this queen of the crater. In glorious young womanhood she went to the halau. The dark body of a great mist enveloped her.

The drum and the voice had led her to Haena, Kauai, to the house of Lohiau, the high-born chief of that island. The house for dancing was long and was beautifully draped with mats of all kinds. It was full of chiefs engaged in the sports of that time. The common people were gathered outside the house of the chief.

The multitude saw a glorious young woman step out of the mist. Then they raised a great shout, praising her with strong voices. It seemed as if the queen of sunrise had summoned the beauty of the morning to rest upon her. The countenance of Pele was like the clearest and gentlest moonlight. The people made a vacant space for the passage of this wonderful stranger, casting themselves on the ground before her.

An ancient chant says:

> "O the passing of that beautiful woman.
> Silent are the voices on the plain,
> No medley of the birds is in the forest;
> There is quiet, resting in peace."

Pele entered the long house, passed by the place of the drums, and seated herself on a resting-place of soft royal mats.

The chiefs were astonished, and after a long time asked her if she came from the far-off sunrise of foreign lands.

Pele replied, smiling, "Ka! I belong to Kauai."

Lohiau, the high chief, said: "O stranger, child of a journey, you speak in riddles. I know Kauai from harbor to clustered hills, and my eyes have never seen any woman like you."

"Ka!" said Pele, "the place where you did not stop, there I was."

But Lohiau refused her thought, and asked her to tell truly whence she had come. At last Pele acknowledged that she had come from Puna, Hawai'i,—"the place beloved by the sunrise at Haehae."

The chiefs urged her to join them in a feast, but she refused, saying she had recently eaten and was satisfied, but she "was hungry for the hula—the voices and the drum."

Then Lohiau told her that her welcome was all that he could give. "For me is the island, inland, seaward, and all around Kauai. This is your place. The home you have in Puna you will think you see again in Kauai. The name of my house for you is Ha-laau-ola [Tree of Life]."

Pele replied: "The name of your house is beautiful. My home in Puna is Mauli-ola [Long Life]. I will accept this house of yours."

Lohiau watched her while he partook of the feast with his chiefs, and she was resting on the couch of mats. He was thinking of her marvelous, restful beauty, as given in the ancient chant known as "Lei Mauna Loa":

> "Lei of Mauna Loa, beautiful to look upon.
> The mountain honored by the winds.
> Known by the peaceful motion.
> Calm becomes the whirlwind.
> Beautiful is the sun upon the plain.
> Dark-leaved the trees in the midst of the hot sun
> Heat rising from the face of the moist lava.
> The sunrise mist lying on the grass,
> Free from the care of the strong wind.
> The bird returns to rest at Palaau.
> He who owns the right to sleep is at Palaau.
> I am alive for your love—
> For you indeed."

Then Lohiau proposed to his chiefs that he should take this beautiful chiefess from Kauai as his queen, and his thought seemed good to all. Turning to Pele, he offered himself as her husband and was accepted.

Then Lohiau arose and ordered the sports to cease while they all slept. Pele and Lohiau were married and dwelt together several days, according to the custom of the ancient time.

After this time had passed Lohiau planned another great feast and a day for the hula-dance and the many sports of the people. When they came together, beautiful were the dances and sweet the voices of Lohiau and his aikane (closest friend).

Three of the women of Kauai who were known as "the guardians of Haena" had come into the halau and taken their places near Lohiau. The people greeted their coming with great applause, for they were very beautiful and were also possessed of supernatural power. Their beauty was like that of Pele save for the paleness of their skins, which had come from their power to appear in different forms, according to their pleasure. They were female mo-o, or dragons. Their human beauty was enhanced by their garments of ferns and leaves and flowers.

Pele had told Lohiau of their coming and had charged him in these words: "Remember, you have been set apart for me. Remember, and know our companionship. Therefore I place upon you my law, 'Ke kai okia' [Cut off by the sea] are you—separated from all for me."

Lohiau looked on these beautiful women. The chief of the women, Kilinoe, was the most interesting. She refused to eat while others partook of a feast before the dancing should begin, and sat watching carefully with large, bright, shining eyes the face of Lohiau, using magic power to make him pay attention to her charms. Pele did not wish these women to know her, so placed a shadow between them and her so that they looked upon her as through a mist.

There the chiefs took their hula-drums and sat down preparing to play for the dancers. Then up rose Kilinoe, and, taking ferns and flowers from her skirts, made fragrant wreaths wherewith to crown Lohiau and his fellow hula-drummers, expecting the chief to see her beauty and take her for his companion. But the law of Pele was upon him and he called to her for a chant before the dance should commence.

Pele threw aside her shadow garments and came out clothed in her beautiful pa-u (skirt) and fragrant with the perfumes of Puna. She said, "It is not for me to give an olioli mele [a chant] for your native dance, but I will call the guardian winds of your islands Niihau and Kauai, O Lohiau! And they will answer my call."

Then she called for the gods who came to Hawai'i; the gods of her old home now known through all Polynesia; the great gods Lono and his brothers, coming in the winds of heaven. Then she called on all the noted winds of the island Niihau, stating the directions from which they came, the points of land struck when they touched the island and their gentleness or wrath, their weakness or power, and their helpfulness or destructiveness.

For a long time she chanted, calling wind after wind, and while she sang, soft breezes blew around and through the house; then came stronger winds whistling through the trees outside. As the voice of the singer rose or fell so also danced the winds in strict harmony. While she sang, the people outside the house cried out, "The sea grows rough and white, the waves are tossed by strong winds and clouds are flying, the winds are gathering the clouds and twisting the heavens."

357

But one of the dragon-women sitting near Lohiau said: "The noise you think is from the sea or rustling through the leaves of the trees is only the sound of the people talking outside the great building. Their murmur is like the voice of the wind."

Then Pele chanted for the return of the winds to Niihau and its small islands and the day was of the singer softened at peace as the voice toward the end of the chant. Hushed were the people and wondering were the eyes turned upon Pele by the chiefs who were seated in the great halau. Pele leaned on her couch of soft mats and rested.

Very angry was Kilinoe, the dragon-woman. Full of fire were her eyes and dark was her face with hot blood, but she only said: "You have seen Niihau. Perhaps also you know the winds of Kauai." By giving this challenge she thought she would overthrow the power of Pele over Lohiau. She did not know who Pele was, but supposed she was one of the women of high rank native to Kauai.

Pele again chanted, calling for the guardian winds of the island Kauai:

> "O Kauai, great island of the Lehua,
> Island moving in the ocean,
> Island moving from Tahiti,
> Let the winds rattle the branches to Hawai'i.
> Let them point to the eye of the son.
> There is the wind of Kane at sunset—
> The hard night-wind for Kauai."

Then she called for kite-flying winds when the birds sport in the heavens and the surf lies quiet on incoming waves, and then she sang of the winds kolon-ahe, softly blowing; and the winds hunahuna, breaking into fragments; and the winds which carry the mist, the sprinkling shower, the falling rain and the severe storm; the winds which touch the mountain-tops, and those which creep along the edge of the precipices, holding on by their fingers, and those which dash over the plains and along the sea-beach, blowing the waves into mist.

Then she chanted how the caves in the seacoast were opened and the guardians of the winds lifted their calabashes and let loose evil winds, angry and destructive, to sweep over the homes of the people and tear in pieces their fruit-trees and houses. Then Pele's voice rang out while she made known the char-acter of the beautiful dragon-women, the guardians of the caves of Haena, calling them the mocking winds of Haena.

The people did not understand, but the dragon-women knew that Pele only needed to point them out as they sat near Lohiau, to have all the chiefs cry out against them in scorn. Out of the house they rushed, fleeing back to their home in the caves.

When Pele ceased chanting, winds without number began to come near, scraping over the land. The surf on the reef was roaring. The white sand of the beach rose up. Thunder followed the rolling, rumbling tongue of branching lightning. Mist crept over the precipices. Running water poured down the face of the cliffs. Red water and white water fled seaward, and the stormy heart of the ocean rose in tumbled heaps. The people rushed to their homes. The chiefs hastened from the house of pleasure. The feast and the day of dancing were broken up. Lohiau said to Pele: "How great indeed have been your true words telling the evil of this day. Here have come the winds and destructive storms of Haena. Truly this land has had evil today."

When Pele had laid herself down on the soft mats of Puna for her long sleep she had charged her little sister, who had been carried in her bosom, to wake her if she had not returned to life before nine days were past.

The days were almost through to the last moment when Lohiau lamented the evil that his land had felt. Then as the winds died away and the last strong gust journeyed out toward the sea Pele heard Hiiaka's voice calling from the island Hawai'i in the magic chant Pele had told her to use to call her back to life.

Hearing this arousing call, she bowed her head and wept. After a time she said to Lohiau: "It is not for me to remain here in pleasure with you. I must return because of the call of my sister. Your care is to obey my law, which is upon you. Calm will take the place of the storm, the winds will be quiet, the sea will ebb peacefully, cascades will murmur on the mountain sides, and sweet flowers will be among the leaves. I will send my little sister, then come quickly to my home in Puna."

Hiiaka knew that the time had come when she must arouse her goddess sister from that deep sleep. So she commenced the incantation, which Pele told her to use. It would call the wandering spirit back to its home, no matter where it might have gone. This incantation was known as "Hulihia ke au" ("The current is turning"). This was a call carried by the spirit-power of the one who uttered it into far-away places to the very person for whom it was intended. The closing lines of the incantation were a personal appeal to Pele to awake.

> "E Pele e! The milky way (the i'a) turns.
> E Pele e! The night changes.
> E Pele e! The red glow is on the island.
> E Pele e! The red dawn breaks.
> E Pele e! Shadows are cast by the sunlight.

> E Pele e! The sound of roaring is in your crater.
> E Pele e! The uhi-uha is in your crater [this means the sound of wash
>   of lava is in the crater].
> F Pele e! Awake, arise, return."

The spirit of Pele heard the wind, Naue, passing down to the sea and soon
came the call of Hiiaka over the waters. Then she bowed down her head and wept.

When Lohiau saw the tears pouring down the face of his wife he asked why
in this time of gladness she wept.

For a long time she did not reply. Then she spoke of the winds with which
she had danced that night-the guardians of Niihau and Kauai, a people listening to her call, under the ruler of all the winds, the great Lono, dwelling on the
waters.

Then she said: "You are my husband and I am your wife, but the call has
come and I cannot remain with you. I will return to my land—to the fragrant
blossoms of the hala, but I will send one of my younger sisters to come after you.
Before I forsook my land for Kauai I put a charge upon my young sister to call
me before nine days and nights had passed. Now I hear this call and I must not
abide by the great longing of your thought."

Then the queen of fire ceased speaking and began to be lost to Lohiau, who
was marvelling greatly at the fading away of his loved one, As Pele disappeared
peace came to him and all the land of Kauai was filled with calm and rest.

Pele's spirit passed at once to the body lying in the house thatched with ti
leaves in Puna.

Soon she arose and told Hiiaka to call the sisters from the sea and they
would go inland.

Then they gathered around the house in which Pele had slept. Pele told
them they must dance the hula of the lifted tabu, and asked them, one after the
other, to dance, but they all refused until she came to Hiiaka, who had guarded
her during her long sleep. Hiiaka desired to go down to the beach and bathe
with a friend, Hopoe, while the others went inland.

Pele said, "You cannot go unless you first dance for the lifted tabu."

Hiiaka arose and danced gloriously before the hula god and chanted while
she danced—

> "Puna dances in the wind.
> The forest of Keaau is shaken.
> Haena moves quietly.
> There is motion on the beach of Nanahuki.

The hula-lea danced by the wife,
Dancing with the sea of Nanahuki.
Perhaps this is a dance of love,
For the friend loved in the sleep."

Pele rejoiced over the skill of her younger sister and was surprised by the chanted reference to the experiences at Haena. She granted permission to Hiiaka to remain by the sea with her friend Hopoe, bathing and surf-riding until a messenger should be sent to call her home to Kilauea. Then Pele and the other sisters went inland.

MEETING WITH WOVOKA

Tradition Bearer: Porcupine, Big Beaver, and Ridge Walker, as recounted to Abe Somers.

Source: Gatschet, Albert S. "Report of a Visit to Jack Wilson, the Payute Messiah." *Journal of American Folklore* 6 (1893): 108–111.

Date: 1891

Original Source: Cheyenne
National Origin: Native American

In 1889, the Paiute prophet Wovoka proclaimed a new revelation and initiated what came to be called the Ghost Dance Religion. According to Wovoka, while he was alone chopping wood he passed out and had a vision in which he was transported to Heaven. This heaven was a distinctively Indian one. There he saw all the Indian people who had ever died living in the traditional way. Before his spirit returned to his body and he returned to consciousness, he was given the doctrine and the rites of the Ghost Dance. As indicated in the following **personal experience narrative**, the religion he taught was pacifistic. During the two years of the Ghost Dance's heyday, whites became increasingly concerned about the movement, interpreting it in all cases as warlike. Finally, in 1891 on the Teton Dakota Reservation at Pine Ridge, South Dakota, troops from the Seventh Cavalry that had been sent to suppress the "uprising" opened fire on a group composed primarily of women, children, and old people—an event that has been labeled the Wounded Knee Massacre.

From information just received from Mr. James Mooney, who has seen the Payute prophet in person, I present the following biographic facts, with reference to this personage.

As near as can be ascertained, Jack Wilson is now (1893) thirty-five years old. He was called after the family name of David Wilson, the white farmer who brought him up in Mason Valley, Nevada, after the demise of his father. In the same valley, about thirty miles from the capital, Carson, he resides now. His stature nearly reaches six feet, which is more than the native Payute generally attains, and this magnitude of bodily proportions may have contributed to his success. He is a full-blood Indian and was married in his twentieth year; no other language but Payute is spoken by him, and he is but imperfectly acquainted with English. There is no doubt that his religious teachings rest on a well-ordained religious system, and, in spite of the numerous false reports that are spread about him, he does not claim to be either God or Jesus Christ, the Messiah, or any divine, superhuman being whatever. "I am the annunciator of God's message from the spiritual world and a prophet for the Indian people," is the way he defines the scope of his work among men. The first revelation he received of God himself took place about four years ago, after he had fallen asleep. God admonished him to work zealously among his fellow-men in promoting good morals and delegated special powers to him to this effect. Thus he considers himself a messenger of God appointed in a dream, and has, on that account, compared himself to St. John the Baptist. When he had that dream he thought himself to be in heaven.

* * *

In the fall of the year 1890, they say, they first heard of this new Christ, at the Arapaho and Shoshone Agency, Wyoming Territory. When they and other Cheyennes of Tongue River went on a visit to said tribes in the autumn of 1890, an Arapaho Indian named Sage, who had been to the southwestern country in 1888, told them that a new Christ had arisen for the Indians; he said where he could be found and explained his doctrine to them.

Farther on, Porcupine said that he and the other Cheyennes were much interested and determined to see the Messiah, but as all could not go so far, nine of these Cheyennes were sent back to Tongue River Agency to tell the people what they had heard. Porcupine and several of the Cheyennes went on. When they arrived in Utah, they received large accessions to their caravan, Indians joining them en route at the different points, and so at last their meeting took place at Walker Lake, to hear the new Christ speak. There were many people present, including women and children.

Then Mr. Porcupine says to the Messiah: "I and my people have been living in ignorance until I went and found out the truth." He sat with his head bowed all the time, and after a while he arose and said he was very glad to see his children, "I have sent for you and I am glad that you have come, and I am going to talk to you after a while about our relations who are dead and gone. My children, I want you to listen to all I have to say, and I will teach you how to dance a dance, and I want you to dance it; get ready for the dance, and then when the dance is over I will talk to you."

He was dressed in a white coat with stripes; the rest of his dress was that of a white man's, except that he had on a pair of moccasins. And then we commenced to dance, everybody joining in with the Christ, singing while we danced. We danced till late in the night, and he said we had danced enough. And in the morning after breakfast we went in the circle and spread grass over it on the ground, the Christ standing in the midst of us, and told us that he was going away on that day and that he would be back next morning and talk to us.

In the night, when I first saw him I thought he was an Indian; but the next day, when I could see him better, he looked different; he was not so dark as an Indian, nor so light as a white man. He had no beard or whiskers, but very heavy eyebrows; he was a good-looking man, and we were crowded up very close.

We had been told that nobody was to talk; and even if a thing was whispered, the Christ would know it. I heard that Christ had been crucified, and I looked to see, and I saw a scar on his wrist and one on his face and he seemed to be the man. I could not see his feet.

He would talk to us all day. On that evening we were all assembled again to part with him. When we assembled he began to sing, and he commenced to tremble all over violently for a while, and then sat down; and we danced all on that night, the Christ lying beside us apparently dead. The next morning we went to our breakfast; the Christ was with us again. After breakfast four heralds went around and called out that the Christ was back with us, and wanted talk with us; and so the circle was made again; they assembled and Christ came amongst them and sat down. He said they were to listen to him while he talked to us.

"I am the man who made everything you see around you. I am not lying to my children. I made this earth and everything on it. I have been to Heaven and seen your dead friends, and seen my father and mother. In the beginning, after God made the earth, they sent me back to teach the people; and when I came back on the earth, the people were afraid of me and treated me badly. This is what they have done to me (showing his scars). I did not try to defend myself, and I found my children were bad, so I went back to Heaven and left them; and in so many years I would come back and see to my children, and at the end of this time I was sent back to teach them. My father told me that the earth is getting old and worn out, and the people getting bad, and that I was to renew everything as it used to be, and make it better; and he said all our dead were to be resurrected and they were all to come back to the earth, and that the earth was too small for them and us; he would do away with heaven and make the earth large enough to contain us all, and that we must tell all the people we meet about these things.

He spoke to us about fighting, and said that was bad and we must keep from it, that the earth was to be all good hereafter, that we must be friends with one another. He said that in the fall of the year the youth of all the good people would be renewed, so that nobody would be more than forty years old. The youth of everyone would be renewed in the spring. He said if we were all good he would send people among us who could heal all our wounds and sickness by mere touch, and that we could live forever.

This is what I have witnessed, and many other things wonderful, which I cannot describe. Please don't follow the ideas of that man. He is not the Christ. No man in the world can see God at any time. Even the angels of God cannot.

THE MAN WHO BROUGHT WATER TO ATAMI

Tradition Bearer: Unavailable

Source: Sparkman, P. S. "Notes of California Folklore: A Luiseño Tale." *Journal of American Folklore* 21 (1908): 35–36.

Date: ca. 1907

Original Source: Luiseño

National Origin: Native American

The holy man Nahyam in the following **legend** gives his life to provide water to his people. According to Luiseño tradition a Pavawut is a spirit who inhabits springs. "Pavawut," translated below as witchcraft, is also known as "ayelkwi," more properly translated as "knowledge" or

"power." Snake is often entrusted with guarding the secrets of the supernatural powers. Revealing secrets, improperly performing ritual, or
telling myths out of season elicit Snake's retaliation.

Many years past, people named Nahyam were living in Atami. One of
them had a son, who grew up and became wise and excelled everyone
in witchcraft. He understood the language of the wild animals, and
when he became a grown-up man, married, and lived together with his wife.

One day he went to a mountain known as Kolo, and on arriving there saw
much yucca. And then he dug up yucca-heads, and roasted them, and worked
hard all day, and got thirsty and hungry. And then he remembered a pond of
water known as Pavawut's house, and went there to that water.

He was very tired and thirsty, and though he knew well that no one used to
go to that water, all being afraid of it, as it was said to be where the Pavawut
lived. Yet, knowing that, he went there. He had great faith in his witchcraft, and
on coming to the water spoke before drinking. He asked permission and knelt
to drink, and his hat fell from his head into the water. Seeing it in the water, he
entered to recover it, and was carried away to a dry place.

And there he saw a black-rattlesnake, and went to him, and the rattlesnake
asked him what he was going around there for.

He said, "I come looking for my hat."

Then the rattlesnake said to him, "Pass on ahead. Your aunt is there." The
man passed to where his aunt (po-pamai) was, and went to her. She was making a basket.

He said, "How are you, my aunt?"

And she said, "How are you, my nephew (no-alamai)? What are you going
around here for?"

And the man said, "Yes, my aunt, I am looking for my elut." And then his
aunt said to him, "Pass on ahead, there is your cousin (o-yuksum), the Pavawut."

And he went to the Pavawut, and said to it, "How are you, my cousin?" And
the Pavawut did not answer him, and he sat on the ground, and he was about
to faint with thirst and hunger. And the Pavawut knew that he was hungry and
thirsty.

And the Pavawut stood up, and took a small shell, and dipped up water and
gave it to the man.

And he took it discontentedly, seeing the small shell; but though he drank
much, he did not finish it, and he stayed a little. And then the Pavawut gave

him honey again in that same small shell. And the man ate much and did not finish it. And he filled himself, and remained some days with the Pavawut. And the Pavawut knew the man was wishing to go away, and did not wish to tell him. And in the morning it said to him, "My cousin, you are going away now, and I will paint your body." And then it painted him.

And the Pavawut said to him, "Now you are going away this day, and I will tell you positively. You will tell nobody what you have seen here, or that you have been in my house. If they should ask you if you have been in my house, or if you have seen me, you will say you have not seen me. I tell you that no one has ever been in my house at any time, except you. Should you tell anyone that you have been in my house, you will be bitten by a black-rattlesnake, and you will die at that place. And you will be put in the valley, and at that place will burst out water."

And the man heard all that the Pavawut said, and it again repeated to him that he should tell nobody; should he tell, a black-rattlesnake would bite him.

And his relations were looking for him in his house, and they did not know where he had gone.

And the Pavawut said to him, "Already it is best that you may go, my cousin." And the man was looking up to see where he might go out, and he saw a small light.

And the Pavawut said to him, "Go here," and took him and showed him where to go, and the Pavawut went back. And then the man went away. He thought that he would go out at the place where he had entered, but he went out at another place far away. And at that place where he went out he remained a little, and then went to his house at Atami. And at that place where he jumped out, water burst out, and its name was Person where he jumped out. And the man arrived suddenly at his house at Atami, and his wife did not know what to do when she saw him, also all his relations.

And that night he slept with his wife, and all the night she continually asked him to tell her where he had been; and the man did not wish to tell her, as he knew well that he would die if he did so. And it got light on them.

And the next day his wife continually questioned him, and he did not wish to tell her; but at last he thought that he would tell, and then he notified his wife and got together all his relations and notified them where he had been.

And then his relations cried: they all knew that a black-rattlesnake would bite him. And after he had finished his speech, the man went outside, and a black-rattlesnake bit him.

And they put him in the valley and cremated him, and at that place burst out water. Now it still runs at that place the same.

COYOTE AND HIS SISTER ROBIN

Tradition Bearer: Molly Kinsman Pimona

Source: Gifford, Edward Winslow. "Western Mono Myths." *Journal of American Folklore* 36 (1923): 343–44.

Date: 1918

Original Source: Western Mono (California)

National Origin: Native American

As noted in the introductory notes to "Prairie Falcon's Contest with Meadowlark" (p. 335), Prairie Falcon is an important figure in Western Mono tradition. He served as an agent of justice in the former narrative. In this **myth**, he upholds the moral order by punishing murder and incest. Here he is matched against his moral opposite, the egocentric **trickster** Coyote.

Bluebird had a son, Coyote, and a daughter, Robin. Robin was the elder. Coyote told his sister to paint her breast red and that is why robins today have red breasts. Bluebird and her children dwelt close to a hot spring, which formed a large deep pool. Salamander was a suitor for Robin's hand and was favored by Robin's mother, Bluebird, but not by Robin herself. Coyote likewise objected to the match, saying that he did not want Salamander for a brother-in-law. Coyote wanted his sister to marry Swallow, but to this Bluebird had objections. To settle the difficulty Coyote suggested that they pull sticks ("draw straws") to determine who should marry Robin. Bluebird's wishes were gratified, for the lot made Salamander the bridegroom.

Finding his wishes set at naught, Coyote fell to planning a means of killing Salamander. Finally he hit upon a plan. He instructed his sister, Robin, to go to gather clover near the hot spring. "Tell Salamander," he said, "that we are going to have a swim in the pool."

Poor Salamander suspected nothing and, when his wife invited him to swim with her, he acquiesced. She said to him, "You jump in first. I shall follow." He promptly jumped into the boiling water and was scalded to death.

After a while Coyote joined his sister and asked, "What shall we tell our mother, when we return without Salamander?" Then he suggested, "Let us tell her that he has gone deer hunting."

When Robin returned home she said nothing about her husband, Salamander, until her mother asked her where her husband was. She answered, "He has gone deer hunting and will be gone several months."

Bluebird suspected that there was something wrong. Prairie Falcon now came to make love to Robin. Rattlesnake did likewise, which made Prairie Falcon quite jealous. He suggested to Robin that she invite Rattlesnake to a bath, just as she had done with Salamander. Bluebird, Robin's mother, did not want either Prairie Falcon or Rattlesnake for a son-in-law. So Robin and Coyote took Rattlesnake to the hot spring and, by the same subterfuge, induced him to plunge in; he, too, was scalded to death. When Bluebird heard of this she was incensed. Even though she did not wish Rattlesnake for a son-in-law, she did not approve of her daughter's method of getting rid of husbands and suitors. She now learned that Salamander had met with the same fate.

Robin remonstrated. "Mother, what do you want me to do? Do you want me to marry my own brother?" Coyote, who was listening, jumped up at once and declared that he wished to marry his sister. They married and Bluebird became furious over the incest in her family. So wrought up was she over the affair that she committed suicide by leaping into the hot spring.

Prairie Falcon returned before long and killed the incestuous pair.

WALKING SKELETON

Variant A

Tradition Bearer: Molly Kinsman Pimona

Source: Gifford, Edward Winslow. "Western Mono Myths." *Journal of American Folklore* 36
(1923): 311–26.

Date: 1918

Original Source: Western Mono (California)

National Origin: Native American

The three **variants** of the "Walking Skeleton" narratives are tied together
by the character of a being who, after having eaten its own flesh and
reduced itself to a skeleton, pursues fresh human victims. Like the villains
of contemporary horror movies, Walking Skeleton apparently is destroyed
but reconstitutesitself almost immediately. The familiar Western Mono
figures of the brothers Wolf and Coyote and Prairie Falcon also put in
appearances. Other **motifs** such as an attack on a house filled with gamblers and the abuse of children permeate the variants. In other ways, however, there are wide variations. **Variant** A is a horror tale with brothers
Wolf and Coyote coming to the rescue at the end. **Variant** B combines the
supernatural tale with a **myth** of the origin of Native American tribes by
means of the marriage of Walking Skeleton's prey to her protector, Eagle.
Variant C finally spills over into apocalyptic chaos with the destruction of
major characters and traditional heroes behaving less than heroically.
Overall, the variations of this story demonstrate the radical differences
that may exist between versions of the "same" tale.

A boy's father went hunting, hunting deer. The boy's mother sent him
down to the spring near their house to get water. While the boy was at
the spring his mother drank his portion of manzanita cider.

When the boy returned, he accused his mother of having drunk his manzanita cider, saying, "You drank all of my manzanita cider." Then he cried and
would not cease.

His mother tried to quiet him, saying, "I threw the old manzanita berries
away. I will make some fresh manzanita cider." This promise did not stop his crying and he went on sobbing just the same.

The boy's continual crying attracted a ghost woman, who sobbed also as she
approached. The boy's mother warned him of the ghost's approach; but her

warning had no effect upon the child. She ran away and hid, leaving the child to his fate.

The ghost woman came and picked him up, saying, "My son's child, what are you crying for? Your mother has treated you meanly, my grandson. We will go away together. I am going to give you a basket to wear as a hat." She produced a small basket lined with pitch and warmed it over the fire. Then she jammed it on to the boy's head and said, "I am not your grandmother." Thereupon she tore the hat from the boy's head, ripping off his entire scalp, which adhered to the pitch. This caused the death of the boy. Then the ghost went to the place where people were playing hand games.

Meanwhile, the boy's father returned from hunting. As he approached their dwelling, he said to himself, "Where is my son? He is not coming to meet me as usual." Upon arriving home, he inquired of his wife as to the whereabouts of the boy.

She replied, "The ghost took away our boy."

The woman ghost proceeded, singing, to the place where the people were playing hand games. She steadily approached that place.

A woman warned the players, "The ghost is coming." They scoffed at the warning and said that there was no such a thing as a ghost, and that there was nothing approaching. As the ghost drew near, the woman who was aware of her approach went out and hid under a large burden basket. The ghost came to the door of the house, where the players were, and whistled at them. They looked at her and all died in consequence. Then the ghost went on her way to Lizard's house.

A baby girl who had been asleep when the ghost came, cried, and the woman who had escaped by hiding under the burden basket heard it and went to its rescue. Then the woman said, "We will go to my father's sister's house." However, the woman knew very well that something was going to happen to the child. When she came to a meadow, she made a fire for her, left her, and went out to dig some wild potatoes.

Walking Skeleton, a monster who had eaten all of his own flesh except a little on his shoulder blades, which he could not reach, came along and killed the baby, while the woman was digging wild potatoes. He carried a pestle with him with which he pounded the bones of victims.

The woman now heard him pounding the bones of the baby girl and she wondered how she herself was going to escape him. She felt that she was in great danger. In order to decoy her within reach, the giant called to her, "Come here, your baby is crying. Come here, your baby is crying."

The woman played for time, saying, "I have hardly enough potatoes yet for the baby."

Then Walking Skeleton said to himself, "I will go down and catch her. What is the use of my sitting here? I might just as well go down there, catch her, and eat her." But by the time the monster had arrived at the place where the woman had been digging potatoes, she was already far away in flight. With her digging stick, she vaulted over a mountain. Then she sought refuge under a rock, as large as a house. Walking Skeleton, in pursuit, was calling for her in every direction.

In order to mislead him, she called to him, "I am back here near the fire" [where he had killed the baby].

"Oh my," exclaimed Walking Skeleton, "I shall have a fine feast now." But when he came to a creek, he fell to pieces. Then he called his parts together again, "My foot come to me. My arm come to me. My head come to me," and so on. He went on to the woman's deserted fire, but of course failed to find her there.

Then Walking Skeleton grumbled over his ill fortune. "Where are you?" he called. He looked all around and finally went to the mountain where the woman was hiding, and there he found her. Still she was inaccessible, for she was under a huge rock. He dug around the rock and almost pulled it up. At nightfall, he decided to cease his exertions until morning. "I will lie down right here and watch you," he said.

Then the woman wished to herself, "I hope that monster will go to sleep, so that I may escape." After a time he fell asleep and snored. She made the most of the opportunity and escaped.

With her digging stick she vaulted over two hills.

At daybreak, Walking Skeleton awoke and pulled up the great rock under which the woman had hid. The rock fell on him and broke him to pieces. Nevertheless, he regained consciousness and shook himself. Then he called to his parts, "O my parts, come to me." When he had been reconstituted, he set out in search of the fugitive again. He passed over the two hills and found the woman in her hiding place under a bush.

The monster decided to forego digging her out until morning; so he lay down again. He said to himself, "I shall not go to sleep this time. I shall remain awake." However, slumber overcame him and he fell to snoring. With this signal that escape was possible, the woman made her way from her hiding place and vaulted over two more mountains. Again she took refuge under the roots of a bush.

Once more Walking Skeleton discovered her refuge and worked hard at pulling the bush from the ground. He had almost succeeded, when the sun set, and he decided to desist until morning. When he ceased his efforts, he said, "This time I am not going to sleep. I am going to remain awake and watch to see that this woman does not escape." Nevertheless, he fell asleep, and the woman once more escaped.

This time she took refuge at the house of two brothers, Wolf, the older, and Coyote, the younger. She asked them to aid her, saying that Walking Skeleton was in pursuit of her. They wrapped her in buckskin and put her on top of their house. Then the two brothers set out and intercepted the monster. They killed him with their bows and arrows and then burned his remains.

While Wolf and Coyote were slaying Walking Skeleton, the woman extricated herself from her buckskin wrappings and set out for the house of her father's sister. She married Chicken Hawk (puna) and had six children by him. They all went to a ceremonial gathering. There they decided to fly away and be birds.

Variant B

Tradition Bearer: Singing Jack

The people were about to play hand games in the house. Walking Skeleton (Ninitikati), was traveling towards the house. He was climbing the mountain ridge below the house just at dawn. He was singing. The people in the house were getting ready to play hand games and were just getting kindling for their fire, for the opposing groups played on opposite sides of the fire. At this juncture Walking Skeleton appeared. "What are those people doing?" he asked as he thrust his head in the door and whistled. All of the people died, because they looked at Walking Skeleton when he whistled.

The people in the house had previously sent a girl outside of the house as a lookout. She put on a rabbit skin blanket when she went outside as guard. She had failed to see the approach of Walking Skeleton. Consequently, when she returned to the house she was astonished and grief-stricken to find the occupants dead, with the exception of a female child, who had been asleep and had not looked upon Walking Skeleton or heard his whistle.

The child awoke about sunrise, and the girl opened the door for the little one to go out. When the two were together outside the girl began to sob and cried, "What am I to do all alone in this world?" Finally she said to the child, "We shall have to depart," and she proceeded to collect what food she could. She could not tear herself away from her home at once, so she went about the house tidying things; she went around and around the house, back and forth.

"What shall we do now?" she queried as she took the little child by the hand. "You gamblers certainly look fine now," she said, ironically addressing the dead. After removing the things she wished to take, she set fire to the house and cremated the dead. Then she started with her belongings and the child, as the sun was mounting the sky.

The girl started on her wanderings, but she had not gone far before she thought of some buried pine nuts near the house. She returned for these and, after securing them, started again with the child and a large bundle. After she had gone half way up the ridge, the child became exhausted. The girl decided to stay there beside the trail. After depositing her bundle and leaving the child with it, she went out to dig some "Indian potatoes." She gathered a basketful, made a fire and roasted them in the ashes. All this consumed considerable time, but finally the two sat down to partake of the potatoes. The girl kept looking about her apprehensively, fearing that Walking Skeleton might be about. Sure enough, he came along and sat down between the girl and the child.

"Eat some potatoes with us," the girl invited.

"I surely will eat some," responded Walking Skeleton. "They certainly taste nice," he said, after sampling them.

"Just help yourself," said the girl, and she started away to dig more of them. She looked back when she got on the ridge and said, "What am I going to do with myself now?" She looked about her and saw a rock pile, which might serve as a refuge. She thought longingly of the people who dwelt safely far back in the mountains. Then she walked back to the edge of the ridge and had another look below at Walking Skeleton, for she thought she smelt something roasting. She saw that the little child had disappeared, and she perceived Walking Skeleton licking the child's blood from a rock. At the sight tears poured down the girl's cheeks.

When the monster had finished, he called to the girl, "Your child is crying."

She responded, "I shall be there in a few minutes."

Walking Skeleton called to her again, but she slipped behind a clump of bushes. She said, "I will leave an echo here, so that when he calls, it will answer him. I think that I had better set out for a safer place." She went to the edge of the ridge and peered over once more. Walking Skeleton was busy going through the bundle that she had been carrying. She stood there and watched him. "Oh dear, what am I to do now?" she sighed. Then she started on her journey. She crossed two ridges. Then she said, "This will not do. I will have to travel faster." Thereupon she took a long pole, pressed one end of it against the ground and vaulted over a high mountain.

About this time Walking Skeleton started to track her.

Beyond the mountain over which she had vaulted, she found a sage bush growing beside a big rock. She pulled the bush up by the roots and hid herself in the hole beside the rock, then she put the bush into place.

About sundown Walking Skeleton reached the girl's hiding place. He dug around the bush a bit and then he said, "I believe that I will wait until morning. I will sit up all night, so that she cannot escape." He burned some logs, so as to have plenty of light. He lay there and kept turning and turning. "I wish it were morning," he said, after he had become weary of waiting.

The girl heard him all night long and she was very much distressed over her precarious situation. "I do not know what I shall do. I fear this will be the end of me," she thought to herself.

Daybreak, however, found Walking Skeleton sleeping soundly. The girl heard his welcome snoring and said to herself, "He is sound asleep. I do not think that he can catch me, if I leave now." When she came out she stood right above him, stood there and looked at him, while he was sound asleep.

She departed and crossed two ridges before Walking Skeleton awoke. When he awoke he looked around for a minute or two, then he set to work to dig up the sage brush, seeking the girl for his breakfast. As he pulled the bush up by the root, he turned over and fell to pieces. His parts came together again and he exclaimed, "Why did I sleep? My fresh meat has escaped."

The monster now set out in pursuit of the fleeing girl and about sundown he overtook her again. She eluded him, however, and entered a cave. He went on by it, without realizing that his quarry was so near.

Once he had passed, the girl set out for the camp of her mother's brothers, Wolf and Coyote, who lived in the vicinity. Wolf, the older brother, had sent Coyote to the spring for a basket of water. There Coyote espied the girl. He ran back to the camp, telling Wolf, "Why, Why, elder brother, there is a very pretty girl at the spring."

"All right," said Wolf, "I will go to see her." He told Coyote to keep behind him, but Coyote ran ahead.

When Wolf arrived, Coyote said, "I got here first. I want to marry this girl."

Wolf said, "Stop that sort of talk," and then addressing the girl, Wolf continued, "My sister's daughter, how did you come here?"

The girl explained and then asked, "What are you two going to do to help me? Walking Skeleton is close behind me."

Wolf replied, "I fear that we can do nothing for you. However, I have a big pelt in which you might hide. I will wrap you in it." The two brothers wrapped the girl and placed her on a platform in a tree. They had scarcely secreted her, when Walking Skeleton appeared.

"I want you to give me that girl, for I know that she is here," declared Walking Skeleton.

"We know nothing about her," protested Wolf and Coyote. "I tracked her to your camp," the monster continued.

"We like fresh meat ourselves," retorted the brothers. Walking Skeleton kept walking about, getting closer and closer to the girl's hiding place. "I believe that I will stay here all night," he said, so he had a meal with the two brothers. They brought out two pelts for him to sleep upon.

Wolf said aside to Coyote, "Younger brother, we will not sleep tonight. I do not like the looks of this man." Coyote made no response, but just rolled his eyes.

After Walking Skeleton had gone to sleep, the two brothers roasted trout for the girl. They wrapped them in tule and took them to her. "You had better go along now, while he is sound asleep. We cannot do anything against him. When you eat this fish, drink water with it." The girl took their advice and departed. When she had climbed to the top of the neighboring ridge, she paused to look down in the canyon below.

When Walking Skeleton awoke, he said to Wolf and Coyote, "You had better give me that girl. There is no use for you to try to conceal her from me."

"What are you going to do with her, if we give her to you?" the brothers asked.

"Oh, I shall take her home and she will wait on me and get water for me," replied the monster. Upon discovering that his quarry had again escaped him, Walking Skeleton once more took to tracking her.

Meanwhile, the girl had pushed back into the mountains and reached the camp of an aunt, who was named "Joined-to-Willow," because she was continually scraping willow bark for basket making. "Aunt, what can you do for me? Walking Skeleton is after me. He is coming right now. Where are you going to hide me?" anxiously inquired the girl.

Her aunt's response was not reassuring. "I fear that I can do nothing for you. Nevertheless, I will do the best I can. I will put you somewhere for the night." So saying, she placed her niece in a burden basket and covered her with tule roots. She put the burden basket with its human load back among her other large baskets, so that it would not be conspicuous.

The girl had not been long ensconced in her hiding place when her pursuer arrived. The tracks led him unmistakably to the old woman's camp and he said to himself, "It is useless for me to track further, for I know that the girl is right here. I am going to capture her this time." He remained all night at the old woman's camp, but slept soundly.

Towards daybreak the old woman went to the girl and said, "You had better leave, for he is sound asleep now." The girl took her aunt's advice and departed.

At daybreak Walking Skeleton was again on her trail, exclaiming to himself, as he discovered her track, "Ah! Here is her track." However, the girl reached Skunk's house in advance of her pursuer. "What are you folks going to do for me?" was her first question.

Skunk possessed a quantity of pitch. He heated it so that it became exceedingly adhesive. Then he put it in holes dug in the trail over which Walking Skeleton would travel.

Walking Skeleton came hastening along the road, stepped into the pitfalls, and perished miserably, disappearing beneath the surface of the pitch.

The girl walked about Skunk's place for a while. She was very grateful for her deliverance. She said to Skunk, "What a wonderful thing you did in catching Walking Skeleton."

After a time she decided to travel to Eagle's home. With her pursuer dead, she took a renewed interest in life and fell to admiring the beautiful things in Eagle's country. "What beautiful flowers there are in this country," she thought to herself, "and how pretty the stars look at night. This is real life now."

Finally she reached Eagle's house. As she stood on the top of the great cliff, she surveyed the whole country. "Well, this country looks like an ocean. This is the best part of the world that I have ever been in. I am smiling all over with joy."

Eagle brought in a deer. He greeted his visitor. She returned the greeting. Then Eagle went in and made a fire. He invited the girl into his house as it was cold outside. "There is room for you on one side there," he said. "Keep yourself warm." After seeing her comfortably settled he set to work to skin the deer he had brought. After he had finished he came in and put the pot on the fire to make stew. When it was done he said to the girl, "Come now, we will have our lunch. You may have the pot of stew." He gave her the pot, only taking out a small piece of meat for himself.

"All right. This is quite a treat for me," said the girl.

Then Eagle directed her, "You must sleep in the same corner you are sitting in. Sleep right there. Tomorrow night you may move your bed a little closer to my bed."

"All right," said the girl. "I will share this house with you." Then Eagle said, "We will cohabit in ten days, but not before."

Nevertheless, in two days the girl bore two children, and in a few days a big band of children had been born. "Now we are getting too many. We had better pair them off," Eagle said. "My wife, we will pair them off and name them. They will be different tribes of people."

He proceeded to pair them off. "This pair will be Usomu (Miwok)," he said. "This pair we will call Chukchansi. This pair we will call Mono." Then he sent all the pairs out. Thus he paired the tribes and sent them out. "Now you all establish homes and settle down. This will make the world. You people increase, for this world looks too bare. Fill it."

All went to their places. They all went away happy. Eagle looked over the cliff himself to see them start. "How beautiful it is to see people walking," he said. "The world certainly looks nice." Then addressing the girl, he said, "Now we are going to kill deer, as I did when we first met. We are only two now, paired off."

Variant C

Tradition Bearer: Molly Kinsman Pimona.

The people were playing hand games in the house. They played without cessation. A woman heard Walking Skeleton approaching when she was still miles away.

Walking Skeleton had flesh only on the shoulder blades; a condition arrived at through extreme hunger, which had caused her to eat herself. She carried a pitch-lined conical burden basket for the transportation of victims. Into this she threw people, who stuck in the pitch. When she reached the cave, which served as her abode, she stooped and precipitated her victims from the basket to the floor.

Because of the approach of this monster, the woman warned the people to stop playing; but they were reluctant to cease and said, "No! Let her come."

When Walking Skeleton came closer the woman again warned her companions, saying, "Stop! She is drawing near." It was of no avail; the people retorted as before. Then the woman decided to go out of the house and hide herself under a burden basket.

Hardly had she done so, when Walking Skeleton arrived and opened the bark door of the house. The monster whistled, causing the people to turn to look at her. They were instantly stricken dead. Walking Skeleton then departed, and went to the house of Lizard who lived close by.

After Walking Skeleton's departure the woman who was hidden under the burden basket heard a baby crying within the house. She entered and picked up the baby to quiet it. The baby had escaped because it was asleep when Walking Skeleton came. The woman now went with the baby to the house of her father's sister. She knew, however, that Walking Skeleton would capture the baby and eat it. She left it in a little meadow, while she went to dig some wild sweet potatoes for it.

Walking Skeleton carried a slippery pestle, with which to pulverize human bones. It was so slippery that none but she could pick it up. As the woman dug the wild sweet potatoes, she heard the blows of Walking Skeleton's pestle and she knew that the baby had been captured and killed. Then she was in great fear, for she knew not how to escape the monster. She dug a hole and attempted to bury herself, but was unsuccessful, as part of one leg remained exposed. Then she tried to hide herself under some bark, but it fell to pieces exposing her. She could not hide and she was so terrified that she hardly knew what to do.

Walking Skeleton now tried to entice her within reach by calling to her, "Your baby is crying. Your baby is crying."

The woman, however, played for time and replied, "I have not dug enough wild sweet potatoes yet, with which to feed the baby." In desperation the woman pushed over the dead tree, under the bark of which she had tried to hide.

She found Bat in the tree. He was rolled into a ball, so that his legs and wings were hard to see. She knew that Bat would help her if she could only awaken him. She said, "Quick! Walking Skeleton is coming after me now." Bat still slumbered, so she started to beat him into the ground with a feathered arrow.

After a bit Bat awoke and asked, "What are you doing to me? Are you awakening me? I was quite sound asleep."

The woman implored, "I want to go somewhere, for Walking Skeleton is trying to catch me. I want to go to my mother's brother's house." Her mother's brother was Skunk.

The obliging Bat said, "Get on my back. I will carry you."

Upon their arrival Skunk agreed to give his niece refuge. "All right. I will keep you," he said. Skunk spread pitch on the ground, hoping to ensnare Walking Skeleton. Skunk now said to his niece, "Paint your face with red clay and with white clay." She mixed the paint and applied it as her uncle had requested. Then Skunk ordered her to sit down in the middle of the area of pitch.

She protested, "Why do you wish me to do that, uncle?"

He replied, "Because a nice-looking man has been stealing my watermelons."

"I do not want to sit there, uncle," the woman remonstrated, "he might eat me." She knew very well that her uncle was putting her up to some mischief.

In spite of her protests Skunk put her in the pitch that he had placed in the middle of his watermelon patch. "When two handsome men come by, greet them," he commanded.

After nightfall Coyote and Puma came to the watermelon patch. They were brothers; Coyote was the younger, Puma the older. They saw the woman and departed without stealing watermelons.

Next morning Skunk visited his niece at her position in the middle of the watermelon patch, and inquired if anyone had come during the night.

She answered, "I saw two handsome men."

"Did they steal any watermelons?" queried Skunk.

"No," the woman replied, "but they looked as though they might eat me, uncle. I want to go to the house."

Skunk was obdurate and refused, saying, "They have been stealing my watermelons and I cannot find any way to catch them. You stay here and we will try again to catch them."

Coyote and Puma meanwhile had returned home, where they fell to fighting over the woman they had seen. One declared, "I am going to marry her."

The other retorted, "No. I am going to marry her."

They fought until Coyote was killed. Puma thus killed his younger brother. That night Puma returned to Skunk's watermelon patch and attempted to reach the woman, but he stuck hard and fast in the pitch.

In the morning Skunk visited his watermelon patch, to see if the thief had been caught. Puma tried to bargain for his release. He promised to marry Skunk's niece and make a good home for her, if Skunk would only release him.

Skunk rudely interrupted him, saying, "You quit your talking," and thereupon seized a handful of dirt and threw it into Puma's eyes. "You stay there until you die," said the heartless Skunk, declining to release his prisoner.

Then Puma threatened, "I am going to call my mother's brother. He is going to eat all of your people." Puma's uncle was Bear.

The woman, Skunk's niece, was beside herself with fear. "I do not know what I shall do," she said. "I will be eaten by his uncle."

Skunk quieted her fears, saying, "You keep quiet. When Bear comes, he is going to be saucy like his nephew and I am going to punish him."

When Bear came, he pursued Skunk, who took refuge in a small pine tree. Skunk warned Bear, "Look out, Bear, it will be the death of both of us, if you climb this tree," for the tree was bending ominously as Bear started to climb it. "Look out, look out! You are going to kill both of us, for there is a big canyon below," said Skunk.

Bear persisted in his endeavors to reach Skunk. "I am going to settle with you now," said Skunk, as the tree bent out over the canyon. It bent clear across the canyon, so that Skunk jumped from the tree top to the opposite wall of the canyon. The tree flew up violently, causing Bear to lose his hold, so that he was dashed to pieces in the canyon below.

Let us turn to Walking Skeleton and her adventures with Lizard. Upon reaching Lizard's house, Walking Skeleton asked him if there were living with him any of his brothers or sisters, or his father, or his mother.

Lizard replied that he had no father or mother, but that he had a brother, who was at that moment engaged in setting traps for mice. Walking Skeleton then picked up some hot ashes and threw them on Lizard's back, burning him slightly. Lizard had an elderberry stick, from which he had removed the heart. To escape his tormentor, he entered it, holding it erect, and proceeded through it up into the sky.

The baffled Walking Skeleton set fire to Lizard's house, incidentally burning Lizard's elder brother to death. The elder brother had returned and, not knowing that his younger brother had gone to the sky, had hidden himself under the bark of the house. Walking Skeleton set fire in a ring around Lizard's house, so that Lizard's elder brother could not escape from his hiding place in the bark of the house, and thus he was burned to death.

When Lizard reached the sky, he entered Coyote's house. Coyote made fun of Lizard's hand and asked him why he wanted to have five fingers. "Why do you not have a hand like mine?" asked Coyote. Coyote had hands just like a dog. He had to pick up things with his mouth. Coyote wanted to kill Lizard, but was unable to catch him. He tried, tried many ways, but each attempt failed, though all the time he was wishing most earnestly that he could catch him. Then Coyote asked Lizard if he had seen Deer. Deer was Lizard's mother's brother.

Finally Coyote devised a scheme for the murder of Lizard. He asked Lizard to accompany him to the top of a high precipitous rock there to assist him to capture Deer, Lizard's own uncle. It was Coyote's intention to shoot Lizard, once he got him there. When they arrived at the edge of the precipice Coyote looked down first and told Lizard that he could see Deer far below at the bottom of the cliff.

Lizard looked down, but could not see Deer. Thereupon Coyote said, "Move a little further over. Stand right on the edge of the rock." Lizard did as he was bidden and the treacherous Coyote pushed him over the precipice. However, Lizard was fortunate enough to lodge in a crevice. Coyote looked down and said, "I think I killed him."

He was greeted mockingly by Lizard who thrust his hand out from his place of lodgment and said, "You did not kill me."

As Coyote returned home he thought to himself, "I do not know what I shall do. It looks as though I could not kill Lizard. I suppose I shall have to give him one of my daughters to marry. That is the only way I can kill him." Coyote had three daughters. Lizard returned to Coyote's house.

Coyote had an elder sister named Raccoon who lived near him. She had two daughters, who were both Snow Birds. These two daughters went down to the spring for water and found Lizard sitting there. Coyote's three daughters repaired to the spring for water also and likewise saw Lizard sitting there.

Lizard said to Coyote's daughters, "Come, give me some water."

Coyote's daughters said, "No. We will give you no water. Our father told us to have nothing to do with you." They returned to their house and told their father that they had seen Lizard at the spring.

"What did Lizard say to you?" asked Coyote. They replied that he had asked for water.

"Did you give him any?" queried Coyote.

"No," the girls replied, "because you told us to have nothing to do with him."

"But I did not tell you to go and tell him that," was Coyote's angry criticism. "I intended to set some traps for him and catch him and kill him."

Lizard received a more friendly reception from Raccoon's two daughters. "May I go to your house?" asked Lizard and they replied affirmatively.

So Lizard went to Raccoon's house with her two daughters. Coyote watched him as he went along in order to see what he was going to do.

Coyote said, "Now that he has entered that house, we are going to kill him. I know that he intends to marry one of my sister's daughters." Happily for Lizard one of Coyote's daughters, who had taken umbrage at her father's scolding, came and made a hole through the house wall where Lizard was sitting, and informed him of her father's plans. Upon receiving this intelligence, Lizard thrust his elderberry stick downward and took Raccoon, her two daughters, and himself down to earth. When Coyote entered Raccoon's house to kill Lizard he found no one.

After he had de-parted Lizard thrust his elderberry stick up again and he, Raccoon, and her two daughters all returned to the sky. Coyote heard a roaring like thunder, made by their arrival in the sky.

Raccoon said to Lizard, "I will get some chaparral and wrap you and the two girls in it, so that it will look merely as though I were carrying some wood home to burn." By this means she brought them to the house without Coyote's knowledge.

Coyote asked his daughters, "What did you dream about?"

One replied, "I dreamed of rain and hail."

"Can you make it come true?" questioned Coyote. His daughter thought that she could. Then the wily Coyote sent one of his three daughters to Raccoon's house, saying, "Go and see if Lizard is in that house."

Coyote's daughter went to the house and peered in, but Raccoon threw a handful of dirt into her eyes, which made her cry, so she gave up in despair. Then Coyote sent a second daughter to see if Lizard was in Raccoon's house, but Raccoon threw dirt into her eyes also. Then Coyote sent his third daughter, saying, "You go. I will gamble so that she may not get dirt into your eyes."

The third daughter went, and, every time that Raccoon threw dirt at her, she turned her head. She saw Lizard sitting in the house. This girl was the one who dreamt about the rain and hail.

The girl returned to Coyote's house. "Yes," she said, "Lizard is there."

Coyote was pleased and said, "We are going to sing to bring the rain and hail. We will freeze them to death with rain and hail. We are going to kill all of them." They commenced singing and dancing in their house, with the result that rain and hail came pouring down, so that it filled Raccoon's house. Lizard put his elderberry stick horizontally across the upper part of the house and sat on it, together with Raccoon and her two daughters.

After a time Coyote thought that his victims must be dead, so he sent one of his daughters to ascertain if they were. After looking into Raccoon's house she returned and reported to her father, saying, "I think they are dead. The water inside is nearly up to the top of the house."

Lizard, Raccoon, and her daughters were two days on the elderberry stick, before the water subsided. When it went down and they were again on the floor of the house, Raccoon asked her daughters if they had dreamt of anything.

One daughter said, "Yes. I dreamed of hot weather."

Then Raccoon said, "Let us sing and dance and make it come true, thereby revenging ourselves on Coyote and his family."

Lizard pleaded for Coyote, saying, "No. Do not do that. We do not want to abuse your brother that way."

But old Raccoon was not to be appeased and she said, "See how Coyote and his daughters have treated us. They have pretty nearly killed us. On account of you they pretty nearly killed us. They wanted to kill you too." Then Lizard acquiesced and they began to dance and sing.

After a while Coyote went out and cut some small oaks to make a sun-shelter as it was getting hot. He and his daughters became very thirsty, and Coyote went down to a pool to bathe. The water was cool and he said to his daughters, "This is all right. We are going to take a bath this way." The second time he took a bath the water had become lukewarm, and the third time it had become rather hot. The fourth time when Coyote and his daughters jumped in, the water had reached the boiling point. They were all scalded to death.

When Raccoon saw their dead bodies she said, "That is the way I punished you. You were mean to me, you, my own brother."

Having finished burning Lizard's house, Walking Skeleton continued her travels. She encountered Prairie Falcon and his wife's brother, Crow, gathering tobacco. She asked them what they were going to do with it.

Prairie Falcon replied, "We are going to feed you upon it." She went to her camp and secured her carrying basket. As she was walking along she again met Prairie Falcon and Crow. They were on their way to the country of the people without mouths.

She said, "Let me carry you, my nephews (brother's sons)."

"Let us get into your basket ourselves," they said. Nevertheless, she chased them, for she wanted to catch them and throw them into the basket, so that they would adhere to the pitch therein. In vain she pursued them for nearly a day. Then she went home and the two men proceeded to the country of mouthless and speechless people.

There they saw great quantities of meat hanging on the bushes drying, also much meat that had been thrown away, meat that had not been eaten. They discussed what they saw and wondered why so much meat was wasted and how the people ate.

A mouthless man, named Rainbow, came along. He took Prairie Falcon's hand and put it on his (Rainbow's) forehead. As soon as Prairie Falcon's hand rested there mist and rainbows appeared every-where. Prairie Falcon and Crow stayed all night in that country. The mouthless people cooked meat, which they sniffed with their noses and then threw away.

After seeing them do this, Prairie Falcon said to his brother-in-law Crow, "I do not know what we are going to do with them."

Rainbow motioned to them to cut open his mouth. Then Prairie Falcon and Crow cut them all open, so that they could eat meat. After they had cut open Rainbow's mouth, he suggested to them that they go and play shinny. "Let us go and play shinny," he said. "We will make some balls and sticks and play."

"All right," said Prairie Falcon, "I will play shinny with you."

Upon looking around Rainbow's habitation Prairie Falcon found his own mother, Wild Turkey, staked out with her legs cut off. He did not know her, but his mother recognized him and said, "I think you are my son. I had a pretty son named Prairie Falcon." Prairie Falcon did not reply to his mother, whereupon his mother besought him, saying, "Come here and visit with me and talk with me." Nevertheless Prairie Falcon said nothing; he just hung his head. He had been wondering if he had a mother.

Rainbow's plan to play shinny with Prairie Falcon and Crow was part of a scheme to encompass their destruction, over which he had pondered for some time. He went to the ground where the game was to be played and dug holes into which he put boiling pitch.

Meantime Rainbow and his companions had interviewed Prairie Falcon and Crow and set the time for the game. "We are going to play shinny in about two days," they said. "You can make yourself a stick and ball."

Then Prairie Falcon, although a male, made a nest and laid eggs to use for balls. He took one of his feathers to use as a stick to play shinny. When the time to play came, he told Rainbow that he had no stick and not even a ball. Rainbow therefore loaned him a stick and a ball, of which he said he had plenty.

They started to play and Rainbow said, "We are going to play two games. These two pines are the goals. We will drive around them twice and then into the hole in the middle between them. If I win, I am going to throw you into that pitch."

Forthwith Rainbow drove his ball around once, whereupon he boasted, "One more round and I am going to beat you." When Rainbow got half way around again, Prairie Falcon produced his own ball and stick and drove ahead of him.

Rainbow said, "We are even."

It was now Prairie Falcon's turn to boast and he said, "One more round and I am going to beat you." Just about the time that Prairie Falcon was nearing the finishing hole, Walking Skeleton put in an appearance and chased the players about. She caught Rainbow and threw him into her basket. Immediately it became so foggy that no one could see. Prairie Falcon and his brother-in-law had to send for Great Horned Owl (muhu) to make daylight.

Great Horned Owl came to Prairie Falcon and Crow and asked, "What do you want?"

"We want daylight so that we can see where we are going in order that Walking Skeleton may not catch us," they said. They asked Great Horned Owl how he was going to make daylight.

He replied, "I am going to say, 'Who are you (Ca hage)?'" He said it and made daylight.

Then Prairie Falcon and Crow proceeded homeward. After arriving at home, they went hunting and again encountered Walking Skeleton.

The following day they went out to get Prairie Falcon's mother, Wild Turkey. She was nearly starved to death and they had to put wooden legs on her, to replace her real legs, which had been cut off. As they were accompanying her, Walking Skeleton came up and gave chase. She caught Wild Turkey without difficulty, because she could not run. Then she pursued the two men.

They said to her, "Let us jump into your basket ourselves."

"All right," she said. Then they jumped into the basket. They made fire with a buckeye fire-drill.

Prairie Falcon said, "I dislike burning my mother," for she was stuck in the pitch in the basket, "but she would have died anyway if I had not taken her from Rain-bow's place." Then he told Crow to make the fire, saying, "I am going to get my mother's heart and eat it while you are making that fire."

Crow remonstrated with him, "Do not do that."

Prairie Falcon asked, "Why should I not do that?"

His brother-in-law answered, "You will turn into a rock if you eat your mother's heart." Prairie Falcon persisted and said that he was going to eat it, to see if he did turn into a rock.

His mother was already dead, so he took her heart and ate it. Prairie Falcon died when he ate that heart. His brother-in-law, Crow, did not know what to do, for Prairie Falcon had turned into a little bag of feathers. Crow made the fire, as Prairie Falcon had directed, and burned Walking Skeleton. Then he jumped out of Walking Skeleton's burden basket with the little bag of feathers and took it home to Prairie Falcon's sister. When Prairie Falcon's sister took the bag of feathers, it turned into eggs and shinny stick. She threw the stick into the fire. When all but an inch or two of it had burned, Prairie Falcon popped out and flew around the house.

He said, "You people are burning me. You awakened me. I was sound asleep." Then Prairie Falcon became furious and uncontrollable. They could not catch him, as he dashed wildly about the house. His sister made a carrying cradle and finally did catch him and lashed him into it. Then they stood him against a tree, thinking that he would grow as tall as the tree. However, before he grew as tall as the tree, his mother Wild Turkey untied him. It seems that she was in the basket with him. From her heart, which he had eaten, she had been formed anew, after Prairie Falcon had been tied in the carrying cradle.

After Prairie Falcon had been freed by his mother, she said to him, "I am going to get you a brother. Would you prefer Eagle or Vulture?" Prairie Falcon objected to both, saying, "They are both bald-headed. I do not want either of them for my brother." Mean-while his brother-in-law Crow was listening behind the tree and almost bursting with laughter.

While this conversation was going on, Salamander came along with a cane made of a king snake. Prairie Falcon jumped up and seized his cane, saying, "Give me that cane of yours." So Salamander parted with his king-snake cane. Immediately the cane turned into a large and active king snake, which bit Prairie Falcon, so that he died.

That was the last of Prairie Falcon. Crow, his brother-in-law, went across the mountains, where he fell into a large lake and was drowned. Prairie Falcon's mother, Wild Turkey, caught a gopher snake, which she tied about herself as a belt and which squeezed her to death. Eagle came along to carry away the body of Prairie Falcon's mother, but she turned into Vulture. She said that she was going to get Prairie Falcon's body and eat his heart, but Eagle would not let her. Eagle killed her.

Glossary

anecdote: Single episode narrative, regarded as true and commonly concentrating on an individual

animal tale: Narratives told as conscious fictions in which the characters, though they speak and behave like human beings, are animals. These animal characters are commonly stock types. For example, in many Native American traditions, Coyote is regarded as an exploitive, impulsive manipulator. In African American tales, Rabbit is typecast in the same role. The tales are most often moralistic ("don't be greedy") or etiological (why the frog has no tail) in intent.

belief tales: Legends or personal experience narratives that are told with the purpose of validating a particular folk belief.

culture hero: Character in myth who finishes the work that brings technology (usually symbolized as fire), laws, religion, and other elements of culture to humans. Culture heroes may take over the business of creating order out of chaos where a Supreme Creator left off. Therefore, the culture hero serves as a secondary creator or transformer of the universe. The culture hero transforms the universe by means of gifts into a universe in which humans can live. In some myths, the culture hero cleanses the universe of those things which threaten human existence: monsters, cannibals, or meteorological phenomena.

fable: Fictional narrative ending with a didactic message that is often couched in the form of a "moral" or proverb.

family saga: Chronologically and often thematically linked collection of legends constituting the folk history of a particular family, usually over several generations. The term was coined by folklorist Mody Coggin Boatright.

formulaic: Refers to conventional elements that recur in folk narrative. Examples include clichés, structural patterns, and stock characters or situations.

framing: The act of setting apart a traditional performance from other types of activity by words, occasions of performance, or other distinguishing features.

genre: Type or category

legend: Narrative told as truth and set in the historical past, which does not depart from the present reality of the members of the group

local legend: Legends derived from and closely associated with specific places and events believed to have occurred in those locales

motif: Small element of traditional narrative content; an event, object, concept, or pattern

myth: Narratives that explain the will (or intent) and the workings (or orderly principles) of a group's major supernatural figures. Myth is set in a world which predates the present reality.

natural context: Setting, in all its elements, in which a performance would ordinarily take place.

numskull: Character who behaves in an absurdly ignorant fashion, also called "noodle."

ordinary folktale: Highly formulaic and structured fictional narrative that is popularly referred to as "fairytale" and designated by folklorists as *märchen* or "wonder tale." Term coined by folklorist Stith Thompson

personal experience narrative: First-person narrative intended as truth

personal legend: Narrative intended as truth told about a specific (usually well-known) individual

stock character: Recurrent narrative character who invariably plays a stereotyped role such as trickster or fool

tale type: Standard, recurrent folk narrative plot

tall tale: Fictional narrative often told as a first-hand experience, which gradually introduces hyperbole until it becomes so great that the audience realizes the tale is a lie

trickster: Characters who defy the limits of propriety and often gender and species. Tricksters live on the margins of their worlds by their wits and are often regarded as possessing supernatural powers. Often a mythic figure such as Coyote or Hare will function as both culture hero and trickster.

validating device: Any element occurring within a traditional narrative that is intended to convince listeners that the tale is true.

variant: Version of a standard tale type

Bibliography to Volume III

Angermiller, Florence. "Interview of Jack Robert Grigsby." American Life Histories: Manuscripts from the Federal Writers' Project, 1936–1940. Manuscript Division, Library of Congress. 12 October 2005. http://memory.loc.gov/ammem/wpaintro/wpahome.html.

Batchler, E.V. "Interview of E. V. Batchler." American Life Histories: Manuscripts from the Federal Writers' Project, 1936–1940. Manuscript Division, Library of Congress.12 October 2005. http://memory.loc.gov/ammem/wpaintro/wpahome.html.

Beckwith, Martha Warren. *Hawaiian Mythology*. New Haven: Yale University Press, 1940.

Boatright, Mody Coggin. *Mody Boatright, Folklorist: A Collection of Essays*. Austin: University of Texas Press, 1973.

Bourke, John G. "Notes on Apache Mythology" *Journal of American Folklore* 3 (1890): 209–12.

———. "Popular Medicines, Customs and Superstitions of the Rio Grande." *Journal of American Folklore* 7(1894): 119–46.

Bowman, Earl. "Interview of Harry Reece." American Life Histories: Manuscripts from the Federal Writers' Project, 1936–1940. Manuscript Division, Library of Congress.12 October 2005. http://memory.loc.gov/ammem/wpaintro/wpahome.html.

Bushotter, George, and J. Owen Dorsey. "A Teton Dakota Ghost Story." *Journal of American Folklore* 1 (1888): 68–72.

Cushing, Frank Hamilton. "A Zuni Folk-tale of the Underworld." *Journal of American Folklore* 5 (1892): 49–56.

Davis, Nita. "Interview of Bill Holcomb." American Life Histories: Manuscripts from the Federal Writers' Project, 1936–1940. Manuscript

Division, Library of Congress. 12 October 2005.
http://memory.loc.gov/ammem/wpaintro/wpahome.html.

———. "Interview of Dick McDonald." American Life Histories: Manuscripts from the Federal Writers' Project, 1936–1940. Manuscript Division, Library of Congress. 12 October 2005.
http://memory.loc.gov/ammem/wpaintro/wpahome.html.

Dixon, Roland B. "Achomawi and Atsugewi Tales." Journal of American Folklore 21 (1908): 159–77.

———. Oceanic Mythology. Boston: Marshall Jones, 1916.

———. "Some Coyote Stories from the Maidu Indians of California." Journal of American Folklore 13 (1900): 267–68.

Dorsey, George A. "Legend of the Teton Sioux Medicine Pipe." Journal of American Folklore 19 (1906): 326–29.

———. The Mythology of the Wichita. Norman, OK: The University of Oklahoma Press, 1995.

———. "The Two Boys Who Slew the Monsters and Became Stars." Journal of American Folklore 17 (1904): 153–60.

———. "Wichita Tales. 1. Origin." Journal of American Folklore 15 (1902): 215–39.

Doyle, Elizabeth. "Interview of Mollie Privett." American Life Histories: Manuscripts from the Federal Writers' Project, 1936–1940. Manuscript Division, Library of Congress. 12 October 2005.
http://memory.loc.gov/ammem/wpaintro/wpahome.html.

Emery, W. M. "Interview of Jack Zurich." American Life Histories: Manuscripts from the Federal Writers' Project, 1936–1940. Manuscript Division, Library of Congress. 12 October 2005.
http://memory.loc.gov/ammem/wpaintro/wpahome.html.

Espinosa, Aurelio. The Folklore of Spain in the American Southwest: Traditional Spanish Folk Literature in Northern New Mexico and Southern Colorado. Edited by J. Manuel Espinosa. Norman: University of Oklahoma Press, 1985.

———. "New Mexican Spanish Folklore." Journal of American Folklore 223 (1910): 345–418.

Farrer, Claire. Thunder Rides a Black Horse: Mescalero Apaches and the Mythic Present. 2nd edition. Prospect Heights, IL: Waveland Press, 1996.

Fewkes, J. Walter. "The Destruction of the Tusayan Monsters." Journal of American Folklore 8 (1895): 132–137.

Fife, Austin E. "The Legend of the Three Nephites Among the Mormons." Journal of American Folklore 53 (1940): 1–49.

Fornander, Abraham. *Fornander Collection of Hawaiian Antiquities and Folk-lore.* 3 vols. Honolulu: Bernice Pauahi Bishop Museum, 1916/1917–1919/1920.

Gatschet, Albert S. "Report of a Visit to Jack Wilson, the Payute Messiah." *Journal of American Folklore* 6 (1893): 108–11.

Gayton, A. H., and Stanley S. Newman. *Yokuts and Western Mono Myths.* Millwood, NY: Kraus, 1976.

Gibson, Robert O. *The Chumash.* New York: Chelsea House, 1991.

Gifford, Edward Winslow. "Western Mono Myths." *Journal of American Folklore* 36 (1923): 301–67.

Grinell, George Bird. "Pawnee Mythology." *Journal of American Folklore* 6 (1893): 113–30.

"Interview of Bones Hooks." American Life Histories: Manuscripts from the Federal Writers' Project, 1936–1940. Manuscript Division, Library of Congress. 12 October 2005. http://memory.loc.gov/ammem/wpaintro/wpa-home.html.

James, George Wharton. "A Saboba Origin Myth." *Journal of American Folklore* 15 (1902): 36–39.

Kawaharada, Dennis. *Ancient Oahu: Stories from Fornander & Thrum.* Honolulu: Kalamaku Press, 2001.

Knox, Robert H. "A Blackfoot Version of the Magical Flight." *Journal of American Folklore* 36 (1923): 401–3.

Kroeber, Kroeber, Alfred L. "Cheyenne Tales." *Journal of American Folklore* 13 (1900): 161–90.

———. *Handbook of the Indians of California.* Smithsonian Institution Bureau of American Ethnology Bulletin 78. Washington, DC: U.S. Government Printing Office, 1925.

———. "Ute Tales." *Journal of American Folklore* 14 (1901): 252–85.

Kroeber, Henriette Rothschild. "Papago Coyote Tales." *Journal of American Folklore* 22 (1909): 339–42.

Lowie, Robert H. "Shoshonean Tales." *Journal of American Folklore* 37 (1924): 1–242.

Lummis, Charles. *Pueblo Indian Folk-Stories.* New York: Century, 1910.

Matthews, Washington. "A Folk-tale of the Hidatsa Indians." *The Folklore Record* 1 (1878): 136–43.

———. *Navajo Legends.* Memoirs of the American Folklore Society 5. New York: American Folklore Society, 1897.

———. "Noqoìlpi, the Gambler: A Navajo Myth." *Journal of American Folklore* 2 (1889): 89–94.

Parsons, Elsie Clews. *Kiowa Tales*. Memoirs of the American Folklore Society 22. New York: American Folklore Society, 1929.

———. "Pueblo Indian Folk-tales, Probably of Spanish Provenience." *Journal of American Folklore* 31 (1918): 216–55.

———. *Tewa Tales*. Memoirs of the American Folklore Society 19. New York: American Folklore Society, 1926.

Phipps, Woody. "Interview of Robert Lindsey." American Life Histories: Manuscripts from the Federal Writers' Project, 1936–1940. Manuscript Division, Library of Congress. 12 October 2005. http://memory.loc.gov/ammem/wpaintro/wpahome.html.

Russell, Frank. "Myths of the Jicarilla Apaches." *Journal of American Folklore* 11 (1898): 253–71.

Sapir, Jean. "Yurok Tales." *Journal of American Folklore* 41 (1928): 253–61.

Smith, Janet. "Interview of Elfego Baca." American Life Histories: Manuscripts from the Federal Writers' Project, 1936–1940. Manuscript Division, Library of Congress. 12 October 2005. http://memory.loc.gov/ammem/wpaintro/wpahome.html.

Sparkman, P. S. "Notes of California Folklore: A Luiseño Tale." *Journal of American Folklore* 21 (1908): 35–36.

St. Clair, H. H., and R. H. Lowie. "Shoshone and Comanche Tales." *Journal of American Folklore* 22 (1909): 265–282.

Stewart, Omer C. *The Northern Paiute Bands*. Millwood, NY: Kraus, 1976.

Stirling, Matthew W. *Origin Myth of Acoma and Other Records*. Smithsonian Institution Bureau of American Ethnology Bulletin 135. Washington, DC: U.S. Government Printing Office, 1942.

Strong, William D. *University of California Publications in American Archaeology and Ethnology*. Vol. 26, *Aboriginal Society in Southern California*. Berkeley: University of California Press, 1929.

Tejada, Simeon. "Interview of Manuel Jesus Vasques." American Life Histories: Manuscripts from the Federal Writers' Project, 1936–1940. Manuscript Division, Library of Congress. 12 October 2005. http://memory.loc.gov/ammem/wpaintro/wpahome.html.

Totty, Francis. "Interview of Maurice Coates." American Life Histories: Manuscripts from the Federal Writers' Project, 1936–1940. Manuscript Division, Library of Congress. 12 October 2005. http://memory.loc.gov/ammem/wpaintro/wpahome.html.

Townsend, Edward. "Interview of A. Harry Williams." American Life Histories: Manuscripts from the Federal Writers' Project, 1936–1940.

Manuscript Division, Library of Congress. 16 October 2005. http://memory.loc.gov/ammem/wpaintro/wpahome.html.

Walden, Wayne. "Interview of Annette Hamilton." American Life Histories: Manuscripts from the Federal Writers' Project, 1936–1940. Manuscript Division, Library of Congress. 16 October 2005. http://memory.loc.gov/ammem/wpaintro/wpahome.html.

———. "Interview of Mrs. R. Ivanoff." American Life Histories: Manuscripts from the Federal Writers' Project, 1936–1940. Manuscript Division, Library of Congress. 12 October 2005. http://memory.loc.gov/ammem/wpaintro/wpahome.html.

Weigle, Martha, and Peter White. The Lore of New Mexico. Albuquerque: University of New Mexico Press, 1988.

West, John O. Mexican-American Folklore. Little Rock, AR: August House, 1988.

Westervelt, W. D. Hawaiian Legends of Ghosts and Ghost-Gods. Boston: Ellis Press, 1916.

———. Hawaiian Legends of Old Honolulu. Boston: G. H. Ellis Press, 1915.

———. Hawaiian Legends of Volcanoes. Boston: G. H. Ellis Press, 1916.

Will, George F. "No-Tongue, A Mandan Tale." Journal of American Folklore 26 (1913): 331–37.

———. "The Story of No-Tongue." Journal of American Folklore 29 (1916): 402–6.

Wissler, Clark. "Some Dakota Myths." Part 1. Journal of American Folklore 20 (1907): 121–31.

———. "Some Dakota Myths." Part 2. Journal of American Folklore 20 (1907): 195–206.

N.A. "Witchcraft in New Mexico." Journal of American Folklore 1 (1888): 167–68.

Wrenn, Sarah B. "Interview of Annie Cason Lee." American Life Histories: Manuscripts from the Federal Writers' Project, 1936–1940. Manuscript Division, Library of Congress. 11 October 2005. http://memory.loc.gov/ammem/wpaintro/wpahome.html.

General Bibliography

Aarne, Antti, and Stith Thompson. *The Types of the Folktale: A Classification and Bibliography.* 2nd rev. ed. Folklore Fellows Communications 184. Helsinki: Academia Scientiarum Fennica, 1964.

Aaron, Abe. "Interview of Cab Drivers." American Life Histories: Manuscripts from the Federal Writers' Project, 1936–1940. Manuscript Division, Library of Congress. 12 October 2005. http://memory.loc.gov/ammem/wpaintro/wpahome.html.

Abrahams, Roger D., ed. *African American Folktales: Stories from Black Traditions in the New World.* New York: Pantheon, 1985.

———. *The Man-of-Words in the West Indies.* Baltimore: Johns Hopkins University Press, 1983.

Alaska Judicial Council. "Resolving Disputes Locally: A Statewide Report and Directory." Alaska Judicial Council. 9 December 2005. http://www.ajc.state.ak.us/index.htm.

Algren, Nelson. "Interview of Davey Day." American Life Histories: Manuscripts from the Federal Writers' Project, 1936–1940. Manuscript Division, Library of Congress. 11 November 2005. http://memory.loc.gov/ammem/wpaintro/wpahome.html.

Allen, Barbara, and Thomas Schlereth. *A Sense of Place: American Regional Cultures.* Lexington: University Press of Kentucky, 1990.

Ancelet, Barry Jean. "The Cajun Who Went to Harvard: Identity in the Oral Tradition of South Louisiana." *The Journal of Popular Culture* 23 (1989): 101–15.

Angermiller, Florence. "Interview of Jack Robert Grigsby." American Life Histories: Manuscripts from the Federal Writers' Project, 1936–1940. Manuscript Division, Library of Congress. 12 October 2005. http://memory.loc.gov/ammem/wpaintro/wpahome.html.

Bacon, A. M., and E. C. Parsons. "Folk-Lore from Elizabeth City County, Virginia." *Journal of American Folklore* 35 (1922): 250–327.

Backus, Emma M. "Animal Tales from North Carolina." *Journal of American Folklore* 11 (1898): 284–92.

———. "Folk-Tales from Georgia." *Journal of American Folklore* 13 (1900): 19–32.

———. "Tales of the Rabbit from Georgia Negroes." *Journal of American Folklore* 12 (1899): 108–15.

Backus, Emma M., and Ethel Hatton Leitner. "Negro Tales from Georgia." *Journal of American Folklore* 25 (1912): 125–36.

Baker, Ronald L. *Hoosier Folk Legends*. Bloomington: Indiana University Press, 1982.

Balilci, Asen. *The Netsilik Eskimo*. Garden City, NY: Natural History Press, 1970.

Banister, Manly Andrew C. "Interview of James E. Twadell." American Life Histories: Manuscripts from the Federal Writers' Project, 1936–1940. Manuscript Division, Library of Congress. 12 October 2005. http://memory.loc.gov/ammem/wpaintro/wpahome.html.

Barden, Thomas E., ed. *Virginia Folk Legends*. Charlottesville: University Press of Virginia, 1991.

Bates, William C. "Creole Folk-Lore from Jamaica II: Nancy Stories." *Journal of American Folklore* 9 (1896): 121–28.

Baughman, Ernest W. *Type- and Motif-Index of the Folk Tales of England and North America*. The Hague: Mouton, 1966.

Beauchamp, W. M. "Onondaga Tales." *Journal of American Folklore* 6 (1893): 173–89.

Beck, Horace. *Gluskap the Liar and Other Indian Tales*. Freeport, ME: Bond Wheelright, 1966.

Beckwith, Martha Warren. *Hawaiian Mythology*. New Haven: Yale University Press, 1940.

———. *Jamaica Anansi Stories*. New York: American Folklore Society, 1924.

"Beliefs of Southern Negroes Concerning Hags." *Journal of American Folklore* 7 (1894): 66–67.

Bergen, Fanny D. "Borrowing Trouble." *Journal of American Folklore* 11 (1898): 55–59.

———. "On the Eastern Shore." *Journal of American Folklore* 2 (1889): 295–300.

———. "Two Witch Stories." *Journal of American Folklore* 12 (1899): 68–69.

Bierhorst, John, ed. *White Deer and Other Stories Told by the Lenape.* New York: W. Morrow, 1995.

Boas, Franz. *Chinook Texts.* Smithsonian Institution Bureau of American Ethnology Bulletin 20. Washington, DC: U.S. Government Printing Office, 1894.

———. "Notes on the Eskimo of Port Clarence, Alaska." *Journal of American Folklore* 7 (1894): 205–8.

———. "Traditions of the Ts'ets'ā´ut I." *Journal of American Folklore* 9 (1896): 257–68.

———. "Traditions of the Ts'ets'ā´ut II." *Journal of American Folklore* 10 (1897): 35–48.

Boatright, Mody Coggin. *Mody Boatright, Folklorist: A Collection of Essays.* Edited by Ernest B. Speck. Austin: University of Texas Press, 1973.

Botkin, Benjamin A. *A Treasury of American Folklore: The Stories, Legends, Tall Tales, Traditions, Ballads and Songs of the American People.* New York: Crown, 1944.

———. *A Treasury of New England Folklore.* New York: Crown, 1944.

Bourke, John G. "Notes on Apache Mythology." *Journal of American Folklore* 3 (1890): 209–12.

———. "Popular Medicines, Customs and Superstitions of the Rio Grande." *Journal of American Folklore* 7 (1894): 119–46.

Bowman, Earl. "Interview of Harry Reece." American Life Histories: Manuscripts from the Federal Writers' Project, 1936–1940. Manuscript Division, Library of Congress. 12 October 2005. http://memory.loc.gov/ammem/wpaintro/wpahome.html.

———. "Interview of William D. Naylor." American Life Histories: Manuscripts from the Federal Writers' Project, 1936–1940. Manuscript Division, Library of Congress. 12 October 2005. http://memory.loc.gov/ammem/wpaintro/wpahome.html.

Brendle, Thomas R., and William S. Troxell. *Pennsylvania German Folk Tales, Legends, Once-upon-a-time Stories, Maxims, and Sayings.* Norristown: Pennsylvania German Society, 1944.

Bullock, Mrs. Walter R. "The Collection of Maryland Folklore." *Journal of American Folklore* 11 (1898): 7–16.

Bunter, Rosa. "Ghosts as Guardians of Hidden Treasure." *Journal of American Folklore* 12 (1899): 64–65.

Burrows, Elizabeth. "Eskimo Tales." *Journal of American Folklore* 39 (1926): 79–81.

Bushotter, George, and J. Owen Dorsey. "A Teton Dakota Ghost Story." *Journal of American Folklore* 1 (1888): 68–72.

Byrd, Frank. "Interview of Leroy Spriggs." American Life Histories: Manuscripts from the Federal Writers' Project, 1936–1940. Manuscript Division, Library of Congress. 12 October 2005. http://memory.loc.gov/ammem/wpaintro/wpahome.html.

Carey, George. *Maryland Folklore.* Centreville, MD: Tidewater Publishers, 1989.

Carter, Isabel Gordon. "Mountain White Folk-Lore: Tales from the Southern Blue Ridge." *Journal of American Folklore* 38 (1925): 340–74.

Chance, Norman A. *The Eskimo of North Alaska.* New York: Holt, Rinehart and Winston, 1966.

Chase, Richard. "Jack and the Fire Dragaman." *The Southern Folklore Quarterly* 5 (1941): 151–55.

———. "The Lion and the Unicorn." *The Southern Folklore Quarterly* 1 (1937): 15–19.

Claudel, Calvin. "Louisiana Tales of Jean Sot and Boqui and Lapin." *Southern Folklore Quarterly* 8 (1944): 287–99.

Claudel, Calvin, and J.-M. Carrier. "Three Tales from the French Folklore of Louisiana." *Journal of American Folklore* 56 (1943): 38–44.

Clough, Ben C. "Legends of Chappaquiddick." *Journal of American Folklore* 31 (1918): 553–54.

Comhaire-Sylvain, Suzanne. "Creole Tales from Haiti." *Journal of American Folklore* 50 (1937): 207–95.

Conant, L. "English Folktales in America: The Three Brothers and the Hag." *Journal of American Folklore* 8 (1895): 143–44.

Cooke, Elizabeth Johnston. "English Folk-Tales in America. The Bride of the Evil One." *Journal of American Folklore* 12 (1899): 126–30.

Cross, Tom Peete. "Folk-Lore from the Southern States." *Journal of American Folklore* 22 (1909): 251–55.

Currier, John McNab. "Contributions to the Folk-Lore of New England." *Journal of American Folklore* 2 (1889): 291–93.

Curtin, Jeremiah. "European Folklore in the United States." *Journal of American Folklore* 2 (1889): 56–59.

———. *Seneca Indian Myths.* New York: W.P. Dutton, 1922. Reprint, New York: Dover, 2001.

Cushing, Frank Hamilton. "A Zuni Folk-tale of the Underworld." *Journal of American Folklore* 5 (1892): 49–56.

Davis, Nita. "Interview of Bill Holcomb." American Life Histories: Manuscripts from the Federal Writers' Project, 1936–1940. Manuscript Division, Library of Congress. 12 October 2005. http://memory.loc.gov/ammem/wpaintro/wpahome.html.

———. "Interview of Dick McDonald." American Life Histories: Manuscripts from the Federal Writers' Project, 1936–1940. Manuscript Division, Library of Congress. 12 October 2005. http://memory.loc.gov/ammem/wpaintro/wpahome.html.

Deans, James. "The Doom of the Katt-a-quins: From the Aboriginal Folk-lore of Southern Alaska." *Journal of American Folklore* 5 (1892): 232–35.

Dixon, Roland B. "Achomawi and Atsugewi Tales." *Journal of American Folklore* 21 (1908): 159–77.

———. *Oceanic Mythology*. Boston: Marshall Jones, 1916.

———. "Some Coyote Stories from the Maidu Indians of California" *Journal of American Folklore* 13 (1900): 270.

Dorsey, George A. "Legend of the Teton Sioux Medicine Pipe." *Journal of American Folklore* 19 (1906): 326–29.

———. *The Mythology of the Wichita*. Norman: University of Oklahoma Press, 1995.

———. "The Two Boys Who Slew the Monsters and Became Stars." *Journal of American Folklore* 17 (1904): 153–60.

———. "Wichita Tales. 1. Origin." *Journal of American Folklore* 15 (1902): 215–39.

Dorsey, J. Owen. "Abstracts of Omaha and Ponka Myths, II." *Journal of American Folklore* 1 (1888): 204–8.

———. "Omaha Folklore Notes." *Journal of American Folklore* 1 (1888): 313–14.

———. "Two Biloxi Tales." *Journal of American Folklore* 6 (1893): 48–50.

Dorson, Richard M. *American Folklore*. Chicago: University of Chicago Press, 1959.

———. *Bloodstoppers and Bearwalkers*. Cambridge, MA: Harvard University Press, 1952.

———. *Buying the Wind: Regional Folklore in the United States*. Chicago: University of Chicago Press, 1964.

Douglas, Sir George. "The Witty Exploits of Mr. George Buchanan, the King's Fool." *Scottish Fairy and Folktales*. New York: A.L. Burt Company, 1901.

Doyle, Elizabeth. "Interview of Mollie Privett." *American Life Histories: Manuscripts from the Federal Writers' Project, 1936–1940.* Manuscript Division, Library of Congress. 12 October 2005. http://memory.loc.gov/ammem/wpaintro/wpahome.html

Dubois, Sylvie, and Barbara M. Horvath. "Creoles and Cajuns: A Portrait in Black and White." *American Speech* 78 (2003): 192–207.

Dubois, Sylvie, and Megan Melançon. "Creole Is; Creole Ain't: Diachronic and Synchronic Attitudes Toward Creole French Identity in Southern Louisiana." *Language in Society* 29 (2000): 237–58.

Edwards, Charles L. *Bahama Songs and Stories.* Memoirs of the American Folklore Society 3. New York: American Folklore Society, 1895.

———. "Some Tales from Bahama Folk-Lore." *Journal of American Folklore* 4 (1891): 47–54.

———. "Some Tales from Bahama Folk-Lore: Fairy Stories." *Journal of American Folklore* 4 (1891): 247–52.

Emery, W. M. "Interview of Jack Zurich." *American Life Histories: Manuscripts from the Federal Writers' Project, 1936–1940.* Manuscript Division, Library of Congress. 12 October 2005. http://memory.loc.gov/ammem/wpaintro/wpahome.html.

Espinosa, Aurelio. *The Folklore of Spain in the American Southwest: Traditional Spanish Folk Literature in Northern New Mexico and Southern Colorado.* Edited by J. Manuel Espinosa. Norman: University of Oklahoma Press, 1985.

———. "New Mexican Spanish Folklore." *Journal of American Folklore* 223 (1910): 345–418.

Farrand, Livingston, and Leo J. Frachtenberg. "Shasta and Athapascan Myths from Oregon." *Journal of American Folklore* 28 (1915): 207–42.

Farrer, Claire. *Thunder Rides a Black Horse: Mescalero Apaches and the Mythic Present.* 2nd ed. Prospect Heights, IL: Waveland Press, 1996.

Fauset, Arthur Huff. "Negro Folk Tales from the South (Alabama, Mississippi, Louisiana)." *Journal of American Folklore* 40 (1927): 213–303.

Fewkes, J. Walter. "A Contribution to Passamoquoddy Folklore." *Journal of American Folklore* 3 (1890): 257–80.

———. "The Destruction of the Tusayan Monsters." *Journal of American Folklore* 8 (1895): 132–37.

Fife, Austin E. "The Legend of the Three Nephites Among the Mormons." *Journal of American Folklore* 53 (1940): 1–49.

Fischer, David Hackett. *Albion's Seed: Four British Folkways in America.* New York: Oxford University Press, 1989.

Fletcher, Alice C. "Glimpses of Child-Life Among the Omaha Indians."
Journal of American Folklore 1 (1888): 115–23.

Fornander, Abraham. *Fornander Collection of Hawaiian Antiquities and Folk-lore.*
3 vols. Honolulu: Bernice Pauahi Bishop Museum, 1916/1917–1919/1920.

Fortier, Alcee. "Louisianian Nursery-Tales." *Journal of American Folklore* 1
(1888): 140–45.

Frachtenberg, Leo J. *Coos Texts.* Columbia University Contributions to
Anthropology 1. New York: Columbia University Press, 1913.

———. "Myths of the Alsea Indians of Northwestern Oregon." *International
Journal of American Linguistics* 1 (1917): 64–75.

Gard, Robert E., and L. G. Sorden. *Wisconsin Lore: Antics and Anecdotes of
Wisconsin People and Places.* New York: Duell, Sloan and Pearce, 1962.

Gardner, Emelyn E. "Folk-Lore from Schoharie County, New York." *Journal of
American Folklore* 27 (1914): 304–25.

Gatschet, Albert S. "Oregonian Folklore." *Journal of American Folklore* 4
(1891): 139–43.

———. "Report of a Visit to Jack Wilson, the Payute Messiah." *Journal of
American Folklore* 6 (1893): 108–11.

Gayton, A. H., and Stanley S. Newman. *Yokuts and Western Mono Myths.*
Millwood, NY: Kraus, 1976.

Gibson, Robert O. *The Chumash.* New York: Chelsea House, 1991.

Gifford, Edward Winslow. "Western Mono Myths." *Journal of American Folklore*
36 (1923): 301–67.

Glimm, James York. *Flatlanders and Ridgerunners: Folk Tales from the Mountains
of Northern Pennsylvania.* Pittsburgh: University of Pittsburgh Press, 1983.

Golder, F. A. "Aleutian Stories." *Journal of American Folklore* 18 (1905):
215–22.

Green, Archie. *Calf's Head and Union Tale: Labor Yarns at Work and Play.*
Urbana: University of Illinois Press, 1996.

Grinell, George Bird. "Pawnee Mythology." *Journal of American Folkore* 6
(1893): 113–30.

Haight, Willliam C. "Interview of Charles Imus." American Life Histories:
Manuscripts from the Federal Writers' Project, 1936–1940. Manuscript
Division, Library of Congress. 14 October 2005.
http://memory.loc.gov/ammem/wpaintro/wpahome.html.

Hale, Horatio. "Huron Folklore I: Cosmogonic Myth, The Good and Evil
Minds." *Journal of American Folklore* 1 (1888): 177–83.

———. "Huron Folklore II: The Story of Tihaiha, the Sorceror." *Journal of
American Folklore* 2 (1889): 249–54.

————. "Huron Folklore III: The Legend of the Thunderers." *Journal of American Folklore* 4 (1891): 189–94.

Hall, Julien A. "Negro Conjuring and Tricking." *Journal of American Folklore* 10 (1897): 241–43.

Halpert, Herbert. *Folktales and Legends from the New Jersey Pines: A Collection and a Study.* Bloomington: Indiana University Press, 1947.

————. "Pennsylvania Fairylore and Folktales." *Journal of American Folklore* 58 (1945): 130–34.

Harper, Francis. "Tales of the Okefinoke." *American Speech* 1 (1926): 407–20.

Hartman, George. "Interview of Ed Grantham." American Life Histories: Manuscripts from the Federal Writers' Project, 1936–1940. Manuscript Division, Library of Congress. 12 October 2005. http://memory.loc.gov/ammem/wpaintro/wpahome.html.

————. "Interview of E. O. Skeidler." American Life Histories: Manuscripts from the Federal Writers' Project, 1936–1940. Manuscript Division, Library of Congress. 18 October 2005. http://memory.loc.gov/ammem/wpaintro/wpahome.html.

Hayward, Silvanus. "English Folktales in America II." *Journal of American Folklore* 3 (1890): 291–95.

Henning, D. C. "Tales of the Blue Mountains in Pennsylvania." *Miners' Journal* (Pottsdam, PA), March 26, 1897.

Herrick, Mrs. R. F. "The Black Dog of the Blue Ridge." *Journal of American Folklore* 20 (1907): 151–52.

Hoffman, W. J. "Folklore of the Pennsylvania Germans III." *Journal of American Folklore* 2 (1889): 191–202.

Hubert, Levi. "Interview of Joseph Madden." American Life Histories: Manuscripts from the Federal Writers' Project, 1936–1940. Manuscript Division, Library of Congress. 12 October 2005. http://memory.loc.gov/ammem/wpaintro/wpahome.html.

————. "Interview of Mary Thomas." American Life Histories: Manuscripts from the Federal Writers' Project, 1936–1940. Manuscript Division, Library of Congress. 12 October 2005. http://memory.loc.gov/ammem/wpaintro/wpahome.html.

Hudson, Arthur Palmer, and Pete Kyle McCarter. "The Bell Witch of Tennessee and Mississippi: A Folk Legend." *Journal of American Folklore* 47 (1934): 46–58.

Hufford, David. *The Terror That Comes in the Night: An Experience-Centered Study of Supernatural Assault Traditions.* Philadelphia: University of Pennsylvania Press, 1982.

Hurston, Zora Neale. "Dance Songs and Tales from the Bahamas." *Journal of American Folklore* 43 (1930): 294–312.

"Interview of Bones Hooks." American Life Histories: Manuscripts from the Federal Writers' Project, 1936–1940. Manuscript Division, Library of Congress. 12 October 2005. http://memory.loc.gov/ammem/wpaintro/wpa-home.html.

"Interview of E. V. Batchler." American Life Histories: Manuscripts from the Federal Writers' Project, 1936–1940. Manuscript Division, Library of Congress. 12 October 2005. http://memory.loc.gov/ammem/wpaintro/wpa-home.html.

"The Irishman and the Pumpkin." *Journal of American Folklore* 12 (1899): 226.

Jack, Edward. "Maliseet Legends." *Journal of American Folklore* 8 (1895): 193–208.

James, George Wharton. "A Saboba Origin Myth." *Journal of American Folklore* 15 (1902): 36–39.

Jarreau, Lafayette, "Creole Folklore of Pointe Coupee Parish." MA thesis, Louisiana State University, 1931.

Jenks, Albert Ernest. "The Bear Maiden: An Ojibwa Folk-Tale from Lac Courte Oreille Reservation, Wisconsin." *Journal of American Folklore* 15 (1902): 33–35.Johnson, Clifton. "The Twist-Mouth Family." *Journal of American Folklore* 18 (1905): 322–23.

Johnson, John H. "Folk-Lore from Antigua, British West Indies." *Journal of American Folklore* 34 (1921): 40–88.

Johnston, Mrs. William Preston. "Two Negro Folktales." *Journal of American Folklore* 9 (1896): 194–98.

Jones, William. "Notes on the Fox Indians." *Journal of American Folklore* 24 (1911): 209–37.

Kamenskii, Annatolii. *Tlingit Indians of Alaska.* Translated and with an introduction and supplementary material by Sergei Kan. Fairbanks: University of Alaska Press, 1985.

Kawaharada, Dennis. *Ancient Oahu: Stories from Fornander & Thrum.* Honolulu: Kalamaku Press, 2001.

Kercheval, George Truman. "An Otoe and an Omaha Tale." *Journal of American Folklore* 6 (1893): 199–204.

Kittredge, George Lyman. "English Folktales in America." *Journal of American Folklore* 3 (1890): 291–95.

Knox, Robert H. "A Blackfoot Version of the Magical Flight." *Journal of American Folklore* 36 (1923): 401–3.

Kroeber, Alfred L. "Cheyenne Tales." *Journal of American Folklore* 13 (1900): 161–90.

———. *Handbook of the Indians of California.* Smithsonian Institution Bureau of American Ethnology Bulletin 78. Washington, DC: U.S. Government Printing Office, 1925.

———. "Tales of the Smith Sound Eskimo." *Journal of American Folklore* 12 (1899): 166–82.

———. "Ute Tales." *Journal of American Folklore* 14 (1901): 252–85.

Kroeber, Henriette Rothschild. "Papago Coyote Tales." *Journal of American Folklore* 22 (1909): 339–42.

Lightfoot, William E. "Regional Folkloristics." *Handbook of American Folklore.* Edited by Richard Dorson. Bloomington: Indiana University Press, 1983.

Lowie, Robert H. "Shoshonean Tales." *Journal of American Folklore* 37 (1924): 1–242.

Lummis, Charles. *Pueblo Indian Folk-Stories.* New York: Century, 1910.

Mallery, Garrick. "The Fight with the Giant Witch." *American Anthropologist* 3 (1890): 65–70.

Matthews, Washington. "A Folk-tale of the Hidatsa Indians." *The Folklore Record* 1 (1878): 136–43.

———. *Navajo Legends.* Memoirs of the American Folklore Society 5. New York: American Folklore Society, 1897.

———. "Noqoìlpi, the Gambler: A Navajo Myth." *Journal of American Folklore* 2 (1889): 89–94.

McHenry, Lawrence. "Interview of Minnie Wycloff." American Life Histories: Manuscripts from the Federal Writers' Project, 1936–1940. Manuscript Division, Library of Congress. 12 October 2005. http://memory.loc.gov/ammem/wpaintro/wpahome.html.

McMahon, William H. *Pine Barrens Legends, Lore, and Lies.* Wilmington, DE: Middle Atlantic Press, 1980.

McNeil, W. K. *Ozark Country.* Oxford: University Press of Mississippi, 1995.

Michaelis, Kate Woodbridge. "An Irish Folktale." *Journal of American Folklore* 23 (1910): 425–28.

Miller, E. Joan Wilson. "Ozark Culture Region as Revealed by Traditional Materials." *Annals of the Association of American Geographers* 58 (1968): 51–77.

Minor, Mary Willis. "How to Keep Off Witches." *Journal of American Folklore* 11 (1898): 76.

Monroe, Grace. "Interview of Middleton Robertson." American Life Histories: Manuscripts from the Federal Writers' Project, 1936–1940. Manuscript

Division, Library of Congress. 12 October 2005.
http://memory.loc.gov/ammem/wpaintro/wpahome.html.

Mooney, James. *James Mooney's History, Myths, and Sacred Formulas of the Cherokees*. Asheville, NC: Historical Images, 1992.

———. "Myths of the Cherokees." *Journal of American Folklore* 1 (1888): 97–108.

———. *"Myths of the Cherokee." Nineteenth Annual Report of the Bureau of American Ethnology 1897–1898, Part I*. Washington, DC: U.S. Government Printing Office, 1900.

———. *"The Sacred Formulas of the Cherokees." Seventh Annual Report of the Bureau of American Ethnology*. Washington, DC: U.S. Government Printing Office, 1891.

Mosley, Ruby. "Interview of Eldora Scott Maples." American Life Histories: Manuscripts from the Federal Writers' Project, 1936–1940. Manuscript Division, Library of Congress. 12 October 2005. http://memory.loc.gov/ammem/wpaintro/wpahome.html.

Newell, William Wells. "English Folktales in America I." *Journal of American Folklore* 1 (1888): 227–34.

———. "English Folk-Tales in America." *Journal of American Folklore* 2 (1889): 213–18.

———. "The Ghost Legends of the Blue Mountains in Pennsylvania." *Journal of American Folklore* 11 (1898):76–78.

———. The Ignus Fatuus, Its Character and Legendary Origin." *Journal of American Folklore* 17 (1904): 39–60.

Oswalt, Wendell H. *Bashful No Longer: An Alaskan Eskimo Ethnohistory 1778–1988*. Norman: University of Oklahoma Press, 1990.

Owen, Mary A. "Ol' Rabbit an' de Dawg He Stole." *Journal of American Folklore* 9 (1890): 135–38.

Paredes, Américo. *With His Pistol in His Hand: A Border Ballad and Its Hero*. Austin: University of Texas Press, 1958.

Parsons, Elsie Clews. "Accumulative Tales Told by Cape Verde Islanders in New England." *Journal of American Folklore* 33 (1920): 34–42.

———. "Barbados Folklore." *Journal of American Folklore* 38 (1925): 267–92.

———. *Folk-Lore of the Sea Islands, South Carolina*. Memoirs of the American Folklore Society 16. New York: American Folklore Society, 1923.

———. *Kiowa Tales*. Memoirs of the American Folklore Society 22. New York: American Folklore Society, 1929.

———. "Pueblo Indian Folk-tales, Probably of Spanish Provenience." *Journal of American Folklore* 31 (1918): 216–55.

405

————. "Tales from Maryland and Pennsylvania." *Journal of American Folklore* 30 (1917): 209–17.

————. "Ten Folktales from the Cape Verde Islands." *Journal of American Folklore* 30 (1917): 230–38.

————. *Tewa Tales.* Memoirs of the American Folklore Society 19. New York: American Folklore Society, 1926.

————. "A West Indian Tale." *Journal of American Folklore* 32 (1919): 442–43.

Phipps, Woody. "Interview of Robert Lindsey." American Life Histories: Manuscripts from the Federal Writers' Project, 1936–1940. Manuscript Division, Library of Congress. 12 October 2005. http://memory.loc.gov/ammem/wpaintro/wpahome.html.

Porter, J. Hampden. "Notes on the Folk-Lore of the Mountain Whites of the Alleghenies." *Journal of American Folklore* 7 (1894): 105–17.

Pound, Louise. *Nebraska Folklore.* Lincoln: University of Nebraska Press, 1959.

Powers, Stephen. "North American Indian Legends and Fables." *Folk-Lore Record* 5 (1882): 93–143. Reprinted from *Contributions to North American Ethnology. Vol. 3, Tribes of California.* Edited by Stephen Powers. Washington, D.C.: U.S. Geographical and Geological Survey Rocky Mountain Region, 1877.

Radin, Paul. "Literary Aspects of Winebago Mythology." *Journal of American Folklore* 39 (1926): 18–52.

Radin, Paul, and A. B. Reagan. "Ojibwa Myths and Tales: The Manabozho Cycle." *Journal of American Folklore* 41 (1928): 61–146

Randolph, Vance. *Hot Springs and Hell; and other Folk Jests and Anecdotes from the Ozarks.* Hatboro, PA: Folklore Associates, 1965.

Rath, Richard Cullen. "Drums and Power: Ways of Creolizing Music in Coastal South Carolina and Georgia, 1730–1790." In *Creolization in the Americas,* edited by David Buisseret and Steven G. Rheinhardt. College Station: University of Texas at Arlington Press, 2000.

Ray, Marie. "Jean Sotte Stories." *Journal of American Folklore* 21 (1908): 364–65.

Rink, H., and Franz Boas. "Eskimo Tales and Songs." *Journal of American Folklore* 2 (1889): 123–31.

Romanofsky, Fred. "Interview of Cabbies." American Life Histories: Manuscripts from the Federal Writers' Project, 1936–1940. Manuscript Division, Library of Congress. 22 October 2005. http://memory.loc.gov/ammem/wpaintro/wpahome.html.

Roth, Terry, and Sam Schwartz. "Interview of Mr. Wollman." American Life Histories: Manuscripts from the Federal Writers' Project, 1936–1940.

Manuscript Division, Library of Congress. 16 October 2005.
http://memory.loc.gov/ammem/wpaintro/wpahome.html.

Russell, Frank. "Myths of the Jicarilla Apaches." *Journal of American Folklore* 11 (1898): 253–71.

Sapir, Jean. "Yurok Tales." *Journal of American Folklore* 41 (1928): 253–61.

"The Sea Tick and the Irishman." *Journal of American Folklore* 12 (1899): 226.

Seip, Elisabeth Cloud. "Witch-Finding in Western Maryland." *Journal of American Folklore* 14 (1901): 39–44.

Sherbert, Andrew C. "Interview of George Estes." American Life Histories: Manuscripts from the Federal Writers' Project, 1936–1940. Manuscript Division, Library of Congress. 12 October 2005.
http://memory.loc.gov/ammem/wpaintro/wpahome.html.

———. "Interview of William Harry Hembree." American Life Histories: Manuscripts from the Federal Writers' Project, 1936–1940. Manuscript Division, Library of Congress. 12 October 2005.
http://memory.loc.gov/ammem/wpaintro/wpahome.html.

Showers, Susan. "Two Negro Stories Concerning the Jay." *Journal of American Folklore* 11 (1898): 74.

Shuman, Amy. "Dismantling Local Culture." *Western Folklore* 52 (1993): 345–64.

Simpson, George E. "Loup Garou and Loa Tales from Northern Haiti." *Journal of American Folklore* 55 (1942): 219–27.

Simpson, George E., and J. B. Cineas. "Folk Tales of Haitian Heroes." *Journal of American Folklore* 54 (1941): 176–85.

Skinner, Alanson. "European Folk-Tales Collected Among the Menominee Indians." *Journal of American Folklore* 26 (1913): 64–80.

Smiley, Portia. "Folk-Lore from Virginia, South Carolina, Georgia, Alabama, and Florida." *Journal of American Folklore* 32 (1919): 357–83.

Smith, Janet. "Interview of Elfego Baca." American Life Histories: Manuscripts from the Federal Writers' Project, 1936–1940. Manuscript Division, Library of Congress. 12 October 2005.
http://memory.loc.gov/ammem/wpaintro/wpahome.html.

Smith, Pamela Coleman. "Two Negro Stories from Jamaica." *Journal of American Folklore* 9 (1896): 278.

Sparkman, P. S. "Notes of California Folklore: A Luiseño Tale." *Journal of American Folklore* 21 (1908): 35–36.

Speck, Frank G. "European Folk-Tales among the Penobscot." *Journal of American Folklore* 26 (1913): 81–84.

———. "European Tales among the Chickasaw Indians." *Journal of American Folklore* 26 (1913): 292.

———. "Penobscot Transformer Tales." *International Journal of American Linguistics* 1 (1918): 187–244.

Spencer, J. "Shawnee Folk-Lore." *Journal of American Folklore* 22 (1909): 319–26.

Spitzer, Nicholas R. "All Things Creole: Mout de tour le monde." *Journal of American Folklore* 116 (2003):57–72.

St. Clair, H. H., and R. H. Lowie. "Shoshone and Comanche Tales." *Journal of American Folklore* 22 (1909): 265–82.

Steiner, Roland. "Braziel Robinson Possessed of Two Spirits." *Journal of American Folklore* 13 (1900): 226–28.

———. "Sol Lockheart's Call." *Journal of American Folklore* 48 (1900): 67–70.

Stewart, Omer C. *The Northern Paiute Bands.* Millwood, NY: Kraus, 1976.

Stirling, Matthew W. *Origin Myth of Acoma and Other Records.* Smithsonian Institution Bureau of American Ethnology Bulletin 135. Washington, DC: U.S. Government Printing Office, 1942.

Strong, William D. *University of California Publications in American Archaeology and Ethnology.* Vol. 26, *Aboriginal Society in Southern California.* Berkeley: University of California Press, 1929.

Suplee, Laura M. "The Legend of Money Cove." *Journal of American Folklore* 31 (1918): 272–73.

Suttles, Wayne, ed. *Handbook of the North American Indians.* Vol. 7, *Northwest Coast.* Washington, DC: Smithsonian Institution, 1990.

Swanton, John R. *Myths and Tales of the Southeastern Indians.* Smithsonian Institution Bureau of American Ethnology Bulletin 88. Washington, DC: U.S. Government Printing Office, 1929.

Swenson, May. "Interview of Anca Vrbooska." American Life Histories: Manuscripts from the Federal Writers' Project, 1936–1940. Manuscript Division, Library of Congress. 12 October 2005. http://memory.loc.gov/ammem/wpaintro/wpahome.html.

———. "Interview of John Rivers." American Life Histories: Manuscripts from the Federal Writers' Project, 1936–1940. Manuscript Division, Library of Congress. 12 October 2005. http://memory.loc.gov/ammem/wpaintro/wpahome.html.

Taylor, Archer. "An Old-World Tale from Minnesota." *Journal of American Folklore* 31 (1918): 555–56.

Taylor, Helen Louise, and Rebecca Wolcott. "Items from New Castle, Delaware." *Journal of American Folklore* 51 (1938): 92–94.

Tejada, Simeon. "Interview of Manuel Jesus Vasques." American Life Histories: Manuscripts from the Federal Writers' Project, 1936–1940. Manuscript Division, Library of Congress. 12 October 2005. http://memory.loc.gov/ammem/wpaintro/wpahome.html.

Thomas, Howard. *Folklore from the Adirondack Foothills*. Prospect, NY: Prospect Books, 1958.

Thompson, Stith. *The Motif Index of Folk Literature*. Rev. ed. 6 vols. Bloomington: Indiana University Press, 1955–1958.

Totty, Francis. "Interview of Maurice Coates." American Life Histories: Manuscripts from the Federal Writers' Project, 1936–1940. Manuscript Division, Library of Congress. 12 October 2005. http://memory.loc.gov/ammem/wpaintro/wpahome.html.

Townsend, Edward. "Interview of A. Harry Williams." American Life Histories: Manuscripts from the Federal Writers' Project, 1936–1940. Manuscript Division, Library of Congress. 16 October 2005. http://memory.loc.gov/ammem/wpaintro/wpahome.html.

Trowbridge, Ada Wilson. "Negro Customs and Folk-Stories of Jamaica." *Journal of American Folklore* 9 (1896): 279–87.

Walden, Wayne. "Interview of Annette Hamilton." American Life Histories: Manuscripts from the Federal Writers' Project, 1936–1940. Manuscript Division, Library of Congress. 16 October 2005. http://memory.loc.gov/ammem/wpaintro/wpahome.html.

———. "Interview of Fred Roys." American Life Histories: Manuscripts from the Federal Writers' Project, 1936–1940. Manuscript Division, Library of Congress. 12 October 2005. http://memory.loc.gov/ammem/wpaintro/wpahome.html.

———. "Interview of Mrs. R. Ivanoff." American Life Histories: Manuscripts from the Federal Writers' Project, 1936–1940. Manuscript Division, Library of Congress. 12 October 2005. http://memory.loc.gov/ammem/wpaintro/wpahome.html.

Weigle, Martha, and Peter White. *The Lore of New Mexico*. Albuquerque: University of New Mexico Press, 1988.

Weippiert, G. W. "Legends of Iowa." *Journal of American Folklore* 2 (1889): 287–90.

Welsch, Roger. *Shingling the Fog and Other Plains Lies*. Chicago: Swallow, 1972.

West, John O. *Mexican-American Folklore*. Little Rock, AR: August House, 1988.

Westervelt, W. D. *Hawaiian Legends of Ghosts and Ghost-Gods*. Boston: Ellis Press, 1916.

————. *Hawaiian Legends of Old Honolulu.* Boston: G.H. Ellis Press, 1915.

————. *Hawaiian Legends of Volcanoes.* Boston: G.H. Ellis Press, 1916.

Will, George F. "No-Tongue, A Mandan Tale." *Journal of American Folklore* 26 (1913): 331–37.

————. "No-Tongue, A Mandan Tale." *Journal of American Folklore* 29 (1916): 402–6.

Williams, Ellis. "Interview of Zenobia Brown." American Life Histories: Manuscripts from the Federal Writers' Project, 1936–1940. Manuscript Division, Library of Congress. 20 October 2005. http://memory.loc.gov/ammem/wpaintro/wpahome.html.

Williams, Mentor L., ed. *Schoolcraft's Indian Legends.* East Lansing: Michigan State University Press, 1956.

Wilson, Howard Barrett. "Notes of Syrian Folk-Lore Collected in Boston." *Journal of American Folklore* 16 (1903): 133–47.

Wiltse, Henry M. "In the Southern Field of Folk-Lore." *Journal of American Folklore* 13 (1900): 209–12.

Wissler, Clark. "Some Dakota Myths I." *Journal of American Folklore* 20 (1907): 121–31.

————. "Some Dakota Myths II." *Journal of American Folklore* 20 (1907): 195–206.

"Witchcraft in New Mexico." *Journal of American Folklore* 1 (1888): 167–68.

Wrenn, Sarah B. "Interview of Annie Cason Lee." American Life Histories: Manuscripts from the Federal Writers' Project, 1936–1940. Manuscript Division, Library of Congress. 11 October 2005. http://memory.loc.gov/ammem/wpaintro/wpahome.html.

————. "Interview of Jane Lee Smith." American Life Histories: Manuscripts from the Federal Writers' Project, 1936–1940. Manuscript Division, Library of Congress. 12 October 2005. http://memory.loc.gov/ammem/wpaintro/wpahome.html.

Wrenshall, Letitia Humphreys. "Incantations and Popular Healing in Maryland and Pennsylvania." *Journal of American Folklore* 15 (1902): 268–74.

Zingerle, Ignaz and Joseph. *Kinder- und Hausmärchen,* gesammelt durch die Brüder Zingerle. Innsbruck: Verlag der Wagner'schen Buchhandlung, 1852.

410

Cumulative Index

Boldface numbers refer to volume numbers.

"A Bewitched Churning," 2:174
"A Bewitched Gun," 2:6, 2:179
"A Drunkard's Promise," 1:303
"A Giant's Rock-Throwing," 3:281
"A Loup Garou Disguises as a
   Beggar," 2:289
"A Messenger to the Indians," 3:241
"A Patriot's Answer to an Iraqi,"
   4:183
"A Pioneer Crossing the Midwest,"
   1:148, 1:243
"A Sight of Alligators," 2:124
"A Wonderful Testimony," 3:242
A`yûn'inï ("Swimmer"), 2:28
"A Zange Disguises as a Snake,"
   2:287
Abenaki, 1:4, 1:12, 1:29; tales, 1:18,
   1:64
"Above Ground and Below Ground,"
   1:281

Abrahams, Roger, 2:39, 2:205
Achomawi, 3:271; tales, 3:271
Acoma Pueblo: corn/agriculture
   influencing mythology, 3:7; kinship
   structure, 3:8; sacred number
   "four," 3:7–8; tales, 3:7
"Adam and Eve," 2:231, 2:291
"The Adams Diggings," 3:4, 3:92
"The Adventures of Haininu and
   Baumegwesu," 3:305
African American jokes: ethnic
   jokes, 1:309, 2:42, 2:73, 2:74,
   2:75, 2:223; master/slave, 1:263,
   1:358, 1:360, 2:122; preacher as
   stock character, 1:315, 2:78,
   2:167, 2:206
African American tales, 1:138; and
   Brer Rabbit, 2:5; Caribbean,
   2:231–44, 2:245–75, 2:277–90,
   2:291–300; with cowboy, 3:224;
   and dangers of nonsensical behavior motif, 2:39; and dangers of
   "putting on airs," 2:92; and dog
   ghost motif, 1:327; Jamaica, 1:292;
   Mid-Atlantic, 1:265–70, 1:272–82,
   1:283–323, 1:326–29, 1:334–44,
   1:347, 1:350, 1:353, 1:357–62;
   Northeast, 1:138; Plains and

Plateau, 3:223; and "signifying"
   (rhetorical device), 2:85, 2:104;
   South, 2:20, 2:25–28, 2:31–34,
   2:36–46, 2:56, 2:62–71, 2:73–76,
   2:77, 2:83–87, 2:91, 2:96, 2:106,
   2:121, 2:126, 2:130, 2:131, 2:149,
   2:159–71, 2:194, 2:199–209,
   2:223, 2:226; tradition in Mid-
   Atlantic, 1:261, 1:263; Trinidad,
   1:42, 1:363
African tales: Cape Verde, 1:94,
   1:141, 1:365; and influence in
   South and Caribbean, 2:4, 2:277,
   2:280, 2:286; Zomo the Hare, 2:94
Ahahe, 3:212
"Aiini," 1:148, 1:178
"Akua," 3:292
Alabama, 2:2; tales, 2:21, 2:98,
   2:100
Aleuts, 4:3, 4:5, 4:42; tales, 4:42,
   4:146, 4:148, 4:151. *See also* Inuit
Algonquian cultures, 1:4, 1:291:147;
   migration to Midwest, 1:148,
   1:149; push west, 3:179
"All Dressed Up and No Place to
   Go," 2:223

"Chef Sampson Lands Mr. Trout," 1:138

"Chef Watkins' Alibi," 1:139

Cherokee, 1:32–33, 1:262, 1:298, 2:2, 2:76; belief in "the immortals," 2:213; North Carolina (Eastern Band), 2:2–3; ravens in sacred formulas, 2:176; tales, 2:11, 2:29, 2:35, 2:101, 2:175, 2:213

Chesser, Allen, 2:46, 2:123, 2:124, 2:305

Chesser, Sam, 2:217

Cheyenne, 3:132, 3:179; tales, 3:178, 3:185, 3:262, 3:361

Chickasaw, 2:2; moieties, 2:76; tales, 2:76

"The Chief's Daughters," 1:149, 1:176

"The Children of the Dog," 4:51

Chinook tales, 4:43, 4:100, 4:113, 4:127

Chipo, 3:305, 3:335

Chippewa (Ojibway) tales, 1:147

"The Chloroformed Roommate," 4:204

Choctaw, 2:2, 2:21, 2:76

"The Chosen Suitor," 2:205, 2:277, 2:298

"The Chosen Suitor: The Forbidden Room," 2:204; original version, 2:311

Christensen, Julian, 1:225

"Christians Charged for Reading Bible in Prison," 4:241

Christophe, Henri, 2:294

"Chronic Dehydration," 4:169

Chumash, 3:268

Circuses, 3:68

"Citibank Boycott," 4:271

Civil War: and Mid-Atlantic, 1:261; and Midwest, 1:149, 1:248; and Plains and Plateau, 3:132; and West, 3:267

Clarke, Alexander, 1:9

Clatsop, 4:43

Clayton, W. O., 1:286

"Clothing Caught in a Graveyard," 1:115

Coates, Maurice, 3:83

"Cock's Breakfast," 2:242

Cody, William Frederick "Buffalo Bill," 1:148, 243; Wild West Show, 3:68

Comanches (Southern Plains), 3:132, 3:230; tales, 3:231. See also Shoshonean Comanches

Comic anecdotes, 4:120

"Contempt for His Torturers," 1:6, 1:131

Cook, Captain James, 3:269

"'Coon in the Box," 2:121

Coos, 4:12; tales, 4:12, 4:55, 4:66

Corbett, James John "Gentleman Jim," 3:238

Coushatta/Cousatti, 2:2, 2:20

"The Cow Is Taken to the Roof to Graze," 1:310

"Coyote and Beaver," 4:86

"Coyote and His Sister Robin," 3:268, 3:367

"Coyote and Pitch," 4:84; tar baby similarities, 4:85

"Coyote and Raccoon," 4:82

"Coyote and the Buffalo," 3:132, 3:228

"Coyote and the Grizzly Bears," 3:339–41; formulaic closing, 3:339

"Coyote and the Old Woman," 4:73

"Coyote and the Stump-Man," 4:92

"Coyote and the Sun," 3:344

"The Coyote and the Woodpecker," 3:109, 3:115

"Coyote and Wolf," 3:342

"Coyote Arranges the Seasons of the Year," 4:20

"Coyote Creates Taboos," 4:4, 4:127, 4:141

"Coyote Frees the Salmon," 4:25

"Coyote's Amorous Adventures," 4:83

"Coyote's Theft of Fire," 3:132, 3:164, 3:173

Creation myths. See Origins

"Creation of Man," 3:274

"The Creation of the Indians," 3:278

Creek Confederation, 2:2, 2:21, 2:58, 2:76, 2:105; tales, 2:59, 2:103, 2:105, 2:151; and ties to African Americans, 2:105

Creole traditions, 2:3, 2:224

"The Crop Division," 1:281

"Crossing the Plains from Kentucky," 3:132, 3:181

Cultee, Charles, 4:43, 4:100, 4:113, 4:127

Cultural contact, 1:262, 1:298, 1:344, 2:5, 2:56, 3:4, 3:17, 3:77, 3:115; among Pueblo peoples, 3:47; Lapin/Bouqui/Rabbit examples, 2:4, 2:49, 2:101, 2:103, 2:105

Culture heroes, 1:4, 2:20, 3:20, 3:165, 3:189, 3:306, 4:14, 4:279; abilities, 1:202; characteristics, 3:173; coyote, 4:93; divine twins, 1:9, 1:12, 3:47, 3:59, 3:206, 3:213; and flow of power, 3:135; Papa, 3:293; Prairie Falcon, 3:268; Raven, 4:40, 4:99, 4:134; and technology, 2:99, 3:22; Uuyot (Wuyoot), 3:289; Wakea, 3:293. See also Trickster legends

"Curanderas and Brujas," 3:5, 3:124–26

"Curanderas and Brujas II," 3:125 "Cures of a Maryland Witch," 1:264, 1:330, 1:352

Imus, Charles, 4:156
"In Liquor," 1:303
"In the Bee Tree," 1:300
"In the Cow's Belly," 2:257
"Incriminating the Other Fellow," 2:62; original version, 2:309
Indian Removal Act (1830), 2:2
Indian Territory, 2:2, 2:105, 3:132
Inuit, 4:3, 4:5
Irish American tales: Mid-Atlantic, 1:344; Midwest, 1:194, 1:225; Northeast, 1:81, 1:91; Northwest, 4:156
"The Irishman and the Pumpkin," 1:225, 2:73, 2:223
Iroquois Confederacy, 1:4–5, 1:128, 1:164; contact with the French, 1:5; legends, 1:4; and Shawnee, 1:148
Irving, Washington, 1:122
Isleta Pueblo: moieties, 3:42; tales, 3:41, 3:47, 3:109; Tiwa, 3:42
"It Was So Cold That…," 1:147, 1:216
Ivanoff, Mrs. R., 3:238

"Jack and the Bean Pole," 1:262, 1:275
"Jack and the Bean Tree," 2:5, 2:98
"Jack and the Beanstalk," 2:6, 2:134
"Jack and the Fire Dragaman," 2:140
"Jack-O'-M-Lantern," 1:371
"Jack-O'-My-Lantern," 1:265, 1:327; original version, 1:371
"Jack the Giant Killer," 2:6, 2:79
Jackson, Henry, Jr., 1:190

Jackson, "Pappy," 2:220
Jackson, Thomas, 4:116
"Jake Strauss," 1:6, 1:115; original version, 1:368
"James Harris," 2:199
"Jane Fonda Nomination," 4:189; variant B, 4:191
"Jean Sot Feeds Cows Needles," 2:4, 2:110
Jean Sot, 2:4; stock character, 2:113
"Jean Sot Kills the Duck," 2:4, 2:111
"Jean Sot and the Cowhide," 2:113
Jeffries, James Jackson "Jim," 3:238
Jenkins, Julius, 2:204
Jenks, Albert Ernest, 1:173
"Jim Johns and the Tiger," 2:217
John and Master tales, 1:263, 1:360, 2:122, 2:126
"John Kerry's Medals," 4:166
"John the Fool and John the Smart," 2:262
Johnson, Arthur John "Jack," 3:238
Johnson, Elsie, 1:321
Johnson, Josephine, 1:306
Johnson, Robert, 1:354, 2:37, 2:162
Johnson, Sextus E., 3:241
"Joke on Jake," 3:132, 3:233
Jokes, 1:104, 1:148, 1:263, 1:357, 1:359, 2:73, 2:120, 2:167, 2:208, 4:100; articulating intergroup strife, 2:259; beleaguered wife stock character, 2:167; Boudreaux stock character, 2:119; Cajun jokes, 2:119; drunkard stock character, 2:167; ethnic, 1:225, 1:263, 1:309, 1:310, 1:312, 1:313, 1:317, 2:73, 2:74, 2:75, 2:223, 2:260, 3:233; master/slave, 1:263, 1:358, 1:360, 2:122; myth parody, 2:243; practical, 4:100; Preacher as stock character, 1:315, 2:78, 2:167, 2:206. *See also* African American jokes; John and Master tales
Joseph, Termeus, 2:286

Joshua, 4:7; tales, 4:7, 4:74, 4:86
"Judgment Day," 1:357
"Jumping into the Breeches," 1:310

Kalapuya, 4:142; tales, 4:142
"Kamapuaa on Oahu and Kauai," 3:318
"Kampuaa Legends: Legends of the Hog God," 3:312
"Kanati and Selu: The Origin of Corn and Game," 2:11,
Karok, 4:14; tales, 4:14, 4:16, 4:25
"Katrina Blunders," 4:275
"Katrina Worker Report," 4:208
Kearny, Stephen W., 3:5
"Keeping off Witches," 1:343
"Kentucky Fried Chicken Becomes KFC," 4:165
Kickapoo, 1:147, 1:149, 1:162, 1:164–65; tales, 1:188
Kidd, Captain, 1:27
"The Killing of the Dutchman," 4:94
"The Kind and the Unkind Girls," 2:224
"The King and Old George Buchanan," 2:132
Klamath Billie, 4:18, 4:28, 4:71, 4:79, 4:82, 4:83, 4:84, 4:91, 4:92, 4:96
Kroeber, A. L., 3:179, 4:37

La Foria, 3:17, 3:19, 3:22, 3:114
La Patten, 1:292
Lakota, 3:132; Ogalala (Sioux), 3:188, 3:227, 3:254; tales, 3:188
"Lazy Jack and His Calf Skin," 1:77, 2:115
"Lazy Maria," 1:97
" Legend of Sattik," 4:4, 4:140
"Legend of the Breadfruit Tree," 3:269, 3:292
"Legend of the Teton Sioux Medicine Pipe," 3:132, 3:251
"Legendary Origin of the Kickapoos," 1:149, 1:164

Mono, 3:268, 3:277; tales, 3:277, 3:306, 3:335, 3:367, 3:369
"Moon Cheese: Two Irishmen at the Well," 1:263, 1:312
Mooney, James, 2:176
Morgan, John Hunt, 1:248
Morgan, Richard, 2:242
Mormons, 3:133, 3:241
Morris, Lucy, 1:278
Moses, 1:45
Mother Corn Ceremony, 3:160
"Mother Holle," 1:97
"The Mother of All Urban Legends," 4:223
Motifs/tale types, 4:280; aimless wandering of trickster, 1:202; animal/fish allows itself to be taken, 4:4; animal motifs, 1:45, 1:55; animal spouse motif, 1:337, 2:277, 2:298; "awl elbow witches," 1:179; bargain with death, 2:161; belief tales, 1:120; brain over brawn, 2:238; cannibal figure, 2:98, 2:100, 3:173, 3:200, 4:55; Cinderella, 1:50, 3:4, 3:77; composites (examples of), 1:304; dead horse, 2:59; demon lover, 2:199; Devil's questions, 2:199; divided village (Wichita motif), 3:213; dog ghosts, 1:327; "earthdiver," 1:9, 1:151, 1:160, 3:277; Earth Mother, 1:9; evil father-in-law, 1:179; exile, 1:45; exploiting trust of romantic rival, 1:270; extraordinary birth, 1:45; "fall from grace," 2:19; "fatal deception," 1:297; girl helper in hero's flight, 1:52, 2:272; Jack tales, 2:5,

2:149; John and Master tales, 1:263; jokes, 1:148; kind and unkind, 1:73; lying, tales of, 1:91, 1:92, 3:103; magic canoe, 1:179; magic object, 1:69; magic stick beats person, 1:69; "mock plea," 1:295; numbskull stories, 1:311, 2:75, 2:121; Obstacle Flight, 2:199, 2:205, 3:255; ogres duped to fight each other, 2:79; *ordinary folktales*, 1:179; orphan and grandparents, 4:79; personal experience narratives, 1:148, 1:149; pirate legends, 1:4, 1:26; rolling skull, 1:239; rope to climb to heavens, 4:93; sacred numbers, 3:7, 3:36; shape-shifting, 1:122, 1:337, 2:86, 2:249, 2:286; "squeezing the stone," 2:79; Star Husband Type I (wish to marry a star), 4:61; stupid stories depending on a pun, 2:111; tarbaby, 2:55; task for suitors/bride as prize, 1:69; theft of butter (honey) by playing godfather, 2:64, 2:240; transformation motifs, 1:110, 3:257; trial of three brothers, 2:273; trickster greed, 1:196, 1:289, 2:106; twins, 1:9, 1:12, 2:11, 3:47, 3:52, 3:206, 3:213; two sisters, 3:8; "unfinished business," 1:324; and validating devices, 1:227; wisdom of age, 2:107, 2:221; wish to marry a star (Star Husband Type I), 1:176; witches "riding" victims, 1:110; young woman defying parent, 4:38
Mountain Chief, Walter, 3:257
"Mr. Deer's My Riding Horse," 1:290, 2:4, 2:56, 2:58; original version, 2:307
"Mr. Hard-Time," 1:310, 2:260
"Mr. Hard-times," 1:310
"Mr. Jones's Advice," 4:175

"Mr. Peacock and the Deadly Ghost," 1:328; original version, 1:376
Miss K.'s Father, 1:346
Murray, Harry, 2:243
"Muskrat's Tail," 1:149, 1:168
"My Son Ali," 1:100
"The Mysterious Deer," 2:197
Myths, 4:280; alternative look at original sin, 2:231; and legends (examples), 3:251, 3:282; memory culture vs. sacred narrative, 3:279; and primary food groups for Native Americans, 2:18; uses, 3:297; Ute, 3:173

Nakassungnaitut, 4:37
"Nancy and the Honey Tree," 2:235
Nancy, Ann, 2:33
"Nancy fools His Wife," 2:248, 2:270
Narcom, W. P., 1:301
Narrative performance, 1:41
Natchez, 2:2; tales, 2:18, 2:53
Native American cultures: in Caribbean, 2:1–2; Indian Removal Act (1830), 2:2; of Mid-Atlantic, 1:262; of Midwest, 1:147–49; of Northeast, 1:4; in Northwest, 4:3–5; in Plains and Plateau, 3:131–33; of South, 2:2; in Southwest, 3:4–5; in West, 3:268
Native American tales: Achomawi, 3:271; Acoma Pueblo, 3:7; Alabama, 2:21, 2:98, 2:100; Aleut, 4:42, 4:146, 4:148, 4:151; Alsea, 4:117; Apache, 3:17, 3:20, 3:22, 3:115; Arikara, 3:159; Biloxi, 2:54; Blackfoot, 3:257; Cherokee, 2:11, 2:29, 2:35, 2:101, 2:175, 2:213; Cheyenne, 3:178, 3:185, 3:262, 3:361; Chinook, 4:43, 4:100, 4:113, 4:127; Comanche, 3:230; Coos, 4:11, 4:55, 4:66; Creek, 2:58,

"Origin of the Bear: The Bear
   Songs," 2:28
"The Origin of the Narwhal," 4:34
"The Origin of the Sauks and
   Foxes," 1:165
"The Origin of the Seasons and of
   the Mountains," 4:27, 4:30; simi-
   larities to Tlingit narrative, 4:27
"Origin of the Universe," 3:132,
   3:213
"The Origin of Vegetation," 1:149,
   1:158
"The Origin of Woman," 2:243;
   original version, 2:314
Origins: tales of, 2:25; Caribbean,
   2:231–44; Cyber Region,
   4:165–74; Mid-Atlantic,
   1:265–74; Midwest, 1:151–71;
   Northeast, 1:9–44; Northwest,
   4:7–49; Plains and Plateau,
   3:135–84; South, 2:11–48;
   Southwest, 3:7–45; West,
   3:271–96
"The Orphan and the Turkeys,"
   1:196, 1:202
Osagiwag`. See Sauk
Otos, 1:148, 1:149; tales, 1:149,
   1:176
"Out of Her Skin," 1:263, 1:334,
   1:335
"Out of Their Skins," 1:335, 1:341
"Outwitting the King," 1:7, 1:89
Ozarks, 2:5

Pa-skin, 1:173
Paiute: "football," 3:327; Northern
   (Paviotso), 3:287; Southern

(Moapa), 3:278; tales, 3:278,
   3:288, 3:326, 3:331, 3:342
Palmer, Francis L., 1:54
Papa, 3:293
Papago, 3:111; tales, 3:111
Parsiow, Alonzo, 1:91
Parsons, Elsie Clews, 1:94, 1:262,
   1:298, 1:309, 2:5, 3:77
Passamoquoddy: tales, 1:17, 1:64
"Paul Heym, the Wizard of
   Lebanon," 1:122
Pavawut, 3:365
Pawnee: Skidi and Arikaras, 3:160
"Pele and Kamapuaa," 3:322
"Pele's Long Sleep," 3:269, 3:353
Pennsylvania Dutch, 1:6
Penny, Charles, 1:42, 1:363
Penobscot, 1:4, 1:12; tales, 1:5,
   1:16, 1:45, 1:61, 1:69
People of the Red Earth. See
   Mesquakie (Fox)
"Perfume Mugger," 4:199; variant B,
   4:200; variant C, 4:201
Personal experience narrative,
   1:148, 1:149, 1:243, 1:264,
   1:330, 1:334, 1:343, 1:347, 2:6,
   2:46, 2:123, 2:124, 2:162, 2:168,
   2:217, 3:68, 3:80, 3:86, 3:224,
   3:233, 3:362, 4:95, 4:121, 4:124,
   4:157, 4:280; "testimony," 2:163
Personal legend, 4:280
Personal vision quests, 3:193
Peterson, Albert, 1:93
Phillips, Percy, 3:251
"Phoebe Ward, Witch," 2:172,
   2:181
Phratries, 1:170
Pickett, William "Bill," 3:224
Pilgrims, 1:5
Pimona, Molly Kinsman, 3:277,
   3:369, 3:377
Pirate legends, 1:4, 1:26
Plains and Plateau: extent of, 3:131;
   heroes/heroines/tricksters/fools,
   3:185–239; Hispanic influences,
   3:132; horses, introduction of,

3:132, 3:179, 3:230; Mormons,
   3:133; Native American inhabi-
   tants, 3:131–33; origins, tales of,
   3:135–84; sacred tales of the
   supernatural, 3:241–63
Plains people, 3:4
"Playing Dead Twice in the Road,"
   1:263; variant A, 1:285; variant
   B, 1:286; variant C, 1:286
"Playing Godfather," 1:287, 2:64,
   2:67, 2:240
"Playing Mourner," 2:64, 2:240
Poe, Edgar Allan, 1:27
"Poison Payphone," 4:205
"Poison Perfume," 4:198; variant B,
   4:199
"Poisoned Coca-Cola," 4:269
Polish tales, 1:131
Ponca, 1:149
Poohegans, 1:64–65
Porcupine, 1:21; tale bearer, 3:361
"Possessed of Two Spirits," 2:164,
   2:167
"Possum and Weasel Have a Falling
   Out," 1:288
Pow-wowing, 1:122, 1:264, 1:330
Power and social stratification
   theme, 1:41, 1:86
"Prairie Falcon's Contest with
   Meadowlark," 3:335, 3:367
Pratt, 1:359
"President Bush's IQ," 4:255
"Priceless," 4:188
Privett, Mollie, 3:68
Privett, Samuel Thomas ("Booger
   Red"), 3:4, 3:68
"Proctor and Gamble and Liz
   Claiborne Confess to Church of
   Satan on Sally," 4:242
Protest tales, 2:227; and modeling
   oppression, 2:233
"Providence Hole," 1:148, 1:236,
   1:238
Pueblo, 3:4; matrilineal clans, 3:8
"Pumpkin Sold as an Ass's Egg,"
   2:73

von Münchhausen, Baron Karl
   Friedrich Hieronymus, 3:99
Vrbooska, Anca, 1:40, 1:85, 1:132

"Wabasaiy," 1:147, 1:162, 1:193
Waí-hu-si-wa, 3:52
"Wailing Wall," 4:250
"Wait Until I Get Dry," 1:303
Wakea, 3:293
"Wal-Mart Boycott," 4:185
"Walking Skeleton," 3:369; variant
   B, 3:372; variant C, 3:377
"Wanted for Attempted Murder,"
   4:234
Ward, Monroe, 2:87, 2:140
Ward, Miles, 2:87, 2:140
"The Watcher Tricked," 1:306
Waterspirits, 1:227
Wendat (Wyandot), 1:4, 1:9
West (California and Nevada),
   3:267–69; gold rush, 3:268;
   heroes/heroines/tricksters/fools,
   3:305, 326–46; origins, tales of,
   3:271, 277–81, 287–92;
   post–Civil war pressures, 3:268;
   pre-European contact cultures,
   3:268; sacred tales of the supernatural, 3:361, 364–86; Spanish
   influence, 3:268; terrain, 3:267
West (Hawaii), 3:267, 269; extent,
   3:269;
   heroes/heroines/tricksters/fools,
   3:297, 312–26; nature gods
   ("akua"), 3:292; origins, tales of,
   3:274, 3:281, 3:284, 3:292;
   sacred tales of the supernatural,
   3:353; terrain, 3:269; ti plant,
   3:284

"When Brer Deer and Brer Terrapin
   Runned a Race," 2:92
"When Brer Frog Give a Big
   Dining," 2:106
"When Brer 'Possum Attend Miss
   Fox's House-Party," 2:64, 2:91
"When Brer Rabbit Help Brer
   Terrapin," 2:96
"When Brer Rabbit Saw Brer Dog's
   Mouth So Brer Dog Can
   Whistle," 2:40
"When Brer Rabbit Was Presidin'
   Elder," 2:77
"When Brer Wolf Have His Corn
   Shucking," 2:69
"When Mr. Pine Tree and Mr. Oak
   Tree Fall Out," 2:25
"When Mr. Terrapin Went Riding
   on the Clouds," 2:218
"When Raven Wanted to Marry
   Snowbird and Fly with the
   Geese," 4:98
"When the World Was Formed,"
   3:17
"Where Did Adam Hide," 2:166;
   original version, 2:310
"Where's Mr. McGinnis?" 1:313
White, Joseph (Mandarong), 1:36,
   1:116
"White Substance Delays Aggie
   Football Practice," 4:230
"Whiteberry Whittington," 1:52,
   2:152
"Why Frog Lives in the Water,"
   1:270
"Why Mr. Owl Can't Sing," 2:38
"Why Rabbit Has a Short Tail,"
   2:239
"Why the Deer has a Short Tail,"
   1:149, 1:170
"Why the People Tote Brer Rabbit
   Foot in their Pocket," 2:26, 2:40
"Why the Spider Never Got in the
   Ark," 2:159
"Why We Love Children," 4:172

Wichita, 3:131–32, 3:135; divided
   village motif, 3:213; tales,
   3:136–59, 3:212
"Wild Bill," 1:148, 1:243
Wild Bunch, 3:221
Wiley, Betty, 1:353
Wilkenson, Susie, 2:132
Will, George F., 3:193
Willoughby, Loneva, 1:281
Wiltse, A. S., 2:197
"The Wine, the Farm, the Princess,
   and the Tarbaby," 2:4, 2:49, 2:53,
   2:64, 2:233, 2:258
Winnebago: cosmology, 1:227; tales,
   1:188, 1:207, 1:227; War (1827),
   1:148
"Wisa'kä," 1:149, 1:159
"The Witch and the Boiler," 2:174,
   2:178, 2:180
"Witch Flights," 3:5, 3:121, 3:124
Witchcraft: punishment for, 3:125;
   vs. hoodoo, 1:348
Witches, 1:65; ability to slip out of
   their skin (cross-cultural belief),
   1:334, 4:136; "awl-elbow," 1:179;
   borrowing object of victim motif,
   1:112; cross-cultural "hag experience," 1:112; little boy witch,
   2:204; "riding" of victims motifs,
   1:110, 2:178; salt as antidote to
   evil (cross-cultural belief), 1:334;
   shape-shifting, 1:122, 2:27; transformation motifs, 1:110, 2:171;
   with two hearts (Hopi), 3:58. See
   also *Brujeria*; Pavawut
"Witches Discovered," 3:5, 3:122,
   3:124
"Witch's Apprentice," 1:347, 1:350
Wolf Clan, 1:128
"Wolf of the Greenwood," 1:6, 1:52,
   2:152
"The Wolf Overeats in the Cellar,"
   2:109
Wollman, Mr., 1:131
"Woman Cat," 1:338, 3:123; variant A, 1:339; variant B, 1:340

About the Editor

Thomas A. Green is Associate Professor of Anthropology at Texas A&M University. His many books include *Martial Arts in the Modern World* (Praeger, 2003), *Martial Arts of the World: An Encyclopedia* (2001), *Folklore: An Encyclopedia of Beliefs, Customs, Tales, Music, and Art* (1997), and *The Language of Riddles: New Perspectives* (1984).